Native Recognition

THE SUNY SERIES

HORIZONS OF CINEMA

MURRAY POMERANCE | EDITOR

Also in the series

William Rothman, editor, *Cavell on Film*

J. David Slocum, editor, *Rebel Without a Cause*

Joe McElhaney, *The Death of Classical Cinema*

Kirsten Moana Thompson, *Apocalyptic Dread*

Frances Gateward, editor, *Seoul Searching*

Michael Atkinson, editor, *Exile Cinema*

Bert Cardullo, *Soundings on Cinema*

Paul S. Moore, *Now Playing*

Robin L. Murray and Joseph K. Heumann,
Ecology and Popular Film

William Rothman, editor, *Three Documentary Filmmakers*

Sean Griffin, editor, *Hetero*

Jean-Michel Frodon, editor, *Cinema and the Shoah*

Carolyn Jess-Cooke and Constantine Verevis, editors, *Second Takes*

Matthew Solomon, *Fantastic Voyages of the Cinematic Imagination*

Native Recognition

Indigenous Cinema and the Western

Joanna Hearne

Cover art jacket image: Film still of Kraig Craig from *Wish Henry, on July 4th, 2010*, courtesy Dustinn Craig. http://vimeo.com/13121992. With thanks to Elizabeth M. Claffey for help with the cover design.

Published by State University of New York Press, Albany

For information, contact State University of New York Press, Albany, NY
www.sunypress.edu

Production by Eileen Nizer
Marketing by Michael Campochiaro

Library of Congress Cataloging-in-Publication Data

Hearne, Joanna.
    Native recognition : indigenous cinema and the western / Joanna Hearne.
        p. cm.
    Includes bibliographical references and index.
    ISBN 978-1-4384-4397-3 (hardcover : alk. paper)
    ISBN 978-1-4384-4398-0 (pbk.: alk. paper)
    1. Indians in motion pictures.   2. Indigenous films—United States.
3. Western films—United States.   I. Title.

    PN1995.9.I48H43 2012
    791.43'658730497—dc23   2011047986

10 9 8 7 6 5 4 3 2 1

A portion of the proceeds from this book will be donated to the
non-profit organization Vision Maker Media
(formerly Native American Public Telecommunications, NAPT),
in support of media workshops and fellowships
for young Native filmmakers.
Please visit their website: www.visionmakermedia.org

Contents

List of Illustrations

Most of the silent film images in this book are from the Library of Congress's Motion Picture, Broadcasting, and Recorded Sound Division (LC). Promotional stills are courtesy of the Academy of Motion Picture Arts and Sciences (AMPAS). Photographs and stills from other sources are attributed in the caption. The images from *The Return of Navajo Boy* are courtesy of Groundswell Educational Films, and the dedication photograph from *Husk of Time: The Photographs of Victor Masayesva* is courtesy of Victor Masayesva. Images not otherwise attributed are frame enlargements.

Introduction

Chapter 1

Chapter 2

Chapter 3

Chapter 4

Acknowledgments

Throughout the years writing this book, my thinking about Indigenous images and image-making has been influenced by conversations with artists, intellectuals, and scholars who expanded my understanding in innumerable ways. I owe a special debt to Larry Littlebird, Scott Momaday, and Rick Morse for sharing their stories about the making of *House Made of Dawn*. Victor Masayesva fielded many questions and shared resources, including the beautiful dedication image from his book *Husk of Time: The Photographs of Victor Masayesva*. Sherman Alexie and Chris Eyre took time from busy schedules to talk with me about *Smoke Signals*. Jeff Spitz, who shared his thoughts about *The Return of Navajo Boy* over several conversations, later provided frame enlargements and offered welcome support and feedback on the manuscript. Dustinn Craig generously shared the still image from his film *Wish Henry, on July 4th, 2010*, for the cover. And this project was influenced by many other filmmakers who shared films and ideas over the years, including Adrian Baker, Nanobah Becker, Greg Coyes, Michelle Danforth, Joseph Erb, Jacob Floyd, Diane Glancy, Sterlin Harjo, Melissa Henry, Simon James, Georgina Lightning, Patty Loew, Blackhorse Lowe, James Luna, Catherine Martin, Darren Kipp, Alanis Obomsawin, Randy Redroad, Leslie Marmon Silko, and Misty Upham.

As I conducted research, the project benefited from the expertise of the incredible archivists and librarians at the National Museum of the American Indian's Film and Video Center and Cultural Resources Center in New York and Washington, D.C., including Amalia Cordova, Millie Seubert, Michelle Svenson, Chris Turner, and Elizabeth Weatherford among others. NMAI programs such as the restoration and screening of the film *House Made of Dawn* and the 2005 "First Nations/First Features" film festival allowed me to see films not in distribution and to talk with filmmakers in person. The staff at the Library of Congress, the Academy of Motion Picture Arts and

Sciences Margaret Herrick Library, the University of Southern California special collections, the University of California at Los Angeles archives, and the University of Missouri libraries all provided essential research guidance. Charles Silver at the Museum of Modern Art helped me to locate the 1928 film *Ramona*, and Veroslav Haba at the National Film Archive in Prague provided wonderfully gracious and knowledgeable help in viewing the print. I'm also grateful to numerous individuals and organizations for providing images and permissions, including Rob Wallace at Keep America Beautiful, Inc.; Scott Krafft of the Charles Deering McCormick Library of Special Collections, Northwestern University Library; Richard Tritt of the Cumberland County Historical Society; and Claire Brandt and the staff at Eddie Brandt's Saturday Matinee in Los Angeles.

Chadwick Allen and Michelle Raheja deserve very special thanks for their generosity, intellectual rigor, and patient support. The list of people who have shared their thoughts, advice, questions, and encouragement—in conversations near and far, some fleeting and some over many years—stretches long. In and around film festivals, cinema studies conferences, and Native studies conferences, many colleagues have helped me better understand Native cinema through their questions, comments, camaraderie, and scholarship, including Susan Bernardin, Joseph Bauerkemper, Denise Cummings, Kristin Dowell, Gabriel Estrada, Michael Robert Evans, Tamara Falicov, Stephanie Fitzgerald, Faye Ginsburg, Penelope Kelsey, Angelica Lawson, Randy Lewis, Deborah Madsen, Elise Marubbio, Danika Medak-Saltzman, Anya Montiel, Joshua Nelson, Dean Rader, Jolene Rickard, Ken Roemer, Channette Romero, David Delgado Shorter, Lisa Stefanoff, Michelle Stewart, David Tafler, Dustin Tahmahkera, Lisa Tatonetti, Theo Van Alst, Debra White-Stanley, Pamela Wilson, and Houston Wood. Feedback from Gerald Vizenor helped shape the project; Michael Marsden and Armando José Prats lent support from afar; Dydia DeLyser, Hugh Neely, and Phil Brigandi traded information with me as we built our understanding of Edwin Carewe's 1928 Ramona; and Robert Warrior provided welcome advice and conversation about the film. Shirley Sneve at Native American Public Telecommunications—and the entire staff there—have created wonderful networks of filmmakers and scholars for social change. At SUNY Press, Gary Dunham's enthusiasm for the project energized my writing toward the end, and I extend thanks as well to Amanda Lanne, Larin McLaughlin, James Peltz, and Murray Pomerance. An early version of chapter 1 first appeared in the *Journal of Popular Film and Television* in 2003 (and a revised version appears in *Westerns: The Essential Journal of Popular Film and Television Collection*, edited by Gary Edgerton and Michael Marsden, Routledge 2012);

fragments of chapter 3 appeared in an earlier form in *Western Folklore*; and chapter 5 is expanded from a version published in *Visualities: Perspectives on Contemporary American Indian Film and Art*, edited by Denise Cummings (Michigan State University Press, 2011).

At the University of Missouri I've had the guidance and support of wonderful colleagues across campus and in the English Department and Film Studies Program. This book and my other projects have grown through the sustaining and brilliant fellowship of Elizabeth Chang, Sam Cohen, and Donna Strickland, who read many drafts. Roger Cook and Nancy West provided cogent readings of individual chapters, and Maureen Konkle came through with long-distance archival sleuthing. Elisa Glick, Elaine Lawless, Karen Piper, and Anand Prahlad offered mentoring and advice, and Pat Okker supported my work throughout her time as department chair. Noor Azizan-Gardner and Pablo Mendoza at the University of Missouri; Paul Sturtz and Polina Malikin of the True/False Film Festival; and Kerri Yost and Paula Elias of the Citizen Jane Film Festival collaborated to bring filmmakers to campus. I'm grateful to the graduate and undergraduate students who worked with me on projects and transcriptions, and who listened and contributed to ongoing conversations about Native film both in the classroom and beyond. The University of Missouri Research Council and Research Board supported the archival research and leave time that made writing this book possible. Further support came from the University's Center for Arts and Humanities and the College of Arts and Science Alumni Organization.

I began this work at the University of Arizona, where Susan White introduced me to the joys of teaching and writing about film, and to the world of archival research—her influence was truly life-changing. Larry Evers provided incredibly generous support and advice over many years and shared his ideas about the poetics and politics of Native American literature and film. Barbara Babcock helped me to both expand and focus my thinking about representation in ways I still find helpful every day. Earlier in my studies at Utah State University, Bonnie Glass-Coffin, David Lewis, Steve Siporin, and Barre Toelken created a nurturing environment for graduate study and positive professionalization. My initial research in silent film was funded by grants from the University of Arizona Graduate Final Project Fund and the Oberlin College Alumni Fellowship Program. The University of Arizona's Department of English and the University of Arizona Foundation, along with ArtsReach Native American Student Writing Programs, the Southern Arizona Women's Fund, and the Yavapai Tribal Council and the University of Arizona American Indian Studies Program's

Ft. McDowell Wassaja Memorial Fund enabled the earliest stages of my immersion in this work.

All of my family members near and far have earned my thanks many times over. From talking musical terminology to preparing digital images to giving pep talks and sending article clippings—I could fill another book with stories about all the ways they have made everything possible. My mother, Betsy Hearne, was my first writing teacher and is still my favorite editor, mentor, and intellectual colleague, not to mention a best friend. And words can't express my gratitude to Chris Morrey for his patient support, technical genius, and copious wisecracks over the years, and to my sons, Desmond and Leo, for making it all worthwhile.

Joanna Hearne
February 2012

Introduction

Before-and-After

Vanishing and Visibility in Native American Images

During location shooting in Monument Valley for the 1925 Paramount film *The Vanishing American*, based on the Zane Grey novel of the same title, a photographer shot a promotional photograph of the film's non-Native star, Richard Dix (see figure I.1; see also figure 2.12). Dix plays a Navajo (Diné) man in the film, and in this photograph he is in "redface"—bronze makeup and full costume—surrounded by the children of local Diné families (some of whom served as amateur actors and crew for the film). The image turned up in a Bureau of Census file in the U.S. National Archives—perhaps inadvertently misfiled there by government officials because it appeared to be an authentic photograph from the 1930 census or perhaps placed there deliberately for the images of the children—with a caption that presumably referred to the many children in the photograph: "Each one of these bear individual names."

The captioner's withholding the children's names, like the frequent practice of withholding Native actors' names from film credits, suggests an unwillingness to engage with Native personhood, relationships, and epistemologies. The original photographer's appropriation of Native children's images to authenticate Hollywood's Western star results in an implied scenario, one that imagines a reconstituted family organized around Euro-American custody. This amalgamated, staged family supports a visual narrative privileging the power of white racial transformation, a theatrical "passing" in a constructed "West" that would undergird the soon-to-burgeon tourist development of the southwest. Long after it was archived in the records

1

Figure I.1. Hollywood star Richard Dix with Diné children. NA/RG29 NR. Bureau of Census. Prints: Navajo Indians. 1930. Box 1. No. 29–NR–31. National Archives.

of the Bureau of Census, the photograph was included in James C. Faris's 2003 book *Navajo and Photography* as a census image, with Faris's additional explanation that it was "probably taken by a weary census taker" (104–05). Faris argues that such photographs reduce "all histories . . . to those of the West" (19), a reading I discuss in later chapters of this book. Yet the case of mistaken identity (Dix is not Diné) and hidden identity (the Diné children are unnamed in the caption, but would of course be recognizable to relatives who knew them) suggest not just the foreclosure of Native history but also its potential retrieval. Embedded in the politics of seeing and being seen are the possibilities of recognition and repatriation. The critical uptake of this image in scholarly studies of cross-cultural photography and image stereotypes such as Faris's book illustrates the intricacy of archival retrieval in the face of the complex histories of Native presence in the film industry and in film audiences across the span of the twentieth century. The photograph's shifting categorization as fiction and nonfiction suggests the slipperiness of images—their tendency to escape their makers' intended signification—and at the same time the stickiness of the attached scenarios that inform the way contemporary viewers understand images from the past.

Indigenous filmmakers' engagement with archival images, genre conventions, and industrial film practices can alter the frame through which viewers see "images of Indians," actualizing dynamic visual processes of political and genealogical recognition. Contemporary Native American film directors have noted the importance of their relationships with the visual archives of popular images of Indians, while at the same time they have appropriated and renarrated these images in their films in ways that strengthen connections to ancestral homelands and reassert Indigenous ownership of images through processes of visual repatriation. Blackfeet filmmaker George Burdeau, for example, describes his first encounter with images of his tribe taken by Edward Curtis as having the effect of bringing him back to his own tribal lands and community. Burdeau specifies a turn-of-the-century photograph by Curtis, titled "The Three Chiefs—Piegan" (see figure I.2), as one of these meaningful images.

Figure I.2. "The Three Chiefs—Piegan." Edward S. Curtis. Image courtesy of the Charles Deering McCormick Library of Special Collections, Northwestern University Library, used with permission.

The photograph follows the pictorialist tradition in its intensely expressive composition; the use of long-shot, the stance of the men, their blurred reflections in a waterhole, and the wide horizon isolate the central figures, separating them from their community context, while suggesting for some viewers (in the caption as well as the image) a clichéd nobility and an elegiac sense of impending loss. Yet Burdeau describes viewing these images, as well as the act of filmmaking itself, in personal terms as part of an active process of "going home": "When I first discovered Curtis, I found this photograph of three Piegan chiefs out on the plains and I still hadn't come home yet, so for me, this was like—coming home . . . it allowed me to go on my own journey, and I knew that . . . I needed to come home."[1] In fact, in Burdeau's 1997 documentary *Backbone of the World: The Blackfeet* about the tribe's struggle to prevent gas and coal mining in the Badger-Two Medicine mountain range, he not only uses many of Curtis's images of the Blackfeet, but he also documents his own return to his tribe and the community filmmaking workshop he organized while directing the film. Both on camera and in voiceover, he describes this process early on in the film:

> It's really been an incredible experience for me to be able to actually come home as a result of this film project. . . . I've been making films for a long time and most of that time has been spent working with other Indian tribes. I always would have this sort of lingering thought in my head when I would be with the Pueblos in New Mexico or the Utes in Utah, I would always envy people who had some sort of connection to their homeland, and had the ability to connect to not only the community and their family . . . but also that cultural connection. Because I really didn't know much about my own heritage, and didn't know . . . what really belonged to me. I didn't even know what was Blackfeet. Now that I've had the opportunity to come back home, I'm beginning to . . . feel that I have a place.

Illustrating this story of return and integrating it with oral histories from community members, Burdeau superimposes Curtis photographs of Blackfeet individuals over footage of the Badger-Two Medicine wilderness area during various seasons. Thus he essentially renarrates the photographic portraits cinematically in order to highlight the perspectives of the subjects' descendants, who reiterate in their stories both the decimation of the tribe from starvation in the 1880s, when many buffalo herds were destroyed, and their ongoing land claims in the Badger-Two Medicine area. The process of renarration and reflexive community self-representation also parallels the strong presence in the film of the young videographers in Burdeau's film-making workshop, who deliberately insert themselves into the cinematic frame as they discuss their goals for the film, technical problems encountered, and their views about the community and homeland.[2] This strategy of deploying past and present media images to revisit shattering events in the tribe's history—massacres and the loss of lands—becomes in Burdeau's film not only a memorial but also part of a testimony of contemporary presence that involves strategic and political claims to ongoing rights based in genealogy and cultural heritage. These reflexive filmmaking strategies register the power of active Native vision at all points across the arc of image production, text, and reception, to assert a Native presence and politics of seeing. Vanishing becomes visibility, absence becomes presence, when an image once symbolic of Indian finality instead elicits tribal recognition and supports discourses of contemporary political sovereignty.

Despite their differences, these two photographs—the 1900 portrait and the 1929 production still—and the changing narratives that inform them have some important qualities in common. Like many historical photographs, these were first narrated in one way and then renarrated in another. The photographs also function in different ways as extracinematic visual texts, both revealing and influencing film production practices. In both photographs, the Native subjects are excerpted from their family and community contexts for the purposes of illustrating an implied narrative. The original images are posed in ways that embed their subjects in preexisting Euro-American scenarios, which the images helped to reconstitute and to circulate into another sphere of signification. The Native subjects are not named or credited in the original images, yet their identities are crucial to shifting, politicized processes of staging and transmission: a Hollywood promotional still becomes a government document, and an artist's ethnographic photograph becomes a filmmaker's personal mnemonic.

The generic arena of the Western—especially the sympathetic Western and its precursor, the Indian drama—informs the constellation of popular representations from which a range of Native filmmakers have drawn a counterdiscourse advocating tribal autonomy in familial terms. *Native Recognition* is about these images of and by Native people in the cinema. Its chapters trace representational scenarios taken up in mainstream and independent cinema from the early silent-era "Indian dramas" of Cecil B. DeMille, D. W. Griffith, and Ho-Chunk director James Young Deer, to the "home dramas" of Cheyenne/Arapaho director Chris Eyre at the turn of the twenty-first century. Images of Native familial separation and reunion in sympathetic Westerns and Indigenous films provide an organizing principle for this book's exploration of the larger relationship between historical Western genre conventions and the emergence of Native American filmmaking. These filmed images of Native generational relationships encode political discourses about civic allegiance, custodial authority, land rights, and tribal futures. I argue that both silent-era and contemporary Native films have resignified cinematic images of familial rupture in order to catalyze family reunification both on and off the screen. My analyses focus on cinematically constructed "families" as contested public images rather than on actual Native family structures or domestic practices, and I combine this textual focus with attention to historical and contemporary Native participation in film production and reception.[3] Native and collaborative film productions have overturned long-accepted mass culture images of supposedly vanishing Indians, repurposing the commodity forms of Hollywood films to envision Native intergenerational continuity. In doing so, they have effectively marshaled the power of visual media to take part in national discussions of social justice and political sovereignty for North American Indigenous peoples.[4]

I ask several questions in this book about how Native writers, actors, and filmmakers have worked both within and against established American film genres and Hollywood production methods. How have films by and about Native people complicated the overdetermined frontier trope of the settler "family on the land"? And how have filmed stories of interrelated Indigenous and settler domesticities disturbed the linear, assimilationist narratives driving U.S. custodial transfers of Native children in institutional schooling and foster care? How have Native filmmakers navigated the power structures of Hollywood, speaking from within established genres, working outside of Hollywood's financial and generic demands, and modeling alternative relations with media? How have contemporary filmmakers responded to the historical archive of Western genre images, establishing Indigenous ways of seeing across film production and reception? To begin to answer these questions, *Native Recognition* explores historical, ongoing relationships between Native filmmaking and the Western genre by addressing the intersections of Indigenous expression, shifts in U.S. federal policy, and the history of visual representations. The project involves two related strands of historical recovery. First, I situate Native directors' strategic interventions in the cinema of their time by historicizing sympathetic forms of the Western in light of contemporaneous public discourses and government policies. Second, I recognize contemporary filmmakers' own historical work as they bridge temporal distances by returning our gaze to the Western and its influence across the twentieth century. Each chapter describes retrievals of Native images in the context of Western genre representations. These recovered texts—of extant silent and "orphan" films as well as contemporary Native perspectives on the Western genre cinematic archive—consistently reveal the cinema to be a site of public contestation over images of Native families.

While some of the relationships between Indigenous projects and mainstream Western genre forms are embedded in historical production cycles and practices, others span historical periods as contemporary directors take up the cinematic and photographic legacies of the past. Rehistoricizing cycles of sympathetic Westerns in light of U.S. Indian policies involves bringing the disciplines of cinema studies and Native studies into closer contact. Documents and social programs related to Native nations' relationships to the United States have gone unremarked in most book-length critical studies of Westerns, except in studies by scholars of Native film images such as Jacqueline Kilpatrick (Choctaw and Cherokee), Beverly Singer (Tewa and Diné), and Angela Aleiss. This book builds on their path-breaking work with a focused thematic study of individual films, historical production cycles, and strategies of remediation. Throughout I emphasize the interrelatedness of visual media: photography and film; documentary and feature films; studio and independent films; documentary "visible evidence" and generic fantasy features. As I discuss later in this introduction, cinematic scenes of familial separation both animate and destabilize the sequential "before-and-after" photographs of turn-of-the-century Native students at government boarding schools. These photographs convey both vanishing and visibility, both the costumed poses of assimilation and the recognizable faces of Indigenous youth. I argue that the before-and-after images represent a formative intertext for several kinds of film, from the Indian drama form of the early Western genre film to contemporary Native documentaries that reframe the photographs as historical documents. The following sections set up this discussion and situate images of familial separation and reunion within a larger schema of Native invisibility and visibility in the arena of popular culture.

The "Vanishing Indian" and the Western's Invasive Pedagogy

The "West" of the Western is a theatrical space in which family formation and the shaping of youth take place within a politicized mise-en-scène. The genre's legacy of intensive racial coding is a central target of many contemporary Indigenous activist reappropriations of screen tropes and performances. My focus in this book is not primarily on Hollywood's canonized body of sound-era A-Westerns, which have dominated the critical literature on the genre and have been the subject of detailed critical readings. Although I frequently refer to these films for comparative purposes, this study emphasizes little-known productions from a parallel, related tradition of representation that has both shaped and departed from mainstream Western genre conventions. By suggesting that the subgenre of sympathetic Westerns carries forward the early generic category of the Indian drama as an overtly didactic, sentimental, and racially discursive form, I am making an argument for the importance of this form's political work at key historical moments. At the same time, I do not wish to suggest a chronological narrative of Western genre evolution leading to a contemporary phase of Indigenous revisionism as a millennial development. Nor do the critical categories of revisionism or "post-Western" quite fit, for rather than contemporary films "ghosting" an old genre, Indigenous directors and performers participated and shaped this cinematic heritage from the beginning, working with and against the generic conventions of Hollywood.[5]

The first two chapters focus particularly on the category of the "Indian drama," which can be seen as an antecedent to what has variously been called the "sympathetic Western," "Indian Western" and "Pro-Indian Western." Indian dramas, I suggest, functioned as foundational yet also contrapuntal production cycles, embedded in the larger phenomenon of frontier representation in cinema.[6] These productions claimed authenticity yet partook of the mythos of frontier melodramas. They were rooted in emergent Hollywood practices, and like the classical Western's generic forms of looking and knowing, Indian dramas also imaginatively staked claims to territory. Yet at times these films also offered a space for Native directors, actors, and consultants to influence or alter the dominant representations of Native peoples on screen. Rhetorically persuasive narrative texts, Indian dramas responded to contemporary changes in public policy by situating cinematic "Indians" in modern and urban contexts, and in this way they sometimes counterweighted the limited historical horizons of the Western genre as a whole.

While these films are sympathetic to their Indian characters, especially by comparison to such silent and sound-era films as D. W. Griffith's *The Battle of Elderbush Gulch* (1913) or John Ford's *Stagecoach* (1939),[7] their stories of tragedy—of interrupted political and romantic relationships—nevertheless refuse to imagine the continuation of Native families. In that refusal, sympathetic Westerns constitute and repeat one of the dominant tropes in the history of both the Western and federal Indian policy rhetoric, the "vanishing Indian." This "vanishing" refers to the mistaken but widespread public belief that Native peoples were destined to disappear from the continent, either through depopulation or amalgamation with settler populations. Brian Dippie's 1982 study, among others, has explored how the historical manifestations of these images of "vanishing" have impacted the seemingly contradictory U.S. Indian policies of removal and assimilation. Emerging from this ideology of the vanishing Indian that drove both policies and popular representations in the early twentieth century, many Westerns simply omit any images of Native families or children, focusing instead on white settler families threatened by groups of (exclusively male) Indian warriors.

This omission or "Indian absence" is central to the visual organization of the Western. Anishinaabe writer and theorist Gerald Vizenor points out the ways that Hollywood's substitutions actively suppress Native representational presence: "the simulation of the *indian* is the absence of real natives—the contrivance of the other in the course of dominance" (*Manifest Manners* vii). A growing number of studies theorize and describe the power of these generic absences to shape the national imaginary, tracing the forms that specific stereotypes of Indians have taken over time.[8] In a nuanced discussion of visual representations in Indian Westerns, Armando José Prats describes how cinematic Indians are indicated by signs of their absence, rendered as "invisible natives" in Hollywood films, which represent the threat of otherness through synecdoche and other paradigmatic textual absences and invisibilities.

This study extends these critical frameworks along a different trajectory, pressuring the Western's discourse of vanishing by exploring those productions that keep images of Native families and youth obsessively in view of film spectators. Although early trade journals declared that the boom in Indian dramas had ended by 1913, I argue that studio and independent producers returned to this genre at strategic historical moments, often coinciding with shifts in federal Indian policy. The emergence of Indigenous filmmaking as a movement in the second half of the twentieth century constitutes both a departure from and a politicized dialogue with these uneasy and ideologically burdened images of Native youth.

Envisioning Native families in the cinema is always a political act, and representations of youth in particular stake claims about the future of Indigenous nations as legitimate, and legitimating, heirs to the land. Controlling the signs of Indigeneity in visual representations engages issues of identity and the ongoing presence of Native tribes as distinct peoples with claims to their homelands and, in the United States, to the sovereignty acknowledged in nation-to-nation treaties. New critical work on Western history and the

Western film genre has emphasized the extensive, symbolic links between land ownership and inheritance. Historian Patricia Limerick maintains that "if Hollywood wanted to capture the emotional center of Western history, its movies would be about real estate" (55), and indeed some of the most cogent recent scholarship on the Western genre has focused on what Virginia Wright Wexman calls the "family on the land," referring to the dual issues of property and dynastic progression. Janet Walker maintains that the trauma at the core of many captivity narratives and the obsession with "generational accession" in many Westerns emerge "precisely at the point where property informs intergenerational conflict" (221, 229). My point in attending to the images of children and families who occupy the land in Indian dramas—and in later film productions—is to suggest that these figures have everything to do with both property rights and intergenerational relations.

For the center of gravity in the Indian drama, broadly defined, is the collapsed and interrelated domesticities of Indigenous and settler families. In the silent era, Indian melodramas were preoccupied with issues of sexuality, child-rearing, education, and personal appearance, which were also funda-mental to the regulation of private domestic spheres by government policies of racial distinction, education, property claims, and issues of succession and heirship. Borrowing from historians working in the field of colonial studies, and particularly Ann Stoler's work on "microsites of familial and intimate space," I take up what she terms "racial discourses as historical processes of rupture and recuperation" in this context of the early Western ("Tense" 19). In these films, the visually persuasive and very public narrative form of cinema speaks through a racialized rhetoric of the domestic. Westerns depend on both rigid categories of racial visibility and interracial mixture in their narratives of domestic inheritance. This traffic between fixed and unfixed racial signage is most evident in photographic and cinematic depic-tions of Native children and youth, the populations targeted by the U.S. government's educational and social policies designed to alter their cultural allegiance, beginning with names and appearances. Western dramas—from *The Squaw Man* in 1914 to *Redskin* in 1929 to *Duel at Diablo* in 1966—cast Native children as the nation's children. Films that depict Native families and youth both contribute to and are constituted by debates about the boundaries of racial identity, social class, land stewardship, treaty rights, and the public management of domestic practices.

In his far-reaching study of the American "myth of the frontier," Richard Slotkin, building on the work of earlier studies by scholars such as Will Wright, Jim Kitses, and John Cawelti that identify the genre's binary structures of civilization and savagery, asserts that Western genre narratives of

American "regeneration through violence" became "the structuring metaphor of the American experience." He writes, "the moral landscape of the Frontier Myth is divided by significant borders, of which the wilderness/civilization, Indian/White border is the most basic. The American must cross the border into 'Indian country' and experience a 'regression' to a more primitive and natural condition of life so that the false values of the 'metropolis' can be purged and a new, purified social contract enacted" (14). Slotkin's vision of a narrative dependency on structures of opposition, based in regressive temporality, offers a compelling account of the Western's obsessive emphasis on violent masculine combat—especially vigilantism.[9] While sympathetic Indian dramas partake of this phenomenon, I argue that they also address their audiences in a different register. Violence and vigilantism are subsumed within emotional melodramas of interracial domestic separation, maternal anguish, and child custody. Critical focus on the constitutive binary oppositions structuring the Western tends to elide the ongoing public contestation over Indigenous futures in the United States. The Western's narrative investment in the chronology of U.S. national origins further obscures Native priority on the land. The orientation of the Western to the national past also encodes a national future, and the genre's visual representation of kinship stages a drama of Native absence and presence that is crucial to this "backward-looking" future charter.

The pedagogic work of Westerns is closely tied to the genre's emotional investment in telling stories about history. Often targeted toward children and marketed as family fare, Westerns teach history by claiming frontier realism, even within the genre's more melodramatic modes of storytelling. That silent Westerns functioned as spectacular "Americanizing" history lessons for youthful and adult audiences—especially for young boys—has been demonstrated by scholars such as Richard Abel.[10] As early as 1914, D. W. Griffith claimed for motion pictures both educational and general public influence in an eerie prediction of the political power and global eye of contemporary television media: "Just think of what it [the motion picture] would mean as an educational force. Think what could be done with the picture if it came into the hands of a rival political party with a big issue like that of slavery before the voters. Think of the possibilities as a newspaper, with up-to-the-minute illustrated areas of the world."[11] For decades, Western genre costumes and accessories were the very sign of white American boyhood.[12] Sympathetic Westerns, claiming (but not delivering) ethnographic content and newly "authentic" representations of American frontier history, are as sites of education that also include scenes of education. Indian dramas and other films about institutional education of Native people have functioned pedagogically, miseducating generations of young viewers about the nature of cultural difference and the history of U.S. settlement. Lee Clark Mitchell argues that narratives of education—the processes of "making the man"—in 1950s Westerns such as *Shane* (Stevens 1953), *Hondo* (Farrow 1953), and *High Noon* (Zinneman 1952) demonstrate broad cultural ambivalence about childrearing and the work of enculturation. The mise-en-scène of education seems to evoke a middle-class utopian wish for experiential frontier education in some Westerns (for example, *Hondo*), while others advocate for systemic progressive reform through the exposure of hardship and loss in military-style boarding schools for Native children (*Redskin*, Schertzinger 1929). In fact, Westerns consistently emphasize the intergenerational transmission of racial knowledge as a foundation of continental settlement, as we see in the images of white women schoolteachers and children learning in frontier settings that pervade its visual discourses of cultural reproduction in films such as *Shane* and *The Man Who Shot Liberty Valance* (Ford 1962).

Sympathetic Westerns as a didactic, sentimental medium combining theatrical and realistic modes have often been marketed as presenting the "real" story—specifically the "real Indian" story—of the Western frontier for the first time. Promotional declarations of new authenticity in production and cultural spectacle seek to legitimate the genre's power to write history and to stage, through the films' pedagogical and enculturating work, a visual articulation of public or collective memory. Claims to the mimetic production of a real frontier have functioned at the industry level to bring in middle-class and youth audiences, and to stave off censorship efforts, even as these constructions of realism in Westerns depended on theatricality and the marketing of casting and costuming. Audiences have responded to various cinematic ways of locating claims to realism, including historical content, documentary truth claims, counterculture politics, low production values, high production values, and immersive technologies. The financial success of such strategies is evident in the blockbuster arc of *The Squaw Man* (DeMille 1914), *Broken Arrow* (Daves 1950), *Billy Jack* (Laughlin 1971/1973), and *Dances with Wolves* (Costner 1990), all films that tell nostalgic or "sympathetic" stories about threatened Indigeneity. In early frontier dramas with melodramatic storylines, trends in stylistic realism also supported the reform impulses and assertions of pedagogical authenticity. Early ethnographic documentaries such as *In the Land of the War Canoes* (1914) and *Nanook of the North* (1922) share with Western frontier melodramas this pedagogical function, bending rhetorically powerful visual narratives to the task of public persuasion. The early and reciprocal influences of ethnographic filmmaking and the Western genre have lent fictional narratives the authority of historical truth claims while infusing ethnographic image-making with the melodramatic conventions of frontier dramas. This exchange and pedagogical subtext is traceable in public discourses regarding government education of Native children as a civilizing process and cinema as a site of education for white youth. But in remaking cinema as an educational theater, Indian dramas also stage a theatrical presentation of education. The dramatic articulation of federal policies of "Indian education" took place in visual and even proto-cinematic form, I argue, through the production and circulation of before-and-after images of Native boarding school students in the late nineteenth and early twentieth centuries. These images constitute a precinematic visual narrative of Native tradition and modernity that profoundly influenced the development of the Western, especially the sympathetic Western, a form that in turn has undergone subversive use by Native filmmakers.

Indigenous Visibility, Visual Sovereignty, and Fourth Cinema

Working with Native crews or with non-Native partners on collaborative productions, Native filmmakers and performers have critically assessed and appropriated the language of American cinema, rerouting the codes and performative idioms of the Western to reveal the instability of its generic world-making. The films I discuss in this book are politically oppositional but semiotically articulated with the expressive generic codes and conventions of Hollywood Indians. And when revisiting the Western's scenarios of extralegal violence and of domestic rupture and repair, some Native filmmakers have deployed the expressive possibilities of cinematic reclamation in specifically familial terms. Contemporary films such as Hopi director Victor Masayesva's 1993 *Imagining Indians* and Jeff Spitz's 2001 *The Return of Navajo Boy* return to earlier recorded images for purposes of political revitalization and even the reconfiguration of fragmented families. The films have voiceover narration and embedded scenes of viewing, situating the older images within contemporary Indigenous hermeneutic frames and within the trajectory of a reconstructed past. The filmmakers' close attention to multigenerational storytelling permeates all points of media circulation, including production, performance, and spectatorship. Through narration and other strategies, conventional codes and icons are reoriented in service of viewers' emotional investment in Indigenous histories. By shifting the established political significations of Western iconic stars, frontier melodrama, and ethnographic display, contemporary Native films such as Chris Eyre's *Skins* target the connections between policies of expropriation, social disruption, and the manipulation of Indian images in mainstream cinema. Using reflexive strategies to reframe older media images, many new Native productions underscore the historically unstable relationship of dependency between racialized policies of state wardship that made a public issue of Indigenous domestic relations, and the performance and technological projection of intimate family matters in the cinema.

Rather than forming a wholly separatist voice of resistance, recent Native-directed and collaborative films richly engage earlier productions as a cinematic heritage and archive, harnessing and reshaping the continuing cultural potency of popular cinematic memory. These productions reflexively take over and reuse existing media images. But their acts of "remediation" serve a distinct social agenda, one that addresses a particular history of colonization in which Hollywood's representational thefts repeated and reproduced U.S. genocidal programs of land expropriation, cultural interruption, and familial rupture.[13] Embedding commentaries on the Western in their feature films and documentaries, contemporary Native filmmakers have accessed multiple audiences and blurred the distinctions between public and private modes of viewing. Rather than suggesting a unified perspective in either Hollywood's construction of Indianness or in the independent, Indigenous productions that "talk back" to Hollywood's Indians, I focus on complex moments of intercultural imaginings when cinematic productions trouble discourses of racial purity and binary opposition with the complex politics and consequences of circulation and exchange.

In many Native films, representational acts of familial or genealogical recognition—which also function as a political recognition of Native claims—support discourses of Native sovereignty in specifically visual ways. Tuscarora artist and critic Jolene Rickard, writing about sovereignty in Native art, argues in an influential 1996 article that "Sovereignty is the border that shifts Indigenous experience from a victimized stance to a strategic one" (51). Beverly Singer developed the term "cultural sovereignty" to describe a "social movement" that involves "trusting in the older ways and adapting them to our lives in the present" (2). Seneca scholar Michelle Raheja has defined "visual sovereignty" as a "reading practice for thinking about the space between resistance and compliance" ("Reading Nanook's Smile" 1161). Her definition stresses the way this practice enables a duel address to both Native and non-Native populations "by creating self-representations that interact with older stereotypes but also, more importantly, connect film production to larger aesthetic practices that work toward strengthening treaty claims and more traditional (though by no means static) modes of cultural understanding" (*Reservation Reelism* 19). In a different formulation that also emphasizes self-determination, Randolph Lewis calls the work of Indigenous filmmakers such as Alanis Obomsawin (Abenaki) a "cinema of sovereignty," defining "representational sovereignty" as "the right, as well as the ability, for a group of people to depict themselves with their own ambitions at heart" (175). Visual sovereignty, then, is an expansive framework that creates a critical space to privilege a range of Indigenous aesthetic strategies and access to traditionality in a political world. This concept also accommodates several specifically cinematic tactics; it begins to account not only for the political interventions of silent-era Native filmmakers in the Indian drama narratives of their contemporaries, but also for twenty-first-century Native filmmakers' power of retrospect over mediated images from the past.

In returning to familial images and stories recorded in the past, Native independent filmmakers at the turn of the twenty-first century remember the consequences of such early policies and persuasive representations, often specifically in terms of a subsequent active claiming, or reclaiming, of land and family. Maori scholar Linda Tuhiwai Smith has emphasized the value for Native communities of the related Indigenous research projects of *claiming* and *returning* (143, 155). Although Smith focuses primarily on the claiming and returning of land and of ancestral remains, the projects she outlines inspire and intersect with the arena of representation. The practical assertion of Indigenous sovereignty in the arena of popular culture parallels other forms of international Indigenous struggle to retrieve "elements of their heritage held by others." James Clifford characterizes this retrieval as "a process of forcefully detaching and reattaching artifacts and their meanings: projects of a dynamic tradition critically reworking its colonial history" ("Traditional Futures" 159).

While this project focuses on Westerns and Native American films produced in the United States, these films have also reached beyond those national boundaries through global circulation. In the silent era, the French company Pathé Frères hired the first Native American director, James Young Deer, to make films in Hollywood for U.S. and European exhibition, and European archives have extensive holdings of Westerns. Chickasaw director Edwin Carewe's films regularly showed in Europe (the only extant copy of his 1928 film *Ramona* was recently repatriated from the National Film Archive in the Czech Republic). From production to circulation and exhibition, the international life of such a seemingly nation-specific genre as the Western parallels the correspondingly transnational scope of Indigenous media production. Films that might at first glance appear to be isolated productions with limited circulation are often localized participants in larger, coterminous international movements, for example the 1972 film *House Made of Dawn*'s concurrent emergence with innovative media productions in the 1970s and 1980s by Indigenous cultural activists such as Merata Mita (Maori) in Aotearoa/New Zealand, Alanis Obomsawin in Canada, and Essie Coffey (Muruwari) in Australia.[14] Key studies in Indigenous media by scholars such as Faye Ginsburg, Eric Michaels, Pamela Wilson and Michelle Stewart, Jennifer Deger, Houston Wood, Shari Huhndorf (Yup'ik), and Corinn Columpar take up this global focus. Pamela Wilson and Michelle Stewart identify "international Indigenism" as a term that privileges Indigenism over nationalism, often appealing to broader discourses of universal human rights in venues of international law such as the United Nations in order to apply pressure on nation-states to recognize Indigenous rights within and across national borders. They describe the concept as one that "may at times appear to be strategically essentialist in its international appeals, identifying Indigenism as a philosophical and cultural attitude toward the world that is shared by all Indigenous peoples, a model for global conduct in its resistance to colonialism, imperialism, environmental destruction, and now, globalization" (8). Michelle Raheja identifies the central resistance articulated by global Indigenous media as redefining racial discourses rooted in United States history: "Transnational Indigenous media production rethinks Audre Lorde's dictum that 'the master's tools will never dismantle the master's house' by insisting that the very foundations on which the master's house is built are Indigenous and should be reterritorialized or repatriated" (18). Key elements of these transnational Indigenous rights include protection or restitution of territories and cultural patrimony, projects for which self-representation in media is and has been essential. Films that follow the transnational repatriation of sacred materials, film footage, and even individuals to their home communities—feature films such as Maori filmmaker and intellectual Barry Barclay's *Te Rua* (1991) and documentaries such as Métis director Gil Cardinal's *Foster Child* (1987) and *Totem: The Return of the G'psgolox Pole* (2003), and Claude Massot's *Nanook Revisited* (1990)—expand transnationally the discourses of repatriation in films such as *The Return of Navajo Boy* (Spitz 2001) discussed in this book.

This broader account of Indigenous cinema and media has benefitted in particular from the work of Barclay, in his films and in publications such as *Our Own Image* and *Mana Tuturu*. Barclay's term for Indigenous cinema, "Fourth Cinema," invokes and extends the classification system first articulated by Fernando Solanas and Octavio Getino's manifesto "Towards a Third Cinema" (Barclay offers the shorthand definition of "First Cinema being American cinema; Second Cinema Art House cinema, and Third Cinema the cinema of the so-called Third World," pointing out that these could all be termed "Invader Cinemas" from an Indigenous perspective).[15] Unlike Third Cinema's focus on colonial legacies in the context of modern nation states, Fourth Cinema describes "how the old principles have been reworked to give vitality and richness to the way we conceive, develop, manufacture and present our films" in ways "outside of the national orthodoxy" (11, 9). Barclay brilliantly encapsulates a paradigmatic Indigenous revision of cinema's form and purpose by appropriating the metaphors of colonialist contact narratives in films such as *The Mutiny on the Bounty* (1935, 1962), identifying "The First Cinema Camera" as one that "sits firmly on the deck of the ship," while "The Camera Ashore, the Fourth Cinema Camera, is the one held by the people for whom 'ashore' is their ancestral home" (10). Barclay's figure for the perspectival reorientation in films by Indigenous filmmakers—"the Camera Ashore"—is balanced by an equally important concept that he develops, in his recent books, around the provenance of Indigenous images.[16] *Mana Tuturu*, or "Maori spiritual guardianship," incorporates traditional Maori protocols into contemporary archival practices while simultaneously establishing Maori ownership as paramount over public claims to Maori images. Barclay's use of traditional Indigenous concepts to reframe dominant discourses of image ownership expands the concept of the "Camera Ashore" to encompass elements of film transmission, circulation, reception, and archiving. His attention to the definitions and strategies of trans-Indigenous cinemas and image archives inform the critical frameworks in this book's close investigation of Native American mediamakers's engagement with the discursively national confines of the Western, while also facilitating the recognition that the production and reception of Westerns and Native films have always been an international phenomenon.

In recovering archival images, Native filmmakers have used mise-en-scène, editing, and sound to assert a representational sovereignty over productions made during a time when Native performers and audiences had little or no voice in cinema, a form of retroactive control over the aesthetic production and political meaning of the films. Establishing Indigenous claims to past media production and reception becomes an act of intergenerational communication, performing social work that Faye Ginsburg describes as a "mediation of rupture."[17] Ginsburg defines the counterstream of Indigenous media in terms of its potential to mediate colonial ruptures through the social relations of film production, circulation, and reception. I want to historicize the surge of energy and activity in Indigenous media-making of the last thirty years, for Ginsburg's paradigm of Indigenous media as mediation can be seen not only as a recent phenomenon but also in the productions of earlier film practitioners such as James Young Deer and Lillian St. Cyr, the Ho-Chunk actors who so intensively participated in the formation of the Hollywood Western (as discussed in chapter 1).[18] Furthermore, Native filmmakers have articulated such mediations using one of the primary modes of mainstream theater and cinema, the generic and affective registers of Western melodramas. The sympathetic Western melodrama makes large-scale structures of colonial power visible in the close-knit arenas of the domestic. While melodramatic stage and cinema productions have functioned to transmit the images that underwrite "scenarios of colonial fantasy," some Native media-makers have been able to harness the social power of public sympathy that emerges from these Hollywood images to connect audiences with Indigenous political agendas.[19] More radically, they have seized and reinterpreted Native characters enmeshed in scenarios of government supervision. The enunciation of colonizing interventions and familial damage in frontier dramas is recognizable to viewers who see a reference to the real in the text and production of the Hollywood West. Paternalistic sentiments associated with sympathetic Westerns become available for hermeneutic realignment and a renegotiation of emotional identification, even in its signature stereotypes, forms, and narratives of the vanishing Indian and the Indian torn between tradition and modernity.

In various ways, images of Native families and generational accession in cinema visualize Indigenous civic allegiance and genealogical futures. Attending to visual discourses of Indigenous families and futures in historical Indian dramas and in contemporary Indigenous films that reframe earlier images addresses a conceptual gap in Western genre film studies, a critical inattention to the ongoing Native presence within, alongside, and outside of Western genre film production. The phrase "Indigenous futures" comes in part from visual anthropologist Eric Michaels's articulation of the relationship between contemporary Indigenous "cultural futures" and local Aboriginal autonomy in media production. The term has been taken up in different ways by James Clifford, Faye Ginsburg, and Fred Myers to break through the rigidly linear temporalities and "constitutive opposition" of tradition and modernity that have dominated Western academic, popular, and political discourses about Indigeneity (Clifford, "Traditional Futures" 152). Similar binaries or "constitutive oppositions" in the Western are the very instantiation of rupture and erasure that discursively suppress Indigenous generational (and hence cultural and political) continuity. The analyses in this book attempt to unravel the binary oppositions that structure both Western and ethnographic documentary genres—civilized and primitive, garden and wilderness. Yet they also take into account the ways that these same generic sign systems, with their cinematically mediated Indian "absences" and racialized melodramatic codes, have become part of the mediascape that shapes the work of Native filmmakers, performers, and viewers.

Thinking about the ways that Native films foreground imaginative visions of Indigenous futures—even as they look back to historical events and archival texts premised on Indian demise—facilitates an overt acknowledgement of the world-making qualities of visual media and articulates the political stakes of public culture images of Indians. U.S. government representatives instituted federal laws and policies such as the General Allotment Act of 1887 and the residential boarding school system because they imagined that Native nations had no future ("vanishing" either through population decline or assimilation). These policies were both promoted and contested through the dissemination of images in the popular sphere. Ginsburg and Myers argue that "Policies . . . are not simply bureaucratic formulations but are given vitality as a social force through powerful and persuasive narratives—most effectively in popular media through which they circulate promiscuously" (29). Frontier film dramas about government interventions in Native American families reveal how linked institutional and representational structures come to dominate our imaginations and make our world. Stuart Hall has famously argued that popular culture matters because it is a political "arena of consent and resistance." It is "one of the sites where this struggle for and against a culture of the powerful is engaged: it is also the stake to be won or lost in that struggle" ("Notes" 239). In this arena of visual popular culture, images of Native families function as sites of contestation over whose vision of the future should become reality. Images of families have functioned as a site where Indigenous media-makers rewrite the imposed imagined futures of Hollywood scenarios with their own autonomous visions.

In the section that follows, I unpack the stakes and arenas of these intersecting discourses in the concrete exemplar of the before-and-after image sequence, initiating an alternative origin story for Indian drama films and sympathetic Westerns in the visual documents circulated by government boarding schools across the turn of the twentieth century. These before-and-after photographs, in their dramatic sequencing and close connection to U.S. policies of assimilation, powerfully shaped the discourses of sympathy in the Western as well as its disinvestment in Indigenous futures. While Western images of Native peoples clearly emerged in part from the legacy of Wild West shows (Buffalo Bill Cody's in particular),[20] critical discussions of the origins of frontier iconography in Wild West shows have eclipsed another paradigmatic point of origin for Indian dramas in the visual representational practices of the Carlisle Indian Industrial School. Carlisle was the first and most well-known of the many federal Indian residential schools established to assimilate Native American children into the dominant culture in the late nineteenth and early twentieth centuries. Understanding the visual influence of school documents on sympathetic Westerns requires a discussion of the history and function of before-and-after images, a discussion that also lays the groundwork for my investigation of the convergence of image and policy in the mobile scenarios of early cinema.

Early Cinema, Photography, and the Visual Iconography of Education

Photographs of Native American boarding school students comprise a colonial archive of staged images that circulated as public documents at the same time that the Western film genre took shape in the early twentieth century. This book is primarily about moving images, but I want to begin by discussing earlier image technology in the form of before-and-after photographs that purported to measure assimilation in separate, temporally sequenced visual frames. This discussion is important because the implied narratives of progress inherent in this style of carefully posed, consecutive photographs underpin the modern scenarios and reformist stance of many silent Indian dramas and Westerns. Frontier and Indian dramas of the 1910s and 1920s were profoundly shaped by these still images, which were originally created to document and market to the public a program of institutional education. Yet, as I discuss in chapters 1 and 2, the films also complicate the tropes and discourses visualized in the photographs.

The sequencing techniques of before-and-after photographs can be considered proto-cinematic in their attempt to make photographs tell iconic stories. According to Martha Sandweiss, nineteenth-century manipulations of photographs strived to make the "literal accuracy" of photographs "symbolic and theatrical . . . an important scene in a longer story" (106, 102). In this period, emerging film technology functioned doubly as a tool of cultural expression through melodramatic storytelling and as a scientific tool for measurement and documentation. The before-and-after sequences, like Eadweard Muybridge's sequenced photographic motion studies, attempt to capture change occurring in time. Muybridge's images render moments in time as discrete photographs that are incomplete on their own; the gridlike mapping of motion is subject to photographic interdependence. As Jonathan Crary notes, the resulting "temporal mutability" and fracturing make possible both visual regimentation and potential alternative sequencing. Muybridge's images "at least suggest the possibility of novel social/historical intuitions, 'flashing up' amid their disruptions of presumed continuities or their shattering of the self-sufficiency of an autonomous image" (147).

Like Felix-Louis Regnault's rapid photography and early film, before-and-after pictures also seek to document racial difference.[21] Regnault, who studied craniometry and body posture in criminals, also frequently photographed Native subjects at expositions and fairs, where they performed in reconstructions of Native villages, providing another link between ethnic and ethnographic spectacle, early cinema, and scientific racial classification.[22] Joanna Cohan Scherer has described the ways that both anthropological photographers and commercial photographers benefitted financially from a thriving market for images of Indians; even such important figures as Major John Wesley Powell, a key force behind the formation of the Bureau of American Ethnology, frequently carried outfits to costume their Native subjects in photographs. The control of the object of the gaze available in ethnographic film was even greater in fictional films such as early Westerns, which explored cross-cultural romances for voyeuristic purposes, combining cultural curiosity, erotic titillation, and a moral anxiety about the displacement of Native Americans in the formation of the United States.[23]

Some of the most hardworking visual documents at the turn of the twentieth century were before-and-after photographs circulated by the Carlisle School as part of its promotional appeal for public support of boarding school education for Native youth.[24] At the request of the Carlisle School, photographer John Nicholas Choate regularly photographed students as they arrived by train to the school and then rephotographed them in their new clothes and haircuts after they had spent several months or longer at the school (see figures I.3–I.6). Some photographs even made students appear lighter-skinned, either through techniques of photographic front lighting, makeup, and exposure or because they had lost their suntans during the time away from home.[25] As Brian Dippie writes, "physical appearance was an obsession at Carlisle" (116). Captain Richard Henry Pratt, a crusader for education at off-reservation boarding schools and the founder of the Carlisle and Hampton schools, believed that race was a "meaningless abstraction" and that racial distinctions could and should be eliminated by total assimilation. He provided persuasive visual evidence of this transformation for legislators, private funders, and others through these before-and-after

Figure I.3. Tom Torlino before education at the Carlisle School. Photograph taken by John Choate in 1882. Image courtesy of the Cumberland County Historical Society, PA–CH2–004a (BS–CH–008) (12–26–03)

Figure I.4. Tom Torlino after education at the Carlisle School. Photograph taken by John Choate in 1885. Image courtesy of the Cumberland County Historical Society, PA–CH2–004a (BS–CH–012) (12–26–04)

Figure I.5. Three Laguna Pueblo students on arrival at the Carlisle School, from left, Mary Perry, John (Chaves) Menaul, and Benjamin Thomas. Photograph taken by John Choate in 1880. Image courtesy of the Cumberland County Historical Society, CS–CH–72 (10B–02–01)

Figure I.6. Three Pueblo students after about four years at the Carlisle School, from left, John (Menaul) Chaves, Mary Perry, Benjamin Thomas. Image courtesy of the Cumberland County Historical Society, PA–CH1–30a (10B–02–02)

photographs, which circulated widely in correspondence, in periodicals such as *Harper's*, and as postcards.[26]

Before-and-after images were already an established visual technique in nineteenth-century representations associated with reform and other social movements. Daguerreotypist Eugene Thibault used the before-and-after image structure to depict a Paris street barricade before and after a conflict between revolutionaries and French troops during the revolution of 1848.[27] Images of children were used by social reform organizations, particularly abolitionists, to raise funds. For example, in 1864 the U.S. Society of Friends circulated before-and-after photographs of African-American children taken from slaveowners and educated at the Philadelphia Orphan's Center.[28] In the latter part of the century, Thomas Barnardo, the head of a British private charity administering group homes and training programs for homeless children, sold before-and-after images of the children to support his organization (about 80 pairs of images were made and sold singly or in packets).[29] These images, like the Carlisle School before-and-after images, privilege institutional discipline within narratives of rescue and social progress, using a visual form that rationalizes the fragmentation and sequencing of temporal frames into a legible organization suggestive of modern industrial production. Although the images appear literal in their photographic claims to the real, the Carlisle School photographs also clearly function as political allegories of state power over Indigenous nations.

Before-and-after photographs are evidentiary records intended to document results. They compress almost any length of time into an instantaneous distillation of difference. Their sequencing conveys a visual moral order and selectively highlights issues of time and transformation. They often demonstrate changes to the landscape—images of San Francisco before and after the 1906 earthquake, for example—and are in this sense related to illustrated and even animated or sequential maps, in which historical territorial shifts are shown through multiple drawings. Late-nineteenth-century advertising trade cards used before-and-after illustrations to sell cosmetics such as hair dyes. By the mid-twentieth century, before-and-after images were routinely deployed as a powerful sales technique for diet plans and women's bras and girdles, and this visual photo-sequencing strategy continues to be primarily associated with cosmetic transformations of the human body.[30] Current advertisements for weight loss programs, acne remedies, antiaging creams, skin lightening, hair replacement, and breast or other cosmetic surgery all rely heavily on the "mission accomplished" effect of before-and-after photographs. Advertising scholar Sut Jhally describes the "before and after advertisement" as a form of "black magic" in a fetishized commodity system: "use of the product changes social relations, such that before its use relations were incomplete and with its use they are complete" (163). This popular advertising technique, already pervasive in magazines by the 1930s, has an important historical origin in rhetorically persuasive visual documents of custodial transfer, specifically the abolitionist use of before-and-after images of rescued slave children and the Carlisle School's promotion of institutional education for Native children. The influence of reformist before-and-after photographs on more contemporary advertising for aesthetic physical manipulation procedures essentially blur the optic forms of racial and cosmetic orders. Advertisements for hair and skin products ask viewers to change their own bodies rather than the bodies of others, yet maintain a regime of visibility and disciplinary control focused on biological qualities of skin color, hair density, aging, and so forth.

Captain Pratt's strategy was distinct from advertising of his time—though in keeping with the practice of social reformers—in his use of photographs rather than drawings or etchings, tapping into public assumptions about the indexical qualities of photography as a closer reproduction of the real world. The before-and-after image sequences, deployed in the context of Indian policy, brought the traditions of racial portraiture and social advocacy together with the proto-cinematic qualities of photography as commercial product, as narrative, and as a form of scientific substantiation. Critic Curtis Marez describes early Indian dramas at the turn of the century as a form of "ritual imperial spectatorship" that encouraged a Euro-American "proprietary relationship to images of Indians." While audiences were only "renting" films, he notes, mass-produced photographic images made individual ownership of Indian images possible on a wide scale and facilitated "the photo-conversion of Indians into property" (340). Thus the narrative of custodial transfer in before-and-after images circulated by social advocacy organizations also engages, through the commodity status of the photograph itself, a narrative of ownership.

The visual technique separating an individual portrait into cellular images articulates a tension between division and wholeness, temporal progression and simultaneity. The images narrate change over time, but are seen all at once in a narrative meant to be read left to right. The before-and-after images of Indigenous students reiterate the structural dichotomies of civilization and savagery that have been important in Western genre studies.[31] The dual photographs become excerpts from a story the audience already effectively knows, functioning as extracinematic texts supporting and supported by Indian drama narratives and other public discourses. Yet the photograph sequences also reveal the ways that the processes, props, and technologies of manufacturing images of Indians both drew from and influenced broader social engineering practices based on regimes of visibility, from children of the African diaspora to orphans of the British lower classes to settler women of the American middle class.

Because they are bound up with the production of desire in their promises to transform the body's appearance, the morally freighted progression of before-and-after photographs carries strong evaluative subtexts regarding the way the body—and the world—should look. Both a document and a wish, the narrative sequencing of the photographs seems to assert that in the case of the body, the way things are can and will surrender to the way things should be. In this assumption the photographers attempt to instill desire in viewers for the solution to a seemingly problematic "before." Concealed hands provide the desired "after" as the images offer testimony to the power of another, unphotographed person or force to transform a passive subject. At the center of before-and-after image sequences is the omission of an event—a transformation by manufacture or a transfer of custodial authority—that divides time between the before and the after, but which is itself unseen, only implied indirectly by its effects on the body. The moment of reordering is visible only in the evidence of difference. Whether testifying to a trauma or suppressing our vision of it, before-and-after images are artifacts that assume linear time and yet skip a step in a temporal progression. They both stop time and demonstrate that time has passed, offering two points of artificial stasis as landmarks that testify to transformation, mysterious and hidden in the unphotographed rift, a destabilizing moment between two apparently stable states of being.

The Carlisle School before-and-after photographs also work to make time visible in the particular form of a narrative of settlement. They do this by envisioning the state reorganization of Native families through processes of colonial removal. The photographer's impulse to document the "before" and "after" presumes a colonial timeline in which forward temporal progression inevitably results in assimilation, an imagined movement from timelessness to modernity. This is the logic of "vanishing," for the "before" photograph documents change by capturing an image of traditionality before it "disappears," creating an artificial stasis. Before-and-after images both retrieve images from change and document the change itself, obscuring the space "in between" where resistance or other strategic actions take place. Thus, the sequences naturalize colonization as a function of the passage of time rather than the effects of deliberate policies. The evolutionary or developmental connotations of this form of photographic sequencing were particularly suited to Euro-American ideas of a progression of races, including the theory that Native people were emblematic of an earlier stage of human development. Such photographs correspond with the peculiar use of time in representations of Indians as relics of the past or emblems of primitivism, what Johannes Fabian has called the "denial of coevalness." The images also imply passivity and political consent through the exclusion of conflict in the middle image. The Carlisle School photographs, by omitting images of parents, elide issues of parental rights and visually reconstitute Native peoples as wards. Sympathetic Westerns that seem to be about cross-racial romance, I argue, are often visual dramatizations of removal that deploy the illustrative tropes of before-and-after photographs.

Richard Henry Pratt used the photographs widely in his efforts to garner public and private support for his program of Native education (Pratt 62).[32] The photographs both promised to solve what was called "the Indian problem" through assimilation, and at the same time contributed to the public construction of an Indian as a person with a problem, a dilemma stemming from bicultural upbringing, alienation from family and home community and eventual encounters with social intolerance. In Indian dramas and later sympathetic Westerns, educated Indian characters are unable to overcome such dilemmas and are almost always in the position of having to make impossible choices in no-win situations. Their only alternative to the vision of vanishing traditionalism in this binary construction is total assimilation—a non-Native future is the only future visually or narratively presented.

These discourses of assimilation were consistently countered with strong public desire to see Native difference expressed through costume, artifact, ceremony, and dancing. Although I have argued here that before-and-after images anticipate cinema in their photographic interdependence, they could also be decoupled; the "before" photographs could be—and were—also sold separately as souvenirs by photographer J. N. Choate from his shop in the town of Carlisle. The crowds of people who gathered at the railroad station to see a group of new Carlisle School students arriving by train in 1879 were primarily interested in seeing what they thought of as "real live Indians" in "native garb."[33] But Pratt himself was vehemently opposed to any form of display of Native cultural practices for either ethnographic or entertainment purposes because he felt these would reinforce interest in the traditions that the Carlisle School was trying to eradicate. These contradictory desires would be played out on the silent screen in the Indian dramas' narratives of education and "reversion."

The Carlisle School photographs attempt to separate "traditional" from "assimilated" children primarily through changes in costuming and hair-styles, indicators that signal to viewers a host of other, implied shifts in citizenship, culture, religion, language, and ongoing political nationhood. The assumption implicit in the photographs, that physical appearance reflects interior identity, also encompasses the reverse possibility—that, to quote Judith Butler, identity is contingent on "the public regulation of fantasy through the surface politics of the body" (173). Butler's question about gender identity raises similar issues regarding racial representation: "How does a body figure on its surface the very invisibility of its hidden depth?" (171).[34] Yet while the photographs divide primitive from civilized and carefully illustrate a typology of difference, their sequencing also implies that one can become the other and invites their disarticulation and separate circulation in other contexts. The images emphasize the already-clichéd idea that contemporary Native young people are "torn" between cultures, although the actual tear—the custodial transfer of children from their families to the institutional setting of boarding school—is suppressed in the linear narrative implied by the image sequence.[35] Carefully dressed and posed for the photographs, the children are only seen "on stage" in costume, never back stage in motion or in transition, denying their mediated, negotiated, or mixed cultural and political identities.[36]

Both Indian dramas and many contemporary Native representations imagine the consequences of institutional interventions in Native families. By "institutional interventions" I mean the assimilationist government policies that included mandatory boarding school education, programs of adoption and fosterage of Native children, and military training and service. These coordinated policies of intervention manifested a public claim to Native children as the nation's children and to tribal lands as "surplus" U.S. land. Jolene Rickard suggests that the Carlisle School before-and-after images "signified the end of the 'Indian' wars and evoked security. They are not overtly photographs of the 'land' but are documents of the systematic removal of Indians from their homelands." In the framing of the image, Rickard argues, "The rigid bodies of the children occupy about 90% of the visual frame with scant detail about their 'environment'" ("Occupation" 60). This isolation, especially in portraits, of the individual from clan, family, and other Indigenous forms of social organization facilitated a "fetishistic observation" that also "disguised the sense of community" and "implied erasure of 'Nation'" (63–64). In visual tropes common to both federal laws and frontier dramas, the Native family is subject to and the subject of the close scrutiny of dual systems of knowledge production and internal colonization. The discourses of the law and the cinema come together in representations that underscore the disjuncture between the paternalistic language of U.S. government documents and Indigenous assertions of genealogical continuity.

Genealogy is one of the most suppressed and contested forces in cinematic representations of Native Americans—especially in the trope of vanishing and in the performative practice of redface—because it is the crucial discourse in rhetorics of policy. Hence, this book explores the cinematic emphasis on the abstract idea of family circulated publicly, a nuclear triad of father, mother, and child, as well as the power and fissures of this visual construction. Custody of Native children in Westerns stands for custody of the land in a semiotic system imported from early-twentieth-century Indian policy, as I discuss in chapter 1. At the turn of the twentieth century, government educational programs for Native American children coincided with the allotment of communal Native lands to individual heads-of-household. U.S. visual and political discourses elided Native families while framing institutional and governmental structures in familial terms.

The special rights of tribes to negotiate with the federal government has been subject, then, to a reinterpretation of tribal peoples as wards of the state under the premise that tribes, incapable of making autonomous decisions, come under federal trusteeship.[37] Nineteenth-century court cases and other federal discourses—most prominently Chief Justice John Marshall's decisions in the 1831 case *Cherokee Nation v. Georgia*—frame Native peoples as children and the U.S. "president as their great father" (Prucha 59).[38] Marshall's defining statement from this case, that Indigenous tribes are "domestic dependent nations," brings tribes into a familial relationship with the United States that is metaphorically that of an adopted child. In fact, Marshall continues, until their "right of possession ceases," Natives are "in a state of pupilage. Their relation to the United States resembles that of a ward to his guardian" (59). The clear and disproportionate assignation of power in the word "dependent" is tied to the progressivist rhetoric of "civilizing" discourses that attempt to disown Native nations through both primitivist and infantilizing images.[39] The language of court statements and government legislation both projected U.S.–Native relations into the distant future with words such as "forever" and "in perpetuity," and at the same time presumed that those relations would be temporary due to population decline and assimilation. This language both guarantees land to Native children and presumes that no such children will actually succeed their elders to claim their inheritance.[40] Imagining Natives to be the nation's children is a legal maneuver to avoid acknowledging the sovereign rights of tribal nations. It is a form of incorporation based on the power differences in a familial model that, in Western legal systems of thought, displaces tribal kinship and political systems to render "Indian" an abstract and rhetorically malleable category.

This category is made and unmade in the cinema through costuming as a theatrical performance and as a sign of racial difference, marking both the desire to classify "Indian" as an exotic, threatening Other and, simultaneously, to blur those distinctions by claiming and Americanizing what is marked as "Indian." Yet the delineation of race by costume destabilizes, rather than stabilizes, racial categories. Costuming, performance styles, and other visual cues are central to my analyses of the film industry's representational strategies—often casting white actors in redface for credited roles while hiring uncredited Native extras—and to connecting Indigenous filmmaking with off-screen activism. The practice of redfacing is both distinct from and related to its sister traditions of blackface minstrelsy and other forms of ethnic performance and masquerade (distinct because redfacing can also invoke Indigenous traditions of the trickster, as Michelle Raheja has noted).[41] The close association of racial identity with theatrical presentation—apparel, accessories—worked to reduce "Indianness" to an accretion of objects, distancing such images from the sense of personhood signaled by familial contexts. But the emphasis on surface appearance in the Western—in particular through hairstyle and costume—as an indicator of Indianness and whiteness has not been limited to popular entertainment and tourist advertisements; it mattered in the realm of Indian policy and education as well.

If Wild West shows stage conquest as violent combat using the signs that would later define the Western—the Plains warbonnet, the cavalry uniform, and the cowboy's outfit—sympathetic Westerns imagine conquest as a form of assimilation in which visual signs of Native traditionality are disassembled. Western genre costumes complicated (rather than clarified) American sign systems of visible difference.[42] Close attention to early Indian dramas expands our understanding of the intertexts shaping the origins of the Western, revealing critically overlooked foundations of the genre in traditions of photographic racial portraiture and in print discourses and cinematic melodramas of political reform.

The analyses in this book explore the ways that many cinematic representations—including the early Indian dramas—dismantle, reverse, confuse, ironize, and otherwise unravel the visual politics of display as well as the linear narratives of transformation in before-and-after photographs. Invoking Vivian Sobchack's description of photographic practices of ownership and the way that "cinematic technology" instead "*animates* the photographic," I am interested in cinema's power to magically "reconstitute" the "visibility" of the photographic image as an immanent presence, a "coming-into-being" that emphasizes the "accumulation—not the loss—of experience."[43] Nanna Verhoeff's work on early Westerns suggests a converse but not contradictory paradigm in which still images are part of a larger system of othering, as the "conventional ante-text" of cinema, function as a "metaphor for stagnation" and "immanent disappearance" in Indian dramas: "The still image evoked, cited, or even incorporated within the moving image thus undermines the transparent representation of vitality that is one of . . . the primary ambitions of film" (56–57).[44] I argue here that Indian dramas build and reflect on photographic image series as a prior discourse; cinematic scenarios of "reversion," for example, depend on visual narratives of "progress" as a point of departure. Indian dramas integrated the before-and-after image-schema in their performances of racial masquerade, visual narratives of "reversion," melodramatic tableaux, and other theatrical conventions. The staging of whiteness and Indianness in cinema not only depends on but also destabilizes prior visual discourses of savagery, modernity, and racial progress mapped onto the bodies of boarding school students. In mobilizing and animating the static portraiture of the photographs, Indian dramas also open up the representational field to imagine moments of trauma, resistance, circulation, substitution, hybridity, and exchange that are suppressed by the rigid, graphic charting of educational conversion in before-and-after images.

The narrative of racial uplift and reform enforced by boarding school before-and-after photographs was also reversed in other photographs meant to document Native people as primitives. Edward Curtis—as well as other photographers and ethnographers—frequently carried costumes with which to dress Native subjects for portraits or later altered photographs to eliminate signs of acculturation or modernity. As scholars such as Jacqueline Fear-Segal and Amelia Katanski have shown, officials' anxiety that returned students might go "back to the blanket," a phrase emphasizing the way costume and appearance came to stand for a sketchily envisioned behavioral and biological evolutionary progression, was a constant in the discourse about residential school education. Narratives of the "reversion" of assimilated Indian characters in literature and film included frequent references to costume—blankets, moccasins—and to hairstyle as racial signifiers. These competing public images of assimilation and reversion, presenting contradictory trajectories for Indigenous futures, were rendered in dramatic narratives of "separation and return" that manifested across media including photography; nonfiction writing and literature about boarding schools; and theatrical venues such as film productions, tourist performances, and entertainment lecture circuits.

Scenarios of Separation and Return

The struggle over Indigenous futures takes place visually in sympathetic Westerns and other films through "scenarios of separation and return" depicting Native youth moving away from and back to reservations and families. These scenes emphasize generational rupture using contrasts in costuming, making the before-and-after sequential photographic articulation of federal policies a visual commonplace in the semiotic field supporting sympathetic Westerns. Unlike the before-and-after photographs, which can take the form of portraits or group compositions but narrate difference across two separate images, two-shots and other cinematic conventions and compositions bring generational relations together in the same frame. Cinematic images can articulate an imagined, paradoxically linear "progression" and "reversion" at the same time while animating and activating the fragmented before-and-after photographic sequence in the more fluid, narrative stream of cinema. The images rely heavily on the symbolic functions of Euro-American and Native costuming in the identifying work of racial portraiture. They project the signs and scenarios of "encounter" between settler and Indigenous nations onto an individual Native family, overlaying an imperial logic of tradition and modernity onto images of Native generational relations. Images from films such as *The Lure of Woman* (1915), *Redskin* (1929), and *Devil's Doorway* (1950), reveal the staged, theatrical pose of this confrontation (see figures I.7–I.9). The melodramatic schema of limited options—a limitation reiterated by the borders of the film frame—suppresses the idea of autonomous self-invention or community identity outside of the narrative trajectories on offer in the genre and excludes the imaginative projection of future tribalism, intergenerational activism, or collective land holding. Scenes of separation and return also generate sympathy through emotional responses that depend on the audience's investment in the narrative world of the characters and family, on assertion of realism, and on the groundwork laid by before-and-after images in staging the "past" and "present" in colonial terms.

The irrelevance of dialogue to these scenes reminds us that their melodramatic qualities are primarily visual, dependent on costume, mise-en-scène, and the gestural pantomime of theater. Scenes depicting the separation of Native children from their families continued to have a central role in

Figure I.7. The Lure of Woman, World Film Corp. (1915) (LC).

Figure I.8. Redskin, Paramount (1929) (AMPAS).

Figure I.9. Devil's Doorway, MGM (1950).

sympathetic frontier dramas, not as an uninterrupted "trope," with its connotations of the verbal and textual, but rather as what performance studies scholar Diana Taylor might call a recurring "scenario," a term that emphasizes theatricality, embodied action, and visual material working "through reactivation rather than duplication" (32). Like the excess of melodrama, proliferations of specific scenarios, such as representations of initial contact between Europeans and Indigenous peoples, suggest an "overflow of meanings" (54). In Western frontier melodramas, scenes of removal function as representations of contact that, like earlier instances of such images, can "work as an act of transfer that literally transports the native *them* into *our* field of vision, into our economic and legal system of operations" (54, emphasis added). The imagined child on screen acts as a symbolic embodiment of an Indigenous future; hence sympathetic Western films often depict the relegation of a child to the status of "ward" when he or she is claimed by government agents.

Scenes of separation and return are common both to films that ultimately present "vanishing Indians" and to films that counter that "vanishing" with narratives and images of continuity. Redeploying scenarios of familial separation and return, later filmmakers seeking ways to answer the visual rhetoric of acculturating and deculturating practices often do so with images of reunion. In the films I discuss in the early chapters of this book, the cultural continuity that depends on familial relationships—and what Chadwick Allen calls "scenes of Indigenous instruction"—are absent or are interrupted by institutional models of instruction.[45] In millennial Native features and documentaries, the act of viewing the televised Western is, in itself, a scene of assimilationist education that can be transformed through politicized viewing practices into a scene of reunion. Indeed, revisiting the Western in order to reframe it critically stages scenes of transmission, recognition, and identification that actively renew the family and community ties in Native terms. In this way, many recent films transform the social function of Westerns, reaching out to reeducate non-Native viewers in order to change the way U.S. history is apprehended and imagined in public culture while protesting the genre's devastating history of invasive pedagogy.

If Westerns typically lock Native characters into the historical frame of the "Indian Wars"—broadly defined, cinematically, to include representations of the treaty-making era in the mid- to late nineteenth century—many of the Indian dramas and later Native productions that I address here also envision characters in a contemporary world. These cinematic engagements with Indigenous modernity are central to my focus on images of Native youth as sites of discursive instability and contestation over the political futures of tribal nations.[46] Scenarios of separation and return constitute the emotional engine of these narratives, confronting viewers with intimate pathos stemming from historical patterns of social disruption and mapping assimilation and traditionalism in the visual differences between youth and elders upon homecoming.

With new Indigenous control over production methods, script authorship, performance, reception, and other aspects of filmmaking and viewing, some recent films influence and repurpose the Western's "scenarios of separation and return" through contextualizing strategies of sound and voiceover and through recuperative strategies of literal identification and recognition. Native films that reframe recovered media texts can leverage the political power of public engagement with images of Indians, reembed documentary content in films produced as colonial fantasies, or model trickster strategies of subversive reading. Contemporary Native and collaborative productions—landmark films in the emergence of contemporary Native American filmmaking—look back critically on the impact and assimilative force of the Western, holding its generic images of Indians accountable to present generations of Native and non-Native viewers. These visual and aural aesthetics of recuperation selectively dissociate individual Native actors and filmed subjects from the structures and scenarios of Western cinema fantasies, instead identifying people, conditions, and histories from the midst of industrial and independent productions.

On the Organization of *Native Recognition*

Native Recognition is organized into three sections devoted respectively to silent film representations, contemporary retrievals and reinterpretations of silent footage and studio-era Hollywood films, and the emergence of Native independent film production. Each section also addresses production circumstances, from the formation of the studio system in the 1910s, to the height of the silent era and transition to sound in the late 1920s, to the established location work of 1950s Westerns, to amateur feature filmmaking in the 1970s and the professional independent, experimental, and documentary filmmaking spanning the turn of the twenty-first century. This organization—simultaneously chronological and dialogic—facilitates close attention to historical moments when influential cinematic scenarios served as a public discourse about major political shifts in U.S. relationships with Native tribes. This structure also allows a fuller exploration, in the early chapters, of the origin of Hollywood's "images of Indians" as context for Native and collaborative productions; rather than devoting a separate chapter to cinematic stereotypes, my intention is that this organization emphasize the interrelation between Native filmmakers and the largely non-Native industry. It also facilitates the juxtaposition of little-known with well-known films, such as *House Made of Dawn* and *Billy Jack,* and the situating of these texts within cycles of film production and ultimately within historical, political, and literary contexts, bringing film theory and visual analysis into conversation with Native studies frameworks. Understanding the reach of popular culture constructions of Native families necessitates work with a wide range of texts, including photographs, periodicals, archived studio documents (marketing materials, censorship memos), government documents and reports, film reviews, and interviews with filmmakers. This diversity of source materials situates the films in the broader context of production cycles, policy changes, and the constitutive role of film reception in the public sphere.

In the first part of the book I survey a wide range of silent Westerns. Chapter 1, "Reframing the Western Imaginary: James Young Deer, Lillian St. Cyr, and the 'Squaw Man' Indian Dramas," locates the influence of Edwin Royle's successful stage play and 1906 novel *The Squaw Man* on the Indian dramas of James Young Deer (Ho-Chunk), D. W. Griffith, and Cecil B. DeMille, among others. Early Indian dramas are rarely included in studies of the Western and have not yet been systematically addressed in critical studies of race and melodrama. This chapter demonstrates both the cinema's melo-

dramatization of Indigenous histories in this period—particularly land allotment policies and residential schooling—and an Indigenous appropriation of
the frontier melodrama as a tool for political discourse. I trace an emerging
Native voice in cinema through the works of James Young Deer and Lillian
St. Cyr (Princess Redwing) during their brief but influential careers, including close readings of films such as *White Fawn's Devotion* (1910) and *For
the Papoose* (1912), that visualize and narrate both interracial custody battles
and mixed-race family coherence. Chapter 2, " 'Strictly American Cinemas':
Social Protest in *The Vanishing American, Redskin,* and *Ramona,*" focuses on
themes of dislocation and displacement in Indian dramas and Westerns of
the 1920s and the early 1930s. Paramount epics such as George Seitz's *The
Vanishing American* (1925) and Victor Schertzinger's *Redskin* (1929) condemn fraudulent appropriations of reservation resources while offering emotionally fraught portrayals of young Navajo characters undergoing cultural
and custodial transition in governmental boarding schools. An independent
production by Chickasaw director Edwin Carewe, the newly retrieved 1928
print of *Ramona*, includes an ethnically reversed massacre scene that suggests Carewe's political manipulation of melodramatic codes. These scenes
of institutional education and frontier vigilantism comment on film itself as
a didactic medium, an arena in which visual racial signifiers are established
and challenged. The chapter ends with a discussion of the archival restoration of *Redskin* by the National Museum of the American Indian and two
Native artists' recent return to this footage with a new soundtrack that
reinterprets its Hollywood narratives.

The second part of the book bridges the studio era with the late
twentieth century by focusing on recent experimental and documentary
films that disassemble Hollywood icons (John Wayne, Monument Valley)
in films from the middle decades of the century. Chapter 3, " 'As if I Were
Lost and Finally Found': Repatriation and Visual Continuity in *Imagining
Indians* and *The Return of Navajo Boy*," describes the ways that several contemporary filmmakers have recovered and retold the historical experiences
of Indigenous subjects and performers in Western and ethnographic films
from the 1930s through the 1950s. Victor Masayesva's *Imagining Indians*
(1993) inserts documentary content into such classic studio-era Westerns
as *The Plainsman* (1936) through production histories and interviews with
Native "extras," while Jeff Spitz and Diné filmmaker Bennie Klain's *The
Return of Navajo Boy* (2001) correlates the repatriation of film footage with
the reunion of the Diné family receiving "lost" movie footage from the
1950s. These films' visual and voiceover strategies of storytelling identify
(or "recredit") people and places from such classical Westerns as *The Plains-*

man, Stagecoach (1939), and *The Searchers* (1956) as well as from independent, ethnographic short films. Masayesva's and Spitz's strategies of aesthetic
reframing and repatriation had already seen·cinematic expression in earlier
television productions, such as Choctaw filmmaker Phil Lucas and Robert
Hagopian's *Images of Indians* series in 1979. These and other independent,
minority-produced films intervene in public memories of the past as well as
public perceptions of Indigenous futures, rerouting frontier dramas' interpretations of history using reenactments, voiceover storytelling, and allusions
to earlier film productions.

The third part of the book extends this discussion of the ways that
contemporary filmmakers reframe Western genre conventions. Independent
artists and viewers have renegotiated the meaning of Hollywood productions by shifting from studio to independent orientation in the 1960s and
1970s with films like *The Exiles* (Mackenzie 1961) and *House Made of Dawn*
(Morse 1972), and into the 1980s with productions such as Laguna author
Leslie Marmon Silko's unreleased film *Arrowboy and the Witches* (1980) and
Victor Masayesva's *Itam Hakim, Hopiit* (1984). These and other films use
temporal fragmentation, experimental editing, and film sound—music and
voiceover narration—to remember, renarrate, and reclaim past and present
media spaces in support of local familial and community ties. Chapter 4,
"Imagining the Reservation in *House Made of Dawn* and *Billy Jack*," discusses
the emergence of local, nonindustrial Native production practices with the
1972 film version of *House Made of Dawn*, a film that moved away from
the pathos of scenarios of separation and focused instead on the mediation
of past ruptures through characters' processes of restoration, repatriation,
and return. Adapted from Kiowa author N. Scott Momaday's novel about
individuals coping with the 1950s assimilationist policies of Termination
and Relocation, the film stages what Chadwick Allen has called an "activist
re-occupation" of Indigenous lands in both its text and production. The film
also initiates new modes of collaborative coproduction while refusing the
Western's instantiations of colonial time and space and dissolving the binary
categories of the genre's representations of settlement. While *House Made of
Dawn* marks a resurgence of Native control in the filmmaking process, the
independently produced blockbuster *Billy Jack* (1971/1973) deploys images
of Indians and reservation lands to articulate broader counterculture politics
of dissent. I link Native acting with political activism in the 1970s, a decade
when key figures in the American Indian Movement caught the attention of
the media, Native American documentary filmmakers such as George Burdeau and the Laguna and Santo Domingo Pueblo director Larry Littlebird
began their careers, and some literary scholars formally named a "Native

American Renaissance" when N. Scott Momaday was awarded the Pulitzer Prize in 1969.[47] Later independent feature films, such as Chris Eyre's *Smoke Signals* (1998) and *Skins* (2002), reimagine the power of Indigenous viewers to interpret Western genre images. Chapter 5, "'Indians Watching Indians on TV': Native Spectatorship and the Politics of Recognition in *Skins* and *Smoke Signals*," explores contemporary reassessments of prior systems of image-making in Eyre's first two feature films. Eyre embeds images of Native audiences in both films, demonstrating through sound and mise-en-scène the potential for these viewers to claim and resignify Western genre and documentary news footage of anonymous, stereotyped Indian characters through politicized forms of viewing.

Each chapter in this book considers Native images in the context of film history, demonstrating the cultural work of the films through the vocabulary of cinema studies. Reading these images and texts in conversation—government reports with films, films with photographs, promotional stills with reform literature, Native films with Westerns—reveals how these varied documents create public stories with political ends. I suggest that we need to understand Westerns in a new way as having emerged, at least in part, out of public discourses about federal Indian policy, and out of the proto-cinematic visual documents that constituted and circulated that public discourse. We also need to understand a historical strand of Native filmmaking as engaging in a conversation with the Western that involves appropriating dominant cinema's conventions and images for autonomous political purposes. Focusing on archival texts and reappropriations demonstrates the value of assessing cycles of American popular culture production across time to see how policies are instituted and resisted visually. We need to read visual culture in this narrative way and to understand the mutually constitutive origins of Westerns and Native cinema because they have powerfully shaped American national imaginaries of Native absence and presence. And we need to read images of Native families at the heart of this confluence because they signify Indigenous futures to a multiethnic viewing public.

Part I

Indigenous Presence in the Silent Western

1

Reframing the Western Imaginary

James Young Deer, Lillian St. Cyr, and the "Squaw Man" Indian Dramas

In 1912 John Ford's older brother, Francis Ford, partnered with Thomas Ince, producer and director of early popular "Indian dramas," to direct *The Invaders*, a three-reel film for Kay-Bee Pictures. The ambiguity of the film's title, which refers to white surveyors illegally trespassing on Lakota lands, draws our attention to competing stories about U.S. imperialism in the West in ways that other Westerns generally sought to camouflage. Later Indian dramas and silent Westerns, centrally concerned with legitimating white settlers' title to land through the manipulation of the Native characters' emotional and political allegiances, typically suppressed any acknowledgment of Indigenous land ownership by inverting history to figure Natives as the invaders of white settlements.[1] *The Invaders* is unusual in that it addresses issues of tribal land rights by returning, insistently, to the text of a treaty no fewer than four times in the intertitles during its 40-minute length (see figure 1.1). Yet this struggle over territory is also conveyed through the visual and narrative conventions of the domestic melodrama, the customary mode for cinematic Indian dramas. These frontier melodramas articulate land ownership as a right of inheritance, yet envision the transfer of legitimate title to land-based resources through profoundly ambivalent representations mixed-race families.

The Invaders was part of a surge in productions of Indian dramas prior to World War I.[2] These short films provide a remarkable window on Euro-American popular representations of the encounter between trib-

43

al peoples and the U.S. military and educational establishments. Their composite narratives depict a white settler "family on the land" emerging from the "broken home" of a previous mixed-race marriage, and equate children, land, and gold as the spoils of failed romance, not of war.[3] The films—epitomized by Apfel and DeMille's 1914 production of *The Squaw Man*, the first feature-length film shot in Hollywood—represent a foundational paradigm in the formation of the Western Indian drama. These narratives of cross-racial romance and disruption of Native and mixed-race families, particularly scenarios of the separation and return of Native youth from their tribal homelands, would prove immensely influential in plotting future revisionist or "sympathetic" Westerns. Cinematic scenes in which Native and mixed-blood children are taken from their families drew moral and emotional power from their direct correlation with actual practices: the removal of children from Native homes in the late nineteenth and early twentieth centuries to be educated in government boarding schools and the often coercive adoption of Native children by missionaries. This chapter traces the political implications of these films about interracial romance and biracial children—films influenced directly and indirectly by the stage play *The Squaw Man*—and the revisions to this story in films by Indigenous filmmakers and performers James Young Deer (Ho-Chunk) and Lillian St. Cyr (Ho-Chunk). I begin by examining the scene of romance in *The Invaders*, in which sexual attraction and the transformation of Native political allegiance coalesce around the technological mediation of interracial relations.

Early in *The Invaders*, the surveying team, having refused an Army escort, sets up camp in the hills and a young man begins to study the landscape through his moveable telescope (a transit or theodolite for surveying; see figure 1.2). Here the film's focus on land claims comes together with one of the most basic and enduring plots in the history of the movies: the young man meets a girl. The reverse-shot, an iris shot[4] to mimic the telescope's viewing apparatus, does not reveal the expected open landscape; instead, the surveyor sees a young and beautiful Native woman leaning on a rock (Sky Star, played by Anne Little in redface). He calls his friends over to share the view and his excitement, and the land and woman come to stand for one another as objects of the technologically enhanced gaze of the white surveyors, the invaders of the film's title, whose economic interests lie in opening Native land to settlers through the railroad.[5]

The young surveyor is a likely figure of identification for audience members at this moment because we have been sutured to his point of view through the shot-reverse-shot construction and the long-shots so frequently used to represent the view through the gun sights of a repeating rifle in later Westerns. Yet this moment also resembles—and seems to represent—the act of filmmaking itself through the surveyor's manipulation of the telescope. The similarity of the equipment suggests an association between surveying equipment and the camera in an extension of the cinematic "gun/camera" trope.[6] Here the action of the film correlates an imperialist gaze with Western settlement. The directorial and spectatorial aspects of viewing in this scene, in which the transit reflexively doubles as a movie camera, link the theatrical work of filming the West with the colonizing work of mapping land for railroad acquisition and resource extraction. These related ways of seeing converge in the act of constructing Indigeneity as a visual object of study and spectacle. Thus the scene suggests the ways that technologies of viewing instantiate as well as visualize imperial invasion and social rupture: filming is a form of claiming.

This mediated gaze as a form of knowledge-making is both desirous and possessive, a visual apprehension of the land that is a prelude to (and a metaphor for) claiming it. The relationship between looking and claiming has been theorized by Mary Louise Pratt, who argues that the colonizing

Figure 1.1. *The Invaders*, Kay-Bee (1912) (LC), Signing the treaty.

Figure 1.2. *The Invaders*, Kay-Bee (1912) (LC), Surveyors look through the viewscope.

gaze positions the gazer as a "monarch-of-all-I-survey" (201), and Anne McClintock has pointed to ways that visual gendering of Indigenous and settler women's bodies "served as the boundary markers of imperialism" (24). In *The Invaders*, land, gold, and women are conflated by the invasive viewing and mapping undertaken by the surveyors.

Crucially, the gaze that maps both mineral-yielding land and the Native woman's body interrupts treaty rights and Native family formation at the same moment. Indeed, the two are intimately connected because treaty rights constitute promises that carry into the future, a future both symbolized and embodied by Indigenous families, especially children. The violence of conquest is allegorized in *The Invaders* as a process of cinematic or directorial vision, and Indigenous political ownership of land takes the visual form of a Native family (distilled here as the young woman's potential reproductivity). In the Western—and in its ur-genre the Indian drama—such prefigurations and images of families are especially freighted with discourses of national origins that negotiate social and political conditions in the historical moment of the film's production. The American West of the cinema, as a theatrical space that mediates societal forces beyond its proscenium, is a stage for social dramas in which families take shape through contestations over land. These politically charged issues of genealogy and staging in representations of Native families are the central focus of this chapter and those that follow.

Indian dramas were produced during a time when federal Indian policy encouraged both Indigenous assimilation and removal from the land. During the silent film era from the turn of the century through the 1920s, the primary national policy structuring Indigenous–settler relations was the drive for assimilation through the General Allotment Act of 1887 and the removal of Native children to government boarding schools. Sponsored by Senator Dawes of Massachusetts, the General Allotment Act (or Dawes Act) broke up reservations by allocating a specific acreage to each tribal member with the "surplus" land made available to "actual settlers."[7] As many scholars have noted, the boarding school and allotment systems went hand in hand, both reflecting the assimilationist impulse that held sway in Indian policy for 35 years. According to Margaret Szasz, "The passage of the Dawes Act . . . was the most significant legislative victory for assimilation, but the boarding school was one of its most effective weapons" (371). Tsianina Lomawaima (Mvskoke) writes that "Government schools were responsible for preparing Indians for the independence envisioned by the Dawes Act" (3), explicitly linking the U.S. policies of separating children from their tribes (through institutional education) with assimilation (through individual land ownership). By the early 1930s more than 65% (90 million acres) of Indigenous land had been transferred to settler ownership under the allotment system (Dippie 308). Francis E. Leupp, Commissioner of Indian Affairs and a strong opponent of the Carlisle Indian Industrial School (the model for later government boarding schools), criticized the boarding school system in 1908 based on the schools' competition for students through a per-capita funding system. He also accused recruiters of engaging in a "regular system of traffic in . . . helpless little red people," suggesting that "ownership" of Native children themselves was as much at issue as ownership of land.[8] In 1900 there were 22,124 Native children reported attending government-run boarding schools (Bolt 227). The boarding school system emphasized separation from family and tribal groups; Native families were often very reluctant to send their children to boarding schools, particularly during the early phase of the policy. Resistance to the boarding school system was demonstrated also by the frequency of runaways and by parents hiding their children from government agents (an act depicted cinematically in Paramount's 1929 film *Redskin*, as I discuss in chapter 2).[9]

Most early Indian dramas capitalized on these powerful racial schema and federal policies to imagine the demise of Indigenous nations. Their versions of mixed-race families end with racial division or sacrificial death. Films that located Native characters in contemporary contexts often narrate failed assimilation as a measure of insurmountable racial primitivity. The ordeal of separating Indigenous children from their families and cultures through the government boarding school policy—and the trauma of their return home as outsiders—is recognized through melodramatic registers in silent Indian dramas. In these tales of interracial romance, captivity, and adoption, defining narrative features include doubling, mistaken identity, and the social and geographic displacement and re-placement of persons. Such narrative strategies formally replicate the physical acts of displacement and re-placement and of coercive assimilation that have been hallmarks of U.S. American Indian policy, from removal in the 1830s through the erosion of reservation lands in the twentieth century. Significantly, although scenarios of separation and return in the "squaw man" plot configuration clearly comment on the removal of children to boarding school and on the impacts of federal policies more broadly, the dramas take place exclusively in the realm of the familial. Indian dramas staged and encoded particular kinds of narratives about frontier family formation and succession through images of mixed-race couples, contested children, and familial disruption. The films translated racial and economic discourses of heritability to the screen using the emotional registers of melodrama in stories of child-swapping, costume exchange, and reorganized family structures.

Film scholar Linda Williams argues that American "melodramas of black and white" stage interracial sympathy by invoking the "nostalgia for a lost home" that is a central driving force in melodrama (58). Indian dramas similarly engage viewers in contemporary social problems by using "tears to cross racial boundaries" (55), dramatizing the suffering of the virtuous to establish "moral legibility" in a world that has become "hard to read" (19). The genre's theater of identity depended on costume in narratives featuring reconfigured families, conventions of coincidence, and emotional scenes of loss and recognition. That pictorial language of costume also informed images of Indians in a more evidentiary mode, one that powerfully influenced public policy—the before-and-after photographs of Native boarding school students. Thus underpinning the films' visualization of familial rupture and reunion were the visual documents supporting the actual institutional interventions in Native families taking place at the turn of the century in government boarding schools. These before-and-after photographs, as I have argued in the introduction, prefigured the mediated scenes of separation and return in Indian dramas, preparing the viewing public to "see" assimilation in the form of costume and to imagine actual children in institutional custody as figures for U.S. wardship over tribal nations. The combined power of realism and melodrama in images of Native familial separation depend, however, on the defining terms for white viewers' emotional engagement: the vanishing of noble primitivism in the face of imperial dispossession. Rendered in terms of pathos and action—what Williams calls the drama of "too late" and "in the nick of time" that characterizes melodrama—white sympathy in Indian dramas is with the "too late" of Indian vanishing rather than the "nick of time" that would instead recognize Indigenous political and familial continuity.

The racial uplift narratives implied by the Carlisle School before-and-after photographs, then, powerfully influenced the short films of the early 1900s and 1910s that were equally obsessed with costume, performance, and inherited identity. Indian dramas manifested converging discourses of Indian policy, tourism, and turn-of-the-century racial theories through a didactic combination of melodramatic and documentary modes, each dependent on costume as a visual key. The films integrated established conventions of racial portraiture in the before-and-after photographs of students with the emerging generic structures of the cinema Western, bringing together the visual racial coding of costuming with frontier melodramas' narratives of interracial violence and interracial sympathy. In doing so, the films established a visual lexicon of domestic mixed-race melodramas in which the semiotics of racial performance encoded political and territorial claims and counterclaims based on shifting identifications of Indigeneity.

Indian dramas, however, could also disturb photographic representations of cultural transition, revealing moments of trauma and resistance that are repressed in the more rigid still image sequencing of before-and-after photographs. Partly because of their expansive temporal fluidity compared with still images, the films frequently depict the very processes of separation and transformation concealed in before-and-after photographs. Just as often, they reverse the traditional image sequence in order to disassemble the signifiers of Euro-American assimilation. Like the tradition of ethnographic photography, Indian dramas could enforce a wider range of transformations than before-and-after photographs. The films' complex array of visual strategies and small variations in scenarios play with temporality and with the raced and gendered politics of civic allegiance, confronting viewers with questions of Indigenous political difference and social mobility in a contemporary framework—what Philip Deloria (Dakota) characterizes as "the problems of postfrontier modernity" (*Unexpected* 108).

We can return to the images of seeing in *The Invaders* as an example of the relationship between paradigms of familial disruption and the politics of cinematic looking relations on screen. In the film, as the smitten surveyor moves from one end of the telescope/camera to the other, he enters the scene to court the young woman. His (and our) surreptitious view is replaced by that of another voyeur, however; Sky Star's spurned Native suitor observes the couple from a distance. Hearing him, she sends the surveyor away and departs while the suitor moves into the center of the frame to occupy the "stage" where the couple had been. He later brings news of the surveyors' trespassing to the Chief (actor unknown), who fetches and rereads his copy of the treaty with Sky Star, his daughter (see figure 1.3). The authority of this contract is superseded in the film's narrative logic by the power of sentiment—here encoded and visualized through the lens of romantic attraction. Sky Star, who is both a child herself (the daughter of the Chief) and a potential mother, never achieves the mobility of the surveyor, who can occupy both the pragmatic and imagined spaces of the West by moving from behind the "camera" to the front of it to enter into the landscape he is mapping and take part in his fantasy. Sky Star's movement in the film

Figure 1.3. *The Invaders*, Kay-Bee (1912) (LC), Rereading the treaty with Sky Star (Ann Little).

is between her tribe and the U.S. military; she must choose between her Native father and her white suitor, a losing proposition that ends with her death at the Army fort.

The film insistently points to the appropriation of land resources and to familial disruption as parallel originary crimes of the American frontier. Furthermore, the tool enabling this shift in perception is thoroughly visual, a mapping apparatus standing in for the camera, a reflection on the prospects of the nascent film industry and the medium itself to facilitate the kind of looking that stakes a claim, while at the same time offering more than one view of frontier settlement and American national origins. Other kinds of looking take place in *The Invaders*—when the Native characters look again and again at the text of their treaty, and the audience looks with them, and when the rejected suitor observes the surveyors and reports the trespass to the tribe's leadership. This imagined Indian gaze sets in motion another perspective, asking audiences to see and acknowledge theft where the settlers and surveyors see free land, sexual availability and easy wealth, and this "other" view becomes the basis for the Natives' response to the violation of their treaty rights later in the film.

In Indian dramas, interracial family plots are the basis for a pose of interracial sympathy invoked by images of familial disruption. To the extent that interracial sympathy enables audiences to imagine detribalization and deterritorialization to be natural and inevitable rather than systematic, that sympathy functions as a narrative of closure that legitimates settler acquisition of land and resources as a form of inheritance. Detribalization is represented as a "natural" shift in political allegiance from Native tribe to U.S. settlers and military using the theatrical signifier of costume, a visual metaphor for the loss of Indigenous sovereignty in the form of assimilation into the United States. Gregory S. Jay, discussing D. W. Griffith's melodramatic treatments of American Indian subjects, argues that "apparently sympathetic representation of the Native American still adheres to the logic of white supremacy eventually enunciated in *The Birth of a Nation*" and that in rendering "political struggle" as "domestic tragedy" Griffith shifted viewers' focus away from political history (3, 7).[10] Yet while melodramatic narratives can release audiences from the desire to change the world outside the theater, sympathetic images of interracial romance and child custody can also facilitate representational space for dissent on screen. Melodramatic racial sympathy makes multiple perspectives legible in film plots, broadening audience expectations and making the dominant cinematic visual lexicon available for directors and performers to use in politically subversive ways. Thus, while Hollywood's silent era Indian dramas did not change the prevailing discourses of civilization and savagery that characterized stereotypes about Indigenous peoples, it did produce limited opportunities for Indigenous performers and filmmakers to intercede in the emergent industry's representations of U.S. national formation.

Scholars in film studies and Native American studies have explored this film cycle in the context of the nascent American film industry, especially the transatlantic dominance of European film companies (such as Pathé Frères) prior to 1910 and the participation of Native actors and directors in early film production. The "Americanization project of early Westerns," according to Richard Abel, translated the spectacle (and the racial lessons) of Wild West shows to the screen, along with American film companies' claims to be the sole purveyors of authentic Western images. The new industrial discourse of authenticity in American filmmaking, beginning in 1907, enabled two Nebraska Ho-Chunk performers, husband-and-wife team James Young Deer and Lillian St. Cyr (stage name Red Wing or Princess Red Wing), to intervene in the cinematic imaginary of the embryonic Western film genre by revising the dominant plot of the Indian drama, the mixed-race romance and ensuing contest over child custody.[11]

Young Deer used the mass culture codes of melodrama and racial costume to tell a different story about Indigenous modernity, racial integration, and tribal guardianship of children. His films about mixed-race romance and Native custody over children ask audiences to imagine Indigenous familial and national continuity. Integration, in Young Deer's vision, is not the same as assimilation. Rather than signaling the end of tribal identity through amalgamation with the U.S. settler population or boarding school education, in Young Deer's films cross-racial marriages and mixed-blood children symbolize the future of tribal nations. From within an emerging Western film genre tradition, Young Deer and St. Cyr's films challenge the Western-genre focus on Indian death by emphasizing Native and mixed-race family ties.

Young Deer and St. Cyr's films reorient melodramatic images of interracial romance and child custody to envision Indigenous futures and territorial sovereignty. Their political intervention in public discourses of Indian policy are made visible through melodrama's theatrical conventions, including tableau, excess, the recognition of virtue in suffering victims, and the tension between pathos and action. The convergence of racial portraiture with melodramatic sympathy is particularly apparent in films that narrate physical separation and reunion of Native and mixed-race families, scenarios that will be the focus of visual and narrative analyses here. Crucially, in addition to their work as performers, Young Deer and St. Cyr's interventions in the field of frontier melodramas take place substantially at the level of plot; they alter the narrative structure and outcomes for Native characters and families in their films in ways that address broad political concerns, rather than attempting to insert documentary content, alter the visual texture of early film melodramas, or express specific tribal aesthetics. These structural interventions are significant because Indian dramas are highly action-oriented, plot-centric genre products. Indeed, a primary element of my argument in this chapter is that we cannot understand what Young Deer and St. Cyr were doing without understanding the larger production cycle of similarly (and complexly) plotted films that was already under way.

Many of the frontier dramas produced during this period suggest public apprehension that despite the rhetorics of assimilation and progressive state wardship, children and land were being siphoned away from Native peoples and placed under white control with devastating consequences. The wresting away of a visually identified "Indianness" through changing costume and the taking of children in these Westerns clearly commented on historical practices. Though the films, as melodramas, depict the twin losses of resources and children as domestic, or private, scenarios, the repeated narration of cross-racial romance from a variety of political perspectives in films such as *The Invaders*, *The Squaw Man*, and *White Fawn's Devotion* (Young Deer 1910) suggests that the films collectively tapped a widespread popular ambivalence about the paternalism of government Indian policy.

Chartering the Western: *The Squaw Man* Paradigm

In the constellation of narratives based on *The Squaw Man* plot, Euro-American family and inheritance patterns reassert themselves, breaking up a mixed-race couple and replacing the Native woman with a white woman while keeping the economic benefits of the previous relationship within the new marriage. Between the turn of the century and the end of the silent era in American cinema, filmmakers developed the Western, a form borrowed in part from postbellum "western" literary romances, as a narrative formula that frequently depicted violent encounters between migrants and Native people on the frontier. A well-established tradition of literary captivity narratives and dramas was also translated onto film in frontier dramas' representations of vulnerable settler domesticity. In particular, Westerns portrayed the frontier as a proving ground where white women, threatened or taken captive by tribes, were the objects of spectacular rescues by white men—narratives adapted from novels such as *The Last of the Mohicans*. But *The Squaw Man* is far removed from the images of Indians pursuing fleeing settlers in Westerns such as D. W. Griffith's *The Battle of Elderbush Gulch*, 1913.

The Squaw Man, the first feature-length film made in Hollywood, offers the defining example of the early Indian drama's mixed-race narrative pattern. The plot—adapted from Edwin Milton Royle and Julie Opp Faversham's successful stage play and 1906 novel—was formative in the early history of the Western, and the film is a major landmark in the evolution of American cinema. Adapted for the screen three times by Cecil B. DeMille in 1914 (with Apfel), 1918, and 1931 (see figure 1.4), *The Squaw Man* launched both his directing career and the Jesse L. Lasky Feature Play Company, which later became part of the major studio Paramount Pictures.[12] The 1914 film tells the story of James Wynnegate (Dustin Farnum), a refugee from the corrupt English aristocracy, as he establishes a new life

Figure 1.4. *The Squaw Man*, MGM (1931), Warner Baxter as James Wingate and Lupe Velez as Naturich, promotional still (AMPAS).

for himself in the American West. Jim's attempt at ranching fails, but in the process he has an affair with Nat-u-Ritch (Red Wing/Lillian St. Cyr), the daughter of the local tribal chief. When he finds her making a tiny pair of moccasins, he rushes to get a pastor, who on arriving refuses to marry the cross-racial couple. Jim's ranch hands try to talk him out of the marriage as well, until he shows them the moccasins. The ranch hands then force the pastor at gunpoint to perform the ceremony in a racially inflected version of the "shot-gun wedding."

When the Earl of Kerhill (Monroe Salisbury)—Jim's elder brother—suffers an accident in the Alps and in a dying confession clears his brother's name, Diana, the Countess of Kerhill (Winifred Kingston), always secretly in love with Jim, travels to America to bring him home. The news reaches Jim, but his excitement is dampened by his realization that his family responsibilities keep him in the American West—he can never take his Native wife home to England. The messenger convinces Jim to send his son instead, "He is the future Earl of Kerhill. He is entitled to the education of a gentleman—send him home with me." Nat-u-Ritch opposes sending away their son and must be forcibly separated from him by Jim. The next morning Nat-u-Ritch watches from a barn window, as the group gets ready to journey back to England with her son. A ghostly presence, her stillness contrasts with the bustle below.[13] Her son, previously clothed in buckskin, now wears a tiny soldier's outfit, and Jim tells him not to take his moccasins. First Jim holds the moccasins, and then Nat-u-Ritch takes them, sneaks away with a gun, and shoots herself in a field behind the house.

In the closing scene, Lady Diana shields the boy from the sight of his dead mother, who occupies the bottom of the frame as all the other characters—the Natives who were about to attack the town, the cowboy ranch hands, and the principal characters—focus on her prone form. Nat-u-Ritch's death "cleanses" her son of his Native identity (represented once again by the tiny moccasins she holds just before her suicide). In this influential final image, a melodramatic tableau of reaction, the assembled onlookers mimic the audience itself while modeling the sentiment of helpless witnessing, a mournful innocence in the face of Native death. This dramatization separates viewers' emotional responses from any impulse to take political action in the world outside the theater, because the object of sentiment (Nat-u-Ritch) is already dead. Furthermore, the temporal suspension between "in the nick of time" and "too late" intersects with cinematic narratives of Indian vanishing that preclude Indigenous modernity. In DeMille's films, white families can be saved in the nick of time, but for Native families it is already "too late"; the stasis or suicide of the Native characters on screen makes visual the already popular misperceptions of impending and predestined extinction. The body of Nat-u-Ritch takes on sacrificial, even Christlike overtones in that her death absorbs the moral consequences of white settler extraction. Her character's silence (first because she cannot speak English, and later because she is dead) imagine and stage both Native traditionality and Native suicide as what Peter Brooks calls a "hyperbolic instance" of muteness in melodrama (61).[14] Nat-u-Ritch's somewhat overdetermined name, William R. Handley notes, might suggest "Not too Rich" (54), though the opposite meaning, "naturally rich," better conveys this character's connection with both natural resources and fertility, as well as her narrative function as the source of her husband's wealth. Her son's survival means that he will inherit western American land as well as an English estate and title, uniting Europe and America through inheritance.[15] The wealth exported from the West in *The Squaw Man* is not land, gold, or oil but the mixed-race child, who will inherit the English title Earl of Kerhill and presumably revitalize a corrupt English gentry with an infusion of Native blood. The representation of that corrupt aristocracy in the figure of the elder Earl of Kerhill, James's dissolute brother Henry, then, alludes to a relationship between Great Britain and the United States as its former colony.

The six-reel film was a critical success and an incredible financial feat—produced for $15,450, *The Squaw Man* netted $244,700 (Birchard 9, 13).[16] These spectacular returns clearly captured the attention of investors and catalyzed the nascent film industry in Hollywood. *The Squaw Man* also preceded D. W. Griffith's *The Birth of a Nation* in finding a middle-class market for moving pictures—in fact, earlier versions illustrate the way this story functioned as a pivotal narrative in the strategic industry shift from shorts to feature-length adaptations. *The Kentuckian* (1908), a one-reel precursor to *The Squaw Man*, contains essentially the same plot elements, except that the "squaw-man" figure is not a titled English aristocrat but a wealthy Southerner fleeing from a murder committed in a duel. However, the scene in which the mother pleads to keep her son and is physically separated from him is almost identical to the scene with Nat-u-Ritch in *The Squaw Man*. The messenger, rather than a white woman, shields the boy's eyes from the sight of his mother's body. While the messenger bringing news of the father's inheritance or pardon (or both) stands in shadows, the father, mother, and son are brightly lit in sunlight. This light play suggests the tragic breakup of a happy and functional family and heightens the mother's impending loss of her child to his new status as heir to a Southern fortune.

The profound influence of *The Squaw Man* on the development of Hollywood feature films leads to many questions. Why does this narrative—

differing as it does from the early Westerns of Tom Mix, and certainly from later iterations of the genre such as John Ford's *Stagecoach*—hold such a crucial place in the development of the Western? And why does it emerge so strongly in the first two decades of the twentieth century? Why does this film, and others based on it, link Native women's marriage to white men with the women's suicide? What is the significance of the forced separation of Native mother and mixed-blood child that forms the heart of the film's conflict as one family gives way to another? How did Native performers and filmmakers like St. Cyr and Young Deer accommodate, resist, or otherwise appropriate the discourses of familial trauma and the melodramatic schema of victim and villain in silent Westerns?

The Squaw Man is also interwoven with subplots. In one of these, Nat-u-Ritch saves Jim by killing his nemesis, Cash Hawkins (Billy Elmer), and is sought years later by the Sheriff for the crime. Nat-u-Ritch, then, takes on the typically masculine attribute of violence in the Western, becoming both victim and victimizer, so that the taint of violent lawlessness dies with Nat-u-Ritch and Cash rather than remaining to complicate the relationship between Jim and Diana. Indianness, in the fantasy world of the Western, is a quality that can be acquired and cast off through one's personal contacts (as with a love affair) or through one's performed identity (as with a costume in a play). The moccasins, for example, remain a symbol of the child's Native identity from their first appearance, connecting him to his mother but easily shed for western clothes when the child is claimed by his father's relatives. In fact, moccasins as a trope for the potential to shed Indianness as easily as clothing appeared frequently in periodicals, such as an 1881 article promoting the Carlisle and Hampton schools in which the author quotes a letter from a father, Brave Bull, to his daughter at the school, " 'Why do you ask for moccasins? I sent you there to be like a white girl, and wear shoes' " (Ludlow 675).[17] Christine Edwards Allred, writing about representations of Natives in *Harper's Monthly Magazine* from 1893–1922, argues that "these domestic fictions depend upon an Indian presence as cultural catalyst for American homes and hearths" (4) and that "the Indian 'touch' resulted in . . . [an] . . . American identity among incoming settlers" (3). *Harper's* itself, according to Allred, created "coveted cultural spaces" in "its readers' own homes" (10). These material signifiers of race on the body and in the home suggest the way "conditions of domesticity often become markers that distinguish civilization from savagery" in the "imperial project of civilizing," as Amy Kaplan has suggested (582). In scenarios of cross-racial domesticity in early Westerns, the "process of domestication" (582) comes to imply both the incorporation and the expulsion of Indianness from an imagined national home.

Manifest Families

Mary Louise Pratt theorizes a domestic incorporation of colonized subjects as a pattern of "loving and leaving" in colonial economies. Travel literatures depict an idealized "mystique of reciprocity" in both capitalist trading systems and cross-racial romances while consistently narrating the failure of that reciprocity and the eventual breakdown of both capitalist trade and mixed-race relationships (96–97). According to Pratt, this "anti-conquest" narrative combines colonizing mastery with the impression of "innocence" and integrity. She writes, "It is easy to see transracial love plots as imaginings . . . in which romantic love rather than filial servitude or force guarantee the willful submission of the colonized" (97). We see similar narratives of seductive imperialism at work in both *The Invaders* and *The Squaw Man*, as well as in news articles from the period.

Representations of cross-racial couples in Indian dramas perform precisely this assimilating or familiarizing function, bringing the Other into the settler family so that their goods and services may be incorporated into the nation's inheritance even as the assimilated Other "vanishes" into obscurity.[18] Rayna Green (Cherokee), along with Michael Marsden, Jack Nachbar, Elise Marubbio, Robert Tilton, and others, have suggested that this pattern has taken specific, gendered forms in which popular representations of Native men and women perform stereotyped Noble/Savage or Princess/Squaw functions, depending on their relationships with settlers. Green argues that the "Princess figure" is a "convert" who rejects or is rejected by her own people for her transgressive attraction to settler individuals and settler culture, and who may die as a result (704). Pocahontas, of course, has been the iconic figure for the organization and transmission of "Indian princess" narratives across media, and the pervasive influence of the Pocahontas mythology clearly supports characters such as Sky Star in *The Invaders* and Nat-U-Ritch in *The Squaw Man*.[19] The representational legacy extended by these films, then, is the national origin story encoded in various imagined versions of the Pocahontas and Captain John Smith romance. Mixed-race relationships, especially those between Native women and white men, are one way in which the landscape and resources of the American West were represented cinematically as available for sexual, economic, and sociopolitical exploitation.[20]

Sociologist Pierre Bourdieu establishes a link between romantic "impulses" and socioeconomic institutions (particularly land use and educational systems) that offers a model for understanding the connection between representation of romantic race relations in early Westerns and the historical context from which such representations emerged. Bourdieu suggests an economic basis for the experience of affect, observing that "Marriage strategies are inseparable from inheritance strategies, fertility strategies, and even educational strategies," functioning as "a kind of socially constituted instinct which causes the objectively calculable demands of a particular form of economy to be experienced as an unavoidable call of duty or an irresistible impulse of feeling" (160–61). Silent Westerns, in the tradition of melodrama, dramatize at the individual and kinship level (mystifying or "enchanted relations," according to Bourdieu), the symbolic domination enacted institutionally through governmental education and land-distribution policies. Mary Louise Pratt's argument that transracial romance plots are central to the visual work of mapping and territorial acquisition can be integrated with Bourdieu's emphasis on the work of social institutions in reproducing class structures. Both theorists link emotional allegiance to economic claims made possible by the structuring and restructuring of kinship. In *The Squaw Man* narratives, settlers' territorial acquisition is associated with Native familial disruption and shift, and images of interracial kissing in Indian dramas are used routinely to narrate the transformed civic allegiance of colonized women. The visual discourse of sexual and maternal devotion in Native women characters invite middle-class white viewers to occupy the frontier in fantasy, attaching images of active colonization and racialized expropriation to the emotional immediacy and sympathetic naturalism of romantic and familial attachment. In her study of Cecil B. DeMille, Sumiko Higashi suggests that DeMille's comedies and melodramas emphasizing spousal swaps reveal "the dominance of exchange value in commodity production." Higashi argues that this process, illustrative of Georg Lukacs's theory of reification as a commodity structure in which "a relation between people takes on the character of a thing" (4), brings the middle-class arbitration of taste to bear on visual narratives that "stressed Americanization as a response to cultural diversity" (3). Thus early Hollywood's visual narratives also commodified social relationships through the boundary-making work of Victorian pictorialism.[21]

   In Indian dramas based on *The Squaw Man* narrative pattern, sequential mixed-race and settler marriages—one relationship enabling the other—are both the result of "irresistible" impulses. The interracial marriage provides actual capital, while the settler's second marriage to a white woman provides what Bourdieu would refer to as "symbolic capital." The displacement and re-placement of characters in silent Westerns—effected through doubling, costume changes, the discovery of white identity, or removal to or return from boarding school in the East—attests to an unsettling of Native identity, and of whiteness, in the formation of the Western genre. These repositionings, because they involve sexual transgression, often signify the displacement of a mixed-marriage by an Anglo marriage with the mixed-blood child serving as an awkward "remainder" who becomes the locus of the ambivalence inherent in the Western's unstable system of representation.

The "squaw man" story circulated in the popular press as well in articles such as the 1910 *New York Times Magazine* full-page story by Bailey Millard, "Indian Brides Who Have Made Their Husbands Rich; Some Received Valuable Land from the Government, Others Knew the Secret of Hidden Wealth—Odd Romances of the West." The article describes the fortunes that accrued to several white men through their interracial marriages, focusing particularly on acreage connected to family size through the allotment policy ("The more children John might have the more land he could get under his control")[22] or, alternately, the location of gold revealed through interracial relationships ("Coe always declared that his Indian wife brought him no end of luck in the mines. Her people knew where the gold was and they took him to it").[23] In the context of the "squaw man" film narratives, we can read these news articles and short stories in periodicals as corroborating narratives that lent extracinematic authority to the fantasies of sexualized acquisitions of Native land already disseminated in nickelodeons.

While the figure of the mixed-blood child could embody shame stemming from a forbidden relationship, in the "squaw man" narratives he or she is prized, suggesting that perhaps such children offered a promise in the national imagination of racial rejuvenation rather than racial taint and of licit Anglo inheritance rather than land theft. Thus the child who represents the illegitimacy of cross-racial unions also becomes a legitimizing agent of white patrimony. The mixed-blood figure in these narratives does the concurrent work of revitalizing the aristocracy through assimilation and defining that aristocracy through abjection and difference. In *The Squaw Man*, James Kerhill gains a fourfold entitlement, becoming titled as Earl, acquiring title to American land, and gaining a familial claim to land and to an heir through his marriage to Nat-u-Ritch and the birth of their son. Through Nat-u-Ritch's death, he becomes legally entitled to marry Lady Diana, gaining her title as well.

The cinematic narration of Native deterritorialization as a byproduct of interracial marriage both masked and enabled concurrent coercive and legislative deterritorialization of tribal nations. The displacement and re-placement of persons in the films resonates metaphorically with the U.S. policies that attempted to detribalize Native people by extricating them from their land base, either through the disintegration of the collective reservation (with the "surplus" land opened for white homesteading) or by removing children from their families for boarding school education. These projects overlapped because many of the children sent to boarding schools were taught menial skills that would allow them to work for low wages in settler towns but that were meaningless in reservation contexts and traditional tribal economies.

Rather than presenting the family as an unchanging haven and retreat (for men) from the rough and changeable outside world of the marketplace, in these mixed-race relationships the home *is itself* a marketplace. The (temporary) domestic sphere of the mixed-race relationship is the site of the genesis of wealth for the white man, but the partnership must be dissolved in order for that wealth to be realized and exported to an exclusively white world. White men look to the West for fortunes with which to found their families, but in the impoverished interim they form cross-racial families, which enable them to acquire what they need to support a white woman of a certain class and wealth. The stasis (or suicide) of a Native woman character enables the upward class mobility of settler men. In this sense, the Native woman or man in the relationship occupies a position in the Western's narrative structure parallel to the gunfighter usually played by a white man (such as Shane, in Stevens's 1953 film). Both make the world safe for white families, and in order to complete that task both must be removed from the world that they have enabled. They cannot participate in the domestic because they themselves are coded as a contaminating factor that the domestic nevertheless relies on to remain pure. The Native element—male and female, costume and artifact—is expelled at the end. Even the mixed-blood child is divested of Native clothing (and moccasins) before being sent off to boarding school.

Tourism on Display: *An Up-to-Date Squaw* and *A Pueblo Legend*

In the staged American West of early cinema, the racial exclusion of Native characters from the combined work of social mobility and frontier family formation is also communicated through comedic play with conventions of costume and tourism. *An Up-to-Date Squaw*, a 1911 comedy from Pathé Frères—made during the time that James Young Deer and Lillian St. Cyr were at the height of their influence on the company's productions, though there is no evidence that they worked on the film—offers an example of this reflexive understanding of costuming and its relationship to racial signification. The film's title alone indicates the source of its intended comedy:

the anomaly of stereotyped Indian figures, generally presented in Westerns as belonging to the past but never the present, suddenly seen in the context of a modern "up-to-date" urban setting.[24] The single-reel film depicts New York tourists visiting a Native camp to buy crafts. As they shop, the Chief's wife, Ko-To-Sho (actress unknown), "dazzled by the elegance of the American fashions," follows the women and later imitates them by putting a flat basket on her head as if it were a hat and dragging a skin behind her skirt to make it longer. The next morning Ko-To-Sho sneaks away from her sleeping husband to go shopping in town; when he wakes, the Chief follows her, putting his ear to the sidewalk to track her movements. The intended comedy stems from the juxtaposition of stereotyped wilderness skills (tracking by listening to the ground) and the modern town with its concrete sidewalks. The Chief's appearance in stores causes fright and panic, while Ko-To-Sho's shopping elicits crowds and laughter. Throughout the film, the Natives' clothing and actions, especially the Chief's headdress and long pipe, are displayed in sharp and deliberate contrast with the tidy row houses and shops of the small New England town. In the end, the Chief "scalps" a dandy who has followed Ko-To-Sho, but emerges with only the man's toupee.

The film reverses tourist roles, its comedic sequences pointing out the importance of costume for locating characters in a story genre while mimicking in its plot and images the work of the Indian drama films themselves, which also brought "screen Indians" into the urban spaces of the viewers in theaters. While Natives appear in the film to be anachronisms in the modern world, they also have the agency to enter into modern American town life at will, partially demystifying stereotypes by organizing comedy around the revelation of incongruity. Ko-To-Sho's character is an example of the "Indians in Unexpected Places" that Philip Deloria describes as occupying the space between "expectation and anomaly" in popular representations. Here, with the anomaly that produces what Deloria describes as a casual "chuckle," audiences are also momentarily made aware of the stereotypes as constructions while remaining embedded in the historical stereotypes that mark the moment as anomalous. These strategies suggest that Pathé Frère's film addressed an audience comprised of sophisticated viewers of Indian dramas even at this early stage in the genre's development.[25] Unlike Indian dramas in which costume exchange between Native and white women allows them to change identities briefly, in *An Up-to-Date Squaw* Ko-To-Sho's attempts to become a tourist by shopping for Euro-American clothes and accessories become a demonstration that the collecting of crafts and clothes (that is, the export of goods and services) and the ability to "cross-over" comfortably as a tourist in another ethnic community is socially organized to work in only one direction—that of settlers exploring Native communities—and never the reverse. This "inappropriate" reversal causes the laughter of the audience. Images of primitive atemporality imply an economic consequence in that that screen Natives are never shown to be consumers of commodities (especially representational commodities, such as films and photographs), but are rather always imagined to be commodities themselves. The proliferation of cinematic and literary Westerns and Indian dramas attests to the extraordinary willingness of the public to underwrite performances of Indianness, performances dependent on costume and racial masquerade. Yet the white characters are shown to be constructed through costume as well (such as when a man's hair is revealed to be just a toupee). The comedy in *An Up-to-Date Squaw*, drawn from the vaudeville tradition, makes Ko-To-Sho an object of ridicule for precisely the imitation of Euro-American culture through appearance so earnestly encouraged by photographs and etchings such as those produced by the Carlisle and Hampton schools. The comedy reveals, and to some extent serves, a racial taxonomy that denies the possibility of interracial class mobility in its closing, yet imagines that very mobility in its unfolding action. Based partly on readings of films such as *An Up-to-Date Squaw*, Nanna Verhoeff argues cogently that, in the films' representations of ethnicity and nationality, "this story of identity construction remains never-ending": "It is precisely the trope of mobility and 'openness' that characterizes many of the Pathé films. This openness is played out in the shifting positions of whites and Indians in the unstable relations between the two" (172). And the premise of economic mobility, coded by costume, was part of the implied promise in the juxtaposed before-and-after images advertising government policies of institutional interventions in Native families.[26]

The embedded structures of tourism and display in Indian dramas take the form of direct address to the audience in D. W. Griffith's 1912 *A Pueblo Legend*, shot on location at Isleta Pueblo, in which Mary Pickford plays an adopted Hopi girl in a drama set in precontact times. Pickford's performance in redface models tourism through cross-racial identification on camera in a scene where, standing apart from a group of male dancers, she acts as both character onlooker and a white spectator's tour guide by breaking the frame of the story to engage the audience with a direct look at the camera (see figure 1.5). Through the veil of redface, Pickford meets the eyes of an assumed settler audience in a shared gaze. Reminiscent of Thomas Edison's earliest actualities, such as *Moki Snake Dance by Wolpi Indians* (1901), *Wand Dances, Pueblo Indians* (1898), and *Eagle Dance, Pueblo Indians* (1898), the dancing

Figure 1.5. *A Pueblo Legend*, Biograp (1913) (LC).

done by the Pueblo men authenticates the star and narrative in *A Pueblo Legend* through the educational realism of ethnographic spectacle. It also provided non-Native viewers with an on-screen white spectator in the body of Mary Pickford, whose embedded presence as a recognizable star "playing Indian" acts as both a model tourist and tour guide. The actress's look toward the audience and the film's focus on display rather than narrative illustrate the Indian drama's historical ties to showmanship and spectacle, as well as what Tom Gunning calls "the cinema of attractions." In this case, Natives function as tourist spectacle for an acknowledged audience, rather than the spectators being sutured into a narrative through continuity editing as in later films, and Pickford's gaze across the screen attempts to produce a homogenous and Americanized audience in the process of that address. Furthermore, the moment reenacts the film's actual production conditions while advertising the company's ability to achieve authentic effects through location shooting: the filmmaking team visits the Pueblo and narrates its intercultural encounter through the dramatic content and visual manifestation of Pickford's spectatorship of the dance. Visual discourses of tourism represent part of the Indian drama's claim to educational value, replicating on screen the film's work of taking non-Native viewers to visit and learn about Native communities.

A similar gaze is embedded in the Biograph film *The Mended Lute* (1909), a drama of precontact Native life starring Florence Lawrence with Mack Sennett, James Young Deer, and Lillian St. Cyr all playing minor roles as "Indians." Alison Griffiths describes this film's technique of having the protagonist "hail" the audience through an inviting gaze. Typical of D. W. Griffith's films of this period, she writes, the white star's direct eye contact acknowledged "the mimetic counterfeit of her 'Indian' performance" (7–8). To some extent, while costumes communicate plot elements in later dramas of assimilation, the emphasis on costumed spectacle in tension with narrative remains a hallmark of Indian dramas and sympathetic Westerns (as I discuss in chapter 2).[27] Together these films manipulate audience awareness of practices of appropriate and inappropriate racial identity through images of power, desire, and identification at work in the film's narratives of tourism. In the 1912 Mack Sennett film *The Tourists*, Trixie (Mabel Normand), a white tourist, arrives at a Pueblo by train and becomes so intensely involved in buying pottery that she misses the train's departure. She continues to avidly consume both objects and experiences, eventually disrupting local social relations when she becomes too familiar with a Native man (see figure 1.6) and must hide under a blanket until she can

Figure 1.6. *The Tourists*, Biograph (1912) (LC).

be rescued and depart on the next train. Here, the interracial romance is embedded in a touristic experience, both rendered as hyperbolic comedy. Tourism is shown to be dependent on the mobility of modern transit, as well as a system of display for consumption, mimicking the viewing experience of the audience. Unlike the self-conscious comedy and tourist play of *An Up-to-Date Squaw*, *A Pueblo Legend*, *The Tourists*, and *The Mended Lute*, however, costume exchange is an earnest and effective strategy for characters in deadly frontier situations in dramas such as *Iola's Promise* and *Maya, Just an Indian*.

"The Cross-Heart People": *Iola's Promise* and *Maya, Just an Indian*

The Squaw Man and its cognates depict the American West and the cross-racial relationships available there as a refuge—though a desolate one—from troubles in the East and England. Well-born men in trouble can wait out the storm in the West, biding their time until news of inheritance arrives or until legal troubles are resolved. However, the children produced by these marriages of convenience become the "property" of the father. Often the child is an eldest son who will inherit the father's legacy (thus becoming a property owner himself) and will accompany him back East, transforming his identity and his destiny along the way. Taking the Native mother back to England or the East Coast is never an option, either because the woman refuses or the man feels she would be unhappy. In *Iola's Promise* (Griffith 1912) and *Maya, Just an Indian* (1913) the cross-racial relationship becomes itself the source of white men's wealth, as well as their justification of and release from life in the West. Rather than producing children, these liaisons produce gold. The gold ore is made available for the white settler by a Native woman, who reveals its location as an expression of her sexual devotion, but who then disappears, enabling the white man to export the wealth to a new relationship with a white woman.

In *Iola's Promise*, Iola (Mary Pickford) is captured by outlaws but saved by Big Bill Kenyon (Alfred Paget), an honest prospector who hopes to strike it rich in the West so that he and his fiancée Dora (Dorothy Bernard), who is in a wagon train on her way to meet him, can marry. Iola, according to the intertitle, is a "simple savage" who, "touched by the goodness of her benefactor, gives him her heart in a sudden ecstasy of gratitude." Before he sends her back to her people, Kenyon teaches Iola two things: first, to identify gold ore, stones with yellow specks, and second, to cross her heart as a mark of her promise to bring any such stones she finds to him. The narrative links the giving of Christian religion through the symbol of the cross with the taking of gold; in this case, both Christianity and gold are connected to Iola's "ecstatic" and sexualized worship of Big Bill Kenyon.[28] For Iola, finding the gold for Kenyon explicitly substitutes for marriage to him; as she leaves she says in an intertitle, "If I cannot stay with you, and be one of the cross-heart people, then I will bring you the little stones with the yellow specks."

While Iola searches for gold ore, her tribe (described as "savage and turbulent" and depicted with a confusing combination of Plains and Pueblo cultural icons including feathered warbonnets, tipis, and Katchina dolls) attacks the wagon train carrying Kenyon's fiancée Dora. Dora and her father are captured and "spared for the slower and more painful death at the stake." Iola's pleas for their lives are ignored, so she trades clothes with Dora in order to lead the warriors away from the captured pair (see figure 1.7). In the confusion that ensues, Iola is shot by her own tribe, while Dora and her father meet up with the prospectors, who protect them from the angry tribe. In a dying gesture, Iola gives the gold ore she has found to Kenyon.

The film ends with a scene strikingly similar to the closing of *The Squaw Man*: Iola lies prone in the foreground, held by Kenyon and Dora, while the prospectors stand in the background looking on (see figure 1.8). Iola's death at the hands of her tribe could be interpreted as a metaphor for racial suicide because she dies by her own tribe's actions, foreclosing the tribe's symbolic future, although the representational complexity of Iola's costumed presentation as Dora at this moment (a white actress performing an Indian character imitating a white character) opens up a range of other interpretations of her accidental death. The doubling between Iola and Dora is emphasized in parallel scenes in which they describe encounters with the other in stories to their own people (Iola tells her tribe of Kenyon's kindness, and Dora tells the prospectors of being rescued by Iola) and in the use of clothing to signal their similar narrative positioning as women devoted to Kenyon.

The confusion of identity caused by Iola and Dora changing clothes underscores Iola's desire to occupy Dora's role as Kenyon's wife and simultaneously imbues Dora with some of Iola's symbolic value, thus legitimating the white family's entitlement to their new western existence and fortune. In *Iola's Promise*, Iola enables Kenyon's marriage to another by providing the wealth he needs to support his white wife, just as Nat-u-Ritch provided a son to Jim Kerhill before his brother's death (and thus the transfer of the

Figure 1.7. *Iola's Promise*, Biograph (1912) (LC), Dora and Iola exchange clothes.

Figure 1.8. *Iola's Promise*, Biograph (1912) (LC), Iola's death.

estate to Jim) made his marriage to Diana possible. Iola's connection with the gold-flecked stones (perhaps representing her own in-between status and double alliance), identifies her with the riches that can be extracted from nature. Iola's correlation with the land's wealth—her figurative fertility—recalls Annette Kolodny's argument that Americans envision the land-as-woman, specifically the land-as-Mother. But Iola, associated with the natural resources, is not incorporated into the American family as a mother; instead she is uncoupled from the wealth she represents.

In *Maya, Just an Indian*, the connection between gold and children as the result of a cross-racial affair is also depicted visually. At the beginning of the film, Maya (actress unknown) returns from the Carlisle School in western clothes, only to find that her family angrily rejects her new appearance and will only accept her if she symbolically reasserts her Native identity by changing into a buckskin dress and headband (see figure 1.9). She is later wooed by a prospector, Bill (actor unknown), who has tried in vain to get her father (the Chief) to divulge the whereabouts of gold in

Figure 1.9. *Maya, Just an Indian*, Frontier (1913) (LC), Maya is ordered to change her clothes.

the area (see figure 1.10). Maya learns the location of the gold from her father (who says, "If you will promise not to see the paleface again, I will tell you"), but she promptly betrays her promise to her father and leads Bill to the riverbed that contains gold ore.

A month later, as Bill packs his bags, Maya (now dressed in a pioneer woman's calico dress, different from both her "reservation Indian" and "Carlisle graduate" clothing) realizes that he plans to abandon her and so replaces the gold with rocks, hiding the real bag of gold in the nearby bushes. Bill does indeed abandon Maya, who collapses in front of their tent and is found by her father's friend. Bill discovers Maya's deception in a hotel room in the East. Two years later, an impoverished Bill returns to the area with his white wife, who has lung fever, and their young baby. Maya overhears this news and retrieves the gold from its hiding place, cradling the bundle and speaking to it as if the gold itself were the baby she and Bill never had (see figure 1.11). Finding Bill's home, she waits until he has left the house and enters as a dark figure hovering over Bill's sleeping wife and child, both dressed in white clothes and lying on white bedcovers. She raises the knife to kill the sleeping woman, but hesitates as she sees the

Figure 1.10. *Maya, Just an Indian*, Frontier (1913) (LC), The courtship.

Figure 1.11. *Maya, Just an Indian*, Frontier (1913) (LC), Maya cradles the bag of gold.

baby. She reaches to touch the baby, pulls back, leaves the knife and gold back on a side table, reaches again for the baby and again pulls back, and then exits the room. Bill returns to find the knife and gold. An intertitle reads "Just an Indian"; in the final scene, Maya climbs to a rocky peak and holds her hands up to the sky, her blanket falling from her to the ground. It is unclear whether she is about to jump from the precipice or whether she is simply praying, but she has clearly relinquished her claim to Bill, gold, and family. This final image, Maya alone at a precipice, is consistent with the iconography of "the vanishing American" as practiced by photographers such as Edward Curtis, and also recalls the images of white women driven to jump from high cliffs to escape from racialized sexual threat in films such as *The Birth of a Nation* and Maurice Tourneur's *The Last of the Mohicans* (1920).

The fluidity of Maya's identity is demonstrated by her changes of costume, which indicate her changing roles. Ultimately, these transformations fail to deliver her from her cinematic fate as "Just an Indian," despite her longing for the family life that she enables Bill to have with his white wife but which she herself cannot attain. Though those around her judge her by her clothes, her very fluctuations of identity to please those near her mean that there is no place for her to make a family either with her tribe or with Bill on the frontier, unlike the fixed whiteness of Bill's chosen wife. Her cradling of the gold bag suggests the substitution of the gold for a mixed-blood child, both of which would have come from the relationship. Though the gold also changes costume, unlike Maya it remains an object of constant desire no matter what it wears. In Maya's moment of hesitation as she holds her knife above Bill's sleeping wife, she reaches for the baby as if to take it in place of the gold she leaves behind, but in the end denies herself this exchange. The film visually equates the gold that will accrue wealth to Bill and his white family with a potential mixed-blood child from his relationship with Maya. In *Maya, Just an Indian*, as in many Westerns, before settlers can achieve ownership—and benefit from ownership—of western American land, they need to extract the gold from the land and the child from the woman (or the gold and child from the land-as-woman). The fertility of the American landscape (figured as female) produces both gold and the potential mixed-blood child. Maya herself is no longer necessary (and indeed disappears in a white fantasy of Native suicide) once Bill has achieved middle-class status through his relationship with her. Her "Indianness"—and her productivity and reproductivity—has already been incorporated into the white family in the form of (legitimated) property.

Like Iola, Maya is moved by her passion for a white man to betray the codes and appropriate behaviors of her tribe, but her sexuality is here represented more explicitly than Iola's metaphorically religious conversion. In several Indian dramas, including *Maya, Just an Indian*; *The Chief's Daughter* (Griffith 1911); and *Comata, The Sioux* (Griffith 1909), white male suitors of Native women awaken their latent sexuality. This dynamic often emerges in scenes that depict the woman touching her lips in wonderment after being kissed by a white suitor and thereafter enthusiastically returning his affections. In all these films, the Native woman's devotion to and sacrifice for a domestic and sexual liaison with a white man leads her to reject tribal bonds to pursue a nuclear, mixed-race family relationship. In the silent Western, whiteness and the reproductive family are synonymous; coherent Native families are rarely depicted because they are presumed to be vanishing. The conquest is domestic: the Native is assimilated into the settler family and eradicated from that family in the same narrative. While the white family's entitlement to the land (or gold or children) is authenticated through the "sacrifice" and "devotion" of the Native woman who provides these things to the settler against the tribe's wishes, the white settler's "debt to her [is] the basis for his *claim* upon her," as Mary Louise Pratt has written in relation to travel narratives (97, emphasis in original).

Both the Dawes Act and the boarding school movement were the result of aggressive policies of total assimilation for Indigenous peoples, and a large part of their assimilationist thrust was economic: to effect "tribal disintegration" and transform Natives into subsistence farmers with nuclear families—or even lone wage earners—rather than extended family and tribal communities (Dippie 175). An 1881 profile of the Carlisle and Hampton schools illustrates the induction of male students (female students are invisible in this economy) into wage-labor and capitalist systems through the payment of government allowances in wages rather than clothes:

> A natural, and therefore valuable, stimulation to their energies, and doing much to make men of them, has been the payment of wages. Part of the government appropriation is given to them in this form instead of in clothing. They are expected to buy their own clothing out of it, except their school uniform. There is some waste, but more profit, in the lessons thus taught of the relation of labor to capital. (Ludlow 666)

Yet, in many of the Western films from the early 1910s, capitalism does not work this way. White men do not make their fortunes from wage labor or subsistence farming; rather, they come West as prospectors to make "easy money" to export back East. They make money from gold (its location often disclosed due to brief romances with Native women), through inheritances from their eastern families, or through the discovery of oil. Silent Indian dramas narrate an imperial West where white men can wait out periods of poverty in comfort or where they can live temporarily while they exploit Native people and natural resources for quick profit. Occasionally they make money in the cattle business, but in *The Squaw Man*, Kerhill's cattle ranch is bankrupt (in what must be one of the great ironic lines in the genre, a minor character in *The Squaw Man* tells Jim that in the West "folks keep their hands in their own pockets").

Silent Westerns reworked colonial narratives that had long been present in nineteenth-century novels, in which past events and marriages in British colonies—Rochester's first wife Bertha in *Jane Eyre*, and Colonel Munro's unnamed first wife in *The Last of the Mohicans* (both women from the Caribbean)—cause marital and racial complications when one family gives way to another, even though the novels are wholly set in the context of England or America. In these novels' allusions to transatlantic sexual economics, the backstory of the first wife becomes a ghost in the machine of the nineteenth-century gothic romance, a part of the story of empire-building that remains untold, the "dark" secret of middle-aged men whose sexual pasts are seemingly beyond the comprehension of young white women, and from which men derive the fortunes and power that make them central narrative figures. Such narratives, then, both reflect and mystify the domestic as it is enmeshed in capitalism and imperialism. The domestic is market-driven even as it proposes to offer sanctuary from the world market.

Other films drawing from the "squaw man" scenario during this early period parody the economy of cross-racial romance. In *Buck's Romance* (Duncan 1912), Buck (William Duncan) inadvertently wins the Chief's daughter (Myrtle Stedman) in a horse race along with the money he needs to buy a house for his white wife. The unnamed Native woman follows him around, encouraged by Buck's cowboy friends who think the escapade is a terrific joke, until Buck finally explains the situation to both women. The film ends with parallel scenes of Native and white family life (the Chief's daughter had married a man from her tribe and had a child, and Buck is living comfortably with his wife and child). In a final scene, Buck dreams that he is still being chased by the Chief's daughter, and wakes in horror to run from her but finds instead, to his relief, that his white baby is by his side. Again, the substitution of the Chief's daughter in the dream for the white baby at the end underscores narratively and visually the way Buck's comfortable family life has been both enabled and threatened by the presence of the Chief's daughter as part of his "winnings" from the horse race.

Yet for all the rigidity of the racial and reproductive schema underpinning these repetitive "squaw man" narratives, early Westerns evinced remarkable fluidity across multiple representations. In addition to *Iola's Promise*, for example, several other films portray white women donning Indian costume to infiltrate or escape a hostile tribe, such as the 1915 Edison film directed by Langston West, *The Corporal's Daughter*, where the white heroine Kate (Gladys Hulette) happens to have an Indian outfit at the ready from prior "Indian theatricals" (see figure 1.12).[29] Other films, such as D. W. Griffith's films *The Red Girl* (1908) and *A Mohawk's Way* (1910), feature closing scenes that emphasize affection between settler and Native female characters (see figures 1.13 and 1.14). And in the 1909 film *The Aborigine's Devotion*, a Native man adopts the orphaned child of a trapper, protecting her against a corrupt frontier trader; the closing scene presents the child in the Native man's lap in a medium-shot as she holds a toy canoe (see figure 1.15).

Some films reimagine and reverse the unidirectional "progress" of the before-and-after assimilationist narrative; in these films Native men and

Figure 1.12. *The Corporal's Daughter*, Edison (1915) (LC).

Figure 1.13. *The Red Girl*, AM&B (1908) (LC).

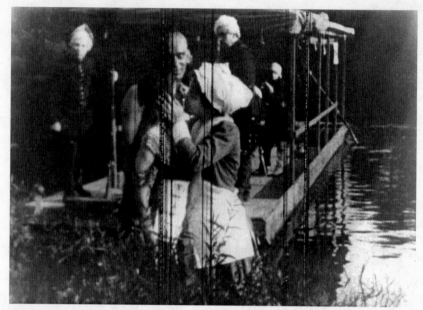

Figure 1.14. *A Mohawk's Way*, Biograph (1910) (LC).

Figure 1.15. *The Aborigine's Devotion*, World Film Mfg. Co. (1909) (LC).

women ultimately choose to return to their tribes. The films imagine a latent, racially based "call of the wild" that could reclaim eastern-educated Native and mixed-blood children from their new lives. Another turn-of-the-century catch-phrase for this idea—the fear on the part of boarding school administrators that Indigenous people would return to the reservation and abandon white teachings—was "back to the blanket," reemphasizing clothing as an indicator of racial and cultural allegiance. In *Her Indian Mother* [*The White Man Takes a Red Wife*] (1910), Moore (Jack Conway), a white Hudson Bay trapper, marries a Native woman and has a daughter, but leaves two years later and forgets his Native family. Fourteen years later, when her Native mother dies, the daughter, Rising Moon (Alice Joyce), inherits the bracelet Moore gave her mother. On a return to the area, Moore recognizes the bracelet and takes his daughter back East with him, away from Rising Moon's Native lover. An intertitle reads, "Four years later, the call": In a parlor, Rising Moon wears a white dress with her hair in a bun and a gold watch hanging from her neck. As she serves tea to her father and a gentleman friend, the visitor drops a beaded necklace—a metonymy for Native identity—that fascinates Rising Moon. She returns to her room cradling the object, writes a note to her father, and begins changing back into her buckskin dress (which she has kept). Though Moore finds Rising Moon, who has gone "back to her mother's people," she stays with her Native lover and refuses to rejoin her father, who rides away. Moore's return to *his* people passes largely without comment in the film, which focuses on Rising Moon's return to her Native community.

In *The Call of the Wild* (Griffith, 1908), after Carlisle School graduate George Redfeather (Charles Inslee) proposes to a white woman (Florence Lawrence) and is angrily rejected by both the woman and her father, he returns to his room and in an extended scene begins to undress wildly, his many layers of white clothing contrasting with his dark skin and the dark doorway framing him. He dons a warbonnet hanging from the wall, and still in a fit of uncontrolled rage and grief, he drinks wine from a bottle, tears up a photo of his beloved, and tears feathers from the warbonnet. In an apparent attempt to reclaim the Native identity that caused his beloved to reject him, he emerges from the house dressed in an unfastened buckskin shirt and headdress with a blanket around his waist. Thus transformed, he rejoins his tribe in drinking and dancing and leads them in pursuit of the woman as she goes for a ride. Pulled from her horse, she pleads with her former lover to release her until finally he repents and protects her from his tribe. In the final scene, he holds a torn piece of her dress or handkerchief to his face, then waves it as he rides dejectedly out of the frame.

As with *Iola's Promise* and *Maya, Just an Indian, Her Indian Mother* [*The White Man Takes a Red Wife*] and *The Call of the Wild* emphasize the transformation of Native characters through costume, as Rising Moon calmly retrieves her buckskin dress and the man in *Call of the Wild* furiously tears off his "white" clothes and puts on his blanket and warbonnet. Whether the films depict the alleged ignoble sexual impulses of Native men or the alleged noble racial loyalty of Native women, ultimately their onstage transformations through changes of clothing cannot withstand the presumption of fixed racial difference. This concept is developed in *The Chief's Daughter* (Griffith 1911) and *The Call of the Wild*, where the presence of Chinese servants in east coast homes and western pioneer settings reiterates visually the connection between race and class. These visual "reversions," in which cross-racial romances always end badly, narrate a racialized basis for the economic boundaries of class (see figures 1.16 and 1.17).

Several films shift the race and gender configuration of the "squaw man" plot, making the reversion an expressly masculine trope of primitivism as in *The Call of the Wild*. In *Strongheart* (Griffith 1914), a Native football star (Henry B. Walthall) at Columbia returns to lead his tribe, leaving his athletic career and settler sweetheart behind. *The Half-Breed* (Dwan 1916) opens with a brief allusion to the "squaw man" narrative—a Native woman, abandoned by her white lover, commits suicide, leaving her mixed-race baby Leaping Brook to be raised by a white naturalist and "self-made scholar." Leaping Brook's (Douglas Fairbanks) experiences with the white settlers in town, especially his confrontation with his father the sheriff, underscore the film's representation of hypocrisy at the heart of America's rhetoric of equality. Leaping Brook eventually turns his romantic attention away from Nellie (Jewel Carmen), the white parson's daughter, to woo Teresa (Alma Rubens), a Mexican woman. Relationships between Mexican and Native characters, as in *Ramona* (Griffith 1910; Crisp 1916; Carewe 1928), often provide the allure of mixed-race relationships without depicting the more socially unacceptable white/Native union. In *The Half-Breed* this dynamic is accentuated when Teresa borrows Nellie's dress and Nellie's suitors mistakenly believe that Leaping Brook has kidnapped Nellie when they see a woman wearing her dress in his camp. Yet the film's sexual focus is really on Fairbanks, who is able to undress in redface for the titillation of the female audience (see figures 1.18–1.19).

In the visual world of the silent Western, Native identity becomes an uncertain negotiation between appearance and blood quantum, between the self-referential playacting of film's costuming and the supposed threat posed by racial and cultural mixture.[30] Writing about the depiction of Pueblo women between the turn of the century and the 1920s, Barbara Babcock

Figure 1.16. *The Call of the Wild*, AM&B (1908) (LC), George Redfeather (Charles Inslee) attends a party in Western clothes.

Figure 1.17. *The Call of the Wild*, AM&B (1908) (LC), George Redfeather (Charles Inslee) changes clothes after his proposal is rejected.

Figure 1.18. *The Half-Breed*, Triangle (1916) (LC), Lo (Douglas Fairbanks).

Figure 1.19. *The Half-Breed*, Triangle (1916) (LC), Changing clothes.

draws on Frantz Fanon's concept of "epidermal schema" as it is reinterpreted by Mary Ann Doane as "the visible prison of race," and by Homi Bhabha as "the most visible of fetishes." Babcock emphasizes the use of costume as a racial marker of Native American identity, noting:

> in the absence of a significant difference in skin color, what is on the body, particularly the head, becomes "the key signifier of cultural and racial difference" in the stereotypes of the Native American . . . the Hopi maiden with her squash blossoms or butterfly whorls; the olla maiden or water carrier; and the Santa Fe Chief Plains brave with feathered war bonnet. (213)[31]

Building on this idea, I want to suggest that the Western film genre's special reliance on costume to signify social roles and ethnic difference inadvertently leads to a fluidity of identity when clothes and props are exchanged during the course of the action. This fluidity, a source of visual pleasure in a medium premised on identity play, also works against the films' ostensible messages about maintaining racial boundaries. Thus, while Westerns appear to present stable binaries,[32] these unstable identities—especially in dramas about mixed-race relationships, mixed-blood children, and Natives educated in boarding schools—challenge apparently clear-cut notions of Otherness and difference. Both whiteness and Indianness, then, are revealed as unstable performances.

Indian Dramas and Child Custody

Themes of shifting familial and racial identities are amplified in films that narrate the actual exchange of babies. Familial separation and the loss of babies and children in particular were extremely common scenarios in cinematic melodramas—one need only think of Anna (Lillian Gish) holding her dead infant in *Way Down East* (Griffith 1920) for example, or the many scenes in Westerns such as *The Battle at Elderbush Gulch* in which Native attackers threaten settler babies to the horror of the mothers on screen and presumably in the audience. The adoptions and child exchanges that dominate Indian drama plots in early cinema are figurations of empathy that facilitated settler audiences' emotional access (through the gestural language of melodrama) to allegories of Native-white relations.

Several Indian dramas use captivity plots to explore family disruptions and separations on the frontier. In *The Indian Massacre* (*The Heart of an*

Indian; Ince 1912) a Native woman (Anna Little) whose baby has died has a chance to adopt a white baby taken in an attack. The Native mother eventually returns the baby, however, and reunites the white family; in the final scene, she prays in silhouette under her baby's high grave. This film reiterates the notion that the disintegration of the Native family makes way for or enables the intact white family to take its place on western land and again frames frontier warfare in terms of the pathos of domestic loss. In the sequence of stills reproduced here (see figures 1.20–1.24), costume accentuates the contrast between families as the baby, clothed in white, passes from settler to Native custody and back again. The scene of separation between settler mother and child supports the narrative's call for urgent rescue through active physical dramatizations of the mother's distress as she is forcibly held back by her Native captors. The Native mother's mourning at the platform grave in the film's closing image is far more static—it is "too late" to save her baby and (by extension) the tribe's genealogical claim to the future. The center image, in which the Native mother returns the stolen baby to its mother, confers the authenticating "Indian touch" to the settler family's political future as the film's legitimate racial unit of national continuity.

In *Tangled Lives* (1911), a settler boy and girl, siblings separated at birth by Native captivity, meet and initially begin a romance until their true relationship is revealed and both are horrified by their incestuous desire. *The Indian* (Klaw and Erlanger 1914) tells the story of Native twin boys who are separated when one is taken captive in a settler raid and raised by a white family. The cavalry captain brings Blue Feather, the Native infant, home with him to be a playmate for his daughter, Gladys, who sees the baby as a replacement for the doll she has outgrown. Red Feather, the other twin, becomes a tribal leader, and when the brothers are reunited as adults they work together to fight government corruption on the reservation until Red Feather is killed in a confrontation. Blue Feather, raised by whites, remains to represent nonviolent political advocacy. These stories of tribes as custodians of settler children also function as legitimating narratives. The acceptance of white children by tribes, usually temporary in Indian drama plots, seems to offer the possibility of a legitimizing "Indian touch" or Indigenous approval to the settler family that implies a political ceding of land.

Native adoption is the central act in the 14-minute, 1908 AM&B production, *The Red Man and the Child*, D. W. Griffith's second directorial effort and his first film to be reviewed in a trade journal (*Variety*, which praised his photographic technique). In this film adaptation of a Bret Harte story, a Native man (Charles Inslee) befriends a white miner and his young

Figure 1.20. *The Indian Massacre*, Bison (1912) (LC), Native mother (Ann Little) and child.

Figure 1.21. *The Indian Massacre*, Bison (1912) (LC), Taking a settler child.

Figure 1.22. *The Indian Massacre*, Bison (1912) (LC), Separating settler mother and child.

Figure 1.23. *The Indian Massacre*, Bison (1912) (LC), Reuniting settler mother and child.

Figure 1.24. *The Indian Massacre*, Bison (1912) (LC), Mourning the Native child.

son, showing the child his own stash of gold nuggets. While the Native character is away guiding some prospectors, however, other miners kill the child's father and force the child to show them where the Native miner's gold is hidden. Seeing the murder of his friend and the beating of the child through the prospectors' telescope (see figure 1.25), the Native miner pursues and kills the white miners, rescuing the child. The film conflates the act of Native looking with the witnessing of a crime; the strategic use of long-shot is integrated into the film's narrative structure as part of his first experience with the telescope, as much a metaphor for the camera here as it would be four years later in *The Invaders*. When the white prospectors first show the Native man the telescope, he draws back in alarm, looking on the other side of the device to find the scene he sees through it. The surveyors

Figure 1.25. The Redman and the Child, AM&B (1908) (LC).

find his astonishment over this technology humorous; they slap one another on the back and laugh, and they move the device so that he can see by panning. The Native character claps his hands once or twice, expressing delight at first, pulling back, looking again.[33] Tom Gunning identifies this moment as a small landmark in the development of narrative cinema: "The Indian's look through the telescope captures the process of transition from a cinema of attractions to one of narrative integration. . . . The point-of-view shot no longer forms the central attraction of the film but is subordinated to the goals of narrative discourse: it interrelates two lines of narrative action and involves us directly in the Indian's reaction to the child's kidnapping" (*D. W. Griffith* 72–73). This technical advance toward a visual narrative system also undergirds an important shift in the way viewers are asked to perceive the "West" of the Western. For although the Native character looks through the same viewfinder as the white miners, he does not see the open land that the white men see, nor does he see a woman substituted for the land, as the prospectors do in *The Invaders*. Instead, the Native character sees the crime scene, becoming both a witness and a vigilante as a result. Distraught and enraged, he retrieves the body of his friend, and reemerges from his tent bare-chested, dressed only in a loincloth and feathered headband. After he chases down the miners, the last scene depicts him rescuing the child, taking him away in a canoe. That Inslee's Native character rescues and adopts a white settler child upsets the Western's professed distinctions between Native and settler families. In this film's adoption there is an echo of the captivity narrative as well as a reference to other Indian dramas in which exchanges of children between Natives and settlers take place with great fluidity. Furthermore, the film contrasts settler technology with Native nakedness in the "reversion" to savagery staged by Inslee's performance. *The Red Man and the Child* activates these images—technologies of vision and the spectacle of nakedness—as metaphors for modernity and primitivism, marks of racial difference that inform scenarios of frontier encounters. The overt theatricality of these sequences is shaped by the film's production practices and the physicality of the actors' performances, yet that theatricality is also masked, in the manner of *A Pueblo Legend*, by the discourses of tourism and authenticity that frame its dramatization.

In playing with the boundaries of identity so rigidly enforced at the Carlisle School, these early films carry forward a theatrical anxiety about who can "pass" as another (onstage or offstage), who holds the rights to the pleasures of racial masquerade and who is subject to the enforced conversions of race-based reeducation. Even when Native characters are center stage, they are subject to (and immobile within) definitions from the outside, whereas white characters, and white actors performing in redface, demonstrate the economic benefits of mobile racial play in defining and maintaining static class borders. In this sense, Indian dramas' costumed narratives of transformation assert the power of theater, and perhaps of cinematic narrative itself, as a race-based privilege.

Performing Assimilation and Reversion: The Politics of Production

The image of the Native character behind the telescope—which I've argued is also a figurative "camera"—in *The Red Man and the Child* suggests a complex process through which settler and Indigenous perspectives are imagined on film. The Native character's lack of familiarity with the telescope becomes, such as Nanook's (Allakariallak) much-remarked encounter with a white trader's gramophone in Robert Flaherty's *Nanook of the North* (1922), a way of classifying primitivism. In *The Red Man and the Child*, the Native man's amazement at Western visual technology, and by extension his act of looking, are themselves marks of the antimodern, and in keeping with this trope, what he sees through the telescope triggers a "reversion to savagery" signaled by his costume change and violent pursuit of the thieves.

His emergence from the tent in feathered headband and loincloth mimics the actor Charles Inslee's own transformation into redface for the film, a reflexive recostuming that invites viewers to engage in the serious play of racial masquerade specifically in the context of a movement from more to less "civilized."

Charles Inslee played many such roles, including his very successful part in *The Call of the Wild*. In early Indian drama plots, these instances of "reversion" are particularly sexually freighted with the construction of a desired body, often either triggering or dissolving a white lover's interest. In her history of early cinema from 1907–1915, Eileen Bowser notes the "allure of nudity (of men only)" in the Indian drama, "which had the same respectability as the nakedness of indigenes in travel films." In a frequently cited passage, she quotes film director Fred Balshofer's assessment of Charles Inslee's appeal in redface: "Inslee made a striking appearance on the screen, and the ladies simply went gaga over him. Oh's and ah's came from them whenever he appeared on the screen in one of his naked Indian hero roles, so naturally most of his pictures were on that order" (173). Inslee's advantageous use of ethnographic tropes of Native nakedness as a "cover" for white nakedness was exploited by many other actors, notably Douglas Fairbanks in *The Half-Breed*. This cinematic erotic of colonial masquerade became typical of later Westerns featuring white stars in redface (among many possible examples: Rock Hudson in Douglas Sirk's 1954 *Taza, Son of Cochise*).

Yet at the same moment that the "Indian" Charles Inslee creates the stage for his own mock reversion, his look through the telescope—in character—ironically retrieves the diegetic potentiality for another perspective, one that parallels the Native characters' repeated return to the text of their treaty in *The Invaders*. Unlike the white surveyor's exclusive possession of the cinematic gaze in *The Invaders*, however, in *The Redman and the Child* the Native character makes use of the scopic technology supplied by surveyors. He then moves from behind the "camera" to literally enter the scene he just witnessed through its lens, enacting justice in an on-camera amplification of the racial masquerade of redface, and "playing Indian" through his change of costume and behavior. Griffith's profoundly contradictory scenario embeds the established signifiers of the antimodern primitive within a narrative framework that hinges on Native vision. This anxiously reflexive scene, then, is animated by the power of representational privilege to reveal frontier colonialism as the site of criminal trauma rather than economic and sexual opportunity, even as the violence of the Native character's enforcement ultimately serves to "project" the future of the nation onto the body of the surviving white settler child.

The routine use of redface in Indian dramas existed alongside another industry practice, already established in the Wild West shows, of seeking out Native American actors and extras for Western film production. These actors, embedded in and responsive to conditions in the emergent Hollywood industry as well as to its dominant representations, created a space for Native participation—and Native looking—both on and off the screen. Though constrained by the conventions of the Indian drama and the nascent studio production practices, Native actors performed in a wide range of roles. Returning to archival records, scholars such as Angela Aleiss, Philip Deloria, Michelle Raheja, Nicolas Rosenthal, and Scott Simmon have recovered information about the careers of many silent- and early sound-era Native actors, including William Eagleshirt (Lakota), Molly Spotted Elk (Penobscot), Luther Standing Bear (Lakota), Richard Davis Thunderbird (southern Cheyenne), Charles Bruner (Muscogee), Charlie Stevens (Apache), Ann Ross (Cherokee), Chief Red Fox (Lakota), Elijah Thurmont (Algonquian), Rod Redwing (Chickasaw), Nipo Strongheart (Yakama), Chief Yowlatchie (Yakama), and the numerous Lakota actors working for Thomas Ince in 1912, many of whom were not credited in the films and remain anonymous. Nicolas Rosenthal has demonstrated the way some of these Native actors and filmmakers tried to control representations of Natives in film scenarios, petitioned and organized for better wages, and helped to create Native communities in urban Los Angeles in the first half of the century, communities that evolved to provide services for the Native people who came to Los Angeles in the 1950s under the Relocation program.

At times Native actors were treated as no more than props and setting for dramas of settlement. For example, in a 1910 letter, Tom Mix reports on his activities recruiting Native actors for Selig Polyscope using the same language that he does in talking about procuring cattle for the set:

> I had Indians lined up and ready for shipment and would have gotten away with them all O.K. but Mulhall endeavored to get the exposition people to hold them on account of a $400 deposit made at Valentine, Nebr., for their return at the expiration of the exposition. . . . In the meantime knowing that I could not get the Indians there, I went to North Carolina and saw California Frank. He has a fine bunch of picture Indians, three of them six foot tall, good clothes and picturesque. I made arrangements for him to send these Indians to Jacksonville from Augusta, Miss.

Letters such as this one also render issues of containment and control of Indigenous movement in stark terms, revealing the tight control government officials maintained over Indigenous peoples' movements to and from reservation lands. In an era of paternalistic restrictions and required permissions for travel, film work could provide opportunities for mobility and income.

Of the Native American actors hired during this period by Los Angeles companies such as the Bison 101 studio run by Thomas Ince, some were able to translate public desire for authenticity in screen representations to ongoing careers. Luther Standing Bear, a Carlisle School graduate, found work in the film industry playing roles that required precisely the costumed "reversion" so feared by boarding school administrators such as Captain Richard Henry Pratt, founder of Carlisle. Yet in Standing Bear's account of his work for the Miller Brothers 101 Ranch in Oklahoma and with Ince in California, he also described his frustration over the limited potential for Native actors to shape their own representations in the movies: "As I look back to my early-day experiences in the making of pictures, I cannot help noting how we real Indians were held back, while white 'imitators' were pushed to the front. One of these was Anne Little, who afterward became a star" (284).[34]

One way in which Native actors were "held back" was in the lack of named credits. The identity of the actor playing the Chief in *The Invaders* is unknown because he is uncredited, yet this actor's dramatic technique is an important part of the film's appeal and is quite different from Inslee's performance in *The Red Man and the Child* and *The Call of the Wild*.[35] Rather than stripping his clothes in order to play Indian, he is fully clothed in a decorated shirt, leggings, and ceremonial warbonnet. And instead of invoking the tradition of minstrelsy and masquerade with exaggerated theatrical gesturing, as Inslee does, the actor's more naturalistic performance underscores his contribution to the film as an authenticating presence. Scott Simmon describes the Lakota performances in Thomas Ince films such as *The Invaders* and *War on the Plains* as "relatively restrained" compared to the "more hieroglyphic gestures" of the white actors, making the Lakotas' "gesturally smaller" performance seem both more modern and more authentic to contemporary viewers (64–65).[36] In fact, the films frequently conflated actor and part, both through the absence of named credits for Native actors and through the naming of film characters after the actors (this is particularly the case for James Young Deer and Lillian St. Cyr). James Naremore writes in his study of acting for the cinema that "people in films can be regarded in at least three different senses: as actors playing theatrical personages, as public figures playing theatrical versions of themselves, and as documentary evidence" (15). If Native actors were often in the latter situation, acting as evidence to validate the racial masquerade of the non-Native Hollywood stars, the Lakota actor playing the Chief in *The Invaders* seems also to be playing a theatrical version of himself, or

at least his community, reenacting a story about the treaty violations and
gold rush that led to the loss of the Black Hills of South Dakota, in a
film that asks viewers to reflect on the role of viewing and representing in
that same story. These and other tensions between Indigenous performers,
production systems (casting, crediting), and plot structures of early Indian
dramas become the key points of intervention for James Young Deer and
Lillian St. Cyr.

Reframing the Western Imaginary:
James Young Deer and Lillian St. Cyr

What were Native actors able to do within an entertainment industry dominated almost from its inception by the "squaw man" narrative scenario, by
conventions of costuming based on assimilationist projections and primitivist fantasies, and by the unequal casting practices of an emerging industrial
mode of film production? James Young Deer and Lillian St. Cyr entered
the film industry as actors and soon used their ability to claim authenticity
in performing Native roles to move into positions of power in an emergent
Hollywood and to exert control over both film scenarios and the politics
of representation. Their performances and narrative revisions of the "squaw
man" plot shifted the political significations of that foundational cinematic
story.

Young Deer and St. Cyr's films differ significantly from the patterns of
suicide, family breakup, and removal from the land in silent Indian dramas
and the "squaw man" plot. Their films manifest an emergent Native voice
embedded within the system of representation already becoming established
in the Western genre. Some of Young Deer's few surviving silent Indian
dramas include *White Fawn's Devotion* (1910), *For the Papoose* (1912), and
The Friendly Indian (*The Falling Arrow*) (1909).[37] Far more films survive that
feature Red Wing and Young Deer in performance, such as the 1911 Bison/
NYMPC film *Little Dove's Romance* (see figure 1.26), with Fred J. Balshofer
listed as director (in which Red Wing plays Little Dove, a Native woman
who falls in love with a white hunter, with a photograph exchanged as a
token between them).

An early example of Young Deer's strategic intervention is *The Friendly
Indian*, in which Young Deer plays a character (also named Young Deer) in
a story of interracial romance with a young Mexican woman named Felice
(who appears to be played by St. Cyr). During their courting, they exchange
tokens including photographs and necklaces. Young Deer, although rejected

Figure 1.26. *Little Dove's Romance*, Bison (1911) (LC), Lillian St. Cyr (left) and James Young Deer (center).

by Felice's family, rescues Felice from a white cowboy who has kidnapped her. She conveys her situation to him by writing a note on a piece of her petticoat and shooting it with a bow and arrow to Young Deer's camp. Here, costume literally "speaks" her predicament: "Young Deer, come, held by Jim the Outlaw." James Young Deer's early vision of Indigenous modernity becomes visible in the characters' use of written notes and photographs to communicate with one another. By exchanging photographs as part of their courtship, Young Deer and Felice become consumers of photographs rather than objects in photographs purveyed and circulated by others (see figure 1.27). Young Deer's primary contribution as a filmmaker, however, was to repoliticize the representations of Native Americans in mainstream cinematic melodramas, using the industry's turn to authenticity to shift the plots and resolutions of Western narratives and emphasize Native familial continuity and political solidarity. He does so by returning to the Indian drama's visual schema of familial rupture in order to revise the "squaw man" images of contestation and closure.

In *White Fawn's Devotion* a South Dakota settler, Combs (actor unknown), receiving news of "An unexpected legacy," is unable to convince his Native wife, White Fawn (actress unknown), to accompany him to

Figure 1.27. *The Friendly Indian*, Gaston Melies, Siegmund Lubin (1909) (LC), Lillian St. Cyr (unconfirmed) and James Young Deer.

England to claim his inheritance, but determines to take their child. White Fawn refuses to let their child go and literally pulls the child from Combs in front of their cabin (see figure 1.28) before the father sends the child away to fetch water. While Combs is inside, White Fawn stabs herself, staggering and falling as her husband emerges from the cabin and catches her. When their daughter returns, she is "deceived by appearances," an important intertitle given the way Western melodramas rely on visual appearances to signify heroism and villainy. Believing her father has murdered White Fawn, she runs to tell the tribe. After an extended chase, Combs is caught and about to be killed by his unwilling and traumatized daughter when White Fawn arrives, explaining that she had tried to take her own life but the knife did not pierce deeply enough. The couple embrace and gather the child between them.

The romance in *White Fawn's Devotion* resembles that in *The Squaw Man* except for the sudden happy ending, a rare fate for an interracial couple in any Western, literary or cinematic. We can see White Fawn's last-minute rescue of her husband as a repurposed "Pocahontas moment,"

Figure 1.28. *White Fawn's Devotion*, Pathé Frères Films (1910) (LC).

using the scene of a Native woman motivated by romantic love to save a white settler (disseminated most widely through fictionalized versions of Pocahontas and Captain John Smith) to direct audiences' attention to a different political vision—one of tribal allegiance. Here, a Native woman rescues her white lover so that he can renounce his fortune, not claim it. Though the concluding reel of the film is missing from existing archival copies, Pathé Frères playbills note that Combs renounces his fortune, feeling he will be "happier with his family on the plains than if he goes east and claims his legacy."[38] In a further difference from *The Squaw Man*, the daughter is loyal to White Fawn and runs to the tribe for help, rather than being surrounded by her father's relatives as is the son in *The Squaw Man* and *The Kentuckian*. This action suggests the child's understanding of the importance of tribal as well as immediate family ties. Combs and White Fawn endure parallel near-death experiences, and both emerge with renewed commitment to each other, their child, and their home on the plains of the Pine Ridge reservation. The ending is one of strengthened—rather than broken—interracial family bonds.

White Fawn's Devotion offers an iconography of mixed-race family survival as an alternative "family on the land" to the white settler model in most Westerns. As the film's director and probably its scenario writer as well, Young Deer was accustomed to the conventions of frontier melodramas and audience expectations from his earlier stage career in Wild West troupes and circuses. Despite Young Deer's immersion in the generic conventions for representing Native characters, several factors set this film apart from the other films discussed in this chapter. First, there is no redface as was common in many Indian dramas and later Westerns. In fact the subtitle, "A Play Acted by a Tribe of Red Indians in America," tenders a specific claim to authenticity by the French film company Pathé Frères, which had hired Young Deer and had begun filming in America to counter trade journal accusations of inauthenticity in costume, set, and behavior. The film is also unusual in that it privileges a female character's perspective on cross-racial marriage. White Fawn, the focal character, inaugurates the action, even when Combs is the object of angry pursuit by the men of her tribe, and the mixed-blood child at issue is a daughter, not a son. Rather than becoming personally enriched through abandonment of his wife and child, Combs ultimately resists the promise of wealth in order to keep his cross-racial family intact. And rather than shielding their daughter from the sight of her fallen mother, as happens in *The Squaw Man*, the child's misapprehension of her mother's failed suicide both brings tribal justice systems into play and delivers a generic critique to an audience already taught by the Western genre to expect Indian death.

For the Papoose, directed by Young Deer for Pathé in 1912 and starring St. Cyr, also narrates an alternative to the "squaw man" story that again begins with the scenario of the separation of a mother and child. In the opening scenes, an intertitle tells us that "Young Buffalo is a Squaw Man tired of his squaw." A white man, living in a Native village, kisses his young daughter tenderly, but when his Native wife (St. Cyr) enters and sees a bottle of liquor in his hand, she pulls the child away from him. For a moment, they struggle over the child (see figures 1.29 and 1.30) before the wife's brother intervenes and confronts the drunken husband while she holds the child. She lets her daughter hug the father good-bye, then holds her possessively. The child holds her uncle's hand, and then he carries her into a tipi. The estranged husband then sets out to create a second family for himself that includes his mixed-blood child, just as Kerhill does in *The Squaw Man*—except here his actions are overtly in the realm of the criminal. Forced to leave the tribe, he makes sexual advances toward a settler woman and is rejected. He provokes the tribe's attack (telling the Native leader that "settlers are taking up your land. Kill

Figure 1.29. *For the Papoose*, Pathé Frères Films (1912) (LC), Settler husband grabs his wife (St. Cyr).

Figure 1.30. *For the Papoose*, Pathé Frères Films (1912) (LC), Settler husband takes his child.

them but save the girl for some brave"). He then kidnaps both his own child and the captive settler woman (leaving a Native woman tied up in her place). The child's uncle reassures his sister—"be not afraid, my sister, I will avenge you and bring back your papoose." Although the print of the film has significant nitrate damage, we can discern the final image of the uncle returning from the chase wiping blood from his knife onto his hand, evidence of a violent retribution.

In this re-vision of the "squaw man" story, the child is taken from her Native mother but is then returned; her family and tribe surround and protect both mother and child. As with White Fawn's attempted suicide in *White Fawn's Devotion*, the initial imagined destruction of Indigeneity (through suicide and forced separation) is invoked early in the film, but these elements are reversed later on. In the scenes of family breakup, the child is a central figure in a custody dispute that is figured gesturally through the codes of melodramatic performance. Each parent lays hands on the child, centering her in the frame as they pull her back and forth between them.

The mixed-blood child is visually marked in these moments as a contested figure in both *White Fawn's Devotion* and *For the Papoose*. This scene of generational rupture—repeated in cinematic variations of the story by Young Deer, DeMille, and Griffith—signifies the suppressed event that goes unseen in the before-and-after photographs that narrate the institutional assimilation of boarding school students. As a moment of melodramatic excess in its pantomimed articulation of unjust social structures brought to bear on individuals, the scenes of struggle over Native children in Young Deer's films present an image of innocent suffering that functions to assert the moral value of intact Native and mixed-race families.

I have argued in this chapter that Indian dramas featuring mixed-race families and children invited viewers to imagine Native Americans as wards of the U.S. government, a strategy for figuratively dissolving the idea of tribal sovereignty through the absorption of Native children into settler families and institutions on-screen. Abstract concepts of race and nation become embodied in the cinematic image of the mixed-race child as a figure for the position of tribes within ongoing U.S. jurisprudence and legislative policy. In Young Deer's films, visualizing interracial contestation over Native familial continuity and national identity—in ways that the boarding school portrait sequences mask—also signals Indigenous resistance to dominant images and narratives of assimilation as progress, underscoring instead Indigenous counterclaims to both children and future civic identity. Settler attempts at substitution and racial masquerade, a staple of Indian dramas, are foiled in *White Fawn's Devotion* and *For the Papoose*; instead, stable identities and political affiliations prevail and tribal identity is safeguarded.

Furthermore, rather than visualizing the child's changing civic identity through changes in costume—a tactic common to both the boarding school before-and-after photographs and other Indian dramas discussed in this chapter—in Young Deer's films the characters' costumes don't change. Instead, the struggle for political and domestic custody over Native children is signaled by touching and specifically by the image of adult hands on the child. The vision of Native parents physically holding onto their children—

an image that is absent from contemporary periodicals—makes material and visceral the domestic scene of resistance to colonial assaults on Indigenous intergenerational relations. This image reinterprets Native assimilation as the work of systems and policies of colonization and rupture rather than the inevitable result of natural evolutionary progress or racial hierarchy. Like the image of a Native character behind the camera, the images of familial contestation over Native children represent a paradigm change in the Western imaginary, one that acknowledges structural systems of claiming to be centered on the image of the Native family on screen.

Unlike both Combs in *White Fawn's Devotion* and Jim Kerhill in *The Squaw Man*, the settler husband is an abusive figure in *For the Papoose*. His actions throughout the film—his alcoholism, rough handling of his wife, kidnapping of his child, attempted seduction of another woman, and deceptive provocation of the tribe—further undermine the legitimating conventions of the "squaw man" story. Rather than "innocently" gaining entitlements through sequentially restructured families (as orchestrated in DeMille versions of *The Squaw Man*), his avarice here clearly destabilizes interracial frontier relations, resulting in his ejection from both communities and eventually in his death.

Young Deer's politicized replottings of the "squaw man" story are complex cinematic strategies that cannot be fully explained in dialectical terms of Indigenous resistance to an established, dominant cultural narrative. Rather, they are mediations that depend for their emotional efficacy on the very language of melodramatic and sentimental performative modes that early cinema inherited from the stage. Yet Young Deer's scenarios also fundamentally reorient the melodramatic progression of transgression and punishment in the "squaw man" story. Instead of coding the originary cross-racial relationship as a transgressive, temporary arrangement that must be cast off to make way for a new frontier moral order based on the white settler family on the land, it is the white settler's very attempt to dissolve his Native family—specifically the separation of his child from mother and tribe—that constitutes his transgression and sets in motion a system consequences *for him*. Unlike *The Squaw Man*, in *White Fawn's Devotion* the allusion to suicide (through White Fawn's failed attempt) neither signals that white settlement and purity are virtues legitimated by Indian death, nor indicates helpless witnessing of the inevitable by innocent settlers. Rather, Young Deer's films index the magnitude of white settler's patterns of extraction and criminalize the frontier economy of "loving and leaving."

In contrast, DeMille's 1914 version of *The Squaw Man* naturalizes the separation of Native mother and child and the displacement of a mixed-race family with a settler family by omitting scenes of Indigenous resistance to familial separation, by suppressing dramatizations of trauma in the filmed sequence, and by narrating Nat-u-Ritch's (St. Cyr) suicide as a form of closure to Native familial and political existence. The film's representation of Native passivity is in tension with accounts of a more active response to the story on the part of the female lead during the production. Actor Dustin Farnum, who played Jim Kerhill in the film, described the way harrowing emotions surfaced while filming the scene of separation:

> When we were rehearsing the scene where the baby is taken from Nat-U-ritch [sic] to be sent back to England this pure-blooded Indian girl broke down and went into hysterics. It was pitiful. It was twenty-five minutes before we could proceed with the picture. In all my years on the stage I never saw anything like it. It was absolutely the reverse of what we have been taught about Indians.[39]

Farnum's story could simply be part of the marketing material for the film, but if his story is accurate, St. Cyr's reaction on the set suggests both her engagement in the story's melodramatic rendering of domestic rupture (and it is important to note here that St. Cyr herself had been educated at the Carlisle School) and her commitment as a performer. Yet the description of St. Cyr's off-screen emotion contrasts with her on-screen gestural silence, a performative mode that better fit with the film's fantasy of Native stoicism and self-sacrifice. DeMille's stylized vision of Indianness required actors to refrain from the new cinematic performance style—what Roberta Pearson has called the "verisimilar code"—that would prove so effective in Griffith's productions for Biograph with Lillian Gish (43). DeMille's literal muting of the potential for interracial identification in the expression of emotion at the scene of child loss is answered in Young Deer's version of the story in *White Fawn's Devotion*, when White Fawn recovers her power of speech at the film's climax.

Through the pathos of melodrama in *The Squaw Man*, viewers become emotionally engaged with (and attached to) a story of Native familial disruption, assimilation, and death. Young Deer's intervention, on the other hand, also takes place through the language of melodrama, but vindicates the child's bonds with birth family and tribe. While these bonds are threatened early on in his films, reprieve always comes "in the nick of time." In further contrast to the racial configuration of the "ride to the rescue" in D. W. Griffith films in which white heroes (such as the Ku Klux Klan "knights" in *The Birth of a Nation*) liberate white women and children from the racial threat of a contaminating blackness, in Young Deer's films it is the mother and child's tribal connection that is recognized, honored, naturalized, and legitimated through melodramatic coincidence and acts of rescue and retrieval.

Young Deer and St. Cyr's films mark a divergence in historical cinematic representations of Native Americans, representing a criticism of the genre from within the genre that is far sharper in its advocacy for Indigenous rights than the "pro-Indian" and "revisionist" Westerns of the second half of the twentieth century. Furthermore, the films look toward the emergence of major Native American literary figures such as Mourning Dove (Okanogan), John Joseph Mathews (Osage), and D'Arcy McNickle (Métis), whose 1920s and 1930s novels recount stories of cross-racial romance and of mixed-race children returning to their reservations after experiences in boarding schools and in settler society. And their films also anticipate later films by performers and directors who criticize the Western from outside its conventions (such as Larry Littlebird, Chris Eyre, and Victor Masayesva).

Young Deer and St. Cyr's films are important early landmarks in Native filmmaking in part because they model later Native appropriation of dominant film industry narratives. In reworking the "squaw man" narratives of Native disinheritance, these filmmakers tell stories that locate Native presence from within the very generic forms that try to erase them. They do this through specifically visual means, by intervening in visual tropes and by dramatizing the familial separations and reunions that are omitted or negated in other visual texts, both photographic and cinematic, then in circulation. The dramatization of familial separation in *White Fawn's Devotion* and *For the Papoose* accesses the foundational engine of emotional excess and moral valuation of maternal suffering in melodrama, carrying the films' political messages across racial boundaries using mainstream generic conventions. Narratives of familial separation can garner "empathy from the wider community," Jackie Huggins writes of the Australian Stolen Generations testimonies; "the fear of losing a child is a universal feeling, transcending social, political, cultural and racial barriers."[40] Yet Young Deer and St. Cyr's films also render experiences of colonial rupture in ways that are specific to Native American political responses to federal policies of assimilation; they do this through images of Native women characters' ultimately successful opposition to attempts to remove their children, and through strategic representations of cross-racial romance. Furthermore, instead of constructing interracial relationships that precede and enable the white settler "family on the land," their films envision Native and interracial family coherence;

instead of crafting narrative closure through images of Indian death, their films end with images of interracial and intergenerational continuity.

The brief period in which Young Deer and St. Cyr rewrote dominant scenarios of Indian vanishing ended with Young Deer's departure from Los Angeles in 1913, although St. Cyr continued her acting career, including performing in Tom Mix Westerns (such as *In the Days of the Thundering Herd,* 1914), until the early 1920s. The post–World War I period saw productions energized instead by a national agenda to reform Indian policy. This second cycle of Indian dramas culminated in the late 1920s with two Paramount epics starring Richard Dix, *The Vanishing American* (Seitz 1925) and *Redskin* (Schertzinger 1929), as well as the Chickasaw director Edwin Carewe's successful production of *Ramona* in 1928. These 1920s "reform dramas," depicting corruption on reservations, more openly narrate and visualize governmental intervention in Native families, including figures such as Indian agents and white schoolteachers and scenes of formal schooling and military training. In these films, melodrama remains an important framework for images of contestation over the custody and education of Native children. The conflicted discourses of assimilation, Americanization, and patriotism that accompany the films' visual and emotional articulations of national identity return us to the idea of filming Native families as a form of claiming their national allegiance while projecting their assimilation into the national future.

2

"Strictly American Cinemas"

Social Protest in *The Vanishing American,* *Redskin,* and *Ramona*

In the late 1920s, Hollywood studios returned to the "Indian drama" form with a cycle of sympathetic Westerns that directly addressed contemporary social movements to reform federal Indian policy. The policies under pressure governed a range of Native American relationships to the United States, including citizenship, land ownership, and education. Melodramatic narratives of Native custodial transition represented conditions of government Indian boarding schools and Allotment-era land policies, and their cinematic tropes, forms, and scenarios emphasized visible signs of Indianness and assimilation: the "lost home" of melodrama, Native youth "torn" between tradition and assimilation, and the violent vigilante attacks of the Western. Tracing these aesthetic strategies of racial representation reveals the deeply articulated relationship between dominant cinema genres, social change, and what might retrospectively be understood as an emergent Native cinema and directorial presence within the studio system at the height of the silent era and at the edge of the transition to sound.

The previous chapter explored Ho-Chunk filmmakers James Young Deer and Lillian St. Cyr's reshaping of early cinematic narrative structures, particularly the formative "squaw man" story that appeared in so many iterations before World War I. In this chapter, we see the ways that films from the smaller, more diffuse 1920s production cycle aligned the cinematic forms and codes of the established late-silent-era studio industry with the social context of shifting U.S. Indian policy. Among the most prominent of these films were two Paramount productions starring Richard Dix: George Seitz's *The Vanishing American* (1925) and Victor Schertzinger's *Redskin* (1929), as well as an Inspiration Pictures production—Chickasaw director Edwin Carewe's 1928 film version of *Ramona*, based on Helen Hunt Jackson's 1884 novel. I take these films as primary examples of the work of Indian melodramas in the 1920s because of their popularity and visibility, but I also survey a range of other films produced between the Indian Citizenship Act of 1924 and the Indian Reorganization Act of 1934. Reading these films together suggests the coherence of this cycle at the height of public pressure for legislative reform. Closely parsing the production of visible Indianness at this historical moment reveals the ways that spectacles of institutional violence (in schools and courtrooms) and frontier violence (massacres and vigilantism) visualized dispossession in terms of personal and domestic trauma, making the relationship of racialized individuals to the broader field of national policy a central component of the films' public intervention.

1920s Western genre epics of settlement located their authenticity and educational value in their representations of the historical past, but the feature-length films that most resemble early silent Indian dramas—films about "Indian subjects" that combined the generic traditions of the social problem film, the domestic melodrama, and the Western within Hollywood's developed system of industrial film production—claimed a different sort of authenticity by representing a more contemporary West within the recent memory of adult spectators. These sympathetic silent Westerns—which really constitute a continuation of the Indian drama—could also be called "reform dramas." They fed public interest in reform by accessing audiences' emotional responses to images of threatened and displaced Native families with melodramatic modes of storytelling. In their scenes of struggle over the custody, enculturation, and marriages of Native youth, these films make visceral the abstract legal position of Native peoples as wards of the U.S. government. Stories about Native youth's institutional education, assimilation, and "reversion" invited national and international audiences to sympathize with Indigenous experiences of colonial rupture while simultaneously registering that interracial sympathy within frameworks of U.S. paternalism. The 1920s Indian dramas built on a range of extracinematic texts and public discourses including government documents, popular periodicals, and especially the before-and-after images of Native children at boarding school circulated by the Carlisle Indian Industrial School and other schools. *The Vanishing American* and *Redskin* in particular illustrate cinematically the static sequencing of the boarding school before-and-after photographs.

Yet many Hollywood dramas also disrupt the linear progression from savage to civilized advertised by the before-and-after images, offering instead images of hybridity—interracial romance and bicultural youth—inflected with melodramatic pathos.

My analyses in this chapter focus on the aesthetic organization of the films to show how filmmakers, using established representational strategies, attempted both to profit from and intervene in shifting views of Indigenous citizenship in the national imaginary. The visual thread that connects these films is the construction and deconstruction of Native domestic space and institutional homes. The cinematic "scene" of home and school as formative sites of Native identity and Americanization focuses viewers' emotions on abstract and systematic processes of land dispossession and institutionalization, but the spectacle of loss speaks in the language of Hollywood melodramatic excess. A surprising number of films appropriated this particular generic framework—with all its particular limitations and strengths—at this moment, within the confines of industrial manufacture, both inside and outside of the major studios.

Paramount, with its two prestige films starring Richard Dix, is arguably the studio most involved in the production of sympathetic Westerns in the 1920s. *The Vanishing American* (adapted from Zane Grey's novel) adopts discourses from early anthropology and condemns fraudulent appropriations of reservation resources by corrupt government agents, whereas *Redskin* explores educational assimilation through the government-run boarding school system. The nonfiction, reformist, and melodramatic impulses of the films come together in scenes of youth's separation from their families and tribes and their return to these communities as outsiders. Countering the films' strategies of redfacing and ideologies of vanishing are their investments in realism as a representational strategy, including location shooting on remote reservation lands (Monument Valley) and attention to traditional practices such as sandpainting and weaving. The 1928 version of *Ramona* is also organized around a Native character's crisis of identity, depicting a family brought together by a process of adoption but torn apart by murder and trauma in the wake of U.S. appropriation of Native lands. As a financially successful Indian drama, scripted and directed by Chickasaw brothers (Carewe's close collaborator was his brother, script writer Finis Fox) and as an important, early-career vehicle for Mexican actress Dolores Del Rio, *Ramona* is a crucial text in American and Native American film history. The surviving print of the film was repatriated to the Library of Congress from the Czech Republic in 2012, and its restoration and availability for scholarly study calls for a renewed consideration of Edwin Carewe's career and influence in Hollywood. Film archivists and Native artists have also worked to recover and restore the print of *Redskin*, and in the conclusion to this chapter I discuss the new live score for the film composed and performed in 2002 by members of the band National Braid.

These films matter because they are part of the way that Native peoples were seen in the 1920s—they were prominent elements of the larger public discourse. In the sections that follow, I describe contextual discourses of melodrama and political reform, outline a range of films produced in the 1920s, and offer close analyses of *The Vanishing American*, *Redskin*, and *Ramona*. These three feature films were marketed to maximize their relationship to public calls for reform, and a comparative reading of films from established studios like Paramount and from independent and intercultural production teams such as Edwin Carewe's Inspiration Pictures, Inc., show the diverse political positioning around seemingly static generic visual tropes. Both non-Native and Native actors and directors worked within the parameters of the studio system's genres, stars, hierarchical structures of production and marketing, and corporate profits. The sometimes-hidden, sometimes-visible identities of directors such as James Cruze, who claimed Ute ancestry, and Edwin Carewe (born Jay Fox), who occasionally spoke publicly about his Chickasaw heritage, complicate readings of the on-screen dramas of masked and revealed Indian identity in the films themselves. Directors' dual claims to authenticity based on Native heritage and to career success within a studio system that regularly relied on redface performers illustrate the uncertain position of Indigeneity as both an identity and a commodity in 1920s Hollywood. Combined with the intertextual work of periodicals and film publicity materials at this time, the films articulated through both realism and pathos the reformist sentiment and public anxiety about Indigenous citizenship and assimilation.

Melodrama and Realism in Sympathetic Westerns

Sympathetic Westerns seem to contradict the dominant political and representational currents of the Western genre while remaining a product of industrial Hollywood's racial semiotics and scenarios of imperial benevolence. The films stake claims to and simultaneously skirt the political issues of racial classification, assimilationist education, and land and treaty rights. The lens of melodrama so conducive to the generation of affect in audiences—and to the films' potential for political influence—almost always renders Native and mixed-blood characters as suspended between two cultures. Like the heroines of maternal melodramas, they are beset by impossible dilemmas and false choices. Lori Muntz asserts that melodramatic representations of Native characters promote "the commodification of Native people's lives," emphasize victimhood over agency, and substitute emotional sympathy for altered behavior or social action (14). Yet, "the melodrama of Native citizenship" can also "provide a ground from which to meditate, to strategize, and to imagine the relationships that are possible with the United States" as well as "to experiment with strategic adaptation as a way to gain political power" (17, 23). Melodrama's promise of moral legibility requires a separation between Native and settler, between traditionalism and modernity, and between Native religion and the tribe as a political entity. Cinematic Native characters must always contend with modernity and traditionalism as binary categories—and they must reject one in order to take on the other. But these boundaries are also destabilized by narratives of assimilation in films depicting the circulation of individuals to and from the reservations and in films that subsume Native characters into settler homes or institutional spaces. The home as a site of cultural and political education is perpetually contested, collapsed, and rebuilt in these dramas in which the violence of wars over land rights erupts on a smaller scale over the bodies, costumes, and futures of Native youth. The "moral legibility" promised by melodrama can become a less-than-legible site of redrawn, rapidly changing political boundaries and confused racial schema.

The disruption of families was a structural element of Indian policy during the boarding school era as well as a common convention of most melodramas. The revelation of identity and reconstitution of the "lost" home in melodrama represents an educational moment for the cinematic characters and appears to map a solution to social contradictions for audiences. The virtue of the protagonist and the injustice of her suffering become clear. In Indian dramas, the interruption of the family is linked narratively with the project of education, racial uplift, and "civilizing" interventions. These moral paradigm changes are manifested in the characters' cloaking and revelation of identity through costume and narrative disclosure, paralleling the process of moral revelation for viewers learning about contemporary Indian policy issues through their consumption of the film.

In the context of public sentiment and political reform, the spaces of interracial violence and interracial sympathy established in Indian dramas of the 1920s revise two related systems of knowledge production: images of assimilation and colonial rupture (including scenes in classrooms and scenes of vigilante violence) and, in a closely related metanarrative, the cinema itself as a site of public education. These systems establish scenes of instruction and spectacles of extralegal violence as spaces of both intercultural sympathy and disjunction. The films seem to call for government reform based on the revelation of frontier and institutional violence and to condemn the separation of Native families. Yet because Native domesticity and familial networks—particularly mothers—are significantly absent as an alternative to foster homes or boarding schools in the films' images, the films imply that reformed U.S. government remains a necessary colonizing entity.

The reformist impulses in Indian dramas in the 1920s can be located in the intersection of realism and melodrama. Silent Westerns, because of their deliberate attempt to increase realism, authenticity, and educational relevance, make truth claims in the politicized context of policy reform. In fact, the claim to offer "the real thing" for the first time is one of the most common clichés of the Western genre—from Buffalo Bill's Wild West show through the "pro-Indian" and revisionist Westerns of the second half of the twentieth century. In the 1920s reform dramas, the realism of location shooting, Native extras, and costuming attempt to authenticate the moments of pathos in spectacles of familial rupture—narrativized moments with the potential to move the spectators to action. As Christine Gledhill notes, realism is not opposed to melodrama but instead supports it: "what realism uncovers becomes new material for the melodramatic project" (31).[1] In Linda Williams's assessment, novels and films in the American melodramatic mode offered white audiences a space in which to sympathize with the plight of racialized characters through images of their suffering—the flight of a mulatta slave from a cruel slaveowner or the beating of the loyal and humble slave in *Uncle Tom's Cabin*, for example. In the "mutually influential" stylistic forms of realism and melodrama (*Playing* 38), realism's shifting center of gravity constantly locates new sources of authenticity in stylistic innovation, casting, setting, narrative voice, and so forth. These become sources of renewal for the melodramatic mode in which sympathy, moral relevance, and the emotional efficacy of spectacle depend on depicting a world recognizable to audiences. In the decidedly fictional world of silent Western Indian dramas, the apparent veracity of images of inequality, struggle, and suffering ally audiences with reform and often very specifically with white female reformers.

Cinematic representations of the removal of children from Native homes and their return from school as outsiders are moments that are fraught with emotional and ideological tensions between the filmmakers' perceptions of Native peoples as emblematic of the past and as contemporary or copresent with viewers. Johannes Fabian's assertion that anthropological discourse provides "temporal distance" between colonizers and colonized through a "denial of coevalness" or shared time holds equally for the discourses of both ethnographic films and Westerns (30–31). In sympathetic Westerns, these issues of history and modernity are brought to bear on representations of Native children in cultural and custodial transition. These transitions are often signaled by changes of costume, a strategy that draws on the visual work of cocirculating documents such as the before-and-after photographs distributed by the Carlisle School. What is veiled in the before-and-after images are the cultural duality and hybridity of Native children at boarding school, their and their parents' aspirations and strategies for resistance, and the emotional and physical challenges of their adjustments and accommodations to the institutional version of American culture in the schools.

Films in the 1920s attempted to encompass contradictory public discourses about Native people, particularly surrounding Indigenous modernity, citizenship, cultural change, and governmental claims to custodial entitlement over Native lands and individuals. Many written accounts, autobiographical and fictionalized, of the early days of boarding school by Native authors such as D'Arcy McNickle (Salish Kootenai/Métis), Charles Eastman (Dakota), Zitkala-Sa (Gertrude Bonnin, Dakota), Luther Standing Bear (Lakota), and Francis LaFlesche (Omaha) acted as a form of individual testimony inflected by situated, particular circumstances and a continuum of choice and coercion. Unlike these autobiographical narratives, cinematic representations, under pressure to recoup production expenses for profit-oriented Hollywood studios, rendered Indigenous experiences as generalized scenarios or formulae recognizable to the widest possible audience.[2] The diversity of actual stories of Indigenous school experiences is portrayed as a singular melodramatic scenario of victimhood and moral imperative with a concomitant call for intervention from the outside.

The Meriam Report and Educational Reform

The Vanishing American, *Redskin*, and *Ramona*, along with other films from the mid-1920s through the early 1930s that narrated the upbringing and education of Native youth—including *Red Love* (Lewis 1925), *Braveheart* (Hale 1925), *The Test of Donald Norton* (Eason 1926), and *Massacre* (Crosland 1934), among others—influenced and were influenced by growing public support in the 1920s for massive changes in federal Indian policy and a media campaign to eliminate the worst abuses of the boarding school system. Those political changes came through a range of official reports and legislation, including the Indian Citizenship Act of 1924, the 1928 report

The Problem of Indian Administration (called the Meriam Report after the committee's chairman, Lewis Meriam), and the Indian Reorganization Act of 1934. The context of these far-reaching policies powerfully informed the production, marketing, content, and reception of 1920s Indian dramas.

D'Arcy McNickle has characterized the 1920s as "a time of reassessment" in Indian policy and a profound public questioning of the U.S. government's record of stewardship over Native tribes and lands. The legal personhood of Indigenous peoples was key to the debate. The U.S. Court of Claims at the turn of the twentieth century summarized the legal limbo of U.S. custody over Native people as a situation without precedent, "unknown to the common law or the civil law or to any system of municipal law. [Native Americans] were neither citizens nor aliens; they were neither persons nor slaves; they were wards of the nation, and yet . . . were little else than prisoners of war while war did not exist."[3] In 1924 the Indian Citizenship Act granted U.S. citizenship to all Native American peoples in a unilateral legislative attempt to assimilate them into the American mainstream. The controversial act, sought by many Native intellectuals as well as non-Native advocates, achieved individual legal rights related to U.S. citizenship (without necessarily guaranteeing civil rights) while further obfuscating legal articulations of tribal sovereignty.[4] Between this act and the major shift away from assimilation and allotment in the Indian Reorganization Act of 1934, the public pressure to reform Indian policy—particularly the allotment and educational systems—became increasingly intense during the 1920s.[5]

In dialogue with a range of extracinematic texts, particularly the media barrage from reformers and their organizations in popular periodicals such as *Good Housekeeping*, *The Nation*, and *Sunset*, Hollywood studios and independent filmmaking companies produced prominent sympathetic Westerns and reform melodramas with themes of dislocation and displacement. The films drew (and then reproduced) social and moral power from public discourses in print; from the visual representations of Native characters removed from their families, homes, and homelands; and from the dynamic combination of stylistic realism and emotional registers characteristic of what Williams calls "the melodramatic thematics of race" (*Playing* 297).

Between the turn of the century and 1934, the failure of assimilationist U.S. Indian policies—particularly land allotment and boarding school systems—were presented to the public in part through a reform movement driven by a range organizations, including (among many others both regional and national) the Indian Rights Association (IRA, founded 1882); the Women's National Indian Association (WNIA, later the National Indian Association, founded 1879); the Eastern Association on American Indian

Affairs (founded 1922); the American Indian Defense Association (AIDA, founded 1923); and the Division of Indian Welfare of the General Federation of Women's Clubs (GFWC, founded 1890). These reformers advocated assimilation and American social tolerance, had access to the press (especially liberal and reform-oriented magazines such as *Collier's*), and throughout the 1920s relentlessly exposed corruption and mismanagement in the Bureau of Indian Affairs (BIA) and on the part of state and local officials. The Society of American Indians (SAI, founded 1911) was one of the few organizations composed of Native American professionals rather than non-Native "friends of the Indians," marking a critical rise in the influence of Native intellectuals in public advocacy.[6]

Public discourse about educational reform in 1920s political rhetoric of racial uplift and the civilizing process had at its core the issues of assimilation, Native cultural futures, and the terms of governmental stewardship. These issues also drove legislation aimed at subsuming Indigenous peoples within the domestic purview of the United States, particularly the Indian Citizenship Act of 1924. If the catalyst for the reform movement was the legislative fight over the Bursum Bill—the 1922 proposal, defeated in Congress, to give non-Native squatters title to Pueblo lands—one of its key testimonials came in 1928 and was one of the most important reform documents in the history of U.S. Indian policy. Prepared by the Brookings Institute, *The Problem of Indian Administration* (Meriam Report) contributed to a sea change in federal Indian policy that was actualized in the Indian Reorganization Act of 1934, the culminating legislation of the reform effort, which attempted to reverse and repair the assimilationist policies of the previous decades. Significantly, the report suggested that education should be the primary task of the BIA, and it attacked the boarding school system, advocating reservation day schools for preadolescent children. According to the report:

> The most fundamental need in Indian education is a change in point of view. Whatever may have been the official government attitude, education for the Indian in the past has proceeded largely on the theory that it is necessary to remove the Indian child as far as possible from his home environment; whereas the modern view in education and social work lays stress on upbringing in the natural setting of home and family life. (346)

Despite its even tone, the report's authors produced a direct and strongly negative assessment of the boarding school system. The report began its discussion of U.S. Indian education by saying that "the survey staff finds itself obliged to say frankly and unequivocally that the provisions for the care of the Indian children in boarding schools are grossly inadequate" (11) based on deficient diet, overcrowding, and epidemics of diseases such as trachoma.[7] The report further condemned the constant routinization, external command, and "military formation" that characterized boarding school life for children of all ages and both sexes (382). Significantly, Hollywood representations of government boarding schools omit most of the penury, material deprivation, and epidemics documented in the Meriam Report, focusing instead on the visual manifestation of cultural change in the institutionalization of military discipline in the schools.

Early nonfiction films depicted boarding schools throughout the silent era. *Club Swinging at Carlisle Indian School* (Marvin 1902), *Viewing Sherman Institute for Indians at Riverside, California* (Sennett, 1915), and, later, *The American Indian: Government Education* (1933) include panoramas of school buildings and drills, and depict Native youth on sports teams, in classes, and in their school uniforms (see figure 2.1). However, these films don't show scenes of travel to or from school, nor do they depict Native students with their families, omitting images that might complicate the representation of total assimilation. Such scenes of transition emerge instead in 1920s Western frontier melodramas in which Native or mixed-blood children are

Figure 2.1. *The American Indian: Government Education*, Harmon Foundation (1933) (LC).

removed from their families by outsiders to be adopted or educated at boarding school. The dislodging of Native characters from their homes and relocation to idealized white domestic spaces in 1920s films corresponds in the actual school system to the "outing" programs, in which children were sent to white homes rather than Native homes for their summer vacations in order to continue their education in (and service to) settler domesticity and wage labor.

The boarding schools, rather than moving children in an orderly way from what were imagined to be "uncivilized" to "civilized" states, as its proponents implied with the circulation of before-and-after images, often had the opposite effect of destabilizing claims of civilization's benefits. The children's very inability to innately recognize the legitimacy of the civilization on offer in educational institutions further revealed its arbitrariness. Thus the boarding school model of compulsory schooling in the 1920s, especially as its abuses were widely exposed in periodicals, called into question the rhetoric of education as the common property of all Americans and suggested instead its relation to the reproduction of a colonial social structure.[8] In cinematic representations of institutional Native education, seemingly legitimate social relations maintained through symbolic violence are revealed to be relations of power based in physical violence, most pointedly in scenes of coerced removal of children from their Native families. Such scenes represent rare moments of ideological slippage in the Western genre, which was more commonly dedicated to upholding the legitimacy of U.S. expansion and which functioned in the 1920s as instruction as well as entertainment for youth.

We can see the Western genre's nationalizing and normalizing function (the reproduction of America in screen form) as an impulse related to the production of American citizens in the boarding schools.[9] In representations of boarding schools on screen, institutional, military standardization perpetuates not integration (or "normality") but trauma, and Native youth are marked, feared, desired, and rejected precisely because they are outside the American mainstream. The vision of normalizing education in sympathetic Westerns is not a middle-class utopian wish, as it is in child-rearing handbooks from this period, but rather a revelation of physical hardship, social rupture, and cultural loss. Thus, sympathetic Westerns in the 1920s not only functioned as a site of education for viewers, but also represented scenes of education as instances of negative institutional intervention. At a moment when the idea of a generic, middle-class childhood was being produced socially, scientifically, and cinematically, sympathetic Westerns engaged a reformist counterdiscourse based on an anthropological and preservationist conception of endangered cultural difference. Yet the films' scenes of assimilationist education as sites of pathos and loss in fact supported their function as vehicles for the ideological, normalizing education of children in the audience; the discourse of vanishing Indians, in its presumption of demographic decline and stylistic emphasis on narrative closure, precluded acknowledgement of continuing Indigenous political identities and rights.

Post-World War I Hollywood Indian Dramas

In the decade between two major legislative landmarks in Indian policy, the Indian Citizenship Act of 1924 and the Indian Reorganization Act of 1934, Indian dramas produced by Hollywood and small independent studios repeatedly returned to the problem of defining Native nations' relations to the U.S. through narratives of interracial romance, assimilation and "reversion," and classroom and courtroom scenes. In order to understand Paramount's reinvestment in the Indian drama form in the mid- and late 1920s, it is useful to survey briefly some of the films from the interregnum period in Indian policy. The fluidity and wide appeal of cross-racial performances before the coming of sound made sympathetic Western films especially appealing for performers or producers attempting to carve out a niche in the industry for their new production companies, as was the case for most of the films discussed here (the exception being Warner Brothers' *Massacre*). In contrast, Paramount clearly had epic ambitions for *The Vanishing American* and *Redskin,* both in the films' representations of education as an Americanizing force and in the educational reach of the films themselves.

After World War I, Hollywood producers largely moved away from the "squaw man" film cycle, with a few notable exceptions (Cecil B. DeMille, for example, would adapt the story again for the screen in 1918 and 1931). The low point in Western production came in 1923 with only 50 films in the genre released, but in that year James Cruze's *The Covered Wagon* achieved runaway success with its sweeping narration of white settlement of the continent in an epic mode (Lusted 130). The film was immediately parodied by Will Rogers (Cherokee) in the short film *Two Wagons, Both Covered,* and other studios and directors rushed to capitalize on Paramount's success with productions such as John Ford's first epic Western, *The Iron Horse,* for the Fox Film Corporation (1924). Despite a declaration in *Motion Picture World* in 1913 that Indian dramas were "played out,"[10] studios also continued to make feature-length films about Native characters, often involving location shooting, major stars, and large budgets—though generally without involving Native participants as scenario writers and directors. The sympathetic Westerns released between 1919 and 1934 never approached the consistent, coherent, intense production level of the pre–World War I cycle of Indian dramas; they became increasingly unusual products and were marketed as such. The field of production ranged widely across the industry from large-scale prestige films by major studios (Paramount, Warner Brothers) to independent productions financed by independent entrepreneurs.

Among the earliest Indian dramas of the 1920s is *The Daughter of Dawn* (1920), directed by Norbert Myles from a script by Richard E. Banks for the independent Texas Film Company. Shot in the Wichita Mountains Wildlife Refuge near Lawton, Oklahoma, the film features an all Native cast of nonprofessional actors for both leading and minor roles, including prominent community members such as White Parker and Wanada Parker (children of the renowned Comanche leader Quanah Parker) and the widely respected Kiowa elder Hunting Horse, who had been a U.S. Army scout. The film depicts a love quadrangle, with White (White Parker, Comanche) and Wolf (Jack Sankey-doty, Comanche) vying for marriage to the Chief's daughter, Dawn (Esther LeBarre, Comanche). In addition, Wanada (Wanada Parker, Comanche) is in love with Wolf, and commits suicide when he dies at the film's end. The film's action includes a buffalo hunt; intertribal raiding between Kiowa and Comanche; the capture and rescue of Dawn; and a ritual contest between White and Wolf involving a potentially suicidal leap from a cliff.

Historian Leo Kelley asserts that the film was "produced by whites for white audiences" (299), and Russ Tall Chief (Osage) agrees: "Tinseltown audiences watch an all Native American cast from Oklahoma perform Hollywood's interpretation of an Indian 'love triangle.'" The film's rediscovery, however, has given it greater resonance. The recovering of a surviving print in 2007 and the subsequent restoration effort led to informal community screenings for Kiowa and Comanche tribal members. Descendants of the cast traced connections to their relatives, and, according to Tall Chief, tribal elders "identified a Cheyenne tipi prominently featured in the film that Sleeping Bear had given to the Kiowa during the 1840s" and which the Kiowa artist Silverhorn had ceremonially restored and repainted with pictorial historical records in 1916. One elderly viewer, Sammy Tone kei White, recognized his mother Em koy e tie: "My mother was walking right at me, she was so beautiful. I'm glad the room we were watching it in was dark, because it was emotional seeing her so young" (McQueeney). Thus the film represents an important site of intergenerational Native recognition as it circulates back to its community of origin (a process I discuss at greater length in chapters 3 and 5). Its Native cast and material culture do not simply authenticate a Hollywood story; rather, the feature film takes on elements of a home movie, and Sleeping Bear's tipi, with its renewed pictographic text, is embedded in the Indian melodrama like a code waiting to be read. Through performance, setting, and elements of the mise en scène, the film—produced by non-Natives and performed by sophisticated tribal community leaders—renews the visual record of generational continuity and aesthetic representations of Kiowa history.[11] Unlike *The Daughter of Dawn*, however, few 1920s Indian dramas have all Native casts; they more often feature interracial love stories, and most remain available only in archives.

Between 1919 and 1925 several independent artists and production companies tapped the Indian drama scenario of mixed-race romance in productions designed as star vehicles. These films—almost all financial failures—have been largely overlooked in studies of the Western, but their attempt to integrate older narrative models into a new political landscape is important to consider here particularly in their emphasis on the legal and educational discourses and physical spaces that defined Indigeneity, an emphasis shared by *The Vanishing American, Redskin,* and *Ramona.* Surveying some of these independent productions—*Just Squaw* (1919), *The Heart of Wetona* (1919), *Red Love* (1925), *Braveheart* (1925), and *The Test of Donald Norton* (1926)—reveals how these industry-based revisions to the genre also began to foreground the films' textual narratives of institutionalized assimilation and citizenship in ways that magnified the political implications of interracial romance and family formation.

Examining these productions also suggests the popular appeal of changeable racial identities in both filmed narratives and star performances. Cinematic racial masquerade was at its height during the silent era, and actors and other industry artists deployed the Indian melodrama formula and its tradition of ethnic mutability as a vehicle for establishing both novel performative identities and new production companies. This versatility, particular to silent film, also made it possible for Latina stars like Beatriz Michelena and Dolores Del Rio to play a range of ethnic characters, including both Native and white Euro-American roles. The adoption of film sound after 1927 made playing a wide range of ethnic roles more difficult for stars because their speaking voices contributed to a stable rather than malleable performative identity, limiting Dolores Del Rio, for example, to roles that justified (and significantly exaggerated) her accented English.[12] White actresses like Norma Talmadge also had greater success in performing varied ethnicities during the silent era than after the introduction of sound. Talmadge, an actress who successfully worked independently of the studio system in the 1920s, specialized in roles as racially exotic and sexu-

Figure 2.2. *The Heart of Wetona*, Norma Talmadge Film Corp. (1919) (LC), Wetona (Norma Talmadge), returned from boarding school, is separated from her father Chief Quannah (Fred Huntley) by her love interest, John Hardin (Thomas Meighan).

ally available women, including a Native woman in *The Heart of Wetona* (see figures 2.2 and 2.3).[13]

These actresses' ethnic versatility facilitated narratives of sequential or substitute Native and white families, domestic images that encode national

Figure 2.3. *The Heart of Wetona*, Norma Talmadge Film Corp. (1919), Norma Talmadge as Wetona, promotional still (AMPAS).

narratives of race and that look back to the prewar "squaw man" plots. Like *Her Indian Mother* [*The White Man Takes a Red Wife*], discussed in chapter 1, two post–World War I films—*Just Squaw* (Middleton 1919) and *The Test of Donald Norton* (Eason 1926)—depict the dilemma of a white child whose adoptive Native "mother" has been abandoned by her settler husband.[14] Beatriz Michelena's character in *Just Squaw*, White Fawn, was a white woman adopted as a baby by a Native tribe. When children in silent Westerns are not mixed-blood but are associated with mixed-race couples in some way, their conditions of confused identity are similar to the narrative dilemmas of mixed-race children. In both these films, a Native woman, rejected by her white lover, has kidnapped his child by his white wife and raised it as her own "mixed-blood" child out of a desire for revenge against the father. These narratives of consecutive adoption end in the discovery that the "mixed-blood" child is really white and can marry his or her white lover.

To make matters of identity in these films even more complicated, both protagonists have been counteradopted: White Fawn's adoptive Native mother died when she was a child, leaving her to be raised by the local parson, and Donald Norton (George Walsh) was taken from his adoptive, abusive Native mother and raised by a Hudson Bay Company trader. In both films, the white children have been raised with whites, have "false" Native heritage suggested by a previous adoption, and long to be white so that they can marry their white lovers (White Fawn is explicit, saying, "Oh, if I were only White," to her half-brother). Finally, both protagonists enact the assimilationist policy of the early twentieth century to the point of literally vanishing as Native characters when they learn of their "pure white blood" at the end of the film, transforming their mixed-blood identities into the promise of an American future of white domesticity. What had begun as a mixed-race relationship involving a settler man and Native woman ends with a white child who can safely be absorbed into the American mainstream. Ironically, Latina star Beatriz Michelena's performance as a white woman mistaken for a mixed-blood woman visualizes whiteness as an innate, unchangeable characteristic by means of a palimpsest of visible and invisible, on-screen and off-screen ethnic presentations. The film seems to assert that racial identity, temporarily disguised by ethnic costume, will ultimately be revealed, thereby righting moral wrongs through increased racial transparency. But the film simultaneously upholds, in both production and on-screen drama, the project of Americanization in early cinema as it was premised on the contradictory practices of theatrical masquerade, racial passing, and "playing Indian."

In contrast to the focus on disentangling interrelated domesticities in the narrative scenarios of *Just Squaw* and *The Test of Donald Norton*, films that hinge on individual cases of mistaken racial identity but don't overtly engage broader social issues, two films from 1925 (the year after the passage of the Indian Citizenship Act of 1924) politicize the depiction of Indigenous nations through Native characters' legal disputes. These films—*Braveheart* and *Red Love*—also illustrate the way filmmakers' attempts to convey realism and authenticity continued to undergird Indian dramas and the way industrial structures catalyzed by the production of *The Squaw Man* in 1914 extended the influence of sympathetic representations into the 1920s. Both films integrate the tradition of sentiment in Indian dramas with elements of realism that resulted from (and resulted in) Indigenous participation—the incorporation of Native performers and consultants in their production.

Braveheart, directed by Alan Hale, was produced by the Cinema Corporation of America, the company formed by Cecil B. DeMille after he left Paramount in 1925 and bought the old Ince studios (the company later merged with the Keith vaudeville chain and then Pathé, and DeMille himself moved briefly to MGM in 1928). DeMille also returned to pre–World War I Indian drama material for the film, having his older brother William C. DeMille's 1905 script "Strongheart," a four-act play and 1914 film, adapted for the screen with the collaboration of Mary O'Hara and Nipo T. Strongheart (Yakama). The story was taken in part from the life story of Strongheart, a Carlisle School graduate, Los Angeles–based actor and technical advisor with a background in Wild West shows, and a powerful speaker and advocate for Native rights on the public lecture circuit (after his lectures, Strongheart often collected signatures on petitions, which he sent to the SAI, directly linking his public performance work with Native political organizations). Throughout his career in Hollywood, he worked as a translator, language coach, and casting agent for Westerns when directors sought to include realistic elements in their films (such as Indigenous languages in the dialogue). In some cases he was able to use this position to agitate for changes, even suggesting the addition of specific characters.[15] He was a consultant for *Braveheart* and played the role of the medicine man, working to shape the film through production and performance.

The film politicizes Indian drama narratives of assimilation by depicting Braveheart's college education as a purposeful choice: he was sent away by his community to study law so that he could pursue tribal claims in U.S. courts against a trespassing canning company.[16] By emphasizing Native American legal rights to fish harvests and by having Braveheart (Rod

La Rocque) give up his white sweetheart (the daughter of the cannery owner, played by Lillian Rich) to take up a tribal leadership position at home, the film highlights the ongoing relevance of treaties for Native communities' economic livelihoods. As Lori Muntz notes in her study of the film, at times *Braveheart* seems a deliberate imitation of Tourneur's *Last of the Mohicans*, produced five years earlier, with its climactic drama involving tribal violence, a white woman captive, and closing physical contest between the "savage" and "noble" Native characters (coded by their costumes). At other times the film prefigures *Redskin* in its depiction of the Native protagonist's complex negotiation of racism and social mores during athletic and social events at an upper-class eastern college, including an extended, dramatically presented football game. The film's most interesting move attaches the tropes of both frontier romance (as in *Last of the Mohicans*) and institutional assimilation (as in *Redskin*), to the static, discursive space of the courtroom.

The court sequence is heavily and multiply textualized, with lengthy intertitles conveying legal arguments and judgments that refer to treaties. The intertitle text of Braveheart's argument brings together the film's melodramatic and legal orientations ("When nations violate treaties with strong neighbors, it means—war! Will you violate this treaty with my people because they are few, unarmed—and helpless?"), while a subsequent title card with the judge's decision parses the meaning of the treaty text itself: "We have examined the Federal treaty with the Indians and find that it gives them the right to fish where and when they please, without limitation by State tax or private ownership." In addition to the attention to inscribed legal rights in treaty agreements, other kinds of commercialized, contested discursive communications are given weight in the film's formal structure, including Braveheart's book *The Redskin* (and its royalties), a written code of team strategies for the football game (which the film's villain tries to sell to the other team), and a front-page newspaper story about the tribal uprising. The latter event creates the deadline structure motivating the film's final action. The film's "drama of the discursive" draws viewers' attention to the legal recognition of Native nationhood written into treaties. While the film narrates both "assimilation" and "reversion" in stereotyped ways in scenes of Braveheart's school experiences and the tribe's rebellion against the cannery, it also intervenes in the trajectory of these popular narratives by ending with images of generational accession that envision a tribal future sustained by their court-protected traditional fishing economy.

Braveheart's story was inspired partly by Strongheart's own life story, particularly his boarding school education. In his description of his work in Hollywood, Strongheart underscores its connections to his boarding school experiences in ways that compare the studio system and the assimilationist project of boarding schools. He writes that his involvement with film production began while he was a student at the Carlisle School in 1905 when the Lubin Film Co. shot footage at the school for the film *The White Chief,* and he was asked to mediate between the film crew, professional actors, and student extras.[17] Much later, when Strongheart was an established consultant in Hollywood, he produced a report critical of a Twentieth Century Fox script for the 1952 film *Pony Soldier*, suggesting significant revisions. He describes a meeting in which studio executives initially resemble the disciplinarians he remembers from the Carlisle School with himself in the role of a defiant student.[18] Although Strongheart was able to convince the studios to make changes to the film, his vividly imagined comparison points out the resemblance between the racialized power dynamics of the studio system and the institutional schools. Strongheart was an active mediator within both systems; according to historian Nicolas Rosenthal, he often hosted boarding school students from the Sherman Institute in Riverside when they were visiting Los Angeles, and he was at the center of the Los Angeles Native community, including serving as president of the Los Angeles Indian Center. Michelle Raheja aptly describes the way that "In their self-conscious interactions with film performance and its myriad possibilities for on-screen and casual, back-lot negotiations of racial representation through redfacing, Native American actors attempted to make a register of images not necessarily of their own creation" (*Reservation Reelism* 74).

Red Love, a 1925 film independently produced by J. Charles Davis and actor John Lowell (for Lowell Film Productions) and directed by Edgar Lewis, tells the story of two brothers educated at the Carlisle School but separated and lost to one another when the elder brother, Thunder Cloud (John Lowell) becomes an outlaw after being led to believe he has killed a white man. Thunder Cloud falls in love with Starlight (Evangeline Russell), the mixed-race daughter of the white sheriff, and then abducts her during the Indian Fair. His younger brother, Little Antelope (F. Serrano Keating), having joined the tribal police, discovers the couple and during the struggle Thunder Cloud recognizes him by a scar on his chest. The two brothers reunite, allegations against Thunder Cloud are cleared in court, and Starlight accepts Thunder Cloud's proposal of marriage at the film's conclusion. Much of the action in *Red Love* hinges on the schoolteacher, Starlight, and her classroom. Starlight's classroom (for both settler and Native children) is a rendezvous point for her and Thunder Cloud, where she nurses him when he is wounded. At the end of the film he proposes to her in the classroom with the chalkboard behind them.

Only a few reels of *Red Love* are currently viewable; several reels are missing from the extant copy in the Library of Congress's "Indians in

Silent Film" collection. The fragments of the film that are available suggest that many elements of *Red Love* continue the production strategies of earlier Indian dramas, including the location shooting in which Native extras appear alongside white leading actors who perform in redface. The scenes at the Indian Fair are remarkably invested in realism, such as representations of Native patriotism when Starlight dances with two older Native men, one of whom carries an American flag because his son died while fighting in World War I. The patriotic opening dance honoring World War I veterans and their families frames the subsequent film action with this visual discourse of citizenship. The film's courtroom scenes, like the scenes in Starlight's classroom, imagine Indigenous presence in institutional spaces, while furthering the film's melodramatic project of adjudicating a moral landscape in a multiracial reservation context. The fair scenes also feature Native extras, a traditional "free-for-all" Lakota cross-country horserace, and an attempt at Lakota language intertitles (the MC says, "Iy okihe kin he isicola tuwe keceyos iny onkapi kte," translated in intertitles as, "Next will be the Free-for-All race"). This use of Lakota in the title cards is unusual since even in silent films Native characters "spoke" broken English in the intertitles. Some audiences were aware of the inaccuracy of this "Indian" speech, especially in films about boarding school students. For example, contemporary reviewers writing about the Norma Talmadge vehicle *The Heart of Wetona* in *Variety* and *The New York Times* noted the oddity of Wetona's broken English in the intertitles, given that she is supposed to have had an East Coast seminary education.[19]

The film foregrounds assimilationist education while also validating both traditionalism and racial mixture. It is also unusual in its focus on a divided Native family coming together, especially the brotherly embrace rather than a rejection between the traditional and assimilated brothers. Starlight's biracial family is portrayed harmoniously as well, in a dinner scene. The separation between the two brothers, as Thunder Cloud takes Little Antelope to boarding school, is seen in flashback (see figures 2.4 and 2.5). The brothers are marked by their costumes—Thunder Cloud wears buckskin and Little Antelope wears knickers—while both Thunder Cloud and the teachers and administrators possessively lay their hands on Little Antelope. Significantly, however, costume is less important as an assimilationist cue here than in other 1920s dramas; in fact, costume disguises the characters' actual identities and a physical scar triggers the familial recognition (see figure 2.6). Starlight also makes statements asserting her Native identity ("I am a Sioux!") rather than rejecting her tribe, and she seems to feel no discomfort or "dilemma" as she moves between settler and Native social circles.

Figure 2.4. *Red Love*, Lowell Film Productions (1925) (LC), sending Little Antelope to school.

The films' representation of traumatic crimes (the attempted rape of a Native girl early in the film and Thunder Cloud's fear of being lynched for the murder of Bill Mosher, indicated by his putting his own hands on his neck before he flees the scene) imagine white violence against Native

Figure 2.5. *Red Love*, Lowell Film Productions (1925) (LC), interracial family dinner.

Figure 2.6. *Red Love*, Lowell Film Productions (1925) (LC), James Logan/Little Antelope (F. Serrano Keating) and Thunder Cloud (John Lowell) are reunited, as Starlight (Evangeline Russell) looks on.

tribes on the frontier rather than sexual availability and tribal violence. *Red Love* doesn't end with a Native woman's suicide undertaken to resuscitate a white family as in *The Squaw Man*. Instead, it ends with a mixed-blood woman marrying a full-blood, more traditional man, and forming a family on the reservation in the very educational space of the classroom that in other films marks the scene of colonization through cultural and familial severance. *Braveheart* and *Red Love* revised early cinema's "squaw man" narrative by including legal discourse, or what Chadwick Allen calls a "discourse of treaties," in the intertitles and restaging classrooms as places of cultural continuity rather than assimilation, but as independent productions these films were not widely seen (*Blood* 14).[20] While retaining the melodramatic form of the Indian drama, they also imagine the possibility of Indigenous control over the extent and processes of assimilation: educated Native professionals—lawyers, schoolteachers, and police officers—work on behalf of their communities and combat exploitation and racism through self-determination.[21]

Later films from major studios, such as the Warner Brothers production *Massacre* (1934), seem to wink at the established genre conventions of the Indian drama by disassembling the signs of Native screen identity. In *Massacre*, Joe Thunderhorse (Richard Barthelmess) embodies for audiences the "dilemma of the modern Indian," recognizable only through costume, and reflexively emphasizes the theatrical qualities of performing Indian-ness. White women consistently demand that the boarding school edu-cated Thunderhorse "play Indian," a sexualized dynamic that mimics and mocks Barthelmess's acting in redface. After the bare-chested, long-haired Thunderhorse performs sharp-shooting and horseback stunts for the "Daw-son's 3-Bar Ranch" Wild West show at the Chicago World's Fair (with the motto "A Century of Progress" prominently displayed with American flags and images of feathered headdresses), eager young women insist that he autograph publicity photos of himself. The camera follows Thunderhorse backstage, however, where he proceeds to remove his long-haired wig and, with the assistance of Sam (Clarence Muse), his African-American valet, dons a sophisticated white suit in preparation for a cocktail party with his wealthy white lover.

The valet's mirror initially reflects his own face, moving aside to reveal Thunderhorse's face. The diegetic reframing underscores the way Thunder-horse's social aspirations are both limited and enabled by visual constructions of his racial identity. Thunderhorse is sandwiched between the whiteness of his suit and the blackness of his valet, a discourse of black and white in America that doesn't account for his Native identity. At the cocktail party, Thunderhorse's girlfriend Norma (Claire Dodd) leads him to a room where she's acquired "absolutely authentic" Native artifacts from the Chicago Field Museum. Joe is nonplussed, but Norma recostumes him in a feathered head-dress before kissing him, saying "Joe—try this on. I see a long procession of red men behind you, riding the plains." When he returns to his reservation to visit his dying father, however, the blind man barely recognizes him, calling him a "white man" after feeling his suit jacket. *Massacre* combines a narrative of "reversion" with an overtly political agenda, advocating New Deal policies and the impending passage of the Indian Reorganization Act of 1934, its story and politics further complicated by the studio's negotiations with various government agencies during production (Aleiss 51).

While a few Indigenous performers and directors attained positions of power in 1920s Hollywood, the identities of these stars and directors were often reconstituted in the context of trade industry marketing—or in some cases remain unknown. The director James Cruze, for example, claimed Ute ancestry but never provided evidence.[22] Unlike later Native filmmakers who would comment overtly in their work on the conventions of sympathetic Westerns, and who often work outside of Hollywood, Chickasaw director

Edwin Carewe and Cherokee entertainer Will Rogers generally appropriated the conventions of mainstream Hollywood cinematic forms, subtly revising the genre (and the industry) from within. I will discuss Carewe's Indian drama (the 1928 film *Ramona*) at length later in this chapter. Will Rogers's important contributions to the political landscape of the Western could easily fill a book—I treat his work only briefly since his Westerns of the 1920s and 1930s operated in a different mode (comedic, rather than melodramatic) than the epic "reform dramas" addressed here. In fact, he parodied the epic and melodramatic elements of the Western genre "Indian attack" scene in his 1924 film *Two Wagons, Both Covered* (Rogers wrote the script and played both a dissolute scout and an Eastern dandy, roles corresponding to scout and hero characters in *The Covered Wagon*). At the end of the film, as the group of settlers finally arrive at a barren "Los Angeles" in California, they are ambushed by a band of "Escrow Indians"—suited and bespeckled real estate salesmen—who use branches to camouflage their approach but who then aggressively sell worthless paper land deeds to the settlers and take their wagons and belongings, leaving them destitute. By recostuming and reversing the ethnic identity of the "Indians," Rogers reveals the land theft underpinning Western real estate transactions, using the racialized trope of the "Indian attack" to establish land speculators and profiteers as the frontier's true aggressors. These reversals prefigure Carewe's later revision of ethnic identities in the traumatic ambush scene in *Ramona*, but engage a completely different emotional register, activating an ironic distance and humorous critique of the dominant narratives and images of Western settlement. Carewe takes the opposite approach to politicized genre revision, immersing viewers in the very epic and melodramatic modes that Rogers's comedy dismantles. Although Rogers's Cherokee identity and political orientation informed his radio show and political commentaries, he played non-Native roles in his fiction films—in fact, he is often coded as a white character by deliberate contrast with exaggerated caricatures of Native and African-American minor characters. In *Mr. Skitch*, the 1933 film directed by Cruze, Rogers's Okie family man encounters an "Indian guide" at the Grand Canyon, dressed in a full warbonnet and speaking broken English. And in the 1934 *Judge Priest*, directed by John Ford, Rogers's Cherokee identity is completely erased on screen in favor of a racial semiotics of black and white as Rogers's white Judge interacts with his servant (played by Stepin' Fetchit). While many of Rogers's films do not engage overtly in Native political issues, his strong, public self-identification as Cherokee and his political commentary in other modes (print and radio) inflect both his screen performances and his regionally specific popular images of the

West in California and Oklahoma.[23] In addition to Carewe and Rogers, the Cherokee dramatist Lynn Riggs was active in the 1930s as a Hollywood scriptwriter for major studios such as Paramount and Universal, contributing to scripts for Cecil B. DeMille's *The Plainsman* (1936), W. S. Van Dyke's *Laughing Boy* (1934), and other major studio productions. Collaborating with friend James Hughes in Santa Fe, he also made an experimental, short silent film in the impressionistic "city symphony" tradition—*A Day in Santa Fe* (1931)—profiling "the Santa Fe burro" (Weigle and Fiore 37–8). Riggs is best known for his play *Green Grow the Lilacs*, which had a successful Broadway run in 1931 and was the source material for the extraordinarily popular Rodgers and Hammerstein musical *Oklahoma!* (produced for Broadway in 1943 and for the screen in 1955).[24]

These films from the 1924–1934 period, which straddled the transition to sound, returned to the Indian drama form, adapting its narrative and visual conventions to address the increasing pressure for changes in national Indian policy. Many of these films accessed images of familial rupture directly and in intensely melodramatic modes, while others did so in more oblique ways through the theatricality of costume and reflexive performance. The steady production of these films through the 1920s created opportunities for Indigenous participants—from occasional consultants such as Nipo T. Strongheart to major international celebrities such as Will Rogers—to assert their perspectives in the public space of the cinema. The remaining sections of this chapter parse the complexities of this representational field by attending closely to images of domesticity, violence, assimilation, and "reversion" in three major productions from this period—*The Vanishing American, Redskin,* and *Ramona.*

Assimilation and Reversion in *The Vanishing American* (1925)

Visual scenes of assimilation in the Paramount epics and other sympathetic films of the 1920s supported articles in print media and periodicals as the movement to reform Indian policy gained energy throughout the decade. *The Vanishing American* was explicitly compared to *The Covered Wagon* in reviews that conflated the films' educational and Americanizing projects; one reviewer claimed that "from the standpoint of importance in an educational way" *The Vanishing American* "has not been equaled. Even 'The Covered Wagon' must, in my judgment, now take second place in this small group of strictly American cinemas." The reviewer noted that both the film's emotional tenor—its "deep, surging element of pathos"—and its authenticity in the acting, in which "Indian babies play Indian baby roles," accounted for its eclipse of the earlier epics (though the reviewer's assertions about the authentic casting are questionable given the prominence of Richard Dix as the lead).[25]

Reviewers and many scholars have focused on the lengthy prologue of *The Vanishing American* in which Paramount's director, George Seitz, narrated an evolutionary vision of the progression of races in the Southwest, each group defeated and replaced by a less "primitive" invader. William R. Handley argues that the prologue works to "externalize, temporally extend and sequentially reverse the internal evolution that [Grey's] characters undergo" ("Vanishing" 52) and that in Westerns like *The Vanishing American* "the simulated presence of the Indian . . . iconically static yet historically charged as it was" negotiates the distance between screen and reality (50). Taking up a third of the film's running time (and a significant chunk of its budget), narrated in intertitles with quotations from social philosophers in an authoritative tone, the prologue lends an evolutionary cast to the educational project of racial uplift that dominates the individual and interpersonal story of heroism and villainy that follows.

The film also seems, in its sweeping introduction, to be attempting to wed the Western Indian drama to the emerging dramatic documentary, which had taken off in the wake of Robert Flaherty's 1922 *Nanook of the North*—Paramount would go on to distribute Flaherty's *Moana* (1926), Merian C. Cooper and Ernest Schoedsack's *Grass* (1925) and *Chang* (1927), and H. P. Carver's *The Silent Enemy* (1930). The result is a stylistically jarring, divided epic form that is rife with ideological contradictions. While the first part of the film rehashes the idea that Native tribes will "vanish" because they are less fit and doomed to fall before the more civilized settlers, the second part presents them as virtuous and even superior people at the mercy of a dominating, corrupt power. The introduction establishes the film's "authenticity" in much the way later historical epics did in the sound era. As Vivian Sobchack observes, in making the experience of history intelligible to popular audiences, historical epics promulgated excess in production, content, and marketing. The historical epic, she writes, "*formally repeats* the surge, splendor, and extravagance, the human labor and capital cost entailed by its narrative's *historical content* in both its *production process* and its *modes of representation*" ("Surge" 287, emphasis in original). Such excesses—the material parallel to the film's emotional excess and staging of virtue—allow filmmakers to profess accuracy in historical reconstructions and an educational public value for their films. Shooting almost all of *The Vanishing American* on location in Monument Valley, Paramount moved 500 crew members to the area, employed 10,000 Native extras and crew, and physically constructed the cliff dwellings used in the prologue as well as the "Mesa" town and government compound (see figure 2.7).[26] The stars and crew complained about the remoteness, rough conditions, heat, and lack of food and water—trials of location shooting that the studios incorporated into their publicity as markers of the film's authenticity.

The theatricality of tourism is also especially evident as the studios exploited the marketing potential of stories about film production. In a still from the 1929 Paramount production *Redskin*, for example, actress Jane Novak (who did not actually play a Native character in the film) is fitted for a Navajo-style blouse and skirt by the Diné seamstresses making costumes for the film (see figure 2.8). Her pose, and the women's attentiveness to her fitting, reminds viewers of the class differences that inform the film's marking of cultural differences. The site of film production itself serves here to reinforce a touristic claim to the rights of outsiders to consume Indianness through the physical and social relations of shopping, as Hollywood stars model the role of the leisure class. This nervous discourse takes place specifically on the grounds of the juxtaposition between the archaic and the modern that Captain Richard Henry Pratt, founder of the Carlisle School, so effectively coalesced in the before-and-after photographs.

Figure 2.7. *The Vanishing American*, Paramount (1925), view of the set, promotional still (AMPAS).

Figure 2.8. *Redskin*, Paramount (1929), staged fitting, promotional still (AMPAS).

After the prologue, *The Vanishing American* centers on the frustrated romance between Richard Dix as the heroic Navajo character Nophaie and Lois Wilson as Marion Warner, a white schoolteacher. The film attempts to reconcile its conflicting ideologies by displacing systemic corruption onto the figure of the crooked reservation agent, Booker (Noah Beery). The dramatic action revolves around government corruption on the reservation and the Army's need for the tribe's horses—and soldiers—for World War I; Indian policy is staged in the context of an Americanizing, nationalist struggle. Marion wishes to absolve the government while convincing Nophaie to support the war effort, saying, "Oh, I know—you have been unjustly treated. But Booker and his men did that—not the government." Booker's melodramatic villainy comes to stand in for widespread abuses of ill-conceived policies—like Harriet Beecher Stowe's Simon Legree of *Uncle Tom's Cabin*, his personal sadism represents the system-as-excess as well as the excesses of the system.

Strategic scenes of melodramatic virtue and distress, and of crime and mis/recognition, occur in the classroom of the reservation school. Like the heavily ironic scene in John Ford's *The Man Who Shot Liberty Valance* (1962) in which white, educated lawyer Ranse Stoddard (Jimmy Stewart) instructs African-American ranch hand Pompey (Woody Strode) on the nature of liberty, the sequence in *The Vanishing American* opens as Marion Warner leads a classroom of Native schoolchildren in the pledge of allegiance with portraits of George Washington and Abraham Lincoln prominently displayed with the American flag in the mise-en-scène (see figure 2.9). Images of Native American patriotism made visible the systemic contradictions between government wardship and tribal sovereignty and were charged with emotion and pathos for much of the American public. There was no more effective rallying point for advocates of policy reform than Native children engaged in patriotic pledges, songs, and flag drills, or Native men in military uniform. Writer Vera Connolly, touring government boarding schools in 1929, witnessed classroom scenes of "Americanization" that she found emotionally intolerable. In closing the second installment of her three-part series about contemporary Native issues for *Good Housekeeping*, she wrote:

> One moving spectacle I shall never forget. It was a roomful of thin, peaked, half-clad, undernourished little Indian children at a compulsory government boarding school—a school which has recently been severely criticized for its atrocious treatment of the pupils—engaged in a flag drill! I chanced to step in just as they broke into "The Star Spangled Banner," waving their flags as they sang. Such eager warmth, in thin little voices! Such a glow on small, pinched faces! I ran from the place. ("Robbed" 259)

Figure 2.9. *The Vanishing American*, Paramount (1925), the Pledge of Allegiance.

Such reactions on the part of non-Native reformers ask readers to recognize the discrepancy between U.S. imperialist policies and rhetorics of freedom as an unbearable moral dilemma. The Native students' virtue is recognized in a melodramatic mode through the image of their tribulations, and this virtue takes the specific nationalist form of patriotic display. The emotional crises of witness in such 1920s images of Native citizenship and allegiance are almost always accompanied by the individual's new understanding of the ways that institutionalized pedagogy masks unequal power relations.

The contextual discourses of policy reform freighted *The Vanishing American*'s patriotic classroom scenes with precisely the questions of assimilation and separatism that drove the slow policy shift of the 1920s. Narrated scenes of contested citizenship in boarding schools, circulating in periodicals, take the expressive form of violence in the classroom in the plot of *The Vanishing American*. For example, after the pledge of allegiance scene in the film, when the flag is hung back on the wall and the children dismissed, the front of the classroom becomes the site of misconduct as Booker enters and his initial advances toward Marion Warner quickly escalate into an assault. When Nophaie sees the struggle through the window in the door, he intervenes and the classroom becomes the stage for a brawl when three of Booker's henchmen arrive to join the fight. Nophaie's perception of the scene, as if on a miniature screen, echoes the viewers' position and allies us with Nophaie's point of view. The chalkboard and classroom furniture are upset as the men fight and Nophaie is cornered several times with the American flag behind him before he escapes on his horse (see figure 2.10). In this scene the classroom as a stage for the attack on Nophaie dramatizes, through the image of physical confrontation, the force behind the "pedagogic action" of detribalization, assimilation, and citizenship. Furthermore, the sourcing of this violence from a corrupt male Indian agent preserves the image of the benevolent female schoolteacher as a basis for reform that can save the system of government paternalism. (In fact, that system of paternalism is ultimately saved in the film through the legitimating power of white domesticity encoded in Marion's eventual marriage to her white suitor Ramsdale.)

Virginia Wright Wexman sees the tight framing of the small window in the door as a strategy for "visually denying the Indian access to the protected interior spaces that connote safe domesticity," and as a deliberate contrast to the more awesome—and resistant—images of the landscape that dominate the film (148–51). Yet this classroom is a porous as well as a protected space. The classroom represents Marion's body as the site of both potential violation in the film and white female viewers' identification

Figure 2.10. *The Vanishing American*, Paramount (1925), Nophaie (Richard Dix) is cornered.

in the theater. However, these classroom and domestic spaces are preyed upon by the white agent Booker, rather than Nophaie. The interior scenes of instruction and Marion herself as a vehicle for assimilationist educa- tion (both Christianity and American patriotism) become threatened from within the system by its supposed guardians. In the process, Native domestic spaces go unseen or are obliterated in the film (to be glimpsed only in hallucinatory flashback near the film's end), replaced by white women as reformers and white women's homes as places of idealized education. Thus, the film genders the reform movement but does not unseat the ideologies underpinning assimilationist education, dependent on the assumption that settler women are the proper domestic incubators of civilization. Because the Native characters have no viable home or space of cultural or political reproduction, the political reform the film advocates is not envisioned as halting the "vanishing" of the film's title. Marion Warner's own domestic space, in which she also engages in instruction during a bible study ses- sion with Nophaie, blurs the work of teaching with the film's foray into interracial romance.

A tableau of the scene, circulated to publicize the film, depicts Nophaie at Marion's feet in a pose that aligns him with the Native children in her classroom and that amplifies visually his (and by extension the tribe's) legal position as a ward in need of custodial guidance during his emergence into citizenship and Christianity. Marion can also be read as a figure for Mary, mother of Christ, in these scenes, especially because she tutors Nophaie in biblical passages. In this, Marion resembles a similar Western film character, the "pioneering Madonna" Molly Wingate, also played by Lois Wilson in the 1923 Cruze epic *The Covered Wagon* (Prats, *Invisible* 48). As Armando Prats points out, the image of Molly in that film, framed by the canvas of the covered wagon as if it were a halo, is itself a quotation of W. H. D. Koerner's 1921 painting *Madonna of the Prairie*, an image that makes the "pioneering Madonna . . . bear the very seeds of empire" while functioning "not as a participant" in westward migration but rather "the very distillation of the process itself" (48–49). The white woman as both settler and schoolteacher is a familiar figure in the Western (John Ford's 1946 *My Darling Clementine* being one of many classic examples), but in *The Vanishing American*, Marion also represents female reformers—people such as Helen Hunt Jackson, or even the scriptwriter for *Redskin*, Elizabeth Pickett—who ran organizations like WNIA.

In *The Vanishing American*, Marion's classroom also becomes the stage for a third scene, an informal "trial" as Marion brings another Indian agent, Halliday, to hear her story. Booker twists her story by accusing her of an illicit affair with Nophaie so that the classroom becomes not only the scene of Booker's crime, but also the stage of misrecognition, misplaced guilt, and the criminalization of Nophaie and of interracial romance. Far from simply connoting a "safe domesticity," the classroom is a state-controlled public space, a theater in which cultural outsiders are Americanized through the performance of allegiance. Here, it is doubly indicted by the filmmakers as the location of both physical and symbolic violence. Marion is a figure of identification for female viewers and is also associated with Indianness and melodramatic cross-racial sympathy when she, too, is targeted by the Indian agent. Marion's word as a victim of Booker's sexual aggression and as a sympathetic witness to Nophaie's actions is discounted, but as a character she claims the stage, in a sense, through this shared marginalization as an outsider. A *Variety* magazine reviewer dismisses the film as having appeal primarily for women, "for to them the idea of having a good cry means a corking time."[27] Here the theater itself as a place for experiencing nostalgia and loss is coded as women's space because of its emotional tenor. It is a space of sympathy, helplessness, and weeping, yet also one of entertainment, suggesting that the catharsis of "a good cry" over Indigenous loss can offer female viewers a "corking time." The pathos of imperialist benevolence—and the capacity of melodrama to articulate its contradictions—is canned here for matinee consumption, highlighting the way melodrama's orchestration of virtue enables and broadcasts but also limits the horizon and scope of political reform. Later in the film, Marion acts as a translator when neither Halliday nor Captain Ramsdell understand a Diné man when he explains why the men won't bring in horses for the war effort. Her translation of the explanation—that Booker's men had previously stolen many of their horses—recovers her virtue and truthfulness in the eyes of the Indian agent Halliday. Her redemption as a melodramatic heroine at this moment foregrounds her role for the audience as a reformer. Her connection with Nophaie is also recognized as a virtue rather than a transgression when, through him, she is able to engineer the delivery not only of horses but also new recruits for the war effort. The emphasis on her role as the go-between—a translator of Native culture for outsiders and a spokesperson on behalf of the tribe and Native characters—aligns her with public figures such as Mary Austin, John Collier, and others who were major voices on Native issues at the time.

In addition to the classroom scenes of Native children pledging allegiance and the abuses and misrecognitions by government agents, images of patriotism outside the classroom dominate the second half of the film as the Native men depart to serve in World War I. As Captain Ramsdell watches them ride away, with one horseman waving a large American flag taken from the agency office, he comments specifically on the scene as one of pathos: "Pitiful—and tremendous! Riding away to fight for the white man!" The subsequent scenes take place on a French battlefield, tinted in red; Nophaie, now a sergeant in uniform, demonstrates heroism and courage in the face of machine-gun units, broken radios, barbed wire, and wounded and dying soldiers. Although one reviewer complained of the inaccuracy of some scenes—such as when men charge out of bunkers wearing full packs and gear, and when, after the war, Native men return to the reservation still wearing bandages—the depiction of Native modernity through the change in costume is striking, especially in contrast to the scene of Captain Ramsdell's arrival on the reservation, when Native men crowd around his automobile in amazement. The war scenes in the film extend the institutionalization of the Diné characters through their military uniforms, while also altering the film's earlier vision of the men as symbolic of primitivism, nostalgia, and an antimodern past. The contrast with earlier costuming functions as a form of before-and-after imagery as the men appear transformed by their change of clothing from traditional dress to military uniforms. The extended, violent action sequences and depiction of physical hardships in battle elicit strong empathetic reactions from viewers, appropriating Native patriotism through the transposition of the "warrior" stereotype to American wars, a strategy that was also common in sympathetic Westerns and in U.S. military appropriations of Native images in its propaganda for World Wars I and II.

The machine gun as an emblem of this modernity comes to the reservation when Booker attempts to use one against the Native men who attack the town of Mesa in their rage at the dispossession of their lands and relocation of families during the war. The soldiers' return to the reservation, where they find that Booker has taken over as the highest ranking Indian agent, triggers their memories of their homes "before and after" the war as an idealized space of innocence, the "lost home" of melodrama. Booker has relocated Native families from agricultural lands to badlands, and as one soldier (on crutches and with an eye patch) looks toward his family's old hogan, his vision of their activities there appears in ghostly superimposition, explained through the intertitle "The visions of a shell-shocked brain—." "Home, home!" he says, calling for his family members, but only one old man lives there now. Another soldier finds that while he was away his sweetheart has died, having worked in Booker's house and been subjected to his abuse. The film's images construct Native homes primarily through nostalgic memory (superimposed flashbacks), never extending their temporality to the present or future. The soldiers' loss of their homes suggests a melodramatic sense of helplessness. For audiences, this narrative move cues the fatalism of bad timing—nothing can be done because it is "too late." The never-present Indian home not only represents a remembered-yet-lost-forever "space of innocence" essential to melodrama but also allows audiences to share in the virtue connoted by that innocence through their emotional sympathy.[28] Furthermore, the "lost Indian home" in *The Vanishing American* might also suggest a symbolic Western "closure" of the frontier, the narratively foreclosed possibility of a continuing Native land base for future generations. The image associated with the audience's excessive emotions also represents a transfer of land title that appears to be irrevocable.

The politics of interracial sympathy underpinning the film's representations of Diné assimilation also organize its anxious depiction of "miscegenation" in the film text as well as in the scripting and publicity materials. The issues of familial disruption and cross-racial domesticity drove frenzied and multimodal revisions of Zane Grey's published versions of *The Vanishing American*, as well as the Paramount script adaptations. Grey's original serialized version of the novel in *Ladies' Home Journal* in 1922 elicited protests from church-based groups for its negative representations of missionary work on reservations, but in revising the manuscript for publication as a novel, Grey also revised the ending to suggest a marriage between Nophaie and the white teacher Marion. Without Grey's permission, his editor at Harper and Brothers publishers changed the plot of the novel back to its serialized ending, in which Nophaie dies of influenza before he and Marion can marry, and deleted some of Marion's more outspoken criticisms of whiteness or "white blood."[29] Paramount reviewers were initially put off by the bleak tone in the serialized version; M. C. Lathrop wrote in 1923:

> Every character (without exception) that earns the sympathy or respect of the reader is either dead or left in a pitiable state at the end of the story; and the miscreants who are the authors of this misery and death, are smugly hale, hearty and prosperous. . . . It is difficult to see how, in view of the harrowing character of the story, it could be made available for pictures without radical revisions.[30]

But the scriptwriters stayed with the bleak ending, focusing their revisions instead on the first half of the story: after adding the extended prologue premised on the "cycle of nations," the writers eventually cut the story of Nophaie's childhood—kidnapped by white tourists and educated at the Carlisle School. In the novel and early script treatments, then, Nophaie is a bicultural character, but the filmed version combines Nophaie's education with his attraction to Marion, signified visually in the tableau of his religious instruction in Marion's parlor (see figure 2.11). In this image, the conflation of settler instructional and domestic spaces narrate a project of racial uplift through both education and intermarriage, yet neither project is carried through to resolution in the narrative. Furthermore, the script changes suppress potential issues of Native domesticity and its disruption,

Figure 2.11. *The Vanishing American*, Paramount (1925), Nophaie's bible lesson.

and of Nophaie's cultural bifurcation, which might have emerged if the childhood kidnapping and education of Nophaie had been filmed.

The seemingly contained issue of "miscegenation" surfaces, however, in the production and publicity photos for the film. If Grey's publishers and Paramount executives were nervous about whether interracial marriage would sell in the popular press and on screen, they confidently staged and used images of integration between the Hollywood-based cast and the Diné to sell the film. Figure 2.12 depicts Richard Dix distributing candy to a group of about eight Diné children, with his arm around the smallest, who sits in his lap. He is wearing his Navajo costume, wig, necklace, and makeup from his early scenes in the film, and apparently his appearance in "redface" is convincing enough for another of the photographs from this session to appear in the National Archives "Records of the Bureau of The Census" from 1890–1959. In a miscellaneous box also containing "photographs and lantern slides of tabulating machinery" are "Photographs relating to the Navajo Indian enumeration" of 1930 as well as "Photographs of bureau activities during the 1940 census." The photo carries the caption, "Each one of these [children] bear [sic] individual names" (see figure I.1 from the Introduction).[31] However, it is unlikely that the photograph was actually shot by a census taker in 1930, since it depicts an actor on location for a major Paramount production in 1925. The ease of the interchanged readings of the image and the confusion between images of a white Hollywood star on location and a Diné man with his children is primarily facilitated by Richard Dix's traditional costuming and demonstrates the power of this form of signification in "reading race" on the bodies of Native and non-Native performers and photographed subjects.[32] The photograph was probably simply misfiled, but it could have been included intentionally as a "generic" image of Diné children for census purposes because the caption refers to them and not to Dix. The staging of a Diné family here might have been seen as a useful addition to the census record; the 1930 Census was the first to include Native peoples as part of the general population and thus participated in the assimilationist project delineated by the earlier Indian Citizenship Act of 1924. The continuing interest of Diné people as visual exemplars of census enumeration is evident in contemporary reuses, such as the photograph of a census taker and a Diné family from the 1930 Census records displayed on the contemporary National Archives press kit website.[33] But the inclusion of images from both the census taking itself and from film sets five years earlier reveal supposedly evidentiary photography to be both product and productive of national fantasies about Native peoples. In figure 2.13, Lois Wilson, also in costume and makeup for her schoolyard scenes in

Figure 2.12. *The Vanishing American*, Paramount (1925), Richard Dix with children, promotional still (AMPAS).

the film, gazes down at a baby, most likely the child of a local Diné family, resting in a cradleboard in her lap. Her soft expression in profile and the careful staging and lighting in the shot suggest that the maternal pose and evocation of possession are deliberate—the child's Diné family members are not in the photograph. Especially as they intersect with government census records and studio marketing efforts, the staged "families" in these images—Dix in redface as benevolent patriarch, Wilson in her schoolteacher costume as a mother figure, each with Diné children—are allegories of custody. They invite audiences to immerse in narrative fantasies of adoptive connection with Indigenous tribes, while asserting government control in the guise of parental bonds.

The transfer of custody—a scene that takes center stage in the filmed plot of the later film *Redskin*—is edited out of *The Vanishing American*, though the suggestion of this plot is visible in the publicity photographs that are meant to suggest the performers' accurate representations of Diné life. The Hollywood stars also signify and "act" as tourists in their staged/

Figure 2.13. *The Vanishing American*, Paramount (1925), Lois Wilson with a baby, promotional still (AMPAS).

photographed encounters with the Diné people of Monument Valley, boosting viewers' desire to visit the same place (in person or vicariously at the movies) through fantasies based on identification with the actors. *Redskin*, released four years after *The Vanishing American*, is in many ways a continuation of the revisions of Grey's story by Lucien Hubbard, Paramount's producer for both films and the head of Zane Grey Productions under the auspices of the studio. In Hubbard's script synopsis of April 10, 1925, the Indian agent expropriates tribal land for oil development rather than an experimental farm, as in the filmed version, and the climactic revolt involves dynamiting the oil wells and setting fire to the "sluggish tide of refuse oil" that was ruining the cornfields. The agent's German name in the script, Blucher, associates the character's local empire-building activities with German actions prior to World War I rather than with the U.S. government's own imperialism. The discovery of oil on the reservation, cut from the filmed version of *The Vanishing American*, is central to the plot resolution in *Redskin*. The casual transfer of land issues from one tribe and region to another (the assumption that Diné once hunted buffalo as a primary food source, and the mapping onto Diné country of the oil industry issues that were centered in Oklahoma territory among the Osage and other tribes in the 1920s) instantiates the studio system's own appropriative practices for which disparate cultural customs and political histories were amalgamated and translated into a single, potent system of visual signs intended for public consumption as generic affect, divorced from the specificity of the local. Both Grey's *The Vanishing American* and Elizabeth Pickett's novel *Redskin* (originally submitted to Paramount as "Navajo") were conceived primarily as films and written after contact with studio executives had been made.[34]

Reviewers in trade journals tended—as they had in the past—to include their own views about Indian affairs in evaluating sympathetic Westerns, blending their evaluations of the film with information culled from other sources, especially popular news media. By measuring the films' representations against their own (often highly inaccurate) perceptions of current Native issues, reviewers treated sympathetic Westerns as if they were, at least in part, intended to be nonfiction. A reviewer for *Variety* reiterates the "vanishing" of the film's title as a documentary fact, but also—contradictorily—recirculates the popular idea in the 1920s that the "vanishing Indians" are actually rich: "the story itself calls attention to the vanishing of the real American, the Indian, off the face of the North American continent. Nothing is said about the Indians who are living in Oklahoma at this time and drawing down a weekly royalty of about $1,750 and riding around in sedans which they discard immediately after a tire blows, so as to get a new car."[35] The gist of the reviewer's assertion that Native people are incapable of navigating modernity—either managing their financial resources or correctly operating Western technology—reinforces an image of tribal incongruity in 1920s America and, in turn, the logic of Indians vanishing in the name of progress; Indians as symbols of the "before" temporarily occupy the cinematic space of the "after."[36] If films like *The Vanishing American* and *Redskin* alienated some viewers (and reviewers) by situating Native characters in a modern context, the films also generalized disparate Native issues into a single visual narrative and exported that narrative as epic spectacle available to middle-class consumers and reformers.

Pedagogic Violence in *Redskin* (1929)

Redskin was the last of the silent Paramount epics to be shot on location in the southwest and, for the final scenes, employed Magnascope, an early 70 mm widescreen technology, as well as other immersive technologies such as Technicolor for footage of Canyon de Chelly, Acoma Pueblo, and other places. An advertisement trumpets the film's technical innovation as "a sensational spectacle in sound and color," which promised to reveal a new Western authenticity embedded in melodrama: "the mysterious Navajo country actually filmed in NATURAL COLORS; a wonderful love story; heart stirring pathos . . . and action" (Sweeney 142). According to Schertzinger, the alternation of color with black and white photography wasn't initially an aesthetic choice—he was ordered by studio executives halfway through the shooting to complete the film in black and white to lower the film's budget. He had already shot the location scenes in the Southwest in color, the remainder of the film, filmed in tinted monochrome, depicted life in the boarding schools and at college. But there is reason to doubt this story, since script treatments suggest the alternation was planned.[37]

Kevin Brownlow describes the Technicolor footage in the film, shot at Acoma Pueblo and other southwest locations, as "documentary scenes," noting that Robert Flaherty had also tried to shoot at Acoma for Twentieth Century Fox (350). Film viewers most likely thought of these scenes as ethnographic representations. However, *Redskin* also anticipates the use of color to externalize characters' interior states in the melodramas of the 1950s in a way that is "thematised in terms of the characters' emotional and psychological predicaments" (Elsaesser 52). The black-and-white footage of the military drill at the school is equally if not more "documentary" in tone—it is indistinguishable from some of the nonfiction shorts depicting boarding schools distributed for newsreels and educational venues during this period.

The film tells the story of a Navajo boy, Wing Foot (Richard Dix), taken by force from his grandmother's care by the Indian agent John Walton

(Larry Steers), and sent to boarding school, where he is whipped by the same agent for refusing to salute the American flag. He is comforted by a Pueblo girl, Corn Blossom (Gladys Belmont), who becomes his lifelong love and who follows him to college at the fictitious Thorpe University where he is recruited as a star athlete and medical student ("Thorpe University" is of course a reference to Sac and Fox/Potawatomie athlete Jim Thorpe).[38] But Corn Blossom is tricked into returning home to her Pueblo by a jealous suitor, Pueblo Jim (played by African-American actor Noble Johnson), while Wing Foot also returns home after a racist incident at the school.[39] At home, Corn Blossom is pressured to marry Pueblo Jim, while Wing Foot struggles unsuccessfully to be accepted by his community. The action culminates in Wing Foot's discovery of oil in the desert and his race against land specula-tors to file a claim on the land; in the end, Wing Foot's oil riches gain him the support of his community and smooth over the conflicts between the Navajo and Pueblo, enabling him to marry Corn Blossom.

After its initial establishing shots of the southwest landscape and the trading post, one of the first scenes in *Redskin* centers on pedagogy: the medicine man, "old Chahi" (Bernard Siegel), lectures young Wing Foot as they sit on a rug in the foreground with sheep running behind them and cliff-dwelling ruins in the far background. Chahi prophecies that Wing Foot will become a leader and cautions him to follow Navajo rather than "White Man's" ways (see figure 2.14). As Chahi points to a pattern in the woven rug on which they sit, the image dissolves and is held for a moment in superimposition with the text of a children's book that Wing Foot is trying

Figure 2.14. *Redskin*, Paramount (1929), Chahi (Bernard Siegel) and Wing Foot.

Figure 2.15. *Redskin*, Paramount (1929), superimposed rug and text.

to read in the next scene, while his grandmother sits beside him, weaving at her loom in their hogan (see figures 2.15 and 2.16). These competing pedagogical iconographies—of oral teaching using the visual aid of the rug design versus the written pages of the book—converge in an indecipherable image in which Chahi's finger seems to point at the text as well as the woven design. The story in the book—of a bird trying to convince a sheep and a horse to fly—further emphasizes the differences in "kinds" of teaching and learning. From the grandmother's conversation in the next scene, we learn

Figure 2.16. *Redskin*, Paramount (1929), Wing Foot and his grandmother (Augustina Lopez).

that the book belonged to Wing Foot's mother, who could read it (as Wing Foot himself cannot), and that "she would be here now—if old Chahi had let me call the white doctor when you were born." The sequence attempts to imagine a Native domesticity and home, but the absence of Wing Foot's mother punctuates the scene; Native women, especially mothers, are largely missing in both *Redskin* and *The Vanishing American*.

In a sequence synopsis on September 6, 1928, and in the first temporary script of August 18, 1928, scriptwriter Elizabeth Pickett drafted an initial scene for the film depicting the death of Wing Foot's mother in childbirth. Alternately named Laughing Singer or Laughing Water in script versions, she has no lines in the film and is spoken for by Yina (Wing Foot's grandmother, played by Augustine Lopez), who attempts to send for a white nurse but is denied. In Westerns such as *Red Love* (1925), *Devil's Doorway* (1950), and *Flaming Star* (1960), racist white doctors refuse to leave their card games or other pursuits to treat Native patients (unless they are forced to at gunpoint), while Native medicines are represented as ineffectual at best, fraudulent at worst. The scene opens the film with ceremonial sandpaintings and singing over Laughing Water, but the script treatment suggests the representation would have stressed primitivist stereotypes: "These drums and faces give to the audience a sense of Voo-dooism, of witch-doctoring, of unholy pagan rites and long-forgotten ceremonies, as did the tom-toms throbbing like the Black Heart of Africa throughout *The Emperor Jones*."[40] The script and sequences deliberately indict Diné medicinal and spiritual systems, depicting Chahi and, in early versions, a midwife, in collusion to maintain fraudulent power while Laughing Water dies "from neglect." The denigration of Native medicine and holy people is a long-standing trope in Westerns, as well as in ethnographic films such as Edward Curtis's *In the Land of the Headhunters* (1914) and H. P. Burden's *The Silent Enemy* (1930). Here the death of Wing Foot's mother becomes an unstated justification for removing him from Diné "superstition"—the film dramatizes the pathos of government separation of Diné children from their families yet presents that act as inevitable through the death of Laughing Water, Wing Foot's educated mother. Her death also suggests a previous generation's failure to reintegrate into the community after boarding school, foreshadowing Wing Foot's ambivalent return later in the film.

After returning from boarding school, Wing Foot characterizes his people as "whipped by your superstitions" and "dying through ignorance." Despite its realism in depicting the trauma of boarding school and despite its politically progressive stance, *Redskin* resembles early Indian dramas in its complete inability to recognize the legitimacy of Indigenous belief systems or to extend its reformist stance to include religious freedom. This ambivalence poses a problem for the filmmakers because despite the pathos of separation in the scenarios of removal when Wing Foot is taken away to boarding school, the film never validates the alternative scenario of leaving Native children with their families to be educated in a traditional manner.

The removal of Wing Foot from his father and grandmother's care is depicted in an extended scene that returns visually to the act of separation three times. After successfully hiding from the Indian agent initially, Wing Foot is caught when the agent returns unexpectedly. First the agent takes Wing Foot from his grandmother inside the hogan, then separates him from her again outside of the hogan (see figure 2.17); finally, the medicine man Chahi takes the child from the agent, who again pulls him away (see figure 2.18). The agent threatens Notani, Wing Foot's father, with military action if he doesn't relinquish his son: "You're too smart to make us bring out the troops again!" Children, like land, become potential sources of armed conflict in the film, and historical records indicate that armed forces were used in some instances in removing Native children to boarding schools.[41]

This extended, repetitive sequence lengthens and heightens the emotional impact of the separation and impending sense of generational rift. Although *Redskin* is deliberately less melodramatic than its precursor *The Vanishing American*, the visual repetition of the agent's removal of the child engages viewers in the pathos of this moment and represents a form of stylistic excess in the mise-en-scène, activating the audience's sympathy with the virtues and suffering of Native families due to systems beyond their control. While the tragic interruption of the coherent family home, figured

Figure 2.17. *Redskin*, Paramount (1929), Indian agent Walton (Larry Steers) takes Wing Foot from his grandmother.

Figure 2.18. *Redskin*, Paramount (1929), Indian agent takes Wing Foot from Chahi.

as a "space of innocence" in the images of Wing Foot's instruction and in the Southwest landscape and hogan, is typical of melodrama as a form, we should also recognize that in *Redskin* and other sympathetic Westerns of the 1920s, images of ruptured *Native* homes take on specific meanings, activated by the intertextual associations with reform literature. Because the scenes refer to and reenact a historical practice of assimilationist education, they draw affective power from viewers' perceptions of documentary actuality and news content while tapping a melodramatic tradition of familial loss (the "good home" of nostalgic memory). This scenario of confrontation is also an act of transfer, rehearsing again the plot of the vanishing Indian—in this case through assimilation and generational estrangement.

In these scenarios the Native child under institutional custody—a literalization of the status of tribes as "wards"—becomes a visual embodiment of "measured sovereignty" or a tribal nation, its assets (including children) overseen "in trust" by the U.S. government. But unlike other representations of contact from the historical past, which invite viewers to participate in a fantasy that normalizes an act of transferring land to new arrivals, the transfer of Native children in these sympathetic Westerns asks viewers to question—and to weep for—the system of institutionalization by drawing our attention to the emotional consequences of the government's moral trespass against Native families. This is particularly the case for films such as *Redskin* that are set in a contemporary, modern moment. Unlike Westerns that envision tribes as perpetual inhabitants of the 1860s frontier, Paramount's films dramatize Native modernity, relying on viewers' intertextual associations with current news media and periodical headlines rather than the dime novels and Wild West shows that constructed the "myth of the

West" as a historical fantasy. *Redskin*'s contemporary call for action requires a strong claim to the documentary realism of the social problem film. The scenes of Wing Foot at boarding school represent at once a recognition of Indigenous modernity and of the contemporary colonization of Native peoples. Rather than returning to a mythical time of national formation, *Redskin* comments on the conflicts generated in traditional and rural communities by the demands of Americanization.

After his separation from his father and grandmother, Wing Foot is taken to a residential school, with sequences shot in sepia-tinted monochrome. When introduced to his Pueblo monitor, Wing Foot tries to escape, but is stopped by the towering adults who hold the door shut—he is framed between the schoolteacher and the Indian agent, both dressed in light clothes that contrast with his dark ones. The agent reprimands Wing Foot for his antagonism toward the Pueblo students: "Young man, we'll have no tribal wars! Pueblo or Navajo—you're all equal here." The irony of this insistence on equality becomes apparent later in the film when Wing Foot encounters racism in an eastern college.

The parallel romances between the Indian agent and schoolteacher, and between Wing Foot and Corn Blossom, model romance that does not cross racial boundaries, but despite this avoidance of interracial romance in the plot, the filmmakers focus relentlessly on the management of Wing Foot's body through images of cross-racial touching and changes of costume. His introduction to boarding school life involves a series of scenes in which he is physically forced to change his appearance and body language to signal his submission and allegiance to symbols of white America. Although the schoolteacher had admired Wing Foot's necklace and herself wears a jacket made from Pendleton blankets (a displacement of Wing Foot's grandfather's traditional blanket), Wing Foot's second encounter with the coercive assimilation of the boarding school system is to be stripped of his traditional clothes and issued new ones. In the locker room a school official denigrates his clothes—"Now young feller, we'll change this Navajo junk for a nice suit o' blue denim"—and proceeds to wrestle the struggling Wing Foot into his new outfit; the image of the fight, with other boys watching from their shower area, fades to black. In the next scene, the children march out and line up for morning roll call and to salute the American flag, standing in military formation as the Indian agent, in military dress, inspects (see figure 2.19). When Wing Foot refuses to salute the flag, the Indian agent threatens to whip him and takes him away over the objections of the schoolteacher. Images of Wing Foot being forcibly stripped in the locker room and his subsequent whipping are hidden from the viewer, but they are implied by the initial scenes of struggle, followed by ellipses, an editing pattern

Figure 2.19. *Redskin*, Paramount (1929), Wing Foot is forced to salute the flag.

frequently used to depict sexual threat and rape in cinema. As in *The Vanishing American*, school buildings and school grounds become the stage for the revelation and recognition of the violence of assimilationist education. Yet this suppression of vision at the moment of physical trauma replicates another concealed moment of transformation (and of custodial transfer)—in before-and-after photographs of Native boarding school students—while at the same time effecting the audience's emotional engagement associated with visual surfeit. Later in the film, the adult Wing Foot eagerly salutes the flag (see figure 2.20), indicating his changed political allegiance as a result of his boarding school education. In *Redskin* and other Indian dramas, the unseen

Figure 2.20. *Redskin*, Paramount (1929), the adult Wing Foot (Richard Dix) eagerly salutes the flag.

violence of the educational "touch" has a counterpart in the film's depiction of excessive handling of Native men by their white teammates and coaches at college sports events (see figure 2.21). In the context of the appropriation of Indianness for team names and mascots, which largely dates from the early twentieth century, the cinematic scenes of touching in sympathetic Westerns represent a specific claim of custodial entitlement to the bodies and identities of Native youth. The more antagonistic version of physical encounter and touching-as-claiming that is shielded from view in the locker room scenes with younger children has the effect of escalating the pathos and emotional currency of the scene by asking viewers to imagine, thereby investing themselves more deeply in the events that take place off screen.

In *Redskin*, the scenario of cross-racial contact is not a gentle clasping of hands or a scene of domestic incorporation, but rather a violent assertion of custody in which a Native boy is forced by the hands of the Indian agent to align bodily with an institutional regime.[42] This moment of excessive force, left to the imagination of viewers, is one climax in the film's reformist agenda; the schoolteacher, Judith Stearns (Jane Novak), a figure resembling many of the women involved in federal Indian policy reform and "friends of the Indian" organizations in the 1920s, breaks off her engagement with the Indian agent Walton over the incident. Returning his ring, she says, "Love is greater than discipline. Until you realize that—until you acknowledge that you've wronged that boy—we must go separate ways." As in *The Vanishing American*, the trajectory of the romance plot is closely linked to

Figure 2.21. *Redskin*, Paramount (1929), after Wing Foot wins a footrace for Thorpe College.

the gendered trajectory of reform and assimilationist pedagogy. Unlike the "squaw man" cross-racial marriage plot that dominated early Indian dramas in which a cross-racial marriage is destroyed to enable a subsequent white, middle-class marriage, in *Redskin* a white marriage becomes dependent on a white man's acceptance of a white woman's Indian policy agenda—only progressive-thinking couples, aligned in their political work of benevolent custodial supervision in the colonized West, can successfully marry. This white settler family is still centrally at stake in the 1920s sympathetic Western form, which continues to represent Native and settler homes as distinct, competing domesticities and to represent reform as a consequence of white romance. The schoolteacher's stance of sympathy is here meant to proclaim her innocence rather than her complicity with the boarding school system, although of course she is a key actor in the staging of Wing Foot's education. As a figure of identification for white audience members, especially women, the schoolteacher demonstrates her social power through her negotiation of the two marriages, while her own incorruptibility releases audience members from a sense of moral culpability.

The violence of transferred custody conveyed by changing costumes is attributed to Native communities when boarding school students return to their reservations, both in earlier Indian dramas and in films from the 1920s. In Pickett's script treatments for *Redskin*, these scenes were to be a series of dissolves that would "show how Grey Eyes [Wing Foot's name in the original synopsis] is changed from a long-haired wild desert imp in tunic and blanket into a submissive over-alled [*sic*] student of Uncle Sam," and on his return from boarding school, the opposite: "Now we see Grey Eyes reverting to type. Once more he dons velveteen jumper and yucca fiber trousers. Instead of a collar he wears his mother's turquoise; instead of a leather belt, embossed silver plates. Once more his hair grows long."[43] Eschewing the sequence of dissolves, the filmmakers instead highlighted Richard Dix's dramatic costume changes through contrast and mise-en-scène, as in the tableau of his initial meeting with his father on returning from Thorpe University (see figure I.8 from the Introduction).

Corn Blossom's return from Thorpe University in Western clothes indicates visually her new assertiveness, coded as a non-Pueblo; when she refuses to marry Pueblo Jim, Jim and her father literally tear her clothes from her (see figure 2.22) and push her into an anteroom with a packet of traditional clothes, tearing her shirt in the process. Though the scene was included in the final film, it was one of the only moments considered censorable by Jason S. Joy, enforcing the Production Code Administration (PCA) codes in the Hays office, who objected to "the scene in which Corn

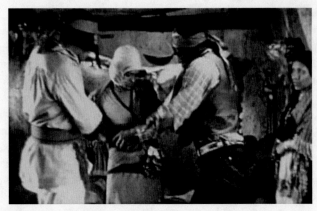

Figure 2.22. *Redskin*, Paramount (1929), Pueblo Jim (Noble Johnson) assaults Corn Blossom (Gladys Belmont).

Blossom, after having been roughly treated by her father and shoved into the hut to exchange her 'civilized' clothes for Indian raiment, half reclines on the bench and exposes her entire breast."[44] Pickett and Hubbard map onto southwest Pueblo and Diné communities a cinematically racialized vision in which costume changes render family members unrecognizable and in which the very picturesque qualities of traditional costuming that the filmmakers took such pains to replicate, including Pueblo olla jars and Diné silverwork, signify both the authenticity and suffering of its focal characters. The coerced return to traditional costuming heightens the pathos of the characters' tribulations and unbearable social dilemma, but complicates the film's reform agenda by presenting Native cultural traditionalism as inherently oppressive.

Yet the violence of the "scene of education" seems only to have reinforced powerful viewers' interest in the film as itself a site of public education because, despite the Hays office objection to actress Gladys Belmont's exposure included in the final cut, the film was selected for promotion as educational entertainment for youth and to showcase in Washington. In January 1929, James Martin Fisher prepared a Secretary's report for the review committee of the National Board of Review recommending *Redskin* for "special use" as a "junior matinee"; the campaign apparently included sending out 38,000 letters to organizations and schools to promote the film. Many letters were signed by New York Governor Milliken and sent to Catholic schools and priests in New York; some were signed by representatives of organizations such as the Daughters of the American Revolution and other New York and East Coast women's clubs. A special screening was arranged for Mrs. Jeannett Emrich, whom Paramount executives called "the most important Protestant church woman in the United States," at the Paramount theater in Los Angeles in order to garner her support for the film.

Both *The Vanishing American* and *Redskin* return in the end to the authority of their white interlocutors, asserting the necessity of government intervention—but a government intervention mediated through the institutionalized, transformative domesticity of white schoolteachers—to address government corruption. In the last scenes of *Redskin*, the two land speculators are apprehended, their crimes standing in for the larger issues of political mismanagement, while the system of wardship itself is preserved through the appointment of the well-intentioned and newly reformed Indian agent Walton as Oil Commissioner for the tribe. The threat to the tribe, then, is transposed from the government onto outsiders—in fact, the speculators become the justification for the continuation of government oversight. This continued emphasis on U.S. government supervision in the closing scenes of *Redskin* underscores Wing Foot's Americanization (he is brought into the fold of citizenship not just in his salute to the flag early in the film but also later in the film, when he files a homestead claim for his own tribal land), just as Nophaie was Americanized through his romance with Marion and his military service in *The Vanishing American*. The films' narrative closures repeat and extend the trajectories of their earlier scenes of Americanizing education. Although both Nophaie and Wing Foot became outlaws, wandering in the wilderness in a literal vision of extralegality and western vigilantism, they are each brought back into the system of U.S. legal custody—by way of military service or homesteading oil land—in ways that further ensure their absorption within the purview of U.S. citizenship. While *The Vanishing American* and *Redskin* challenge but ultimately reinforce custodial models of U.S.-Native relations, the 1928 film version of *Ramona* associates adoptive familial relationships with historical amnesia. *Ramona* appropriates the pathos of melodrama as a political, marketable tool to invert the moral order of the Western, assigning pacifism to tribal communities and unchecked violence to settler groups.

"No sign of recognition":[45] Edwin Carewe's *Ramona* (1928)

The 1928 *Ramona* was long thought lost until its 2010 rediscovery in the National Film Archive in the Czech Republic.[46] This version is unique among other film adaptations of Helen Hunt Jackson's 1884 novel about a displaced Native family in Southern California because it was made by the Chickasaw director Edwin Carewe—the first Native American director since James Young Deer and the first Native director of feature-length films—and starred the Mexican actress Dolores Del Rio. This critically and financially successful production of *Ramona* represents a rare and important moment of Chickasaw–Mexican presence and power within Hollywood's industrial star and studio systems. And unlike most of Carewe's films, which were on non-Indian subjects, *Ramona* is an Indian drama adapted from a well-known story: Jackson's novel was in its ninety-second printing in 1928, and film versions of the story had already been made by D. W. Griffith in 1910 and Donald Crisp in 1916. Carewe's visual interpretation of frontier race relations in *Ramona* expanded the scope of the sympathetic Western production cycle in the late 1920s, using generic forms of the Western in politicized ways to alter public perceptions of Native–settler relations. Appearing alongside the films about assimilation produced by Paramount in the mid- to late-1920s, the 1928 film version of *Ramona* tells another kind of story common to the Indian drama form, a story about "reversion" as its heroine comes to identify with her Native heritage over her wealthy Mexican-American adoptive upbringing.

Using his partnership with Del Rio and his creative control over production—he had his own production company at the time, Inspiration Pictures—Carewe renders Jackson's complex portrait of ethnic mixture to the screen as a frontier melodrama. He effectively anchors the story's emotional freight to a communicative spectacle around the action of land loss, marked in familial terms. The film's central scenes of removal and massacre repeat and reinterpret visual tropes of the Western and the configuration of frontier melodramas in order to shift the popular vision of Native history, lands, and families. Crucially, he reverses the dominant racial organization of such representations, realigning spectatorial identification by depicting a prosperous Native village uprooted by nomadic bands of white marauders. Unlike James Young Deer and Lillian St. Cyr's intervention in Hollywood's emergent Western genre scenarios, which involved changing structural plot elements (such as the Native characters' survival at the end of the story), Carewe maintains the tragic scenarios of the Indian drama and even amplifies visual representation of tragedy. My analysis of *Ramona* hinges on these detailed sequences, largely absent from the novel, in which conventional shots of the Western "Indian attack" are deployed in a reversed ethnic schema.[47] By emphasizing these sequences through techniques of camera movement and montage, Carewe wields the visual language of cinematic melodrama to invest the dispossessed with moral power. In *Ramona*, he fuses the women's sentimental melodrama, the social problem film, and Western genre visual discourses of spectacular violence. Given the extracinematic texts circulating in government documents and periodicals supporting federal Indian policy reforms in the late 1920s—the 1928 Meriam Report and essays in magazines such as *Harper's* and *Collier's*—Carewe's deployment and recombination of highly conventional Hollywood genres in a film that seems to support Indian policy reform necessitates a critical consideration of the extent to which he might have had a personal stake in the film's politics. Carewe's Chickasaw identity is important to my reading of *Ramona* within a biographical framework, and in a more expansive sense, attending to Carewe's deliberate *marketing* of his biography in relation to the film's content, combined with close analysis of the *Ramona's* images, compels a new critical account of the availability of generic forms for Indigenous projects in the commercial environment of 1920s Hollywood.

The story of Ramona, especially with its fully articulated backstory in Jackson's novel, is strongly connected to the "miscegenation" plots of nineteenth-century novels (*The Last of the Mohicans, Metamora*) and, as the previous chapter discussed, early cinema. The story embeds two generationally sequential "squaw man" plots. Ramona is the daughter of a Scottish father and a Native mother, adopted and kept ignorant of her heritage by her strict, wealthy Mexican aunt. In an interracial and cross-class love triangle, Ramona falls in love with Native laborer Alessandro (Warner Baxter), disappointing her smitten, aristocratic Mexican foster brother, Felipe (Roland Drew). After discovering her Native birth and heritage, Ramona elopes with Alessandro, but their child falls ill, and then dies when a white doctor refuses to treat the baby. White gold miners attack the couple and their Native community and expropriate their homes and land, leaving them destitute. Alessandro, traumatized, becomes prone to blackouts and is murdered after he steals a horse during an episode of memory loss. The despairing Ramona loses her own memory, but is found by Felipe, who marries her at the end of the film. Like *The Vanishing American* and *Redskin*, *Ramona* dramatizes social theories of racial progress and reversion, but in *Ramona*, these issues of assimilation and separatism are not represented through institutional and educational settings as they are in the Paramount films; rather, they take the form of familial amalgamation in the domestic sphere. For example, archived promotional stills from the film suggest its investment in images of Ramona's maternal attachment to her Native child (played by Edwin Carewe's daughter, Rita Carewe; see figures 2.23–2.24).[48]

Figure 2.23. *Ramona*, Inspiration Pictures (1928), Alessandro (Warner Baxter) and Ramona (Dolores Del Rio), promotional still (AMPAS).

Figure 2.24. *Ramona*, Inspiration Pictures (1928), Ramona with her child (Rita Carewe), promotional still (AMPAS).

The 1928 *Ramona* represents just one facet of the larger, ongoing staging of the Ramona story. The story had already accumulated massive cultural (and actual) capital by the late 1920s, having migrated across media from novel to stage to film in several versions. It was a story that, like other influential adaptations such as *The Squaw Man* and *Uncle Tom's Cabin*, both reproduced and altered melodramatic racial schema across media. Helen Hunt Jackson's literary and political accomplishments—her nonfiction work *A Century of Dishonor* (1881), her novel *Ramona* (1884), and her voluminous correspondence on Native issues with legislators and others—have received significant attention from literary historians.[49] Recent scholarship has also elucidated the broader parameters of the Ramona phenomenon as a myth-making narrative for Southern California that generated both substantial literary tourism and enduring performative legacies.[50] The story continues to be reproduced in regional spectacles such as the yearly Ramona pageant in Hemet, California, ongoing since 1923. Despite this breadth of work on Jackson and on *Ramona*, there has been a relative paucity of scholarship on the film adaptations, with the notable exception of Chon Noriega's compelling essay on D. W. Griffith's 1910 version starring Mary Pickford. Carewe's *Ramona* is the loosest of the cinematic adaptations of Jackson's novel, yet capitalizes on these earlier performative and cinematic legacies, pointing, for example, in its opening credit intertitle to Griffith's earlier film.[51]

The melodramatic plot device of amnesia marks Ramona's suppression of traumatic familial loss (the death of her baby and Alessandro). This vision and later amnesiac erasure of Ramona's Native family first summons and then ultimately separates her from that heritage, facilitating her assimilation through marriage into an upper-class, non-Native Spanish family (her subsequent marriage to Felipe). Beyond its function as a plot device, amnesia also provides a powerful metaphor for both the existence and the suppression of traumatic frontier history that is part of the cinematic rewriting of historical conquest as a narrative romance in film Westerns. The novel's extensive discussion of legal documentation regarding land titles and government bureaucracy, as well as the ubiquitous textual references to blood and genealogy, are excised in this film version. Instead, the melodramatic lost homes in the story—both the Moreno rancho and Alessandro's Native village—are the film's primary conduits between its own dramatic scenario and the context the 1920s policy reform. Scenes of violence and vigilantism replace these more abstract textual discussions, making visual spectacle bear their representational weight. The film's images of scarcity, natural abundance, and violence are all staples of the Western genre's concerns with colonial settlement, continental resources, and land ownership. In particular, the reverse-massacre scene at the center of the film's story provides a way of visualizing these issues in the language of film violence and action that is the cornerstone of the Western.

In both novel and film, Ramona's amnesia is manifested by her lack of reaction. Late in Jackson's novel, for instance, she shows "no sign of recognition" when she sees Felipe after his long search for her (340). The film's plot also emphasizes this narrative device: Alessandro's madness takes the form of temporary lapses of awareness and memory, while Ramona becomes limp and expressionless after Alessandro's murder. The melodramatic trick of coincidence brings Felipe back to Ramona just at the moment when she cannot recognize him. Yet this thematic emphasis on vacuous incomprehension is contradicted by the film's editing and cinematic language, in which reaction shots function as omnipresent "signs of recognition." Characters register visual spectacle and cue viewers' own emotions with reaction shots, a staple of continuity editing in classical narrative cinema. Carewe floods the screen with images of witnesses who visibly register or "recognize" the scene before them, and these shots insist that audiences acknowledge and remember the very events that drove the story's Native characters toward amnesia as a form of insanity. The Native characters' amnesia dramatizes the legal erasure of their land rights, detailing the impact of abstract laws on individual families through its melodramatic scenario.

Edwin Carewe and Dolores Del Rio

Edwin Carewe's staging and editing of *Ramona*, while unusual in its politics, clearly worked on a formal level within the parameters of Hollywood's representational practices. His career reveals the extent of Indigenous immersion in the film industry and melodramatic mode of the silent era. Indeed, his success in appropriating the dominant mode of melodrama as a storytelling form complicates critical interest in Native studies on comedic irony as a primary means of Indigenous resistance to imposed images of Indians in American cinema.[52] He directed more than 50 films between 1914 and 1934 for major and minor Hollywood production and distribution companies such as Rolfe-Metro, Paramount, First National, and United Artists, and he was an important director during the late 1920s "golden age" of silent film. He ran his own independent studio for a time and was a key person behind the early careers of stars such as Gary Cooper, Dolores Del Rio, Francis X. Bushman, Wallace Beery, and Warner Baxter. Yet his work is largely overlooked by critics in part because so few prints have survived, and no scholarship exists on the Fox brothers' work in Hollywood apart from passing references.[53] Given this lacuna, it is important to take stock of what is known about Carewe before engaging in a more detailed discussion of *Ramona* (see figure 2.25).

Carewe was not avant-garde. Drawing on his extensive experience as an actor and later director, he was thoroughly adept at wielding the conventional dramatic idioms of the American stage and cinema. He was integrated into a well-developed, profitable system of industrial film production in 1920s Los Angeles. And like other directors and producers of the silent era, he was also an experienced global traveler, shooting scenes from *A Son of the Sahara* (1924) on location in Algiers and petitioning Queen Marie of Romania to perform in his 1927 film adaptation of Tolstoy's novel *Resurrection*.[54] In 1927 he merged his own production company, Inspiration Pictures, with Tec-Art and shot films on a lot on Melrose Avenue across from Paramount.[55] His film about the Alaskan gold rush, *The Spoilers* (1929), with its spectacular climactic fistfight scene, helped bring Gary Cooper to

Figure 2.25. Edwin Carewe.

early prominence. His best-known and most lucrative films, from the height of his career in the late 1920s, include *Resurrection* in 1927 (made with Tolstoy's son Ilya Tolstoy), *Revenge* and *Ramona* in 1928, and a version of Longfellow's *Evangeline* in 1929, all starring Del Rio.

Carewe was born Jay J. Fox in Gainesville, Texas, in 1883. He and his brothers, Wallace and Finis, along with their father, Frank M. Fox, are named and identified as Chickasaw on the 1907 "Final Rolls of the Citizens and Freedmen of the Five Civilized Tribes of the Indian Territory," or Dawes Rolls.[56] Although he replaced his birth name with a stage name, Carewe continued to identify as a Chickasaw after leaving home and throughout his Hollywood career. He was profiled in *Who's Who among Oklahoma Indians* in 1927 and in the Indian Council Fires–sponsored book *Indians of Today* in 1936, where his biography appeared alongside other Native professionals and public figures such as Gertrude Bonnin/Zitkala-Sa (Dakota), Charles Eastman (Dakota), Mourning Dove (Okanogan), Molly Spotted Elk (Penobscot), and Jim Thorpe (Sac and Fox).[57] The descriptions of Carewe in that profile and in other sources suggest that he was a forceful personality. Quotations from the author reveal an assertive individualist philosophy: "Show me a man of strong opinions, and I'll show you a man with good ideas . . . conflict is the essence of drama, and a difference of opinion makes conflict." He advises that "There is no substitute for experience" (*Indians of Today* 29). Kevin Brownlow sketches Carewe's background, emphasizing his Chickasaw identity, in these few sentences from *The War, The West, and the Wilderness*, where he also calls Carewe a "director of great importance":

> He was a quarter Chickasaw, his maternal grandfather being the daughter of Chief Tabuscabano. Carewe was proud of his colorful youth among the tepees; he had been expelled from four schools in less than a year, he ran away from home, punched cattle, and wandered the West as a hobo with Jack London. . . . His father, F. M. Fox, loaned the family's precious Indian relics from his ranch at Corpus Christi, Texas, for use in Carewe's Western *The Trail of the Shadow* (1917). (334)[58]

Brownlow's account resembles Carewe's profile in Carolyn Lowrey's 1920 book *The First One Hundred Noted Men and Women of the Screen*, suggesting the consistency of Carewe's public image: ". . . he comes of mixed New England and Indian stock, being a quarter-blood Chickasaw Indian, regularly receiving compensation from the government for the sale of lands inherited from his maternal grandmother, the daughter of Chief Tabuscabano of the

Chickasaws. 'Big Chief' Carewe spent his childhood among the tepees of the Indians and believes he owes his robust health to the outdoor life of the red man" (32). While Lowrey asserts that "One of [Carewe's] chief aims—it amounts to a fad—is to stand solely on the foundation he himself has laid" (32), he frequently enlisted the help of both of his brothers—but especially his older brother, writer Finis Fox—on his productions. Lowrey's profile typifies the contradictory representation of Carewe in various media and publications, where he is depicted as both an independent, self-made man and simultaneously embedded in (and distinguished by) his Chickasaw family and genealogy. He occupied this middle space in Hollywood as well, where he not only directed films for established studios in the 1920s, but also ran his own independent studio. Thus steeped in Hollywood production systems, industry marketing practices, and aesthetic style, he was nevertheless an independent operator, orchestrating his own studio and troupe of actors and writers. Experienced, savvy, and well-connected, he could and did exert an extraordinary amount of autonomy and creative control in shaping his late 1920s films.

After beginning film work for the Lubin Film Company in 1914, Carewe often collaborated on productions with his brothers, producer/director Wallace Fox and screenwriter Finis Fox. In his essay "Directorial Training" from the 1927 book *Breaking into the Movies*, Carewe represents himself as a self-made man who benefited from both experiential training in theater (rather than formal schooling) and professional relationships with his family members. "In all my best pictures," he writes, "I have had the capable cooperation of my brother, Finis Fox, the scenarist. He was my closest collaborator in the production of *Resurrection*. . . . We have worked in similar relationship on my current screen drama *Ramona*. . . ." He goes on to assert that what makes the film industry unique is that "directors have risen from the lowest ranks of the profession. And they have come from all walks of life" (Carewe 189; see figure 2.26). Accounts of Carewe's life suggest that he lived this story; having been a runaway, tramp, and itinerant actor, he worked steadily in Hollywood through the late 1910s and the 1920s, and he was an established insider by the mid-1920s. Richard Koszarski calls Carewe's 1920s literary adaptations "ponderous" and "ill advised" (186), but these films were quite successful financially. Carewe's earnings from his films with Del Rio, particularly *Resurrection* and *Ramona*, made him a millionaire; *Ramona* alone grossed $1,500,000 (Walker 82).[59] However, Carewe quickly lost his fortune to bad investments during the economic crash of 1929 and by 1930 could no longer honor his previous contracts with performers.[60] His Hollywood career had peaked in the late 1920s; neither he nor Del Rio

Figure 2.26. Finis Fox.

achieved the same success in the United States after the transition to sound, although Del Rio continued to work in Hollywood in the 1930s and in the decades after, and went on to a long and acclaimed career in Mexico. Carewe worked with Finis Fox on his final production, the 1934 message film about censorship, *Are We Civilized?*, which was shown nationally but produced little revenue. He retired in 1934 and died in Hollywood in 1940 at age 56. Wallace Fox's work as a director of serials took off shortly after Carewe's and Finis Fox's careers faltered during Hollywood's transition to sound. He continued to write, direct, and produce low-budget films and, later, television shows—including episodes of *The Range Rider* and *The Gene Autry Show*—through the mid-1950s. Taken together, the Fox brothers' careers writing and directing films in Hollywood spanned 40 years, from Edwin Carewe's directorial debut in 1914 to Wallace Fox's last film in 1954—four decades of continuous Chickasaw presence at the height of the studio era in American cinema.

What I wish to emphasize about Carewe's image as a Hollywood entrepreneur is that he retained his Chickasaw affiliation while working in an industry that most often produced representations of Indigenous erasure. This complex negotiation of industrial production and representational practices has been important to a range of Native actors in Hollywood including performers such as Minnie Ha Ha, Molly Spotted Elk, Victor Daniels, and Jay Silverheels.[61] Carewe's own marketing strategies point to the significance of his tribal identity to his film work: he highlighted his tribal heritage, for example, when promoting *Ramona* in 1928. The *New York Times* reported (lifting the material directly from the Press Book for *Ramona* distributed by the studio):

> Edwin Carewe is himself a Chickasaw Indian, so that unusual interest attaches to any film produced by him and concerned with an Indian theme. "Chulla" is the name that was given to Mr. Carewe as a baby and this, according to the director, means "Fox." His brother, Finis Fox, retains the original name, altered by Mr. Carewe when he became a stage actor in Kansas twenty-six years ago. . . . According to Mr. Carewe, his Indian father was a full-blooded Chickasaw and the representative at Washington, D.C., of the Chickasaw reservation.[62]

Given his background, Carewe would have been attuned to the effects of the Dawes Act, the Indian Citizenship Act of 1924, and the Indian policy reform movement of the 1920s due to his upbringing in southern Oklahoma and northern Texas during a particularly turbulent time in Chickasaw tribal history. His and his family's immersion in the events of this period resonate with the politics of settlement in his screen adaptation of Jackson's *Ramona*.

When Carewe was born in the 1880s, economic development and urbanization had begun to emerge in the wake of railroads and large numbers of settlers on tribal lands. Between 1893, when Congress applied the Dawes Act to the Cherokee, Choctaw, Muscogee (Creek), Chickasaw, and Seminole, and 1907, when the Indian Territory was fused with the Oklahoma Territory to form the new state of Oklahoma, the U.S. government worked to liquidate the tribal estates and governments of the Chickasaws and other tribes in the semiautonomous Indian Territory. This process involved the conversion of collective lands to individually owned allotments and the final determining of tribal citizenship via the fiercely contested "Final Rolls of the Citizens and Freedmen of the Five Civilized Tribes of the Indian Territory," on which Carewe is listed by his birth name.[63] The

General Allotment Act of 1887, or the Dawes Act, which some scholars have argued that Helen Hunt Jackson's *Ramona* had helped to pass in Congress, was under pressure in the late 1920s.[64] In light of the massive changes in land ownership, tribal sovereignty, and government purview in the Indian Territory and Oklahoma Territory at the turn of the century when Carewe was coming of age, and in light of the return to vexing issues of Indian policy in the national political scene in the late 1920s, it is hard not to read an embedded response in the dramatizations of expropriation from Carewe's most accomplished films from these years. Because of his own self-positioning in his marketing of *Ramona*, Carewe invites viewers to see the film in terms of his potential identification with the story and indeed in terms of his casting and organization of Del Rio's performance as well.

Carewe's achievements were partly due to his skilled manipulation of the established star system, and he is most remembered in film history for his cultivation of Del Rio as a screen star. Del Rio's Mexican nationality and the story of her "discovery" in Mexico City were an important part of her public image. The Press Book for *Ramona* included several articles connecting Del Rio's background with the character of Ramona, such as her use of family heirloom dresses and jewelry for Ramona's costumes. These claims to realism in casting and costume reveal the film as a vehicle for Del Rio. The story, repeated in most popular and scholarly studies, is that Carewe first met Del Rio with her then-husband Jaime Del Rio in 1925 while Carewe was in Mexico City with his fiancée, actress Mary Aiken. The Del Rios were part of the wealthy Mexican elite, and Dolores often performed the tango or other dances at society events, including the party where she met Carewe. This public narrative is worth noting here because Carewe transformed Helen Hunt Jackson's shy Ramona into a more playful and performative character in order to take advantage of Del Rio's dancing ability, essentially recreating on screen the story of this scene of his first encounter with her in Mexico City. Del Rio's Ramona performs a dance early on in the film, and this dance becomes the trigger that restores her memory—and enables her reintegration into upper-class, non-Native Californio society—in the film's closing scene. The dance also helped to justify the film's incorporation of music and song: Mary Beltrán calls *Ramona* a partial talkie that was actually a musical, with its Movietone musical score that "marked Del Rio's singing debut" (65).[65] Once in Hollywood, Del Rio was closely managed by Carewe, who was also directing her in multiple films.[66] Her image as a wealthy, glamorous figure was constructed through careful handling of her appearance, wardrobe and contact with the press, as well as through fan magazines and other texts. Del Rio herself wanted her on-screen and publicity images to change American stereotypes about Mexicans and to "show the best that's in my nation" (59).

Carewe's organization of Del Rio's early career involved marketing her as an ethnically versatile, thoroughly modern, aristocratic star, and simultaneously as an actress uniquely aligned genealogically with the character of Ramona. In the late 1920s stars like Del Rio had opportunities to play a wide range of ethnic roles (her portrayal of the mixed-blood Ramona was sandwiched between other roles as a Russian peasant and an Acadian emigrant). Her choices narrowed with the transition to sound as risk-averse studios began to typecast Latina and Latino actors based on their accents. *Ramona*, however, hovered at the cusp of that technological shift, and Del Rio's heritage worked to her advantage in the film. She clearly provided what reviewers perceived as a kind of racial authenticity in her performance of Ramona. Yet precisely because she also remained racially unstable as both a character and a star persona, Del Rio's performance "facilitates *emotional* moments of universal identification," as Chon Noriega argues that Helen Hunt Jackson's character Ramona does for female readers (209; emphasis in original).

Joanne Hershfield, in her study of Del Rio's career, contends that reviewers conflated "Mexicanness" and "Indianness" in their approval of Del Rio as a "fitting person to impersonate the Indian-blooded Ramona" (in later U.S. roles, she performed the part of "an Indian woman" opposite Henry Fonda in John Ford's 1947 *The Fugitive*, and the Kiowa mother of Pacer Burton [Elvis Presley] in Don Siegel's 1960 film *Flaming Star*).[67] The *New York Times* reported that Del Rio was "an excellent choice to play Ramona" and that "This is the first time in her brief but rapid screen career that Miss Del Rio has portrayed a character at least partly parallel in heritage to her own nationality." Carewe frequently asserted that "Dolores Del Rio, in my mind, could not act Ramona. She was simply Ramona herself—with that quaint Latin temperament—the high culture—all that Helen Hunt Jackson pictured in the pages of her volume."[68] A *Variety* review concluded that although the film was filled with "drab tragedies," "*Ramona* will make money" because of its valuable "tie-ups" in the popular novel and hit song (the ballad "Ramona," sung by Del Rio).[69] The *Variety* reviewer also complains of "closeups as numerous as deaths in the picture."[70] These close-ups, which exclude the exotic costumes and settings that mark Ramona's Native ethnicity in order to focus on her face, encourage viewers to access and identify with Ramona's emotional sensations of fulfillment and loss while situating that identification in the larger narrative and visual context of cross-racial fantasy.

Ramona's Gaze

Carewe's *Ramona* is structured by an extensive web of visual observation: from Señora Moreno's punitive, investigative gaze; to the exchange of desiring looks between Felipe, Ramona, and Alessandro; to the witnessed scenes that produce trauma, madness, catatonia, and amnesia in Ramona and Alessandro.[71] This frequent dependency on embedded viewers—characters whose gaze we see, and then adopt, through the cinematic grammar of shot-reverse-shot and inserted reaction shots—organize filmic action around characters' visual apprehension using continuity style. This strategy of manipulating diegetic, desiring gazes and lines of sight to construct a cinematic drama of heterosexual romance is among the most common techniques in classical Hollywood narrative film. Here, for example, Alessandro falls in love with Ramona when he spies her doing her washing at a stream; during their later romantic tryst, Señora Moreno finds them and reacts censoriously to seeing the kiss that is evidence of their relationship. In *Ramona*, however, this customary visual structure also conveys the characters' investment in surveillance and visually parsing the ethnic and class identification of Native tribes and Californio elite. This is especially significant in Ramona and Alessandro's case because they comprise a nomadic-yet-land-based racial group, destabilized by colonial settlement and with tenuous connections to rancho culture. Furthermore, the film presents Ramona and Alessandro as uniquely positioned eyewitnesses of atrocity. Caught between the old (Mexican) and new (American) orders of colonization in the historical context of occupation, the Native couple's melodramatic tribulations and agency of vision bear the burden of the film's political focus on transfers of land title, inherited wealth, and Native mobility and immobility. Scenes of witnessing, in particular, accentuate Carewe's reversal of the Western genre's construction of Native aggression in order to refocus audience identification and vest moral power with the Native characters.

The scenes introducing Ramona and Alessandro emphasize both their agency (cued by images of mobility, visual acuity, and emotional expressiveness) and their unstable positions in relation to shifting colonial hierarchies. The film's opening shots of Franciscan priests and devout worshipers (both Native and Spanish) are juxtaposed with images of white settlers panning for gold—and finding it. After introducing the Moreno hacienda in the Southern California mountains with establishing shots, the film follows Señora Moreno (Vera Lewis) as she seeks Ramona in the kitchens. The servant Marda (Mathilde Comont) denies that she's seen Ramona, but after Señora Moreno leaves she looks through a window, where we follow her gaze to find a comedic, even slapstick scene in which Ramona rides and falls from a donkey with Felipe following behind. Carewe returns to this strategy repeatedly in the film: the audience sees through the mediating trope of the embodied viewer (here Marda), who cues us with her reactions (here uproarious laughter, in deliberate contrast to the dour Señora Moreno). Del Rio's Ramona is far more kinetic, playful in her cutoff pants and work shirt, than Helen Hunt Jackson's timid and serious girl, forever bent over her embroidery. Caught by her foster mother Señora Moreno, Ramona is sent to her room as punishment, her ill-treatment underscored by a shot of her weeping figure behind the imprisoning bars of her window.

After the opening view of Ramona in her tomboyish pants and shirt, later scenes show her in expensive, frilly dresses. Her comments, however, more closely associate her with servants, emphasizing her fragile tenancy in the main house. Following the scenes introducing the dynamics of the Moreno household, the film moves to a montage of the Moreno family's vast herd of sheep and their open-air shearing sheds and runs. Señora Moreno's management of this hacienda business and labor is juxtaposed with images of upper-class leisure—Ramona in a ruffled dress feeding parrots, Felipe playing his guitar. Ramona dances for him, a circle of servants quickly gathers, and Ramona is then replaced by the heavyset Marda as the central dancer. This invitation to compare Marda and Ramona, initially established through the metonymic connection of the earlier shot-reverse-shot introductory sequence, recurs in a later scene when Ramona discovers her Native ancestry and shares her news: "Marda, have you heard? I'm an Indian woman!" Ramona's visual and narrative alignment with Marda constructs a race-class continuum of Indianness from Marda's coarse servant-class to Ramona's innate nobility. Carewe, an experienced showman, wields long-standing stereotypes here by evoking what Rayna Green has described as a "squaw/princess" image paradigm based on sexual appeal.[72] In this case, however, we understand Ramona's position in the Moreno household to be unstable, vacillating between a lady and servant, Spanish and Native, daughter and outsider. Alessandro's position vis-à-vis the ranch becomes similarly destabilized when he falls in love with Ramona and begins to loiter near the domestic sphere of the house to watch her when he should be working in the sheep shearing runs.

The next scenes introduce Alessandro's tribe, all on horseback at a full gallop toward the Moreno house as if they were warriors and marauders rather than the peaceful working shepherds and families described in the novel. The effect is augmented by juxtaposition with the arrival of the elderly Franciscan priest Father Salvierderra (John T. Prince) on foot and greeted by Ramona.[73] The high-angle extreme long-shots and low-angle long-shots of bare-chested men riding toward the camera reveal Carewe's turn toward cinematic Western as a visual and generic resource for the story's adaptation. A medium-shot of Alessandro is captioned by the intertitle "Alessandro, the leader of the shearers. A son of the last Chief of Jemecul Indians." This phrasing alludes to both Alessandro's inherited nobility and its impending closure, foregrounding the past and future of his genetic lineage in the intertitle's textual captioning.

Alessandro is introduced wearing a Navajo silver necklace and beaded headband; later, however, when he and Ramona have established their own small household, he wears denim pants and a work shirt, while she wears a dress with traditional Mexican Indigenous embroidery as she works in their kitchen (a costuming choice that is vaguely suggestive of her trajectory of "reversion" as she chooses her Native roots over her adopted Spanish family). This range of costuming contributes to the film's theatrical feel and suggests a somewhat scattershot approach to regional authenticity that is reflected also in the mix of adobe houses and tipis in Alessandro's village.[74] The way the film situates its primary characters through their costumes and the backdrop of the Southern California architecture and scenery indicates the characters' embeddedness and then dispossession from the Moreno hacienda and their village on traditional lands, issues that are manifest in the film's visual grammar as well.

The largely immobile camera supports the film's narrative and thematic focus on Indian mobility and immobility, landedness and landlessness, forced movement and imprisonment. The alternately coerced and restricted mobility of the Native couple Alessandro and Ramona is mirrored in the lack of camera movement (with a few notable exceptions, including the massacre scene) and the emphasis on the mission-style mise-en-scène and Southern California mountains (although some of the sheep shearing scenes were actually shot in southern Utah). Reinforcing the sense of imprisonment, cages and bars are everywhere in the Moreno household. Shots of Ramona caring for her parrots, with a small cage prominently featured, emphasize her isolated and precarious status in the domestic space. Carewe telescopes the extended forbidden courtship between Ramona and Alessandro in Jackson's novel to two brief scenes, one in which Ramona's window bars separate Alessandro from Ramona while he courts her with flowers and a nighttime tryst when they are caught by the Señora Moreno.[75] The immobility suggested by the film's still camera and editing pattern is augmented by these numerous medium-shots and close-ups of Ramona behind the hacienda's window bars, as well as by Del Rio's performative interpretation of Ramona's amnesia as a kind of trancelike physical stasis or catatonia. The bars further visualize the dysfunctional foster relationship between Ramona and the controlling Señora Moreno that is important to the novel's backstory. These shots are juxtaposed with playful moments between Ramona and Felipe that contrast with her traumatized immobility later in the film.

The film establishes a clear connection between colonial appropriation, tribal resources, and the coercive movement or restriction of tribal groups. *Ramona* is a story that hinges on preexisting treasure, slowly unveiling the backstory of that treasure to implicate older and newer orders of imperialism and resource extraction based on ownership of gold and land. Ramona's title to both, and the machination of her exclusion from that title, is central to the film's most dynamic scenes. Though without blood relatives of her own and living under the foster care of her mean-spirited adoptive aunt, Ramona has title to two kinds of wealth: Spanish treasure and tribal land (on which gold has been found). Land-based plenitude suffuses the film's images of mining and herding—there is gold in the streams and sheep in the fields. In fact, the film's scenes of domestic harmony and economic well-being, as well as loss, are important in part because they are so different from the unremitting poverty presented in *Redskin* and *The Vanishing American*; for a time, we believe that Alsessandro and Ramona could be economically successful herders if left alone by settlers. (Just as explicit is the film's presentation of Southern California's scenery and Spanish mission architecture as the basis for a commercially viable heritage industry. The staginess suggests the constructed set of the tourist attraction, and in fact Southern California was full of such establishments developed to draw tourist dollars and boost local real estate. The film's themes and images draw from and augment the larger regional boosterism made possible by the Ramona phenomenon, motivating travel to the sites that the film itself imagines as emblematic of processes of Native confinement.)

In addition to the sheep shearing montage at film's opening that underscores land-based wealth, one of the film's only indoor tracking shots takes place during the scene in which Señora Moreno reveals to Ramona the chest of jewels she will inherit if she refrains from marrying Alessandro. The camera follows first the chest of treasure that Señora Moreno drags from a closet, then a smaller jeweled box, in a marked departure from the film's primary visual organization around human action in the rest of the film. These stylistically dynamic sequences depicting natural abundance and New World treasures connect visual movement through space through cinematography and editing to the film's larger narrative of Native forced migration and settler land acquisition.

The film's alignment of a stylistic and narrative "reformist gaze" is produced most powerfully late in the film (in reel four), the miner's attack on the Native village. This sequence combines fast-paced tracking shots, including shots of the posse riding toward the retreating camera and shots that track alongside the riders as they shoot down the villagers (who have neither horses nor guns). In this sequence, Carewe abandons the lingering close-ups, which connected viewers to the emotions of characters in a love triangle, in favor of medium-shots and long-shots. In a series of shot-reverse-shots, Native characters—the couple Alessandro and Ramona—witness the destruction of their idyllic home and the massacre of their community by non-Native attackers. This scene exemplifies the way the 1920s Indian reform dramas functioned as a cinema of witness within Western generic frameworks. By devoting significant screen time and production value to the spectacle of horrors in this "reverse massacre" and by emphasizing through reaction shots its intermediary witnesses (Ramona and Alessandro), Carewe formally reproduces but ethnically realigns the stylistic language of extended "Indian massacre" scenes that anchored films such as Maurice Tourneur's 1920 *The Last of the Mohicans* (with its 9-minute sequence detailing the slaughter of white settlers by Huron warriors) and Griffith's 1913 *The Battle of Elderbush Gulch*.[76] Although initially we see the posse from an omniscient point of view, and while some shots are from the miners' perspectives (such as the first view, in iris and in long-shot, of the peaceful village), midway through the 4.5-minute sequence we adopt Ramona's view of the disaster from her position nearby the village. She and Alessandro then become surrogate viewers for the audience, and the shot sequence becomes triangulated among the villagers, the posse, and the couple as a third agent from their location of witness.

Carewe deploys the idiom of the Western genre massacre, but instead of Native warriors, the white attackers gallop in a circle around a house to hem it in and shoot down villagers in the fields and roads, men and women praying for mercy, mothers and babies in flight, and those helping the wounded. Made in the wake of Eisenstein's innovations in montage in 1925 with *Battleship Potemkin*, Carewe's *Ramona* makes sophisticated use of fast montage and continuity editing to escalate the emotional impact of violent action by cutting on movement and by using shot-reverse-shot, reaction shots, and variations in angle, movement, and rhythm. Initially, shots from a stationary camera show unarmed villagers being mowed down by pistol fire as the posse gallops past them. Midway through the scene, however, this static camera gives way to dynamic tracking shots, both from the point of view of the shooters, showing the Indian villagers as they are shot and fall, and from the reverse angle depicting the posse as they ride forward through the town.

Interspersed with these mobile shots are longer takes of individuals. Carewe slows forward action, pausing for longer shot-counter-shot duration to isolate particular dynamics in more detail. As a young couple is shot by one of the posse, we see the man's bloody collapse, and the woman crossing herself before she is shot, praying and kissing her statue of a saint as she falls. The camera cuts on action between the couple as they fall and reverse-shots of the shooter on horseback. Additional shots of individual members of the posse firing their pistols are also intercut with villagers fleeing the massacre. One shot sequence depicts a woman falling from gunfire as she runs up a nearby hill slope carrying a baby in a cradleboard on her back. Close-ups of the baby in the cradleboard, still attached to the fallen mother, are intercut with the shooter firing additional shots (the mother here is played by Augustina Lopez, who also played Wing Foot's grandmother in *Redskin*). The deaths of a man helping one of the wounded, and an elderly woman holding a child in her arms, are filmed in the same way. These constructions, emphasizing the supplication, relational bonds, and religious devotion of the unarmed Native villagers expertly wield the visual formulations that establish the suffering of innocents and the culpability of the dominant in visual spectacles of Western genre frontier violence and especially the "Indian attack." But the visual grammar of moral feeling, or what Jane Gaines has called the "logic of the heart," typically assigns images of distress to besieged white settlers surrounded by Indian attackers—even in such overtly sympathetic Westerns as *The Vanishing American* and Tourneur's *The Last of the Mohicans*. These two films elaborately acknowledge Native grievances, yet their Native characters retain a singular capacity for violence. In *Ramona*, not only is the moral legitimacy of nonviolence located with the Native villagers, but the discursive, testimonial power of witnessing the massacre is also vested in Alessandro and Ramona.

These dynamic, formulaic shot sequences making up the massacre scene deploy continuity editing constructions to clearly separate perpetrators from victims, rarely depicting them in the same frame. However, in the next sequence, moving from the disaster at the village to the more individual and emotional story of the destruction of Ramona's home, Carewe uses reaction shots to complicate visual access to the action, integrating Alessandro and Ramona as witnesses with whom viewers identify. In a series of eyeline matches, we see Ramona and Alessandro watch the massacre in horror from their house near the village. This pattern—iris shots of destroyed homes and Ramona and Alessandro's reaction shots—is then immediately repeated after the posse leave the village and ride to Ramona and Alessandro's home. After the couple has fled their home, they watch again from a farther vantage point as the posse set fire to their house and take their sheep, cows, and horses. The stylistic orientation of the camera moves from omniscient view (the initial iris shot opening the massacre sequence) to the embodied point of view of Alessandro and Ramona as focal characters for audience identification, despite the increasing distance of these witnesses from the scene as they retreat. Troubling the clarity of vision established in these scenes, Carewe punctuates the violence throughout the massacre sequence with smoke effects from the pistols, often using backlighting to brighten the clouds of smoke or using the smoke to soften the late afternoon light and cast confusion over the village under attack. These effects are later magnified, reaching a more expressionistic mode when the posse set the village homes and then Ramona's home on fire, and the screen fills with billowing smoke and flames. The smoke effects here, and in Carewe's film *Evangeline,* are comparable to parts of the lynching scene from Oscar Micheaux's 1920 film *Within Our Gates* in their disorienting, aesthetically abstract vision, a vision that reorganizes established tropes of unchecked vigilantism and racial violence.

Carewe and Finis Fox's sequencing in the second half of the film bracket the central action of the massacre between the deaths of individual members of Ramona's family: her child and Alessandro. The illness and death of Ramona's child is connected metonymically to the Western genre vigilante violence that immediately follows it, positioning losses within the domestic unit in the context of the destruction of the larger tribal community and village land. This sequence is set off by preceding images of domestic health and economic prosperity—Ramona tends to her child in the kitchen, then joins Alessandro on their porch where, in a series of eyeline matches, they look with satisfaction at their herds of sheep, cows, and horses.

The extended massacre scene and the destruction of Alessandro and Ramona's home are immediately followed by another sequence depicting the shooting of Alessandro in front of his mountain cabin with Ramona hearing the shots from the nearby stream. This further reduplication of racial violence on the more intimate scale of the individual home brings the pressure of the film's historical sweep to bear on Ramona, underpinning her extended reaction in histrionic performative mode as she flees the scene in distress through a landscape suddenly turned hostile (grasses and thorny vines have become overgrown and entrap her). This moment is adapted from Jackson's novel and reproduces, more generally, the melodramatic torment of heroines from Eliza's flight in *Uncle Tom's Cabin* to Lillian Gish's portrayal of

Anna Moore, cast out in a snowstorm, in Griffith's *Way Down East* (1920). Carewe himself returns to this trope in *Evangeline*, where Del Rio depicts the title character lost in a torrential storm in Louisiana.

Ramona's structural nesting—the pivotal, extended massacre scene bookended by familial deaths and organized around Ramona's vision—points to the larger historiographic work of this film adaptation. Through the witnessing and then amnesiac figure of Ramona, the film "observes" and remembers events that were forgotten in the public history and ongoing treatment of California's Indigenous peoples. The film's first images of Ramona with Felipe—and images of her dancing—are repeated at the end in flashback as Felipe tries to restore her memory. Ramona's suggested emergence from her amnesia through selective memories of her upper-class, non-Indian upbringing with Felipe provides narrative closure, but only by eliding Ramona's memory of the formation and destruction of her Indian family, thus containing that history as a detached element of the past. In Jackson's novel, crucial action hinges on the status of land deeds and titles—various legal papers are issued, signed, obtained, missing, nullified, lost, or cancelled, often involving the lawyers in distant San Francisco. Unlike these allusions to mediating historical documents and unlike the emphasis on the figure of the white schoolteacher as intermediary in films such as *The Vanishing American* and *Redskin*, in Carewe's film Ramona herself is the direct witness to violent dispossession. The historical events she sees are "written" through her vision of them, which in turn comprise the cinematic spectacle of the film. Carewe's film, then, comments upon the unstable place of historical trauma in the sympathetic Western, and Ramona's amnesia evinces the larger potential for Indigenous invisibility in public memory of frontier violence and settler land acquisition. The narrative of forgetting alludes to processes of excising historical records that is part of the work of Hollywood Westerns. Amnesia complicates the film's (and the novel's) reform agenda, an agenda that insistently reminds readers and viewers of established prior land rights that colonizers wish to forget.

Carewe's organization of climactic cinematic action around the representation of violence and community disruption was not unique to his adaptation of *Ramona*—visual tropes of removal are mobile across Carewe's films in the late 1920s. He relied on similar melodramatic forms and histrionic performances in central scenes from his 1929 film *Evangeline* that demonstrate both Carewe's representational strategies beyond the Indian drama and also the potential for reading his broader oeuvre with his Oklahoma experiences and Chickasaw heritage in mind. For example, in *Evangeline*, a film based on the Longfellow poem about the Acadian migration to Louisiana, the effectively rendered chaos in scenes of family separation and forced migration evokes parallels with historical Indigenous displacement and his 1930 film *The Spoilers* situates lawless frontier violence in the context of systematic corruption in the Alaskan gold rush.

My intention in this section has been to bring the 1928 *Ramona* to greater visibility in order to foreground Native American work in the heart of the film industry at this historical juncture. Carewe deliberately foregrounded his Chickasaw identity in marketing *Ramona*, a communication strategy that also supports closer scrutiny of his depictions of land loss and dispossession in this and other Carewe films from this time. His realignment of generic forms of the sympathetic Western, in particular, expands our understanding of Native cinema to include the language of Hollywood melodrama. He brought these Western genre codes to bear on a cinematic adaptation of a reformist text during a time of intense pressure on Indian policy and a small production cycle of reform-oriented Indian dramas. Adapting a non-Native policy reformer's novel to the screen from a distinctive Chickasaw perspective, Carewe used the story of Ramona to exercise a political voice in the 1920s public imaginary and to make space for his ongoing film work in Southern California.

Redskin and the Politics of Restoration

The Western has been widely understood in terms of structural oppositions that produce and reproduce cultural categories. But in the sympathetic Westerns that depict contemporary social problems on Native lands and reservations, representations of assimilation and amalgamation destabilize this internally constitutive generic boundary-making. In these films, produced within the studio system, the "problem" of misidentification and misrecognition signals the potential collapse of political and racial categories—a cinematic illegibility in the "Indian affairs" of the Western. The discourses of assimilation embedded in policies such as the General Allotment Act of 1887, the Indian Citizenship Act of 1924, and the boarding schools, were premised on ideas of equality but instead reproduced race-based economic divisions, a contradiction explored by a wide range of sympathetic Westerns in the 1920s. In particular, scenes of frontier dispossession and spaces of institutional pedagogy dramatize government processes of education and U.S. citizenship comprised of systemic violence. Scenes in which Native youth are handled and forcibly transformed by white teachers and government agents act out in literal and bodily ways the legal custodial transfers and political redefinition of Native nations as wards of the government. The Paramount films *The Vanishing American* and *Redskin* imagine Indigenous experiences of assimilation and familial rupture in ways that are mystified and occluded in the before-and-after photographs of boarding school students, yet in other ways the films draw on the same domestic ideologies of imperialism that underpin these photographic sequences. The post–World War I iterations of the Indian drama articulated a limited reform agenda within the dominant system of industrial production. Through the production of sympathetic Westerns in the 1920s, studios furthered the cause of policy reform at the national level, yet their process of restaging functioned within the parameters of melodrama, revealing the traction of this dramatic form and its potential for complex and contested representations. Edwin Carewe's version of *Ramona* provides a case study and a window into the work of a Native director embedded in the silent-era studio system; it is a film in which Hollywood genres are made to speak to public discourses of Indian policy reform, extending the reach of this "social problem" iteration of the Western. Carewe's *Ramona* extends and complicates the field of melodramatic representations of Indians in the 1920s by reversing the expected, generic racial configuration of traumatic frontier violence, vigilantism, settlement, land ownership, and memory.

The implications of these visual representations in the 1920s films mattered not only in their historical moment, but also as they reached into the sound-era studio and later independent film productions. While Carewe's directing career had ended by the mid-1930s, along with Finis Fox's screenwriting production, Wallace Fox continued working in the film business as a director of B Westerns and later television series into the mid-1950s, a decade that also saw major studios return to production of sympathetic Westerns in films such as *Devil's Doorway* and *Broken Arrow.* The contemporary turn to films from the twentieth-century archive of Native images—such as the restoration of the silent-era films *Redskin* and *Ramona*, the repatriation of found footage, and Indigenous filmmakers' reframing of footage from sound-era studio films—suggest the continued social force of images of Indigenous modernity and citizenship in the popular culture mediascape.

Demonstrating the ongoing revaluation of footage from Hollywood's sympathetic Westerns of the 1920s, in 2002 and 2003 the Native band National Braid created and performed live musical accompaniment for the restored print of *Redskin,* with screenings organized by the National Museum of the American Indian at film festivals in New York and Santa Fe in the United States, Prague in the Czech Republic, and Pordenone in

Italy. Their interpretation of the film through sound reframes its images of a Native boy's removal from his family, his boarding school experiences, and his later return to the reservation. The two members of National Braid—Laura Ortman (White Mountain Apache) and Brad Kahlhammer (tribe unknown)—introduce a measure of what Randolph Lewis has called "representational sovereignty" where there was none in Paramount's original 1929 film, without intervening visually in the original images structured by Hollywood studio production practices. What is the relation of such acts of recovery and revaluation to *Redskin*'s initial claims of knowledge production and emotional sympathy? In a 2003 interview, Laura Ortman described her reactions to the film:

> The film [*Redskin*] really speaks to Brad and me because we were both adopted. It's like trying to fit in Native America through the language of music. The film's main character is taken off the reservation, educated in the white world, and comes back to the reservation with lots of complications, which ultimately resolve. We understand the clash of cultures, and we feel his predicament.[77]

The contemporary personal identifications by the members of National Braid recognize the film's original alignment with political interventions in 1920s Indian policy. In their musical accompaniment, Ortman and Kahlhammer revisit the silent Indian melodrama, not to see it as an outmoded form of representation that limited political avenues, but rather to use it as a tool for cinematic expression of the domestic disruptions wrought by twentieth-century educational and social policies. It is a scenario not for duplication but for *reactivation* within a changed interpretive soundscape. With its minor mode, limited pentatonic melody, and slow movement, National Braid's droning score conveys a relentless emotional darkness in the first part of the film. At times, Ortman's violin departs from this limited modulating capability and circular, slow architecture with brief glissandos and nonharmonic dramatic notes. As the pace of the film's action accelerates, so does the texture of the soundtrack with the addition of drums and staccato fragments of chanted song.

In their performance of a fraught, intense soundtrack, National Braid reclaims the historical and emotional trauma imagined in these older representations through recovered fragments from the archive of Indian dramas, augmenting the very foundation of the film's melodramatic engine—not only its visuals but also its *melos*.[78] While for some viewers the realism of location shooting on the Navajo Nation and the images of ceremonial sandpainting remain the most meaningful aspects of the film because of their documentary value, for others, including the members of National Braid, the moments of emotional excess in the film's visual representation of generational or cultural rift constitute its continued power and relevance. By investing the pathos of *Redskin* with a contemporary emotional valence based on their personal experiences of adoption, the members of National Braid expose the conjoined work of custodial and aesthetic appropriation. They demonstrate the interpretive flexibility of artistic reclamation in the face of colonial traffic in visible Indianness.

Part II

Documenting Midcentury Images

3

"As If I Were Lost and Finally Found"

Repatriation and Visual Continuity in
Imagining Indians and *The Return of Navajo Boy*

The poster for Jeff Spitz's 2001 documentary film *The Return of Navajo Boy* visualizes a scenario of encounter, one not seen in the film itself but rather present everywhere in the visual texts that surround it. Against the backdrop of Monument Valley's rock spires, a man and a woman with their backs to the camera contemplate a life-size cardboard figure of John Wayne (see figure 3.1). The people in the poster are Elsie Mae Cly Begay and John Wayne Cly, Diné siblings from Monument Valley who were separated during childhood when missionaries adopted John as a toddler. The image stages both their separation (the cardboard figure stands between them) and—because of their presence together within the frame—their reunion. As a visual metatext the poster also alludes to Native viewers' confrontations with past media and with mediated pasts as well as the intrusion of media productions and images into the private lives of particular families. The flattened image of John Wayne is a ghostlike presence from the cinematic past, an iconic emissary of imperialist storytelling called to account for the consequences of Hollywood's productions. The life-size figure also embodies the continuation of the stories Hollywood made—the broad impact and long shelf-life of the Western.

In the poster, this two-dimensional image of John Wayne is propped beside John Wayne Cly, who is holding a small home-movie camera. Addressing more than a century of unequal power relations in the production of visual media in which Native people have been the subjects of outsiders'

179

Figure 3.1. Poster for *The Return of Navajo Boy*, Groundswell Educational Films (2001).

cameras, John Wayne Cly's camera figures a turning point in Indigenous peoples' control over the production and circulation of their images. The two John Waynes—the white star and the Diné man—reveal Diné history to be deeply intertwined with movie history. The image highlights the most famous star of sound-era studio Westerns while drawing our attention to the reflexive turn in contemporary film, the impulse in Indigenous films and coproductions not only to reject Western images from the past, but also to revisit and interrogate them by engaging in a conversation with the history of image-making, as the Clys seem to be doing when they face the life-size photographic image. The text of the poster emphasizes this conversational pose: "There are thousands of pictures of us, but we never got to say anything. Until now." Speaking—and corresponding voiceovers framing visual images—as well as processes of assembly in production and editing are underscored here as the film's particular intervention in the replication and circulation of images of Indians produced for the entertainment and tourist industries. In all these ways, the poster imagines and articulates a confrontation with the history of the Western and the social impacts of Hollywood and tourist image production, bringing together the work of telling family stories with the reframing of commercial images.

The Return of Navajo Boy tells the story of a contemporary Diné family receiving footage taken of them by an amateur filmmaker in the 1950s.[1] In the Cly family's process of viewing and discussing the film more than 40 years later, however, other memories and stories emerged, and the film's focus became the legacies of tourism and of environmental contamination in Monument Valley. The reverberations of the family's viewing and commenting on the returned film also led to a reunion with their lost sibling when a newspaper article about the family's new film project helped John Wayne Cly find his birth family. The film is complicated by its multiple, intergenerational, and intercultural authorship—director Jeff Spitz worked with Diné coproducer Bennie Klain, who was hired initially as a translator and later became an essential advisor during postproduction, eventually helping to shape the film's narrative structure.[2] The film was privately financed by Bill Kennedy, the son of the original filmmaker of the 1950s film *Navaho Boy*, and was geared for a PBS television audience. The Cly family collectively articulated what they wanted their images to accomplish, including sharing their story with their family's future generations and the political goal of drawing public attention to injustices in the Radiation Exposure Compensation Act of 1990 (RECA) compensation process for miners injured by exposure to uranium.

This chapter revisits several independent and Hollywood films from the mid-twentieth century through the lens of two contemporary documentaries, revealing how the retrieval of production histories, the "recrediting" of Indigenous actors, and the repatriation of footage expand their field of interpretation (an argument I will expand with a discussion of Indigenous spectatorship in chapter 5). I consider *The Return of Navajo Boy* alongside another, more stylistically experimental documentary film, *Imagining*

Indians, directed by Hopi photographer and filmmaker Victor Masayesva in 1992, and released in 1993. A practicing artist, Masayesva is also a theorist of Indigenous visuality who, along with others such as Tuscarora artist and scholar Jolene Rickard, has turned our attention to issues of sovereignty and accountability across visual media. His insights about the paradoxical qualities of photographic action ("the negative contains the positive") and the ways that the extractive and duplicative functions of photography reveal relations of power ("what people do to people") gauge the social relations of mechanical reproduction in Indigenous terms.[3] An all-Native production, *Imagining Indians* consists of interviews with Native individuals about their work on Hollywood films and about commercial exploitation and commodification of Native spirituality. The interview sequences are framed by a dramatic narrative and the film closes with the radically symbolic act of destroying a camera lens. By subsuming old footage, photographs, and paintings within sound voiceovers, dramatic performances, and technical manipulations of the image, Masayesva shares with viewers a process of "looking again" that is intrinsic to film and photography as well as visual repatriation.[4] Masayesva's work, which has been characterized by critics as both "antivisual" and intensely visual, makes Hollywood footage accountable to identifiable Native viewers and emphasizes diversity within and among Native communities.[5] His theoretical writing on film, photography, and experimentalism provide a crucial framework for theorizing image-making and the rerecognition of images in an Indigenous context, including the critical reappropriation that unfolds in *The Return of Navajo Boy*.

Like *The Return of Navajo Boy*, *Imagining Indians* also repositions Native participants within the actual and constructed landscapes of Western genre films and ancillary tourist industry images. The film opens with a pan (from left) over Monument Valley, empty of people except for a Native woman walking slowly up a low rise. In this and many other shots, Masayesva alludes to Western genre representational appropriation of territories through landscape images while embedding a contemporary Indigenous presence in those landscapes. Later in the film in a montage of images of Indians in western American advertising and tourist commodity display, a Native woman and man pose with their faces inserted into a hole in a painted backdrop, a Native figure, and Monument Valley scene (see figure 3.2). Here, people look through and are seen within an artificial, painted panorama—a manifestation of the "media landscape" itself, saturated with an assembly of kitschy images that oppressively surrounds and defines the human faces. *Imagining Indians* also implicates itself in this spectrum of ethically complex and potentially divisive representational choices that origi-

Figure 3.2. *Imagining Indians*, Victor Masayesva (1993), painted setting.

nate with the Western genre's assault on Indigenous territorial and spiritual coherence.

Imagining Indians and *The Return of Navajo Boy* strongly engage the emotional relationship between filmic vision and world-making in the entrenched discourses of film production and reception. The films tell stories about the effects of filmmaking on the world and the people that they endeavor to document.[6] In the convergence of visual repatriation, formal cinematic techniques, and film production situations, *The Return of Navajo Boy* and *Imagining Indians* address the damage wrought by cameras—the ways of seeing Native people and lands transmitted by Western film production and tourist industries. These documentaries communicate the intrusive, extractive functions of photography and film, in the process of using the generative capacities of that same media to renarrate the earlier footage. From the act of destroying the camera to the reparative work of returning a film canister to the family members who were its filmed subjects, the films insist that viewers recognize the capability of representation to affect people (subjects and viewers) in the world beyond the film frame.

In *Imagining Indians* and *The Return of Navajo Boy*, speaking about the damage images can do is necessary to counteractive representation in the present. In their attention to Native recognition, these and other Native documentaries imagine a contemporary Native visual continuity. In light of these films' strategies, my phrasing is intended to shift the cinematic meaning of "continuity" away from its common signification in film studies where it is understood to mean the illusion of seamlessness or the "reality effect" of the continuity system, including editing that maintains a coherent narrative by effacing the fault-lines of cinematic manufacture and covering over disparities in production. I want to take up an alternate meaning of continuity here as a political, amendatory process that emerges from the narration of social and representational rupture and an acknowledgement (rather than smoothing over) of the discontinuities ongoing from the colonial past.

This disjunctive and reparative work of visual continuity takes place through specific audiovisual strategies. In attending to these films' shared investment in the documentary renarration of photographic images of Indigenous families, I am particularly interested in the proprietary work of attribution. Masayesva's and Spitz's films reframe cinematic processes of identifying land and people and return us to the relationships between production situations and filmed texts by naming and telling stories about individual places, subjects, actors, or extras. Locally embedded production methods intervene in the abstractions of cinematic public memory. Archival footage and photographs are integrated into contemporary documentaries in several ways, including sound (voiceover and recrediting, traditional music, community histories, oral narratives), dissolves and superimposition, point-of-view editing, long-shots and lateral pans, as well as compositional framing and the mise-en-scène of viewing. The films reintegrate popular images, songs, and archival footage into particular tribal contexts, literally changing the stories that give meaning to the images on-screen. These formal techniques come to take on a particular political valence in the context of Indigenous partnerships and decision-making roles in film production. The films' images intercede in the narrative boundaries implied by the visual conventions of Indian images and breach the enclosure of Native lands and subjects within the image frames of photographs and films. The critical value of this tactical reflexivity is its focus on the impact of images and image-making on Indigenous subjects, a public and activist yet also personal and domestic register of intervention.

As filmmakers and their subjects reinterpret and restore old footage, their handling of archived and broadcast media not only asserts a retroactive representational sovereignty over mainstream representations, but also aligns filmmaking with the impulse to remediate in U.S. Indian policy, including the Native American Graves and Repatriation Act of 1990 (NAGPRA). The act asserts Native American right of possession to tribal human remains and cultural objects, mandates the repatriation of remains and objects from federally funded institutions to the tribes, and prohibits "illegal trafficking" in these items (NAGPRA 5). The act defines "cultural affiliation" as "a relationship of shared group identity which can be reasonably traced historically or prehistorically between a present day Indian tribe . . . and an identifiable earlier group" (5).[7] One result of repatriation—the return of ancestors and objects—is to shift the framing narration to address a tribal audience rather than a scientific, scholarly, or mainstream public one. In these terms NAGPRA implies the right of tribes to be the intended audience, beneficiaries, "readers," or "viewers" interpreting their cultural patrimony. NAGPRA registers a crucial shift in federal Indian policy and in public opinion about the national stake in appropriating Indigenous artifacts and a recognition of the way Indigenous perspectives reframe the meaning of objects and images.

While NAGPRA does not address issues of aesthetic or intellectual property rights, the legal endorsement of material repatriation has drawn attention to Native rights to "cultural patrimony" in these categories as well. The particular complexities of visual repatriation are unique to Native communities and are impacted by NAGPRA, which informs the field of reference in films about the return of artifacts (such as Chuck Olin's 1983 *Box of Treasures* and Gil Cardinal's 2003 *Totem: The Return of the G'psgolox Pole*). Films that document the material act of returning a canister of film to Indigenous communities or that document or restore Indigenous narratives of film production excluded from film texts are not merely reflexive; they navigate the intersection between the materiality of archived images and the less tangible qualities of aesthetic and epistemological provenance.

Indigenous repurposing of earlier photographs and footage in a cinematic narrative accomplishes both a critical, pedagogical stance that remembers the history of colonization, and simultaneously a more direct embracing of Indigenous subjects, images, and memories in intimate tribal, clan, and familial terms. *Imagining Indians* and *The Return of Navajo Boy* connect the reviewing of film footage with substantive consequences for Native community relations and environmental rights. Remembering the past in the act of return or restitution is one source of the emotional efficacy of scenes of visual repatriation in Native films, reminding us that formal representational recognition of Native land claims and genealogies is foundational to discussion of sovereignty in Native cinema. In altering the narratives with which images of the West have been affiliated, these Indigenous documentaries actively transform the trajectories of public recognition.

Victor Masayesva's *Imagining Indians*

Imagining Indians models the ways in which Native stories, testimony, and critiques of Western genre images of Indians can expand (rather than constrict) the social possibilities of mechanical reproduction beyond the extractive function that photography and film have so often had in Native communities. This expansion includes expressive historical transmission in service of genealogical continuity, particularly when earlier Hollywood films become attached to Indigenous-language storytelling and information systems, oral histories, and the sharing of family images across generations. Masayesva defamiliarizes Hollywood production styles through sound and speech, recovering the voices of the silent Native "extras" in Hollywood movies.[8] Listening to the performers' stories shifts cinematic images of Indians out of an isolated state of abstraction, imaginatively reclaiming Indigenous familial and community coherence by associating the performers with two concrete relationships: their relationship to the cinema as named actors rather than anonymous figures conflated with their screen roles and their relationships with their own local family, clan, and community networks and lands.

In *Imagining Indians*, Masayesva continually returns to visual and textual documents—including footage from Hollywood Westerns and paintings by artists such as George Catlin—while redirecting viewers' perceptions of the images through contrapuntal sound and voiceovers from interviews with actors. His emphasis on portraits and landscapes as sites of necessary identification and reclaiming expose the Western's erasure of Indigeneity and pervasive inundation of Indian images in commodity culture. Although *Imagining Indians* most rigorously interrogates contemporary film productions such as Costner's 1990 *Dances with Wolves* and Apted's 1992 *Thunderheart* that dominated theater screens in the years immediately prior to the 1992 "Columbus Quincentennial," Masayesva extends the film's historical reach to early silent frontier dramas such as Griffith's 1913 *The Battle of Elderbush Gulch*, classic sound-era studio productions such as De Mille's 1936 *The Plainsman*, and revisionist Westerns such as Brooks's 1956 *The Last Hunt* and Silverstein's 1969 *A Man Called Horse*.[9] *Imagining Indians* reveals these films' close relationship to territorial acquisition and describes the psychological muting and mutilation caused by popular images of Indians with sequences in which Native people tell their own diverse stories about how popular images are produced and how such images affect them. They discuss films that were shot on their lands, their experiences as extras or crew members, and particularly their feelings about cultural and spiritual commodification. Throughout the film, Masayesva returns to footage of these extensive interviews with Indigenous performers, from Cheyenne elders who once acted in Westerns of the 1930s, and to younger Lakota actors, extras, and crew who recount their experiences on the set of *Dances with Wolves*.

The histories and testimonies embedded in the film touch off preconstituted or attached meanings for viewers, and at the same time become available for reinterpretation in a new context. Its stories interact powerfully with the "shadow texts" that viewers bring to bear in their encounters with the films.[10] Masayesva thus foregrounds the way Native communities can intervene in and alter meanings of the images through the contexts and practices of filmmaking.

In addition to voiceover, visual experimentation with computer animation and superimposed posterization convey spiritual connections to land and animals, and the frame narrative of a Native patient in a dentist's office and the use of texts alongside interview footage underscore the disjuncture between individual stories and official news reports and press releases.[11] Masayesva attends to the way his own image-making participates in the "imagining Indians" that his film critiques by drawing viewers' attention to issues of authorship and to productive discontinuities. He describes the film as "a composite process to let people know there were a lot of cracks in the seams. It was *about* imagining Indians, and *I* was part of that imagining. . . . And I was implicating myself . . . by showing the technology, the filmmaking, the transparency *behind* the scenes" (Rony 31, emphasis in original). Masayesva's reflexive, theatrical aesthetics highlight issues of authorship and manufacture, rejoining abstracted screen Indians with diverse yet distinctly authorial voices. His frequent use of computerized manipulations of images (animation, posterization, embedded text) confronts viewers with the constructedness ("the seams") in technology and film language. These introductory and transitional images function as illustrations, as countertexts, and as marginalia, glossing the interviewee's voices. Layers of paint on photographs, according to Fatimah Tobing Rony, add "layers of history" (23–24). The intensive manipulations of images effect transitions between sequences using animation, matrix (or patterned) wipes, and other strategies. These graphics, in their exuberant, experimental realization of visual plasticity as a world-making technique, expand the juncture between visual representation and "the real" in ways particularly suited to spiritual or mythic subjects and to the restrictions on communication and recording that accompany ceremonial contexts.

Early in the film, Marvin Clifford (Lakota) discusses his experiences as an extra in *Dances with Wolves*. As he speaks, a young boy turns on a television in the background. The television plays an image of the interview, and the small screen of this mise-en-abyme becomes the transition to a closer framing of Clifford (see figure 3.3).[12] In another scene, images of red rock formations part in the middle and draw back to the sides of the screen

Figure 3.3. *Imagining Indians,* Victor Masayesva (1993), Marvin Clifford.

before disappearing, like theater curtains, to introduce a new speaker (Diné actor and artist Red Wing Nez). In another sequence, as a woman's voice describes the commodification of Indigenous spiritual relationships with animals, Masayesva animates petroglyph images of antelope on a rock wall; later, a grassland scene with running buffalos is posterized in red tones. In the same sequence, footage of women powwow dancers is superimposed over evergreen trees blowing in strong wind, synthesizing the fringed costumes and tree fronds. The images are beautiful, and contrary to the primitivism naturalized as "realism" by the continuity system in films such as *Dances with Wolves,* they are emblazoned with technological artifice. In many sequences, text appears as intertitles or subtitles carrying newspaper headlines or press releases countering the statements of the interviewees. A Hopi meeting to discuss the 1991 production of *The Dark Wind* is set within a single box of a comic book, and for the full-screen footage, comic-style speech bubbles carry the English subtitles for Hopi language dialogue.[13]

These dynamic graphics visually organize the interviews with Indigenous actors and crew about location shooting while drawing viewers' attention to cinematic rupture—to the discontinuities from which other continuities emerge. The interviews convey that other continuity, the living community behind the scenes, in all its heterogeneity and intergenerational divisiveness and solidarity. For example, early in the film, Masayesva overlays the viewpoints of the Cheyenne extras with film clips from Cecil B. DeMille's classic 1936 Western *The Plainsman.* Northern Cheyenne elder Charles Sooktis Sr. recounts the economic impact the filming of *The Plainsman* had on the reservation community during the hard times of the Great Depression:

There was, uh, money, floating around that camp, a lot of money. There was, ah, armor car came, come in from Sheridan, Wyoming, and they paid cash to every man that was taking part in that movie. And the money was something that people realized, that the money was scarce during the time that that movie company came in. And there were gambling, gambling men and women playing cards. And nobody was hungry—there would always be a couple trucks come in every morning from Sheridan, Wyoming, to bring out food, distribute it to the people that were camping. And they usually killed two cows a day, for the people to have meat, during the camping days there. And it was such a thing that people had never seen before, but after that, nothing ever came by anymore. . . .That was the time that, uh, I met that Cecil B. DeMille and Gary Cooper.

Sooktis's interview footage is shown first—he sits with his arms folded and resting on a table; an elderly woman and an interviewer listen quietly. Following this oral history of the film's production, including further discussion in the Cheyenne language, which remains untranslated, Masayesva cuts to a clip from *The Plainsman*, an "Indian charge" through a stream toward an armed group of soldiers led by Wild Bill Hickok (Gary Cooper) (see figure 3.4). The Indian charge, emblematic of the Western genre trick of making Indians seem to be intruders in their own lands, is the same visual trope that Chickasaw director Edwin Carewe so effectively revised by making the

Figure 3.4. Footage from *The Plainsman* (1936) in *Imagining Indians*, Victor Masayesva (1993).

settlers the attackers in his 1928 film *Ramona* discussed in chapter 2. In the sound-era film *The Plainsman*, the scene displays a classical Hollywood editing construction in which studio shots of the star and his companions are joined with—and authenticated by—location shots of the Indian charge across a shallow river, using intercutting and rear projection techniques. Sooktis's narrative decouples the shot-reverse-shot editing pattern that joins the studio and location footage in illusory unity, instead resituating the extras to make the location footage illustrate local social relationships.

Masayesva overlays the film's original soundtrack with Sooktis's description of preparing for and shooting this scene. In his story, an actual Chief of the northern Cheyenne also wishes to be the "Chief" of the cinematic Cheyenne during the filming of the charge, despite being warned about the trip-wire hidden under the water to make the horses and riders fall under Hickok's gun. Sooktis describes the way the man was outfitted for the shot ("he had too many things in his hands!") and then, after the "Chief"/Chief has fallen in the water, a humorous scene:

> DeMille came around, riding around the riders, and he asked for somebody to be the Chief. Just anybody could be the Chief, during that run you know. But there was a man name of Little Coyote, "No," he says, "I'm the Chief. I been Chief of the Northern Cheyennes for many years," he says. Then, some young guy tried to warn him that, ah, there was a wire strung across the water. The horse would stumble on it. "Ah, no," he says, "I'm the Chief." So he—they took him out. They were gone for about 45 minutes, and they brought him back, and he had—warbonnet, all the buckskin outfit, all—he had too many things in his hands! He had a sword, he had a bow and arrow, and—and a tomahawk. Then, ah, when the leader says "Go!" we all went. Good thing I was behind—or one of the last ones you know, and this Chief took a big leap, and they got to that wire that was strung across the, underwater. His horse stumbled. And he got all wet, and got run over two or three times. And you know how the chickens look when they get wet—the warbonnet was hanging way down there, and dripping with water you know, and buckskin outfit all wet. And the young guy told him "I tried to warn you—let them, some young guy be the Chief for just, just this run." "No," he says, "I'm the Chief." And he was still Chief when he got all wet, you know.[14]

Sooktis' story reframes the Indian charge scene through voiceover and suggests a complex negotiation of authenticity on the set, while invoking the humorous conventions of trickster stories and what Michelle Raheja has called "redfacing."[15] The narrative exposes the content of *The Plainsman* as a manifestation of the cross-cultural relations and practices of its production, but Sooktis is more interested in his own community's politics and values than in the film's Hollywood-based stars or director. The previously anonymous "extras" become the most important figures as they struggle to make the film more accurate in its representations of the tribe's social organization. Little Coyote wishes to make the Hollywood drama recognize his tribal leadership and in doing so resolves to maintain his identity both on the set and on-screen. While the story gently mocks Little Coyote's insistence on his position as Chief, it also recognizes or credits him by name in a way that *The Plainsman*'s credits don't, and furthermore honors his refusal to accept the social disruption that accompanies the misrecognition of Native actors in Hollywood casting (for which "just anyone could be the Chief"). In its image of Little Coyote's survival, coming back to life after both the actual trip-wire and Cooper's cinematic gunfire—still the Chief, despite being all wet—Sooktis's story gives *The Plainsman* a small but symbolic documentary content while rewriting the Western's scenario of Indian death and defeat in the West. Like the visual framing devices (animation, posterization, and speech bubbles), the voiceover narrative here exposes *The Plainsman*'s misrepresentations of the Cheyenne by widening the "seams" in its continuity editing and establishing Cheyenne presence in the film's production. The story unravels the mystique of the Western hero's individualism by showing the complex support structures behind his appearance of frontier competence. Indeed, Gary Cooper's performance of Wild Bill Hickok is largely insignificant to this story about Cheyenne negotiations with the machine of Hollywood production.

Sooktis's voice, given such emphasis in this sequence, foregrounds other community concerns that have little to do with the representation of Indians in *The Plainsman* as the savage threat to a settler nation's individual heroes. He remembers the production for the economic relief that it brought to his reservation during the mid-1930s, the height of the Great Depression. His moving assertion that "nobody was hungry" during the filming and his repeated mention of the distribution of both cash and food transported from Sheridan, Wyoming, to the people at the location camp suggests that the production represented an important—but temporary—flow of resources from distant cities (Los Angeles) and local towns (Sheridan) to the tribe.[16]

Masayesva further recontextualizes images with a dramatic frame narrative depicting a Lakota dental patient (Patty Runs after Swallow) who has been muted by dental drilling and by oppressive stereotypes (see figures 3.5 and 3.6). The many posters decorating the dentist's office, all advertising old Westerns, appear behind shots of the dentist and patient, continuing the stylized layering of the animation and comic book sequences. The drilling indicates the feelings of discomfort, exposure, and voicelessness that accompany the dentist's work on the woman's mouth—the site of speech—while she is forced to listen to his imperialist fantasies about Native peoples and his plans to exploit Lakota ceremonies for profit.[17] But the "drilling" may allude also to the history of mining operations on Native reservations, from gold to oil to coal and uranium, in which sacred lands (and the spiritual practices connected with them) are expropriated, altered, or desecrated, again for the profit of outsiders.

Frustrated, her mouth full of cotton swabs, the woman pushes the dentist to the floor and appears to threaten him with the drill as a weapon. She then turns the drill on Masayesva's camera lens itself at the end of the film (see figure 3.7). This sequence has been the focus of significant commentary. Scholars such as Fatimah Tobing Rony, Elizabeth Weatherford, Stephen Leuthold, Karen Jacobs, and Kerstin Knopf among others have discussed Masayesva's emphasis on restraint—his turning away from photographic images of the sacred—as an important aesthetic strategy for Indigenous filmmakers who remain accountable to their tribes, clans, and families. Karen Jacobs argues that the dentist's drill in the film represents "the

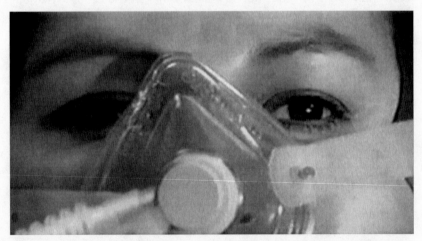

Figure 3.5. *Imagining Indians*, Victor Masayesva (1993), dental patient (Patty Runs after Swallow).

Figure 3.6. *Imagining Indians*, Victor Masayesva (1993), dental drill and Western poster.

phallic means of inscription" (298), as when the patient takes up the drill at the end of the film and "writes back" onto the camera lens. In destroying the viewer's vision and the camera's image-making capabilities by making the clear glass opaque with scratches, the patient literally obliterates the camera's

Figure 3.7. *Imagining Indians*, Victor Masayesva (1993), drilling the lens.

eye in an act that Jacobs calls "anti-visualist" (291). The first scratches in the lens resemble an X, which Jacobs suggests resembles "the image of a gun's crosshair which captures us, the film's viewers, in its frame" (298).

Building on this allusion to the camera as a tool of destructive vision resembling a gun, we can also see the dentist's drill itself and the references to drilling in the film as analogous to the broader symbolic meaning of "shooting" in photography as part of a camera/gun trope. Susan Sontag's assertion that the camera is a "sublimation of the gun," functioning as both a "predatory weapon" and a "fantasy-machine" (14) establishes a core association between duplicative imaging and violent conquest.[18] In an article on Indigenous experimentalism, Masayesva deliberately conflates "the gun/camera/computer" in describing the mainstream cinematic practice of "colonizing through technology" to which experimental filmmaking is opposed. "From this perspective," he writes, "experimental films and videos can be defined by the degree to which they subvert the colonizers' indoctrination and champion Indigenous expression in the political landscape" ("Indigenous Experimentalism" 237). The drill is also, as Jacobs notes, a discursive instrument that, like the animated speech bubbles, "cuts" against the image. The image expands the metaphor of the camera, as a weapon aimed at a person and the land itself, to include the drill as an equally destructive implement. The film opens with a long-shot of a woman walking in Monument Valley, and we can see the dentist's extraction of a woman's tooth as an assault on her body, which also represents invasive harm to the land she occupies.

The increasingly abstract image of (and through) the destroyed camera lens is further complicated by the pattern of the lines that the dental patient drills into the glass, which at first resemble a spider's web. The woman who has been muted and suppressed by "drilling" becomes powerful in this moment because of her association with spiders and weaving. Grandmother Spider acts as a messenger and benefactor of humans in the Hopi emergence stories; spiders are associated with creation through storytelling in Pueblo and other tribal traditions. The image of the camera lens obscured by web-patterned drill lines is intercut with special effects in which paintings by George Catlin—portraits of tribal leaders from the mid-1800s—crumble into dots. This visual disintegration is replaced, finally, by a black screen, and several voices speak in Native languages. In this closing and in his use of Western film clips, Masayesva both embeds oral narrative in the film text and draws attention to the ways that cultures of film production make meaning, thus creating an Indigenous space in and through the very act of renouncing and ejecting the camera. The evocation and rejection of ethnographic portraiture conveyed by the animated dissolution of Catlin's colonial portraits is visually linked to the dental patient through graphic

Figure 3.8. *Imagining Indians*, Victor Masayesva (1993), superimposed close-up and portrait.

matches—the close-up of her face, increasingly obscured by the scratches on the lens, occupies the same space in the frame as the intercut paintings. The woman's silence corresponds to her erasure of her own image along with Catlin's images, whereas the Native speech that takes place in the film's interviews, instead of dissolving older images, returns to them in a process of re-viewing (see figures 3.8 and 3.9).

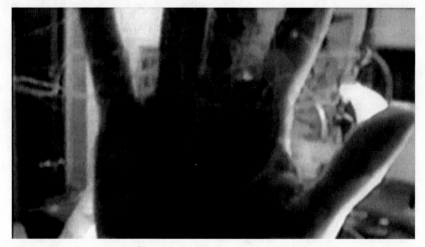

Figure 3.9. *Imagining Indians*, Victor Masayesva (1993), pushing the camera away.

If Masayesva's destruction of his own camera extends one possible strategy of resistance to the commodification of Indian images, his use of interpretive devices—computer graphics, recorded interviews, and the dramatic narrative frame—demonstrates another, specifically the revisiting of sensitive images with new narration. *Imagining Indians* shares this particular approach, a recovery in narration, with *The Return of Navajo Boy*. The event that initiates *The Return of Navajo Boy* is the return of a film reel to the Cly family who were its subjects. Recovered images and films, including not only the materials found in museum archives or private collections, but also the commercialized images available in gas station postcard racks, pose problems of both circulation and containment. The contradictory importance of restraint in the practice of transmission is illustrated in *The Return of Navajo Boy*, as it is in *Imagining Indians*, when the filmmakers recuperate the older footage by incorporating it within another film project.

Indigenous Theories of Mimesis

Reading *The Return of Navajo Boy* through the lens of *Imagining Indians*, then, requires a consideration of the fluid relationships between photography and film, and the specific context of Native American photography. In these documentaries, photographic images become nested within different narratives through cinematic storytelling and histories of production, whereas still images of people are excerpted from cinematic footage for recirculation as family photographs. For example, Spitz derived photographs from the original *Navaho Boy* film, reproducing stills of the actors, which he showed to people while trying to find Cly family members on the Navajo Nation. And photographic portraits persist within *The Return of Navajo Boy* itself, which is dense with scenes of viewing. Cly family members encounter not only the original film footage but also postcards, framed portraits lining pawn shop walls, newspaper images, film stills, family photographs and other images. The original *Navaho Boy* production was part of a broad-based tourist industry in Monument Valley both occasioned and facilitated by photographic images. In that historical context, photographs and footage were taken and circulated both commercially and privately in parallel ways, ending up as magazine articles, Hollywood movies, postcards, pamphlets, advertising, and educational materials.

The history of imagining Indians evidenced in the photographic record is documented in *Navajo and Photography*, James Faris's meticulous study of published and archival photographs of Diné people. From this enormous body of material, Faris describes a range of specific "photographic registers," repetitive tropes of gesture and posture that, he argues, reveal and serve only Western narratives and perspectives. Faris cogently maintains that such photographs are false evidence; they originated within and continue to enforce vastly differential power relations that deny Diné histories and social relations. More problematic, however, is his assertion that "photographs of Navajo allow for no alternative narratives" (19) and that "any social relations that authorize Navajo outside Western terms are simply unphotographed or unphotographable" (306). The totalizing aspects of this argument risk overlooking Indigenous agency during photographing as both subject and photographer, as well as the power of reframing and repatriation. What is demonstrated in *Imagining Indians* and *The Return of Navajo Boy* is that however Indigenous social relations may be evidenced (or absented) in Western images, individual viewers can and often do retrieve the specificity and visibility of pictured familial relations, identifying and recognizing their relatives and negotiating emotional connections to the images in ways that may resist, accommodate, or otherwise mediate the origin of the images.

This sense that singular yet reproducible images can tell different stories simultaneously is articulated in Masayesva's assertion that "Photography reveals to me how it is that life and death can be so indissolubly one; it reveals the falseness of maintaining these opposites as separate. Photography is an affirmation of opposites; the negative contains the positive" (*Hopi Photographers* 90). Masayesva describes his photographic and film work in terms of the Hopi Kwikwilyaqa clown, a ritual figure that mimics or "duplicates" the actions of individual spectators during Katsina ceremonies, to the irritation of the "original" and the laughter of the crowd. For Masayesva, the Kwikwilyaqa clown implicates the duplicative work of photography by "revealing what people do to people" (*Hopi Photographers* 12). Masayesva's eloquent meditation on photography from a Hopi perspective presents an Indigenous theory of mimesis that is profoundly relational. He articulates not only the potential for creative renewal in the linking (or "affirmation") of opposites that is built into the mechanics of mimetic technologies, but also the corollary tendency of those technologies to structure interpersonal relations.

The redeployment of older photographs in these and other Native and intercultural productions suggests ways that the generative capacities of mechanical reproduction can be considered within a model of photographic meaning that emphasizes this surfeit rather than scarcity of interpretive possibility. New repatriations of museum photographic collections have also been important in this regard. As Elizabeth Edwards argues, photographs are not static documents but rather socially performative records of "parallel realities": "This infinite recodability of photographs is the site of fracture and re-engagement and is fundamental to visual repatriations" (84).[19] Thus, she argues, a photograph is an object with its own historicized "social biography" that holds "the seeds for recognition" (*Raw Histories* 235). It is this recognition, in a literal sense, which energizes the encounters with photographs in *The Return of Navajo Boy*, including in the film's conception and production.

Community revaluing of old films and photographs has implications for scholarly discussion of the mimetic power of photography and filmmaking in the context of Indigenous image studies. Native reclaiming of images invites a further reassessment of theories of reproduction that emphasize spectrality and death in the photographic sign, such as Barthes's association of photography with deathlike stasis and the Freudian association of repetition with the uncanny and the death drive. The theorization of photography as premonition or simulation of death and closure begins to account for the colonizing work of Western image-making, but excludes the potential of repetition to function as transmission, bridge, or generative performative utterance or image.[20] In some Indigenous ceremonies, repetition is an essential actualizing force in the efficacy of images or spoken words to alter the material world. In performance, repetition creatively reproduces traditional action. In contrast to the Western theorization of the copy as "subversive" of the power of the original to which it is opposed, Candice Hopkins (Tlingit) writes of Native oral expression that "replication in storytelling, by contrast, is positive and necessary" because the work of oral transmission involves simultaneous repetition and invention (342). "Reading across the contradictions in storytelling is generative, as it reveals a worldview: one in which truth is considered apart from fact, where *originality exists within the copy*, where change is an inherent part of tradition" (341, emphasis added).[21]

The process of "looking again" at reproducible images may constitute a special form of repetition in service of continuity and transmission, one that is not exclusive of change. John Berger defines private photographs as embedded in a context of familiarity and the decontextualization of public photography as an encounter of strangers with the presumption of distance and lack of relationality between viewer and subject. But the very detachability of photographs makes performances or scenarios of colonization materially available for reincorporation into Indigenous frameworks.[22] In *The Return of Navajo Boy*, images from tourist postcards and Western films are redefined as family photographs and home movies.

Jeff Spitz and Bennie Klain's *The Return of Navajo Boy*

The Return of Navajo Boy correlates the repatriation of documentary film footage with the reconstruction of the Diné family receiving (and directing) the film, reassigning the signifying work of tourist and Western genre images based on the recognition of family relations. Dense with interrelated histories, the film links the impact of Hollywood and tourist image-making with other processes of extraction on Diné lands. The repatriation of the silent film *Navaho Boy* to the Clys facilitated other important developments: John Wayne Cly, taken away into foster care as a toddler, was reunited with the Cly family, and Bernie Cly's ongoing compensation claims for injuries stemming from radiation contamination led to broader community and family activism to alert others to the dangers of uranium mining waste on the reservation. The film targets the intensive uranium mining that took place simultaneously with the height of John Ford's Western genre location shooting in Monument Valley in the 1950s. The family's narration of the old film reframes its aesthetically beautiful images to articulate the relationships between tourist photography, uranium mining, and the disruption of Indigenous families through illness and foster care, and to draw attention to the ongoing damage from these practices. The events set in motion by the reactivation of this found footage highlight film as a powerful material artifact; filming the Cly family's reclamation of the old movie and reunion with their lost sibling does not simply repeat or update the photographic practices it critiques. The image of Bill Kennedy returning his father's film to the Cly family is a cinematic scene of visual repatriation (see figure 3.10).

Figure 3.10. *The Return of Navajo Boy*, Groundswell Educational Films (2001), Bill Kennedy and Cly family members watching the original *Navaho Boy* film.

In *The Return of Navajo Boy*, the repossession through recognition that takes place in the voiceover and subtitling is also performed visually in the conventional practices that mark transitions between footage from *Navaho Boy* and *The Return of Navajo Boy* and in the lodging of the older images within newer ones. In his initial attempt to locate the anonymous actors in the then-"orphaned" film *Navaho Boy*, Spitz did not bring a video camera but instead took stills from the film with him to Monument Valley and began asking if anyone recognized the faces of the subjects. He hoped find "people whose faces match or who [could] identify the people in these pictures." Soon, the staff of the hotel where he stayed identified the family and directed him to Cly family members living nearby. When he met "people whose faces lit up when they looked at the pictures" he gave them the color stills—giving pictures back instead of taking pictures—because Cly family members told him that "this is really important because it's the first time we've ever seen our grandma's face."[23] Coproducer Bennie Klain notes that following the family's directives continued in postproduction: "at every stage of the production we were adamant that it wasn't us making the decisions about what they were going to talk about in the film. With every rough-cut we would take it back to the families and get their feedback" (Nesbit). In keeping with Bernie Cly and Elsie Mae Cly Begay's wishes, the film project has resulted in ongoing activism through film screenings, Spitz's organization Groundswell Educational Films, news media coverage, and webisodes (many by Mary Helen Begay, daughter-in-law of Elsie Mae Cly Begay) updating online readers about steps by the U.S. Environmental Protection Agency (EPA) to clean up contaminated tailings from the Skyline Mine (Fahys).[24]

The strategy of coproduction and the use of photographs in *The Return of Navajo Boy* can be usefully contrasted with the anthropological fieldwork practice of "photo-elicitation" in which photographs are used in interviews as mnemonic prompts to increase the range of topics and amount of information an "informant" can and will provide. Scholars in anthropology and museum studies have pointed out the way this premise is based on a model of extraction rather than reciprocity (Brown and Peers 98; Edwards, "Talking" 87).[25] The related practices of extracting information, images, and cultural data (through or in photographs) and extracting natural resources (including mineral resources such as coal and uranium) is explicitly criticized as a form of representational and ecological violence in *The Return of Navajo Boy*. In fact, the film's focus on the related patterns of land use and image-making in Monument Valley reveals the consequences of cinematic claiming in the Western.

Both *Imagining Indians* and *The Return of Navajo Boy* begin with shots that pan across the landscape of Monument Valley. This valley, part of the Diné Nation and spanning the Utah–Arizona border, has also been a symbolic frontier landscape for the Western genre's story of nation-building. It was the location for the 1920s films discussed in chapter 2, George Seitz's *The Vanishing American* and Victor Schertzinger's *Redskin*, as well as seven of John Ford's sound-era Westerns.[26] *The Return of Navajo Boy* describes and interprets Ford's work in Monument Valley from the perspective of the Cly family members who worked as extras, a reading that allows us to see more directly the relation between filmmaking and world-making, evidenced even within the film frame. *The Return of Navajo Boy* demonstrates a relationship between symbolic domination and physical domination by exposing the relentless production requirements of an intertwined tourist and Hollywood image-making system in the valley. Stuart Hall's metaphor of "contested ground" to describe the negotiation of power within the production and reception of popular culture texts takes literal form in competing land uses in the valley and in its consequences for Native families.

Formal techniques that characterize the Western, particularly panoramic landscape shots, further entrench and mystify colonizing social and ecological relations on Native lands. If we think of the work of the camera as resembling the work of a surveying transit (as in *The Invaders*, discussed in chapter 1), the cinematic technique of the lateral pan across Monument Valley's landscape is itself a form of claiming in the act of looking. Establishing long shots that depict the valley enact an imperial gaze and produce a passive visual right of possession, particularly over the course of the many films Ford set in the valley.[27] And embedded in Ford's cinematic landscapes are settler families. In *Stagecoach* (1939) the Apache aggressors are defeated and killed by the Cavalry in a sequence that includes close-ups of two white women and a newborn baby. Critic Jon Tuska aptly summarizes the net effect of this climactic chase, in which "killing Indians is shown to be exciting" (51). Augmenting the passive claims of panoramic long-shots and long takes, then, are rapid shot-reverse-shot and other editing techniques that blur the distinctions between gun, camera, and viewscope through which viewers are invited to partake in a merged directorial and settler point of view. It is a view that works to naturalize and rationalize Indian characters' deaths and settler rights to territory—and rights to represent—in the same act of looking. This more violent and active form of cinematic claiming targets Indian characters and land in the same shot while the lens of the mediating equipment (gun, camera, surveyor's telescope) gives the impression of controlling or containing that landscape, mimicking the boundary-making function of the film frame itself.[28]

Ford's flagrant disregard for actual geography in his films has invited scholarly assessments of the Monument Valley as a purely symbolic landscape, as the definitively emblematic vista of "Indian country" in the Western. His repeated representations of Monument Valley have been variously interpreted as signifying moral, transcendent, or civilizing aspects of American western settlement. Lee Clark Mitchell characterizes Ford's vision of the valley as a nostalgia for "a land clearly inflected by time but not yet marked by human history" and "a terrain only to be recovered imaginatively" ("Why Monument Valley" 145). Jean-Louis Leutrat and Suzanne Liandrat-Guigues assert that the valley is "a cliché, a stereotype, an empty signifier which can accommodate any number of signifieds" (169). While these are important readings of the Western as social parable (an approach to Westerns often shared by contemporary trade journals and news media reviews), this thread in film scholarship allows analyses of Ford's landscapes—and the Western genre itself—to remain isolated from some of the broader implications of its representations of tribes and land.

Furthermore, in treating representations of Indians and even of Western landscapes as abstractions—ciphers that can allegorize any current social problem—critics instantiate and extend the discourses of Indian absence that characterize the genre itself. Hollywood filmmakers have indeed appropriated images of Indians as endlessly available signifiers, to allegorize civil rights conflicts in the 1950s and 1960s and Vietnam War atrocities in the 1970s. These appropriations are based on the assumption of vanishing—that images of Indians and Native lands exist primarily as allegories for frontier relations or codes for conversations about other issues. Scholarship that limits its scope of inquiry to the way images of Indians function to signify non-Native social problems extends popular beliefs that Indian images are public property, and overlooks the Western's manipulation and misrepresentations of specific Native histories, legal rights and relationships to homelands.[29]

Leutrat and Liandrat-Guigues assert that Ford's "repeated use of a single space will create a place in the memory both for Ford to use personally and for everyone who goes to see the film," giving Monument Valley a "commemorative function" as a "theatre of memory" (160, 162, 167). My point is that Ford's influence on public memory through cinematography and editing—his vision of the valley—has affected its current use while diverting public attention from its other uses, including uranium extraction. This memory-making extends to renaming the landscape: Ford's preferred location of the camera for shooting the horizon in sweeping pans is now called "Ford's Point," replicating imperialist tropes of discovery in which setting foot on land, renaming it, and visually knowing it act together in a political assertion (followed by legal recognition) of European rights to Indigenous territories. The custodial work of naming—as in boarding school and census contexts—extended to the Cly family as well. The name "Cly" comes from a local trader's attempt to pronounce the family's Diné name, *Nishtlhaai*, meaning left-handed. And John Wayne Cly's name was suggested by John Wayne himself during a visit to the family when the baby was a newborn.

If Ford's films attempt to deed Monument Valley to a settler-nation audience, Native viewers and scholars have insisted that the Western should answer to different historical perspectives. After a viewing of *The Searchers*, Tom Grayson Colonnese (Santee Sioux) rejects Ford's presentation of Monument Valley as a fantasy frontier space, instead attending to the location shooting "on the reservation" and the use of Native "extras" in the context of the 1950s economic exclusion of Native tribes from postwar prosperity (336). That suppressed economic context, one of the many "graphic silences" of the Western, also includes the industrial appropriation of Diné land for cold war uranium extraction. Many of the Diné men working as extras in Ford films also worked in uranium mines. In the convergence of industrial tourist and dream factory production systems, Monument Valley is visually appropriated for mainstream American consumption as a vacation playground and a stage for the production of colonial fantasies. But in the 1950s the U.S. government and industries also continued to actualize Western expansion into the valley through economic extraction of mineral value from land.[30] Colonnese's assessment exposes the way Ford's narrative exclusions suppress the actual story of U.S. national origins that it purports to narrate.

The visual mastery represented by the camera's eye in Ford's Westerns parallels outsiders' physical occupation of Diné land during the production processes of location shooting by Ford and other directors. Footage from the *The Making of the Searchers* (1956), excerpted in *The Return of Navajo Boy*, depicts the construction of the set and the shooting while Cly family members describe their bewilderment at the activity: "Who knows what they were thinking?" Ford's Monument Valley Westerns were deeply affected by his relationship with local trader and regional booster Harry Goulding. The presence of Ford, along with his cast and crew, was facilitated by Harry Goulding's trading post and tourist enterprises. In fact, several accounts of John Ford's career include a story in which Harry Goulding visited Ford in Los Angeles in 1938 and used photographs as well as descriptions of the Diné to convince Ford to shoot his next film (*Stagecoach*) in Monument Valley (Carmichael 217; Davis 93–94).[31] Ford used Goulding's lodge as a base of operations for location shooting in the valley, and relied on Goulding's knowledge of the area and connections with Diné families and the Cly family in particular.

The lives of the Cly family have been marked by Goulding's activity in the valley as well. Goulding brought tourists to meet and photograph the Cly family almost every day during the tourist season in the 1950s. Cly family members—adults and children—performed Diné traditionality for tourists' cameras, including weaving and carding, doing their hair and dressing in traditional clothes, making frybread, and bringing sheep over sand dunes to a waterhole. In Dean MacCannell's articulation of the semiotics of tourism as "staged authenticity" and "site sacralization," Monument Valley would be constructed as a tourist site—apart from regular social space—through acts of naming, framing, signage, and other mechanically reproduced imaging. The Cly family's performance of traditional life, an "onstage" simulation, masks their wage labor in the "back regions" that tourists ignore, including the restaurants and hotels that make tourist consumption possible. In addition to this onstage work for the benefit of tourist's cameras, for example, Elsie Mae worked backstage in the tourist industry as a housekeeper at the Goulding's lodge—"I did laundry," she said in an interview, "I made beds"—and worked as a tour guide in the summers.[32] It was during an interview in the "John Wayne Room" of the Goulding lodge, in response to Spitz's questions about her memories of the movie star, that Elsie Mae spoke and cried over the loss of her brother.

In *The Return of Navajo Boy*, the Cly family tells the story about their land that Ford's images—and images from other studio-era Hollywood films—withheld and obscured. Asserting the Diné words in conjunction with shots of landscape features during the course of *The Return of Navajo Boy*, narrator Lorenzo Begay (Elsie Mae's son) contrasts the names of various geographic features in English and Diné. In this and other ways, the film counteracts the colonizing reach of Westerns such as *The Searchers* with a visual land charter. Filmmaker David MacDougall describes a relevant dynamic of showing and naming during the production of his film *Familiar Places* (1977), about an Aboriginal family's effort to map and reclaim clan territory in northern Queensland, Australia, and their children's first view of their hereditary lands. MacDougal writes that the film "is an act of investiture, a formal endorsement of their rights to the country. The *showing*, and their *seeing*, stand in place of what we might consider a formal statement or delineation of rights. Showing here constitutes a kind of charter" (162, emphasis added).[33] The landscape shots in *The Return of Navajo Boy* assert land rights—and by extension environmental rights—on film by demonstrating knowledge that constitutes ownership. Scenes of Indigenous *viewing* are as important as *showing*, as I will discuss in chapter 5 with examples from Chris Eyre's feature film *Skins* in which Hollywood misrepresentations are embedded the context of Lakota oral history.

The panning shots across the mesas behind Elsie Mae's home have other functions as well. Unlike Ford's use of the valley to represent nineteenth-century Texas (to continue the example of *The Searchers*), *The Return of Navajo Boy* employs the technique to illustrate the marks left by uranium mining and the contamination from mine tailings. This vision supports a different set of claims and legal recognitions: EPA water and homesite testing for radiation contamination, and reparations under RECA for uranium miners who suffered from lung cancer and other health problems after working in uranium mines in the 1950s (see figure 3.11). In one sequence from *The Return of Navajo Boy*, Bernie Cly points out his family's residences in the valley below, from the vantage of an abandoned mine entrance on a high cliff. "All my family live down there," he says, indicating different houses at the base of the cliff. The eyeline match of Bernie Cly's face, a reverse-shot of the small Cly family houses on the valley floor, a shot of his figure in the foreground pointing down to his family's homes, and earlier shots of

Figure 3.11. *The Return of Navajo Boy*, Groundswell Educational Films (2001), mine tailings above Elsie May Cly Begay's house.

the cliff-face scarred by tailings from the mines visually organize identification of the landscape to tell the stories that Ford's and Goulding's images omit (see figure 3.12). John Ford's films, constituted by and through their interconnection with tourist image-making in Monument Valley, have in turn bolstered the representational techniques of visual mastery that made the valley an icon of the national imaginary. When Bernie Cly points out his family's homes from the closed mine site, the shot-reverse-shots, long-shots, and forensic identification of particular places visually reclaim the Monument Valley land from that public imaginary. By returning the focus of the camera to the lives of a Diné "family on the land," *The Return of Navajo Boy* shifts the sense and purpose of "location shooting," and the associated trope of the camera, gun, and drill to tell a family story.

Identification as Recrediting

As I will discuss in chapter 5, images of Indigenous spectatorship—images of viewing that function to claim older media images of Indians—signal a process of spectatorial identification that functions more literally than has

Figure 3.12. *The Return of Navajo Boy*, Groundswell Educational Films (2001), Bernie Cly points out his family's homes from the mine site above.

been suggested by theories of revisionist identification and disidentification, which emerge from and push back against Lacanian (and ultimately Freudian) paradigms based on nuclear family romance. When Cly family members point out the actual identities of the film's subjects—including identifying relatives who have been missing—they engage in a familial identification that is also a political identification, an act of historical memory that revises past cinematic representations of Indians as generic, iconic, or allegorical figures available to the general public. Of course, other kinds of gazing and identification are also going on at the same time, including not just an "identification of" but also the "identification with" that has held the attention of film studies scholars for so long. This identification is not based in an alignment with a fictional character's point of view, nor in a prosthetic extension of the self onto the screen (except in the literal sense of seeing one's image as a child), as much as a recognition of the faces of relatives. It is a visual identification enabled by a viewing position within a web of familial and clan relations and emerging from knowledge of local history and the impact of colonizing practices. In the context of the systemic, historical practices of renaming or refusal to name Native actors in film credits and Native subjects in photographs, this literal identification through naming and clan affiliation amounts to a politicized "recrediting." The recrediting or recaptioning also functions, like film credits, to ascribe aesthetic and titular rights through the acknowledgement of the origins of the image.[34]

These family claims are a decolonizing strategy in scenes of viewing: the Cly family members do not "misrecognize" themselves in the screen-as-mirror; instead, their recognition, based on specific relations, corrects the colonizing, appropriative misrecognitions of tourist and Hollywood images. The effect of the circulating photographs and film footage in *The Return of Navajo Boy* magnifies the issues of naming and identification that occur when the Cly family members view the old movie.[35] As Lorenzo Begay notes in the voiceover, "One magazine called Happy Cly [Elsie Mae's grandmother] the most photographed woman in America, but in most pictures she's only identified as 'The Navajo Woman.'" This elision of individual identity characterizes tourist and other kinds of popular photography, including Edward Curtis's portraits, which sometimes identify well-known male chiefs but which rarely name female subjects. Instead, the women are identified as a generic example of a racial or physical type: "Hesquiat Woman" or "Navajo Woman." This practice of stripping subjects of their names and identities renders them available as empty signs, manifested for example in casual statements such as this one in the 1955 documentary

The Making of The Searchers: "all it took was a little warpaint to turn them [the Diné extras] into hard-riding, bloodthirsty Comanches."

A classic example of this pervasive refusal to name Native performers is *Nanook of the North* (1922), in which the name of the actor Allakariallak, playing the character "Nanook," was omitted from the credits, blurring the distinction between actor and role and reinforcing the notion—already suggested by the film's content—that the dramatic character "Nanook" was not a performance for the camera.[36] Allakariallak's name and the fictional nature of the nuclear family in the film were not known outside of Inuit communities until recently. Furthermore, in *Nanook of the North*, "Nanook" is not just envisioned as a nonactor, someone unfamiliar with film production. He is also rendered archaic by seeming to be a bad *consumer* in the scene at the trading post, during which he appears to encounter a gramophone for the first time and then bites or tastes the record disk. Thus, the film hides not just Inuit work on the film's *production* but also their *consumption* of commodity entertainment, a consumption that signified a cosmopolitan modernity for contemporary audiences. Claude Massot's film *Nanook Revisited* (1990) stages similar scenes of viewing to those in *The Return of Navajo Boy*: Inuit community members identify their relatives and friends in stills from the original *Nanook of the North* and in interviews discuss the impact of the filmmaking on the lives of the performers who acted out a nuclear family triad under Robert Flaherty's direction. The longevity of public indifference toward named crediting of Indigenous performers is striking—68 years elapsed between the release of *Nanook of the North* and *Nanook Revisited*, and 49 years between the completion of *Navaho Boy: A Monument Valley Story* in 1952 and *The Return of Navajo Boy* in 2001. The emotional scenes of recrediting that take place in *Nanook Revisited* and *The Return of Navajo Boy* attest to the importance of naming and attribution in Native repossession of filmed images.

In *The Return of Navajo Boy*, members of the Cly family consistently introduce themselves in the Diné way, by stating their clan affiliations.[37] Traditional Diné introductions include stating one's clans ("born to" one's mother's clan, "born for" one's father's clan, and one's paternal grandmother and grandfather's clans as well). This genealogical identification locates the speaker in Diné kinship systems, which potentially establish kinship relations between a speaker and addressee even if they have not met before. *The Return of Navajo Boy* begins with such an introduction, as the narrator Lorenzo Begay introduces himself in voiceover this way: "My family has lived here in Monument Valley for a long time. I am from the Tlaashchi'i clan, which means Red Streak Bottom clan. My name is Lorenzo Begay, and I am a Navajo." This is an opening address directed to a dual audience: Diné viewers would not need Lorenzo Begay to declare that he is Navajo because he has already stated his clans, whereas most non-Diné viewers do not know the clans and so need the second introduction.

Later in the film, when Jimmy Cly introduces himself and the film *Navaho Boy* during the screening for the inauguration of the new Navajo Nation museum, he introduces himself in Diné. Viewers of *The Return of Navajo Boy* hear his Diné greeting in voiceover with the English subtitles forming a caption to the image of his youthful face in the *Navaho Boy* footage: "My mother's clan is Towering House [Kinyaa'áanii]. My father's is the Leaf Clan [Bit'aanii]. My maternal grandfather is the Salt Clan [Ashiihi]. My paternal grandfather is the Manygoats Clan [Tlizi'tlani]. This is how I was taught to greet others as I was growing up" (see figure 3.13). The English subtitles, for non-Native viewers, function as an identifying caption, and Cly's voiceover introduces his image and himself in a formal address to both the largely Diné audience at the museum and the viewing audience for *The Return of Navajo Boy*. In a visual transition that parallels the identifying work of the voiceover, Jimmy Cly's face as he speaks at the event is superimposed on his boyhood face in the older film at the conjuncture of two

Figure 3.13. *The Return of Navajo Boy*, Groundswell Educational Films (2001), Jimmy Cly in the original *Navaho Boy* film with contemporary voiceover and subtitles.

dissolves. The dissolve and graphic match as transition from past to present in the film evince the techniques of continuity editing yet call attention to the temporal gaps that the film's work of family reunification addresses. "This summer some white people came. They told me they were returning my pictures. [Pause.] It was as if I were lost and finally found." Cly pauses as he describes his feelings of connection to the images. In another scene, as other Cly family members view the *Navaho Boy* footage, they identify the people in the movie: "There's Shirley's mother, Frieda," Elsie Mae says, "That's my grandma fixing my hair. That's me." Her *naming* also becomes *narration*: "That's my mom that's holding the baby, my brother. His name is John Wayne Cly. He was two years old when they adopt him. I haven't seen him. No, I haven't seen him. He was a baby at that time . . . he never came back."

The film's investment in this kind of literal or "forensic" identification is profoundly emotional. Jane Gaines argues that the engagement of affective registers in documentary—what she calls "documentary pathos"—connects the bodies in the theater and the bodies on-screen ("Political Mimesis" 92).[38] Gaines focuses on the effect that documentary imagery of political struggle can have on the bodies of spectators, which can result in mimetic, real-world political action. This "political mimesis" is based on an appeal to viewers' senses, an appeal that depends on a strong resemblance between the world depicted onscreen and the world experienced or perceived by the audience. The scenes of identification in *The Return of Navajo Boy* ask viewers to respond with intimate emotions not to scenes of mass protest or collective action but rather at the microlevel of the familial embrace. That familial embrace, and the work of identification leading to it, is a highly political act. One facet of this political evocation of emotion in representations of Indigenous familial separation and reunion is to reframe the relationship between documentary and dramatic codes. *The Return of Navajo Boy* binds the documentary with the dramatic characteristics of melodrama—coincidence, engagement of affective registers through images of suffering, a temporal tension between "just in time" and "too late" in the recognition of once-hidden social identities. Thus, rather than negating industry cinema's narrative conventions, *The Return of Navajo Boy* locates stories of unjust suffering, of hidden and revealed identities, of separation and reunion in the historical experiences of Native families. But the Cly family repurposes the communicative efficacy of their story, making their images testify to the urgency of specific social justice claims, such as RECA compensation. The film's point of intervention is to repair earlier documentary misrecognitions of individual people, families, and lands, and to rectify the Western's erasure of Native families and mythic images of open frontier. The film's amendatory recrediting of earlier images—the shift in provenance through corrective identification—underpins its strongest emotional and legal claims.

The Return of Navajo Boy is a story in which the circulation of film footage parallels the movement of its Native subjects away from and back to the Navajo Nation reservation in a pattern of reunification. The material repatriation of footage echoes scenarios of separation and return discussed in other chapters of this book; in this case, the subjects' retrieval of photographic and cinematic images of family members answers the before-and-after images of turn-of-the-century Native students, bookending that assimilationist image sequence with a narrative of familial continuity set in motion by the return of a film canister.

The Hands that Hold the Image

Victor Masayesva opens his 2006 book *Husk of Time: The Photographs of Victor Masayesva* with a visual dedication, a photograph of a photograph. In the photo, weathered hands hold another photograph of a young woman and man seated outside the entrance to a stone house. The bright sun on the stone makes the image gleam, while the framing background—a wooden table and log, the hands holding the photo—are lit more dimly (see figure 3.14). The aged hands seem to be holding a glowing memory from the past. We are invited to understand the couple in the picture to be Masayesva's parents—and that the hands holding the photo belong to his parents also—because underneath the image is a written dedication: "For my beloved mother and father, for all the years they have been there for us." While the photograph is further framed and informed by this textual captioning, the visual and textual dedication in turn frames the rest of the book with its relational crediting, surrounding the book itself with the larger context and purpose of a familial embrace and making visible Masayesva's assertions about the importance of Native filmmakers' accountability to home communities. Nesting the photograph in familial hands suggests, in the gesture of holding, both possession and transmission. The hands imply human work or manufacture, while the bodily contact with the photograph evinces Native presence and an implied spectator sharing his or her interpretive point of view with the camera. Finally, Masayesva's caption and the hands holding the photograph reach across time in intergenerational touch, framing memory with the assurance of continuity. That continuity, implied

Figure 3.14. Dedication page image from *Husk of Time: The Photographs of Victor Masayesva* (courtesy of Victor Masayesva).

by the photograph's embedded story of Native image-making, viewership, and generational recognition, challenges the narratives of assimilation and familial erasure in institutional images such as the before-and-after photographs circulated by the Carlisle School and other boarding schools at the turn of the twentieth century. In making the memory of the past visible, Masayesva assures us of a visible Indigenous future, or that, as Ross Macaya says at the end of his story of Hopi emergence in *Itam Hakim, Hopiit*, Masayesva's 1984 film, "This will not end anywhere."

The circulation, dissemination, and exchange of images of Indians—and the politically loaded redistribution that takes place in repatriation—has a visual analog in the possessory image of hands holding photographs in point-of-view shots (see figure 3.15). These shots, repeated many times in *The Return of Navajo Boy*, distance viewers from direct imaginative access to primitivist fantasy in the older photographic images, reflexively highlighting the photographs and film footage as authored objects and implying (though not always specifying) social relations and power relations in its production, circulation, and reception. This composition effectively narrates a scenario of return, one that answers the interventionist presumptions of before-and-after photographs of boarding school students discussed in the introduction to this book: hands holding the photograph physi-

Figure 3.15. *The Return of Navajo Boy*, Groundswell Educational Films (2001), Elsie May Cly Begay sharing postcard images of her family.

cally embody and reframe the act of "imagining Indians" by visibly taking in hand the power of interpretive guardianship. A mediated touch, these images bring the photographed subject and the embodied viewer together in the same frame while indicating the passage of time that had separated them. Such shots ask viewers to "identify with" Native spectatorial practices of recognition ("identification of") and prepare viewers for more directly emotional scenes later in the film when Elsie Mae is reunited with her brother John Wayne. Like the scenes in which the Cly family view footage of themselves, this arrangement in point-of-view shots stages a scene of Indigenous spectatorship. The metonymic connection of contemporary Indigenous hands holding footage or photographs, and of Native spectatorship in editing, bring contemporary Indigenous generational survivals to bear on older images of vanishing.

In his essay "Portraits and Landscapes," from *Husk of Time*, Masayesva describes taking a portrait of his niece before she performed in a Butterfly Dance:

> The sound of the shutter being released was like a rush of air through wings and appeared in my imagination like a release of time. It certainly was not capturing or freezing a moment of

time, despite all the promising Kodak claims. It was like releasing a moment that had been resigned to living in the steady
current of time. The sound and the release together had all the
appearance of yellow pollen dislodged from plant stems. (5–6)

This understanding of photography as a form of breath or "release"
rather than "capture" changed Masayesva's mind about the work of por-
trait-taking: "Up to that point I had vowed never to be a portraitist in the
manner of Edward Curtis and the many more recent photographers for
tourist magazines that featured Indians posing in Native costumes. Those
images represented the epitome of stereotyping to me, and I would have
no part of it" (5). This moment marks a photographic disengagement from
what Gerald Vizenor calls the "portraiture of dominance," instead expanding
the possibilities of image-making out of and across the mediation of the
camera: "the eyes that meet in the aperture are the assurance of narratives
and a sense of native presence" (*Fugitive Poses* 155). Even Roland Barthes,
who so convincingly articulates the capacity of photography to immobilize
its subjects, to transform "subject into object, and even . . . into a museum
object," refers to the click of the shutter as a "voluptuous" sound "breaking through the mortiferous layer of the Pose" (13, 15). In photographic
equipment's relationship to older forms of artisanal manufacture such as
cabinetry and watches, Barthes suggests that early cameras were "clocks for
seeing" (15). Masayesva's image of photographic action as a "release of time"
counters the assimilationist narrative and temporal straitjacket of the institutional before-and-after photographs of Native boarding school students
discussed in the introduction to this book, extending instead a more fluid
and expansive vision of Indigenous futures.

In *Imagining Indians* and *The Return of Navajo Boy*, renewed attention to the politics of continuity and repatriation form a central component of the films' visual sovereignty. Across both text and production,
mediated images from the past are nested within audiovisual frameworks
that assert ownership through processes of visual interpretation. This form
of claiming through "genealogical testimony" is a witnessing that draws
authority not just from individual experience but also from imagining, reenacting, or otherwise recouping family history—relationships with relatives
and ancestors—in ways that establish continuity with the past and make
Indigenous futures visible. When directed toward a heterogeneous audience,
such testimony also functions as what Roger Simon describes as the "trans-
active address" of "educative space" (68). In the context of documentary,
the politicized, pedagogical address of genealogical testimony makes images
once circulated as evidence of Indigenous defeat, colonization, and vanishing

accountable instead to the communication of Indigenous persistence and the particular needs of decolonization. At the same time, this address shifts the lenses of narratives and names through which non-Native audiences have envisioned landscapes and portraits, insisting that viewers "change the terms of recognition" in the wake of that paradigm change (Worsham 222).[39]

Many Native documentaries share characteristics with a broader field of reflexive documentaries narrating familial separation and return, such as James Hatch and Camille Billops's *Finding Christa* (1991) and Deanne Borshay Liem's *First Person Plural* (2000). And the formal strategies discussed in this chapter—the use of archival photographs and footage, voiceover, and techniques such as lateral pans over expansive landscapes in service of social justice claims—are common to many documentaries. But Native documentaries access political discourses about Indian vanishing, repatriation, and activist intercession that anchor common tropes and techniques in a distinct visual economy based on tribal histories. Despite significant differences in authorship and style, *Imagining Indians* and *The Return of Navajo Boy* bring Hollywood's commodified images of Indians into Indigenous interpretive frameworks, revealing both the heterogeneity of Indigenous perspectives and the stakes for individuals, families and communities in controlling the production and circulation of their representations. Their filmic conventions reappropriate the indexical and possessory qualities of cinematic portraiture and landscape imagery.

Indigenous and collaborative film productions have changed the discourse that speaks and defines "Indianness" on-screen. The figure of the individual Western star—often playing a military hero—comes under pressure in these films. Rather than being authenticated by the Native "extras" on-screen, the location shooting, and the signification of various props and costumes, the authority invested in stars such as John Wayne and Gary Cooper by Hollywood filmmaking is revoked in *The Return of Navajo Boy* and *Imagining Indians*. Masayesva and his interviewees, and Spitz, Klain, and the Cly family, take back the persuasive representational power of cinema and tradition for their own ends, using oral histories to disassemble Hollywood icons through irreverent questions, critique, and storytelling. In particular, film sound becomes a metaphor for voice as the films explore the repercussions of viewing and the conditions of making media. The images of mouths and teeth in *Imagining Indians*—the Lakota woman's teeth under a dentist's drill, the many interviews with actors and crew—become emblems for the experience of being silenced as well as for the right to speak, and through speaking, to transform the discourses about Indigenous identities in the contested arena of popular culture.

Part III

Independent Native Features

4

Imagining the Reservation in
House Made of Dawn and *Billy Jack*

In taking the 1972 film version of *House Made of Dawn* as my central text in this chapter, my object is to trace one point of emergence in the nascent Native filmmaking movement's emphatic disarticulation from the representation of Indians as a practice of industrial manufacture. The film *House Made of Dawn* evinces an aesthetically complex divergence from the melodramatic scenarios of "separation and return" that had characterized those previous representations of Native assimilation, renegotiating the political significance of intergenerational images in both its content and its production. If the generic conventions of frontier melodramas envision Native traditionality as stasis, subject to tragic and impending destruction, *House Made of Dawn* instead understands Indigenous familial relations to be mobilized across temporal and spatial distances through an ongoing and inventive process of instruction and transmission. The film breaks away from the melodramatic "squaw man" plot and interracial custody battles that still circulated in Westerns such as *The Man Who Loved Cat Dancing* (Sarafian 1973) and *Duel at Diablo* (Nelson 1966), and from the figure of the returning Native war veteran as a Western genre vigilante in films such as *The Vanishing American* (Seitz 1925), *Devil's Doorway* (Mann 1950), *Flap* (Reed 1970), and *Billy Jack* (Laughlin 1971/1973).

Directed by Richardson Morse from a screenplay coauthored with N. Scott Momaday, the film *House Made of Dawn* is a milestone in the resurgence of Native American filmmaking.[1] It traces the contours and assimilationist pressures of the federal Relocation program, Western films, and legal and military establishments while modeling systems of independent, interracial, and intercultural coproduction that continue to characterize much of Native filmmaking. This chapter explores the film's intervention in cinematic productions of Indianness at a particular historical juncture—the interstices of the Native American renaissance, the Red Power movement, and the New Hollywood renaissance.[2] The aesthetic and political histories of this moment have already been widely discussed in Native studies scholarship—the literary establishment's recognition of Momaday's first novel, *House Made of Dawn*, which won a Pulitzer Prize in 1969, and the intense surge in collective Indigenous responses to the 1950s federal policy of Termination, which catalyzed grassroots Native organizations and culminated in activist occupations in the late 1960s and early 1970s. This moment—the height of the Red Power movement, and concomitant mass media attention to the American Indian Movement (AIM)—was also a formative period in the history of Native Americans on screen. While images of the Vietnam War saturated public discourses, Native Americans were broadly recognized by producers and consumers of popular culture as emblems for the domestic history of American imperialism, not least in an industrywide cycle of violent, revisionist Westerns clustered between 1969 and 1973, including *Tell Them Willie Boy Is Here* (Polonsky 1969), *A Man Called Horse* (Silverstein 1969), *The Stalking Moon* (Mulligan 1969), *Soldier Blue* (Nelson 1970), *Little Big Man* (Penn 1970), and *Chato's Land* (Winner 1971). Other films synthesized Western genre signs and codes with contemporary urban, small-town, and reservation settings such as *Flap* (Reed 1970) and the extraordinarily profitable independent production *Billy Jack* (Laughlin 1971/1973)—a title I will discuss at some length as a counterpoint to *House Made of Dawn*.

In contrast to the wildly popular revisionist Westerns of this period, and indeed in contrast to the critical longevity of Momaday's novel, the film *House Made of Dawn* went largely unseen for almost 30 years—immobilized by distributors' refusal to purchase and circulate it—before its restoration in 2005 by the National Museum of the American Indian's (NMAI) Film and Video Center. I would like to bring the film *House Made of Dawn* to critical view as both an active response to contemporary popular representations and an early model of alternative, local film production that disengaged from the practices, forms, and sentiments of previous Los Angeles–based representations. The screenplay, for example, was the first to be adapted from a Native-authored novel, and Momaday participated in writing it and in scouting New Mexico locations (the film was shot on location at Sandia and Isleta Pueblos as well as Los Angeles). Casting is one of the most crucial decisions in translating Native narratives to the visual mode of cinema, compounding issues of genealogy and performance in the representation of Indigenous identity. Momaday himself describes both an imag-

Figure 4.1. *House Made of Dawn*, Firebird Productions (1972), Abel (Larry Littlebird).

ined, constructed, individual dimension of Indigenous identity ("an Indian is an idea which a given man has of himself") and a communal narrative written on the body (the "racial memory") ("Man Made of Words" 49, 50). Three of the Native actors in *House Made of Dawn*, including Larry Littlebird, Mesa Bird, and Teddy García, were cast from a Santo Domingo and Laguna Pueblo extended family, and documentary filmmaker George Burdeau (Blackfeet) also performed in a small role (see figures 4.1–4.3).

Figure 4.2. *House Made of Dawn*, Firebird Productions (1972), Francisco (Mesa Bird) and young Abel (Teddy Garcia).

Figure 4.3. *House Made of Dawn*, Firebird Productions (1972), George Burdeau as Abel's friend.

Their presence and influence enabled the finished product to engage in social criticism without imagining Native characters as "ethnic stand-ins" for other minorities, emblems of primitivism and masculine regeneration, or figures that vanish into narratives of imperialist nostalgia.[3]

House Made of Dawn is also situated at a temporal and geographical midpoint (the early 1970s) between several other key texts in a developing corpus of independent, increasingly Indigenous-controlled feature filmmaking—the Los Angeles–based production of Kent Mackenzie's *The Exiles* (1961), the Laguna Pueblo production of Leslie Marmon Silko's *Arrowboy and the Witches* (1980), and the early video work of Hopi photographer and filmmaker Victor Masayesva, particularly *Itam Hakim, Hopiit* (1984). Together these films represent an emerging experimentalism in representations of Native peoples on screen. The films remained underground and invisible for decades even as cycles of Hollywood production repeatedly turned to Native subjects as counterculture political allegory in revisionist Westerns. With the increasing twenty-first-century scholarly attention to Native cinema as a critical category, efforts to locate, restore, and preserve these early independent productions have come from organizations such as the NMAI and Milestone Film and Video.[4] *House Made of Dawn* is, then, historically important for its contribution to the development of Indigenous cinema broadly and to a distinctive, regional Pueblo cinema. The film's participatory and intercultural production style fuses a politicized Pueblo production aesthetic with an avant-garde break from Hollywood-based representational practices.

The chapter's concluding section on the film's production builds on interviews with lead actor Larry Littlebird, author N. Scott Momaday, and director Richardson (Rick) Morse to describe the incorporation of tribal dramatic idioms, community aesthetics, and local knowledge in the film's production, especially through casting.[5] The production of *House Made of Dawn* represents a turning point not only in the history of intercultural collaboration in feature filmmaking, but also in the history of Native documentary. Several Pueblo film directors describe their first film experiences on the sets of studio productions doing location shooting in New Mexico for 1960s Westerns. Before the educational and support infrastructure of the Sundance Film Institute and other organizations, productions such as *House Made of Dawn* functioned as a crucial training ground for documentary filmmakers Littlebird and Burdeau, who would go on to produce—among many other projects—the *Real People* (1976) documentary series for KSPS-TV in Spokane, Washington. This television series was one of the first produced by Native directors and crews and can be seen as a documentary extension of the work begun in *House Made of Dawn* in its focus on contemporary, individual Native voices, urban/reservation migration, and issues of traditionality and assimilation. In the face of the Western's developed grammar of violence based on vigilantism and generic icons (cowboy, Indian, settler, gunfighter), and the absorption of this aesthetic into urban action films during the 1970s, Momaday, Morse, and Littlebird offer a rereading of Western vigilantes and generic Indians informed by the government's post–World War II Relocation policy, a program that profoundly affected Native families and urban communities.

House Made of Dawn and Momaday's "Indispensible Equation"

The central character in the film *House Made of Dawn*, Abel (Larry Littlebird), is a Walatowa (Jemez Pueblo) man traumatized by his combat experiences in Vietnam (a departure from the novel's post–World War II timeframe) and by the isolation and racial brutality of American institutions. Upon his return home from the war he comes into conflict with a mysterious albino (Skeeter Vaughn), and believing that the man is a witch, Abel kills him during a bar fight. After serving a prison sentence, Abel is relocated to Los Angeles where he is befriended by his Diné roommate Benally (Jay Varella); by a white social worker, Milly (Judith Doty), who becomes his lover; and by a charismatic religious leader from the Native American Church, Tosamah (John Saxon). But Abel finds enemies in Los Angeles as well, and after a brutal attack by a sadistic police officer, he returns home to nurse his dying grandfather and to heal himself by restoring his relationship to his homeland through the ceremonial practice of running at dawn. Abel must decide how to respond to evil that manifests itself through both witchcraft and state oppression, and although he seems alone in his struggle, in the end he turns away from extralegal violence to Pueblo ritual action that is communally sanctioned. Unlike the visions of masculine regeneration then dominating the Western's revisionist landscapes, Abel finds voice and active resistance in Pueblo songs and especially in the dawn run, which forms the frame narrative that anchors the film's storytelling structure.

Abel's vigilante impulses are a symptom of his illness, a manifestation of his alienation from his Walatowa community and land. This association of vigilante violence with illness represents a radical divergence from both Hollywood representations of Indians in Westerns and other independent and minority-controlled productions that energized the action film genre, in which physical prowess indexes the hero's spiritual health and connection to his community. And in rejecting vigilantism and spectacles of violence as a form of narrative resolution, *House Made of Dawn* disengages from an entire tradition of representing Native Americans in Western genre cinematic storytelling.

While the film *House Made of Dawn* was never envisioned as a Western, its significance as an intervention in Hollywood's Western genre imaginary and production practices becomes clear when we attend to the context of revisionist cinematic representations of Native characters that saturated movie theater screens in the late 1960s and early 1970s. *House Made of Dawn*'s interruption of contemporary filmic images of racialized vigilante violence and the urban West, in particular, refuses the counter-culture appropriation of Native characters as allegorical figures for social critique while maintaining and even amplifying the novel's invocation of Red Power political claims. Momaday himself was actively thinking and writing about violence and vigilantism in the context of both Western genre frontier historical narratives and urbanization. He described the cinematic turn to the urban occurring in the Western genre when speaking about his screenplay for *House Made of Dawn*: "One of the things that happened to Westerns, at roughly the same time, was the arrival of the urban setting. . . . And I was dealing with Los Angeles as an urban reality at the time. And that's a new thing in Westerns, drugstore cowboys. . . . And I think that was something that I was working with, an urban Indian, in a sense—the relocation program, the '50s."[6] In addition to the post–World War II Indigenous experience of Relocation, Momaday's vision of the urban West may also have developed from his perception of a history of criminality on the frontier. Momaday has described the "Wild West" of the nineteenth century as a place where "freedom was confused with the ability to take the law into your own hands." This view of American frontier vigilantism seems a subset of a broader concept of violence in the West that Momaday describes as the "paradox" or "indispensable equation" of the American frontier ("Poetics and Politics" 13–15, 18, 21). Describing his novel *The Ancient Child*, which explores the allure of frontier violence through the folk hero/outlaw figure Billy the Kid, Momaday suggests that "the equation of the frontier in American history" is not "a pastoral" but "a murder mystery" ("Poetics and Politics" 15).[7] The comment is relevant to Abel's violent acts in *House Made of Dawn*, his ritual murder of the albino and attempt to kill the Los Angeles cop Martinez. In both the novel and film, Abel and Benally frame their discussion of police using frontier tropes: "cowboys and Indians" become "cops and Indians" as the murder mystery of the Western occupies the city.[8]

Abel's alienation from his Pueblo community, his war trauma, and his experience of assimilation and immersion in urban Los Angeles are initially withheld, revealed in a series of nested flashbacks and flash cuts, as well as through crosscutting and, especially, superimposition—techniques that suggest temporal simultaneity and that parallel rather than contrast Jemez land and Los Angeles. The twinning of Los Angeles and Abel's homeland through editing, graphic matches, and doubled characters further connects Abel's identity to tribal land and presents tradition as a modern resource rather than a relic from the past. Freeze frames, negative photography, and posterization express Abel's interior states while voiceovers frame the images in contexts of specific Walatowa traditions as well as U.S. Indian policies and institutions.

In dramatizing Abel's dislocation and his return to his grandfather and the Pueblo community, the film never engages the cinematic strategy of visually coded binarism in the representation of Native generations—so often presented in terms of costume as a visual signifier of traditionality and assimilation—or the sentiments and visual signs of familial separation that mark earlier films such as *The Vanishing American* (1925) and *Devil's Doorway* (1950), films that also depict Native war veterans returning home. *House Made of Dawn* has been characterized critically as a drama that "reveals the dilemma of the modern Indian" (Hilger, *Savage* 142), but the film's experimental aesthetics modify notions of Indigeniety as a crisis of boundaries between clichéd constructions of traditionality and modernity.

That imagined boundary is inscribed and reinscribed in scenes from silent
Indian dramas to revisionist Westerns produced in the Hollywood studio
system. In these sympathetic Westerns, scenarios in which Native children
return home from institutional settings are frequently signified first by costume and composed as a two-shot in which male relatives (often father
and son) confront one another in an uneasy intergenerational reunion. As
I discussed more extensively in the introduction to this book, such scenes
reshape the visual terms of assimilation instantiated so powerfully by the
Carlisle School photographs, extending the visual contrast between the
"before" of the previous generation and the "after" of the current generation's shift to a temporal and spatial modernity signaled by western style
clothing. Costume materializes colonizers' assimilationist ideologies of social
development while separating the visual signs of Indianness from the bodies
of Native actors, a fetishizing move that makes racial schema available for
performative masquerade.

The Vanishing American and Redskin (1929), as I discussed in chapter
2, staged sentimental "scenes of separation and return" that made visible the
violent coercion elided in the Carlisle School's before-and-after photographs
and in discourses of federal assimilationist programs. But these melodramas imagine Native boarding school graduates and military veterans to be
traumatized less by their experience in Western institutions and wars than
by their difficulty in maintaining their assimilated Western identities on
returning to their home communities. Devil's Doorway and Redskin narrate
a "reversion to savagery" through incremental or abrupt changes in costume,
a visual movement "backwards" in the assimilationist timeline such that the
characters' apparent Westernization in fact reiterates the tragic overtones of
racialist discourses of Indian vanishing.

House Made of Dawn, too, foregrounds the violence of assimilationist
programs—in fact, the entire film is structured around an extended "scene
of return" as Abel remembers his experiences within the military, prison,
and Relocation systems after he has returned to his Pueblo. But the film's
vision of Native subjectivity is radically new to cinematic representations.
Its cinematic techniques of superimposition and nested flashback present a
far more complex temporality than the straightforward narratives of classical
Hollywood cinema. The film destabilizes the sequential locations of "before"
and "after" through this formal stylistic experimentation and pulls public
discourse about Indian policies away from the rhetoric of reform couched
in sentimental representations of familial loss. Instead of imagining Abel's
return to the reservation as a study in contrasts, the film focuses in flashback
on Abel's immersion in urban Los Angeles with the frame narrative set in

the Pueblo. The effect is to emphasize the mutual influence of these places on one another and Abel's circulation back and forth between them in the context of *systemic* violence, rather than either an aestheticized culturalism or Native characters captive to the stasis of a personal dilemma. The film aligns Abel's urban experiences with Pueblo knowledge systems while at the level of production integrating Pueblo social relations into a Los Angeles–based system of production.

Locating Indigenous Film Production

The filmed version of *House Made of Dawn* follows a foundational premise of the novel—that stories are linked with places in particular ways. It envisions an Indigenous modernity that is both land-based and characterized by movements between shared geographies—experiences of mobility and migration—rather than the costumed stasis of ethnographic portraiture and melodramatic tableaux. Although much of the film's action takes place in Los Angeles, the site of Hollywood moviemaking itself, its production departs from the Hollywood system of location shooting to authenticate stories written in Los Angeles about settlers and tribes on the frontier. In turning to Los Angeles as both a pan-tribal metropolitan community and a location for new modes of film production, *House Made of Dawn* explores the relationships and boundaries between Native urban and reservation spaces and between the studio-based film industry and independent filmmaking. Indeed, the film expands the field of film production beyond Los Angeles to include Native lands—here, the Pueblos of New Mexico—as positions from which Native stories can be told and from which Native films can be produced and cast. Describing his role as Abel, lead actor Larry Littlebird emphasized this work of retelling Native histories through casting and performance, contending that non-Native actors "stand out rather than speak from the content of Pueblo peoples' history, thousands of years of being" (Littlebird, "*House*"). In order to discuss the ways that *House Made of Dawn* "speaks from the content of Pueblo people's history" through production and casting as well as formal techniques such as flashback and superimposition—and in order to discuss the ways that Hollywood's revisionist "Indian Westerns" do not speak out of that history—it is necessary to see cinematic representation as a place-based social practice that actively mediates Native claims to sovereignty.

House Made of Dawn's visual strategies—particularly the movement between Los Angeles and the Pueblo—tell a story of its break with

Hollywood production practices and its investment in Pueblo-based story-telling. Film scholar David James has asserted that independent cinemas allegorize their constituting social relations, that "a film's images and sounds never fail to tell the story of how and why they were produced—the story of the mode of their production" (*Allegories* 5). In his history of minority film movements in Los Angeles, *The Most Typical Avant-Garde*, James suggests that minority filmmakers in the 1960s and 1970s faced

> two parallel systems of choices: first, on the level of production, the choice between creating manufacturing and distribution apparatuses—alternative cinemas—of their own or attempting to secure positions in the industry; second, on the level of the film text, the choice between searching for the authentic or natural images, languages, or narratives of their own identity, or reworking those of Hollywood, using them against the grain or otherwise disrupting them. (300)

This formulation should not be seen as an either/or construction of limited choice (that is, a dilemma) for minority filmmakers, however, for James calls for dismantling the polarized categories of the industry and the avant-garde. "In neither register did the binaries remain stable" because niche markets resulted from "the new social movements' reconstruction of audience demands" while some minority filmmakers found careers within the dominant production system (300).[9] In a specifically Indigenous context, these choices involved coproduction, alternative private and public financing, and new cultures of production. In revising structures of Native performance and film production, *House Made of Dawn* also envisioned strategies of resistance and social action based in tribalism, intergenerational continuity, and a return to tradition as a *contemporary* source of resilience.

Anishinaabe writer Gerald Vizenor understands place-based Native sovereignty as a form of active "transmotion" (the right to be in motion, to subjectivity through action). Vizenor expands concepts of Indigenous modernity, survival, and sovereignty to include "survivance": "an active sense of presence, the continuance of native stories," and "renunciations of dominance, tragedy, and victimry" (*Fugitive Poses* vii). Survivance, then, is more than passive survival; it is an active resistance. He contrasts "survivance" with "*indian* absence," a pervasive "simulation of the *indian*" that is premised on "the absence of real natives" (vii) and that exists in the context of dominance. For Vizenor, survivance and Native presence are forms of dynamism or motion. "Natives have always been on the move, by chance, necessity, barter, reciprocal sustenance, and by trade over extensive routes; the actual motion is a natural right, and the tribal stories of transmotion are a continuous sense of visionary sovereignty" (ix).[10]

Analyzing Anishinaabe "picture writing" as "possessory" maps that assert a "visual claim" through aesthetic images (170), Vizenor connects political sovereignty with traditional expression:

> . . . the ideas and conditions of motion have a deferred mean-
> ing that reach, naturally, to other contexts of action, resistance,
> dissent, and political controversy. The sovereignty of motion
> means the ability and the vision to move in imagination and
> the substantive rights of motion in native communities. . . .
> The sovereignty of motion is mythic, material, and visionary
> not mere territoriality, in the sense of colonialism and national-
> ism . . . native transmotion is an original natural union in the
> stories of emergence and migration that relate humans to an
> environment. . . . (182–83)

This paradigmatic integration of material, imaginative, and political relation-ships to land is important for analyses of cinematic representations, which are of course both fabricated in form and profoundly material in produc-tion.[11] Another way to understand Indigenous territoriality in the cinema is Michelle Raheja's articulation of the "virtual reservation," or the "space of the film" as one in which "Indigenous people recuperate, regenerate, and begin to heal on the virtual reservation under the direct gaze of the national spectator" ("Reading" 1168).

The ideas of transmotion and the virtual reservation suggest the simul-taneous but very different kinds of movement between Los Angeles and Walatowa in *House Made of Dawn*.[12] The attention in the film to the con-nections between seemingly separate locations foregrounds the conditions of agency and compulsion (such as forced migration) that have character-ized Indigenous nations' interactions with the United States. The relational understanding of place in *House Made of Dawn* thus involves both a reli-gious bond maintained through ritual and a land-based authorization of Native nationhood and sovereignty, including its legacies and projects of political resistance. Abel's act of running over the land is a particular focus for critics discussing this concept of place in the novel's narration of Abel's return; the dawn run synthesizes the moral, spiritual, material, aesthetic, political, and imaginative facets of his relationship to his hereditary tribal lands.[13] Arif Dirlik suggests, in a global context, that Indigenous modernity is premised on an "attachment to place understood concretely" ("Global-ization" 1). His definition of place-consciousness involves not just "places and holisms" but also "translocal or transplace interactions that mediate the relationships between places and imperial centers, national or global" (17). This sense of place is different from (for example) place understood allegorically, as "the frontier" is allegorized in Westerns (in which there also occurs an "appropriation of the Indigenous for the national") (4). If West-erns attempt to imaginatively authorize U.S. nationhood and inventory its resources through representations of landscape, *House Made of Dawn* claims both the Pueblo and Los Angeles as Indian land—but not the same Indian land because Walatowa is Abel's homeland whereas Los Angeles is the site of his displacement to an intertribal community, in a city located on traditional Tongva, Chumash, and Luiseño lands. This political claim to the historical interrelation between places is articulated through images of Walatowa land and urban spaces, locations whose connectedness becomes the framework for the film's visual assertion of Indigenous sovereignty and mobility.

Filming an Activist Text

In moving between reservation and urban spaces, the film's silenced pro-tagonist alludes to another, collective Native voice—the very public procla-mations of AIM and the activist reoccupations of federally held land in the 1960s and 1970s. Momaday's novel understands Abel's generation of post–World War II Native men and women to be deeply affected by institutional interventions in their families and communities—in boarding schools, in the military, in prisons, and in cities—and to be seeking redress through activism. While the filmed version of *House Made of Dawn* is set in the early 1970s, it documents the effects of the Termination policies of the 1950s—a time when many Native families and communities also participated in the federal Relocation programs aimed at urban assimilation.[14] It was one of the first films and still one of the only films to do so.

House Made of Dawn's sharp focus on the way U.S. policies and institutions abetted individual racism, abusive working conditions, and sys-tematic police brutality shifts our attention to Abel's silence and the political implications of Native speech. The context of AIM's activist marches and occupations further politicize the Los Angeles–Pueblo axis in film produc-tion—an axis instantiated by both the film text and film production of *House Made of Dawn*—as a symbolically freighted, composite location from which Native speech occurs. The film's privileging of Native voices, and its emphasis on the relationship of urban and reservation locations, takes shape in this context of policies and urban Indigenous communities that incubated the political activism of the 1960s and 1970s.

"Termination"—the general term for a series of resolutions and public laws enacted between 1953 and 1961—sought to dismantle the U.S. federal treaty relationships with Native tribes, eroding reservation land bases and tribal sovereignty.[15] From the late 1940s through the late 1970s, the Bureau of Indian Affairs' (BIA) "Relocation" program encouraged Native individuals and families to move to urban areas. In adjusting to the new environments of American metropolitan communities such as Chicago, Minneapolis, San Francisco, and Los Angeles, Native people arriving from reservations and rural homelands formed connections through community organizations. These centers—represented in *House Made of Dawn* by the "Indian Friendship House" and Tosamah's Native American church—supplemented the services of the Relocation offices with material help in the form of groceries and clothes, networks for finding jobs and housing, and day-to-day support.

The film *House Made of Dawn*, like the novel, dramatizes the effects of Relocation by interweaving urban and reservation spaces and by staging interruptions of space and voice that indicate Abel's fractured subjectivity. Relocation as a policy and a pan-Indian historical experience is central to my analysis because it impelled the separation of Native individuals and families from reservation lands and because it continues to drive a generationally organized aesthetic in the storytelling of one place through the lens of another place.[16] For Red Power activists and Indigenous filmmakers, telling audiovisual stories about material reoccupations of land in a mass mediated form amplified the stories' political reach by rendering the occupation in the imaginative, virtual space of the screen.

The Indigenous activism so evident in the novel *House Made of Dawn* looks back to these urban pan-Indian communities and culture developed in cities in the 1950s, but the 1972 film version was made at the height of the activist movement—fish-ins, the occupation of Alcatraz Island (November 1969–June 1971) by the group Indians of All Tribes, the AIM "Trail of Broken Treaties," the occupation of the BIA offices in 1972, and the 1973 occupation of Wounded Knee.[17] The birth of the Red Power movement in the 1960s and 1970s took shape through these activist occupations of urban spaces and of places guaranteed by treaty but no longer under Native control, and through dramatic and symbolic actions designed to gain national and international media attention.[18] The increasingly violent confrontations between Native activists, some of them Vietnam veterans, and federal agents amplified and made publicly visible the historical and ongoing police brutality and judicial inequity in Native communities, even as the government tried to portray AIM as a group of isolated vigilantes.[19] In the Red Power movement, reoccupied waters, lands, buildings, roads, battlefields, and blockades became stages for highly symbolic protests, which the U.S. government, already embattled in Vietnam, interpreted as a "theater of war." Commanding symbolic spaces, crossing established boundaries through demonstrations of mobility (such as the cross-country march in the "Trail of Broken Treaties"), and taking up media "screen space" profoundly challenged categorizations of Native people as anterior in time to Western cosmopolitan modernity. That evolutionary representational paradigm had justified the "developmental" impulses of the Relocation program, an assimilationist model that attempted to "advance" people in time by moving them in space.

Chadwick Allen argues that Indigenous protests are performative "events," "instances of ethnopolitical conflict and performances of ethno-drama" with "an immediately discernable dramatic structure" (*Blood Narrative* 11). Such events define and consolidate ethnic identity for political purposes, and like other kinds of dramatic events there are actors, audiences, and stages. According to Lakota leader Robert Burnette, AIM leader Russell Means employed the tactic of strategic occupation of symbolic spaces by "staging demonstrations that attracted the sort of press coverage Indians had been looking for."[20] This close association and orchestration of dual spatial claims—the material and the virtual (or mediated)—in reoccupations of Indigenous land by AIM activists also inform the symbolic geography of the film *House Made of Dawn* in which parallel activist "occupations" take place both in the location production and in the representational space of the cinema screen.

Billy Jack's Reservations: Captivity Narrative and Freedom School

Shooting in Los Angeles locates Abel's story in the proximity of Hollywood and its images of Indians. At the same time that Native activists dominated the mediascape in the early 1970s on the basis of their distinct claims to sovereignty and self-determination, Hollywood revisionist Westerns reimagined screen Indians as publicly available emblems of non-Native cultural dissent. In order to understand the cultural production of Indianness at this moment and the ways that diverging representations of Native people originated from it, I want to briefly explore the complex cinematic performance of the Native "ethnic vigilante" character on screen.[21] In particular, Native histories and political protests were appropriated in Hollywood as spectacles of extralegal, and legal, violence through which to reshape, renew, and profit from the social imaginary of American youth. Producers and directors used conventions of ethnographic spectacle and innovations in the techniques of screen violence to claim new realism in representations of the West.

Western genre filmmakers (and much film criticism of the Western) often cast the virtual Western "frontier" of the cinema as an allegorical space of cultural encounter in which location shooting and dramatic stagings can signify a broad array of non-Native social problems and political views.[22] Native lands are once again appropriated—this time on screen—as a territory available for white American stories of origin, while the specificity of existing policies and politics affecting Native reservations and urban communities remains absent from the screen. The prominence of revisionist Indian Westerns is one example of the way public appetite for images of Indians both covered over and enabled Indigenous expression. In appropriating images of Indians for counterculture messages, revisionist Westerns obscured the specificity and voices of individual tribes and a thriving pan-Indian political movement.[23] *A Man Called Horse, Tell Them Willie Boy Is Here*, and *Billy Jack*, for example, elide and blur distinct tribal beliefs and narratives, instead adopting the sexualized captivity narrative and (in the latter two films) outlaw and vigilante figures as defining plot structures and central metaphors for Native-white relationships. *Little Big Man* and *Soldier Blue* used satirical and graphic massacre scenes to critique U.S. actions in Vietnam by revisiting and revising the racial landscape and bloody history of the American frontier.[24] Reading these films' depictions of Native ceremonial and historical events shows us how Native stories become detached from their material contexts and communities for presentation to non-Native audiences and why it matters who performs Native characters on screen.

Rick Morse's decision to shift the timeframe of *House Made of Dawn* from the immediate post–World War II period to the contemporary moment, making Abel a veteran of Vietnam rather than World War II (done for financial reasons to avoid the cost of recreating a historical set) foregrounds the film's divergence from contemporaneous films that imagined Native characters in the context of postwar trauma, vigilantism, and generational friction between counterculture and mainstream social values. Other films powered by vigilante protagonists—including Vietnam veterans, disenfranchised ethnic minorities, and vengeful Western frontiersmen—exhilarated youth audiences with spectacles of violent problem-solving. These revisionist Westerns advertise newly accurate representations of the West, but instead deliver traditional generic anxiety about racial indeterminacy and the performative and genealogical boundaries of identity. The phenomenon of *Billy*

Jack is important to consider in relation to *House Made of Dawn* not only because it too was independently produced by amateur filmmakers only a year earlier (1971), but also because it played a crucial role in reinventing the tropes of the Western—the melodramatic schema of the white home under threat, the spectacle of violent masculine vigilantism, and the idea of tribal territories as "open land" to fulfill settlers' desires. *Billy Jack* was also instrumental in translating those conventions to the incipient action and kung fu film genres. *Billy Jack* was made for less than $800,000 and grossed more than $65 million, making it a media phenomenon and one of the highest-grossing films to that date.[25] Unusual for its depiction of the contemporary West rather than the post–Civil War era setting of most revisionist Westerns, *Billy Jack* seems to take on similar issues to Momaday's novel—modern Native relationships to reservation homelands, ceremonial healing, and the figure of the Native war veteran, as well as the tensions and contradictions between heritable and performative models of identity. But in imagining reservation land as an allegorical space of freedom for counterculture youth, *Billy Jack* continues the Western genre's central concern with the frontier as a site of setter society's social and generational renewal, and it locates resistance to dominant social policies and Hollywood representations in aesthetically, generically, and genetically coded violence.

    Billy Jack is a title that (like *Shaft, Dirty Harry, Enter the Dragon, Sweet Sweetback's Baadasssss Song,* and other financially successful studio and independent films from this period) advertises visual pleasure specifically in terms of identification with and objectification of the physical mastery and suppressed rage of a charismatic vigilante hero. Laughlin's film succeeded beyond all expectations perhaps because it incorporates into its performative language the multiple modes and genres of a society remaking itself. Like *House Made of Dawn,* its familial drama of interracial relationships is set in a racially tense Western town adjacent to a reservation, and it features a traumatized Native veteran recently returned from Vietnam, reestablishing ceremonial practice under the guidance of an elder. The film's opening credits invoke the Western with spectacular aerial footage of a mustang roundup (and the protest song "One Tin Soldier" on the soundtrack) and through its structural focus on an ethnically marked outsider-hero—the vigilante figure bridging the Western with the incipient action genre—whose ultramasculine competence shields a pacifist, besieged community.[26] Billy Jack's racial politics merge with performative models of identity through the new grammar of film violence in 1970s visual culture. In particular, the violent defense of the pacifist Freedom School echoes the paradoxical mystique/critique of violence so pervasive in New Hollywood Westerns (such as *The Wild Bunch*).

In the film, Barbara (Julie Webb), the white daughter of a small town deputy sheriff, returns from San Francisco's Haight-Ashbury district pregnant with a potentially mixed-race baby. She finds shelter at the Freedom School, a white-run school on reservation land protected by the mixed-blood former Green Beret Billy Jack (played by non-Native actor-director Tom Laughlin in unconvincing redface; see figure 4.4). Billy Jack acts out the film's contradictory paradigms: racial mimicry disguised as tolerance suggests a performative model of identity while the captivity narrative structure and preoccupation with white women's sexuality indicate both racial determinism and a fear of racial contamination. The film employs a heteroglossic language of posture to communicate racial scenarios of what Ella Shohat has called "ethnicities-in-relation"; the acting and choreography appropriate ethnically coded gestures that allude to the African-American civil rights movement, Asian martial arts, and Native American spiritual and activist practices that were newly and profoundly attractive to American moviegoers.

Billy Jack's vision of reservation land as a space for settler alterity is materialized in the Freedom School, located on the reservation. For a century Native American children had been sent away from reservations to

Figure 4.4. *Billy Jack*, National Student Film Corp., Warner Brothers (1971), Billy Jack (Tom Laughlin).

boarding schools to learn the strict performance of white American culture, but in *Billy Jack* the Freedom School reverses the flow, obscuring actual federal Relocation policy by depicting a fantasy exodus of white youth to reservation land and taking Native cultures as teaching models. Rather than imagining reservations as systems of containment—"prisons" or "concentration camps"—as had 1950s policymakers and filmmakers (in films like Delmer Daves's 1950 *Broken Arrow* and Martin Ritt's 1967 *Hombre*), here the reservation is a utopic retreat, a haven for freedom and creative expression.[27] The space and idea of the reservation is given over in service of white counterculture education. Native land is figured as a commune, as well as a place for non-Natives to heal from the traumas suffered outside of its borders and create a better model of whiteness. Scenes of religious ceremony are framed as theatrical spectacle, exhibited, and explained for the consumption of white spectators. Yet in this process, dark-skinned actors are cast as students, not teachers. An example is an early scene when Barbara's Native boyfriend Martin (Stan Rice) asks to be Billy Jack's apprentice during the upcoming Snake Ceremony, making characters such as Martin, with dark skin and black hair, function as sidekicks for the purposes of authenticating Laughlin's redface by creating narrative equivalence between the men as Native characters.

The performative construction of race is also dramatized when Native and white students, having come to town in a bus trip reminiscent of the Freedom Rides, spontaneously enact a civil rights–style lunch-counter sit-in at an ice cream parlor. The Native students are humiliated and beaten by bullies, and the characters' investment in race-mutability is mimicked and mocked when the bully's "solution" to the problem of segregation is to "simply make [our] non-white friends white" with scoops of flour. This, too, is a form of theatricality, "whitefacing" the students in a violent parody of coercive assimilation. Billy Jack is unable to contain his rage at the injustice and removes his cowboy boots to better avenge the children in the fight that ensues. Just before he demonstrates his Hapkido karate skills, Billy Jack moves from calm containment to frenzied action with a speech: ". . . when Jean and the kids at the school tell me that I'm supposed to control my violent temper and be passive and nonviolent like they are, I try, I really try. But when I see this girl of such a beautiful spirit so degraded . . . I just go *berserk!*" Fast cutting, slow-motion, high-angle, and low-angle shots accentuate the gymnastic, choreographed quality of the action, which emphasizes slow, dancelike movements and fleeting glimpses of graceful kicks and leaps. Laughlin combines his Western genre narrative structure and iconography (the cowboy boots and hat) with the performative and kinetic violence of an emerging genre, the kung fu film. It was one of the earliest films—perhaps the first with a non-Asian star—to incorporate extensive martial arts fight scenes, just before Bruce Lee came to American stardom in *Enter the Dragon* (Clouse 1973). While the visual techniques immerse audiences in spectacular violence, the scene is also connected to the film's investment in acting out "psychodramas" and improvisational street theater.

Although many creative activities—weaving, painting, barrel-racing—are initially included in the description of the Freedom School's offerings, the primary focus of every scene involving the students is performance, especially protest songs and improvisational theater (what the school's director calls "psychodrama and role playing"). As a drama teacher tells the sullen Barbara, "all you have to do is come into the scene and discover who you are as the scene progresses," directing Barbara to find her essential self within her performative self and positing role-playing as a powerful agent of social change and personal growth. In the improvisation that follows, Barbara becomes the mother of a black Jesus, who teaches the students to give the Black Power sign, a raised fist, as the "sign of the new religion so that people will know each other." The play incorporates Barbara into the school while rehearsing the film's conclusion in which Billy Jack makes his last stand in an abandoned church. In the final moments of the film, the camera tilts down from the cross above the church door to Billy submitting to handcuffing; the students line the road, stand, and raise their fists with the Black Power gesture as he is taken away.[28] Laughlin "role-plays" AIM occupations and Black Power activism with highly theatrical violence, and the film targeted young audiences who might already be immersed in news media coverage of these movements. Laughlin's Western genre-derived violence in the shoot-out turns out to be, after all, itself a performance on stage when the closing scenes include news cameras recording both the standoff and surrender with the implication that the trial will be well publicized. Earlier in the film, conservative townspeople are won over as they themselves are incorporated into comic improvisational scenes in which they play wayward teens, and Sheriff Cole (Clark Howat) becomes unwittingly involved in a street-theater faux robbery. These and other lengthy sequences of amateur drama, representing the school's nonviolent methods of social change, suspend the tense narrative that frames Billy Jack's theatrical violence in the context of the Western.

Laughlin's playing Indian reveals in the film's production a larger concern with the benefits of performing Indianness; but in making cinematic signs of Indianness available to everyone through redfacing, the film denies and interferes with the specificity of actual Native claims to treaty rights based on the particular histories of tribal nations. The performative process distracts viewers from the actual policies and histories affecting Native people and lands, as well as issues of poverty and social service practices such as the removal of Native children from family custody.[29] This instance of the film's articulation of its modes of production suggests Indigeneity is available to all as a lifestyle choice with cinematic representation as its mode of transmission. At one point, Billy Jack sums up the film's presentation of redface by pronouncing that "Being Indian isn't in the blood. It's a way of life." After undergoing a rigorous ceremonial rite, Billy Jack describes an Indianness that is in service to white youth. Revealing his vision of the Ghost Dance prophet Wovoka, he says, "The time is now when the Indian will triumph . . . the whole spiritual wisdom of the great holy men, of the Indian tradition, is now what the young people of the world are looking for." Billy Jack's outstretched arms echo Christ on the cross through gesture; allusions to sacrificial martyrdom and political assassination are strengthened by cross-cut shots of Billy Jack through the sights of a rifle as Bernard Posner, son of the town boss, takes aim from above. The speech continues: "And lastly you must learn the dance . . . of friendship and welcome in which all whites who come to you with open hearts must be taught the dance in the Indian way."[30] "Indian triumph" consists of white youth taking up "the Indian tradition."

After a climactic Western-style shoot-out in the closing scenes of *Billy Jack*, Laughlin mimics Native American activist occupations and AIM use of the media to affect policy and judicial review, and in fact the film borrowed viewers from audiences already following such events as the occupation of Alcatraz Island in the media. The film itself imagines its youth audiences in the crowds of students who take Billy Jack as their hero. Linda Williams has suggested that violence (gunfights as well as action sequences) acts as a performative "number" in the Western, where "disequilibrium is figured as physical violence" and "through violence, equilibrium is reestablished" (*Hard Core* 130–31).[31] *Billy Jack*'s performances—both the student talent shows and the carefully choreographed fight sequences—function as different kinds of numbers, a spectacle that disrupts the film's narrative progression and at the same time assures audiences that the problem of race hatred can be solved if white youth discover themselves through racial mimicry. This mutable, thespian model of identity is a reflexive manifestation of the film's practice of redface as an expression of social regeneration for American middle-class youth. The ritualized role-playing of both the performance theater and generic violence rehearses in the film's content its production practices of cultural appropriation. The work of the Freedom School—and of the film itself—is to teach white audiences to perform and to consume Laughlin's vision of Indianness. Yet while Laughlin's film returns obsessively to performance and spectacle as a process of alternative education and self-discovery, it simultaneously imagines a biological racial identity so elemental and legible as to be manifest on the skin of the unborn. When Barbara miscarries after a fall from a horse, the town doctor assures the deputy sheriff that the baby "was not an Indian. I told you I handled it and it was a *white* fetus."

At the center of *Billy Jack*, then, is a familiar Western genre focus on racialized threats to white women's reproductivity: Barbara's "real" baby is a "white fetus," her "psychodrama" baby is a black Jesus, and her cinematic savior/captor is the redface Billy Jack. In fact, the film's entire plot hinges on the deputy sheriff's interpretation of Barbara's stay at the school as a kidnapping or "captivity," reprising the sexualized captivity of narratives such as *The Last of the Mohicans*. Barbara's relationship with the Native student Martin is the mixed-race relationship that crosses the lines of propriety in the town. Barbara's father, the deputy sheriff, is unable to accept his daughter's choice or the possibility that her baby is mixed blood. By the end of the film, in a deeply familiar narrative pattern, Barbara's baby, mixed blood or not, is lost, and Martin has been killed for his transgression. But Barbara and Martin, though central characters, are youthful shadows of a more mature couple—the school's director, Jean, and Billy Jack. Married in real life, in the film Jean (Delores Taylor) and Billy Jack (Laughlin) never act on their feelings beyond mutual declarations of love when their separation has already become inevitable. The couples echo each other, creating equivalencies between the white women, Jean and Barbara, and the Native men, Martin and Billy Jack.

House Made of Dawn unravels these formulaic depictions of Native vigilantism, female captivity, and settlement in films like *Billy Jack* by calling attention narratively and stylistically to the failure of heroic violence to effect change, redeem the protagonist, enact justice, or restore the social order. If *Billy Jack*'s source of regeneration is vigilantism, *House Made of Dawn* questions the narrative paradigm that Slotkin calls "regeneration through violence," undermining the currency and efficacy of violence through stylistic and narrative deflation. It engages a very different mode of revisionism from the aesthetically lush critiques of violence in contemporaneous films such as Penn's *Bonnie and Clyde* (1967) and Peckinpah's *The Wild Bunch* (1969), and from the transposition of Western genre spectacles of violence of the Western to contemporary urban settings in films like *Dirty Harry* (Siegel 1971) and *Death Wish* (Winner 1974). Narrating the failure of violent spectacle, Morse instead employs montage, superimposition, and flashbacks to signal Abel's movement toward restoration. These modernist, avant-garde filmmaking techniques counter primitivist readings of Pueblo culture with technologically and aesthetically dynamic methods and an urban setting.[32]

Seeing and Being Seen

The film version of *House Made of Dawn* calls into question the Holly-wood model of violence-as-competence. Abel consistently fails in his use of force. Unable to heal himself or solve social conflicts through violence, he returns to Walatowa strategies for addressing evil by running in a ritual footrace. The film uses complex visual transitions and nested flashbacks to suggest Abel's memories and altered states as he reconstructs his past during the ritual dawn race, and parallel scenes link institutionalized violence with witchcraft. Some of the editing and special effects in postproduction were intended to make the film more saleable and attractive to distributors, but the flashbacks, freeze frames, slow motion, multiple superimpositions, and negative and posterized images effectively translate Momaday's literary experimentation with modernist forms and emphasize Abel's subjectivity as he alternates between memories of urban and reservation experiences. Momaday's novel extends oral storytelling as a contemporary key to an urban post–World War II generation's confrontation with Indian policy. Using his capacity for multiple address and realignment of literary styles and genres, he also merges that oral expressive tradition with literary modernism and pulp Westerns. Louis Owens claims that Momaday's success as a novelist rests partly in his ability to use high modernist forms to dramatize Indigenous experiences, making "the discourse of the privileged center . . . 'bear the burden' of an 'other' world-view" ("Acts" 92).[33] Returning to David James's description of the ways that films materialize or "speak" their modes of production, I am interested in the way that the film version of *House Made of Dawn* has a "metaphorical relation to [its] own manufacture," the way its images make available a "filmic trope—a camera style or an editing pattern" that can be "understood as the trace of a social practice" (*Allegories* 14).[34] In its representation of Abel's coming and going from Los Angeles, the film materializes the relation of the homeland to an urban "imperial center" where Indian images are manufactured for mass consumption. This movement back and forth, then, is both the subject and the work of the film, and comprises a particular intervention in the cinematic purposing of Indian land for white regeneration in films such as *Billy Jack*.

Most significantly, the reservation is the place where images are generated in the film: Abel's memories come to him (and to viewers in the flashbacks) while he is running at the Pueblo. Thus, the film's images represent Abel's act of self-creation as he uses the ceremonial structure of the dawn run to organize his past. Bringing this community framework to bear on his experiences begins the process of reintegrating Abel into his familial relationship to Pueblo tradition; as he runs he recalls his grandfather's stories about running at dawn as a young man, and so he embodies and extends what his grandfather calls "the life that runs through our people." The temporal and geographical linearity and binarism of assimilation (before and after, reservation and city) implicit in the Relocation policy is unraveled by the mobility and simultaneity of these strategies.

The film is structured by an initial moment of generational transition. In the first scene, Francisco speaks to his grandson Abel in the actor's own Keresan language as he lies in bed. His lines are not translated; no gestures or reactions from Abel cue the viewer. The lack of translation through dubbing, subtitles, or other means prevents outsiders from fully knowing or accessing the character and is the first indication of the film's doubled audience, its strategy of simultaneous inclusion and exclusion of the non-Pueblo viewer. Abel's grandfather's death appears to invoke the image of the "vanishing Indian" so common to narratives of the American West, but a brief superimposition of their faces disturbs this trajectory. The film's shift in focus to Abel further revises the "vanishing" trope to consider the effects of assimilationist Indian policy *on the child*. As symbolic and contested figures on screen, and as living proof of continued Indigenous presence in the United States, Native youth disturb and interrupt the narratives that figure them as "problems" and vanishing populations.[35]

The film's movement between urban and reservation landscapes establishes both the disorientation of uprooted individuals and the interconnected relationship between apparently separate geographies. Importantly, as in the AIM occupation of Alcatraz Island, viewers are reminded that urban institutional spaces are also Native lands. Abel and his friend Benally continually seek out and create a Native geography of Los Angeles, finding spaces for themselves in the Indian Welcome House, Tosamah's basement church, Indian bars, and powwows and 49s located on the outskirts of the city.[36] Benally redefines the factory where he and Abel work as a Native space by singing powwow songs that overlay the rhythm of the box-cutting machines with pan-Indian song cadence, and the two men talk and sing together in marginal areas of the city—alleyways, fire exits, and train tracks. The editing collapses and connects urban and rural places through parallel scenes in which white people—factory bosses, policemen, and even Abel's girlfriend Milly—continually occupy, interrupt, and attempt to claim these Native spaces. The usurpation of land-based Indigenous economies for urban and rural wage labor reveals the racial uplift narratives supporting assimilationist policy to be, in actuality, the creation of an Indigenous underclass through deterritorialization. The factory scenes further allegorize and critique the industrial production of Indianness in which Hollywood studios extract the labor of Indigenous actors as "extras" but exclude them from sharing in profits.[37]

Abel's subjectivity drives the narrative structure of the film through the transitions from shot to shot. A recurring editing pattern begins with a freeze frame on Abel's face, followed by tighter shots, superimposed images, and flashback sequences.[38] The freeze-frame effectively visualizes Abel's inability to act or speak on his own behalf and depicts his altered states as the result of trauma, the effects of alcohol and peyote, and the effort of his ceremonial running. As Abel begins his dawn run, increasing slow motion represents his body in transition, and his image gradually becomes its own negative. The negative image is posterized so that the light images become fuchsia, and the film cuts to Abel in a suit and tie leaving a Trailways bus station in urban Los Angeles. He emerges, then, out of his own negative image into a memory of Relocation, by means of a technical manipulation that expands photographic oppositionality to encompass the character's simultaneous relationship to two geographical spaces (see figures 4.5–4.8).

Figure 4.5. *House Made of Dawn*, Firebird Productions (1972), Abel at dawn.

Figure 4.6. *House Made of Dawn*, Firebird Productions (1972), Abel running.

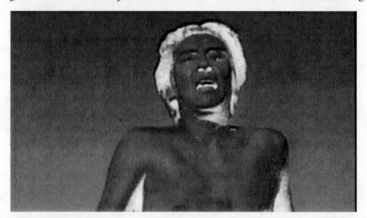

Figure 4.7. *House Made of Dawn*, Firebird Productions (1972), posterized transition to flashback.

Figure 4.8. *House Made of Dawn*, Firebird Productions (1972), Abel in Los Angeles.

This sequence draws from Abel's realization in the novel that "they [those in power in the courts] were disposing of him in language, their language" (Momaday, *House* 90). During this urban montage scene, Abel remembers his trial for the murder of the albino on the reservation. In voiceover a priest, judge, lawyer, and other officials construct Abel's institutional history for the viewer and deconstruct his sense of self as he wanders the streets of Los Angeles looking for the Indian Welcome House. The dominant discourse in voiceover fuses with views of buildings and signs, giving the cityscape an intimidating quality that persists throughout the film. Rather than aligning the viewer with an orienting hero as in revisionist Westerns and urban vigilante films, sounds and images in the Los Angeles montage scene leave both Abel and the viewer disoriented. High-angle shots diminish Abel's figure amid the enormity of the city and suggest that he is lost, and a low-angle shot overwhelms him with views of the Rosslyn Hotel towers. The street and its signs, stores, and diners would be landmarks to city dwellers, but for Abel (shot from his point of view) they become meaningless visual noise multiplied by the mirroring effect of plate glass windows.[39]

Abel arrives at the Indian Welcome House and social services office, located behind (or perhaps under) a street-level insurance and tax office that is itself for sale. An empty school desk and baby carriage sit outside the storefront entrance, props that silently point to the history of institutional intervention in Native families through adoption and boarding school education programs intent on shaping and reshaping Native youth (see figure 4.9). In the office, the poster of Sitting Bull in the background aligns the white

Figure 4.9. *House Made of Dawn*, Firebird Productions (1972), finding the Indian Welcome House.

social worker Milly's bureaucratic language with commercial photographic (and cinematic) constructions of Indianness. The photograph—taken by D. F. Barry in 1885 after Sitting Bull's imprisonment and during the time when he was both on tour and on display—is another emblem that brings together discourses of law and of image as strategies of containment. Brightly lit, Milly and the poster of Sitting Bull face the viewer stacked on the left of the screen, while Abel sits with his back to the camera, his black suit jacket darkening the right screen. The shot composition displays interlocking bureaucratic and commercial "faces" of Indian policy and commodified images, but withholds Abel's face and voice (see figure 4.10). His visual presence in the discourses that frame him is an absence, an exclusion from the resources and representations that circulate in Los Angeles. Through its geographical trope for assimilationist government policies and popular visual representations, the film implies that the law and the cinema "see" and define Indianness in similarly destructive ways. Abel's relocation to the city further integrates the film's commentary about the federal policing of Native spaces with its blurring of the boundaries between the Hollywood industry and nonindustrial filmmaking— Los Angeles represents a site for "an address to and interaction with Hollywood" (James, "Extras" 5).[40]

The film's association of the Los Angeles and Walatowa lines of action revise the trope of confrontation in the Western. Instead of the violent oppositionality of the Western standoff, *House Made of Dawn* is structured accord-

Figure 4.10. *House Made of Dawn*, Firebird Productions (1972), Milly (Judith Doty).

ing to a more integrated relational model. In parallel scenes at the center of the film, the motif of the saloon entrance from the Western destabilizes interior spaces—spaces marked as Native—first in an Indian bar in Los Angeles and then at Paco's Bar on the reservation. The character of the albino is a pivotal figure for this purpose because his trajectory is the same as that of Martinez (Philip Kenneally), the corrupt Los Angeles policeman. In the first scene, Benally, Tosamah, and Abel sit at a table drinking beer and telling stories. Benally finishes a story about a friend from Los Angeles visiting his reservation. As Tosamah goes to the bar, the sadistic police officer Martinez enters. In a medium-shot, his uniformed figure blocks a handpainted "Indian Power" sign on the wall behind him, reminding viewers of the recent AIM activism. Martinez begins to bully Benally and Abel, but as Tosamah returns he locks eyes with Martinez, who then leaves the bar (see figures 4.11 and 4.12). Though Benally offers Abel a model of survival in the city through a pan-Indian culture of powwows and 49s, Abel rejects Benally's subservience to white authority figures such as the factory boss and Martinez, a system of hierarchy that Benally accepts as an inevitable part of participation in the "good life" of Los Angeles. Social power is negotiated in this scene through a web of gazes in which Benally casts his eyes down when confronted by Martinez, Abel holds his gaze steady, and Tosamah meets and bests Martinez's stare. Tosamah is the only Native character able to circulate in both white and Native spaces with equal competence, and his portrayal by white actor

Figure 4.11. *House Made of Dawn*, Firebird Productions (1972), Tosamah (John Saxon) stares down the police.

Figure 4.12. *House Made of Dawn*, Firebird Productions (1972), Tosamah with Benally (Jay Varella) and Abel.

John Saxon complicates this scene by confronting Martinez with a white antagonist in redface. Although Saxon plays a Native character, the racial configuration of the actors places Saxon and Kenneally in the upper frame and Varela and Littlebird in the lower frame. As this staging intersects with the diegetic gazes, we see white actors playing "Cop" and "Indian," locked in conflict, literally over the heads of the actors of color seated below them. After the cop departs, Tosamah contrasts Abel's immersions in white institutional culture through boarding school, military, and prison, with the Pueblo worldview that allows Abel to identify the albino as a snake. The recollection of this crime triggers a nested flashback in which the albino enters Paco's Bar on the reservation, another interruption of interior, Native space that emphasizes—as do their black police and cowboy uniforms—the parallel narrative trajectories of Martinez and the albino.

The visual correlation of these characters links the institutionalized violence that Abel has experienced in the military, in prison, and in the city with Pueblo conceptions of witchcraft. At Paco's, Abel sits alone at the bar, but the mise-en-scène doubles everything around him (two couples sit in the background, two Budweiser clocks hang above them, and in the foreground to the lower right of the screen sit two large candy jars). The albino approaches the door and his figure, with cowboy hat, casts a shadow on the metal screen door that resembles scales (see figure 4.13). These doubled "saloon" scenes, interrupted by the entrance of Martinez and then the albino,

Figure 4.13. *House Made of Dawn*, Firebird Productions (1972), the albino (Skeeter Vaughn).

imply that the narrative patterns of representation in the Western, like the violence of policy and of witchery, are inescapable regardless of locale. The visual doubling of mise-en-scène in the bar also points to Abel's doubled consciousness and couples villain and hero in a way that complicates their otherwise clear-cut narrative positioning as apparent opposites. Given the prominence of twins in both Pueblo and Diné narrative traditions, we can see the visual doubling, also prominent in the novel, as a form of twinning. Susan Scarberry-Garcia argues that the novel creatively adapts and refers to stories about the Jemez Pueblo War Twins *Masewi* and *Uyuyewe* and the Diné Twins, Monster Slayer and Born for Water, sons of Changing Woman. She writes that the "double cyclic or spiral pattern of separation and return, separation and return" is "an example of Momaday's imaginative adaptation of oral traditions. This complex spiral pattern also echoes the theme of twinning or duality in the novel" (18–19). The urban and reservation lines of action are equated or twinned through flashbacks, including parallels between manufacturing and agricultural wage labor personified by the factory and farm bosses. These juxtapositions in Abel's memory suggest that he sees his homeland not as an escape from the systematic oppression of the city but rather as a place where he has recourse to ritual, communal modes of resistance to malevolent forces that exist everywhere.

"I've known for a long time now—who you are," Abel says as the albino smiles. Abel's assertion, his certainty in his knowledge of the demonic, otherworldly figure of the albino/witch, raises issues of identification that have surrounded Abel himself throughout the film. While institutional structures support the racially evaluative gazes of the people around Abel who have an interest in his performance of ethnicity, Abel himself, in gazing at the albino, identifies him not through a system of racial classification but rather to ascertain his status within a Pueblo schema of the supernatural. That is, Abel is not interested in the albino's whiteness or Indianness but in his witchery. It is Abel's *way of seeing*, not of being seen—his identification of the witch and, earlier, his vision of the eagle and the snake—that ultimately establishes both his identity and his resistance to the gazes of others that would determine his identity for him.

But if Abel's belief in witchcraft and his certainty about the albino's identity as a witch determine his Pueblo identity, his actions toward the albino signify the extent of his alienation from that community bedrock. As Larry Evers has discussed in relation to short stories by Leslie Silko and Simon Ortiz that draw on historical incidents of "witch perception," problems with witches are compounded when what should be brought to the community and dealt with as a "public matter" is instead confronted in the context of "a private grievance" (256, 253). Abel's confrontation with the Los Angeles cop occurs in the isolation of a dark alley, but Ben has already revealed the potential absurdity of public action against the cop. When Abel asks "Why'd that cop rough us up like that?" Benally replies, "I dunno, maybe 'cause he's a cop and we're Indians, you know? Like cowboys and Indians—Bang! Bang! We could complain to the police, that would make him really mad. I know what we could do, we could scalp him! But somehow I think they'd know who did it." The institutional framework for violence, manifested by the L.A. cop in uniform, prevents Abel from making a "public matter" of his victimization. Abel's attempt to act against injustice, to "do something about that" (an activist impulse except in its isolation from community) takes the form of vigilante action, which instead of solving the problem of Martinez only contributes to Abel's own illness. Indeed, *House Made of Dawn* suggests that the Western film tradition of vigilantism *is itself* a symptom of illness.[41]

House Made of Dawn imagines the trauma experienced by returning Native veterans as contiguous with the experiences of previous generations and events in tribal history. Trauma is not the result of a discrete event or the fact of biculturalism, but is rather an *ongoing* result of *systemic* oppression and the institutional and political interventions regulating Native families, mobility, and self-determination.[42] During his relocation to Los Angeles, Abel is "profiled" by the corrupt cop Martinez, by his boss at the factory, and less aggressively by the social worker Milly and spiritual leader Tosamah. His ethnic makeup and cultural destiny are contested by the disembodied voices of the priest, judge, and other officials as he wanders the streets. The Relocation program that sends him to Los Angeles both apprehends Native difference as a deficit and works to efface or camouflage that difference in the multiethnic milieu of the city. The disembodied gaze or Foucauldian eye of the law implied by Termination policies, with their bases in systems of racial classification, becomes instantiated in specific situations through specific characters, such as when Milly, in her capacity as social worker, compiles Abel's statistics: "I'll need your name, date of birth, place of birth, and military service." Under Milly's questioning Abel is, in Foucault's words, "seen, but he does not see; he is the object of information, never a subject of communication" (200). Milly is both a vehicle for a kind of panoptic gaze and an individual who cares for Abel and establishes an intimate and private space with him outside of their administrative relationship. But Abel is continually caught up in the fixtures of institutions: government school, the military, the courts, prison, the BIA relocation office, and the factory where he works. In this sense, Abel's experience with the institutional gazes and disciplinary mechanisms of bureaucracy immobilize him and remove his own powers of speech, his ability to act in the world through language. The particular vision of trauma in *House Made of Dawn* calls for recovery based in a return to tradition, and characterizes that tradition as a form of resistance that "speaks out of a specific history."

In the scene in which Abel kills the albino, shaky camera movement, low-key lighting, and canted frames convey the off-balance, atmospheric anxiety of film noir, not the decisive certainty of action films or the aesthetic, lyrical violence of multi-speed montage that characterized new revisionist Westerns such as *The Wild Bunch*. Ultimately, it doesn't matter whether Abel wins or loses his dark-alley fights—evil continues to exist and his attempts at vigilante justice only isolate him from his community. Graphic matches unite these moments of isolation with images of Abel as he begins to heal. The close up of his face, horizontal on the ground after Martinez' assault, reappears when he falls during the dawn run in the film's closing scene, a moment when he gathers the strength to finish the run and seems to connect most strongly to his grandfather's voice (figures 4.14 and 4.15).

Another shot of Abel's face, frozen and unable to pray during a peyote ceremony, is echoed in the next scene's three-way superimposition layering the lights of a Los Angeles freeway, his grandfather Francisco's drill spinning

Figure 4.14. *House Made of Dawn*, Firebird Productions (1972), Abel after the attack.

into turquoise stone, and Abel fluently singing a song that Benally could not remember.[43] The work of this superimposition as a graphic metaphor for Indigenous presence in interrelated locations also depends on Abel's song as a sound bridge, emphasizing the mnemonic value of his traditional knowledge and performative voice. The superimposition answers the

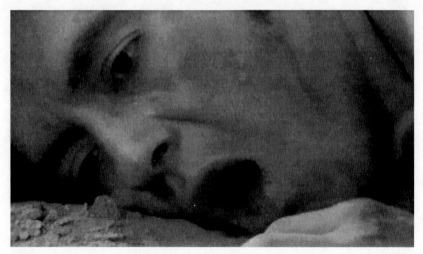

Figure 4.15. *House Made of Dawn*, Firebird Productions (1972), Abel fallen while running.

enforced developmental sequence of the Carlisle School's before-and-after photographs—their one-way assimilation in linear time—with a model of Indigenous modernity that is temporally simultaneous and geographically relational. If the before-and-after images were static, they also circulated through designated routes of dissemination, accumulating meanings and affects across social fields. The images were mobile at the same time that their subjects were prevented from or coerced into movement across reservation boundaries. The close-ups and freeze frames in *House Made of Dawn* might also suggest the more pervasive representational imposition of stasis in portraiture and photography (what Vizenor calls "immoveable simulations"), and Abel's silence in these still images can be seen as a symptom of his illness and alienation from community. As a visual strategy, the extended superimposition sequence in *House Made of Dawn* counteracts the freeze frames and the "scene of return" at the film's opening—the shot-reverse-shot of Abel and his dying grandfather—by making Abel's face as he sings occupy the same cinematic frame as his grandfather's hands crafting beads. While the characters still occupy different geographic locations and different cinematic images, the superimposition—with its more flexible model of temporal and geographic simultaneity than joining shots with a cut—brings grandson and grandfather together in a visual metaphor for the possessory work of memory and kinship (see figures 4.16–4.18).

Figure 4.16. *House Made of Dawn*, Firebird Productions (1972), Abel singing in Los Angeles.

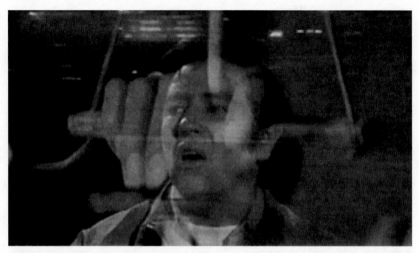

Figure 4.17. *House Made of Dawn*, Firebird Productions (1972), remembering the Pueblo.

Seen through the lens of Vizenor's theory of transmotion, or the "sovereignty of motion" as a form of political action, Abel's dawn run at the close of *House Made of Dawn* represents a political claim by affirming a generational relationship to a homeland through *literal* movement over

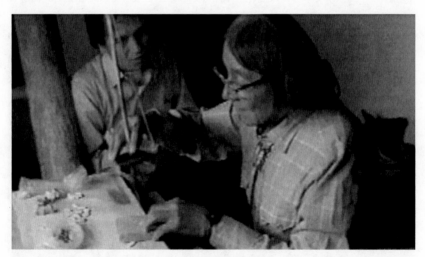

Figure 4.18. *House Made of Dawn*, Firebird Productions (1972), Abel and his grandfather at home.

traditional Pueblo lands (see figure 4.19). His movement is an articulation of a relationship to a place, yet this concrete relationship is reproduced in a virtual screen space. By generating images in his mind while he is running, images that constitute the film itself, Abel assembles his experiences (and thus reassembles himself) through a "vision to move in imagination." This *visionary* movement between Los Angeles and the Pueblo—coded in cinematic editing—takes up memories of coerced migrations mandated by assimilationist policies but is not defined or contained by them. Rather Abel's visionary movement represents an originary and ongoing history emergent from a specific location. In this context, the interaction between grandfather and grandson in the film's opening signifies not a story about closure or an instance of vanishing traditionality but instead a generational exchange that, as Walter Benjamin might describe it, is a form of contemporary "counsel . . . concerning the continuation of a story which is just unfolding" (86). Abel integrates his memories into a chartering practice that is both land-based and traveling. The productive aspects of this project—the work of "re-building the ancestor as the self," to use Chadwick Allen's phrase for Indigenous narrative tactics in this historical moment (219)—are also place-based responses to the paternalistic developmentalism of U.S. policies, particularly the Termination policy's return to coercive assimilation and expropriation reminiscent of the Allotment era. Lead actor Larry Littlebird reiterates this view of Pueblo storytelling as a resource for political resistance: "It's not like you have all these stories, and so they're

Figure 4.19. *House Made of Dawn*, Firebird Productions (1972), Abel's dawn run.

in your memory. No. The words free you to be reminded of all the stories that you have as a resource, from which you can make choices that give you action toward freedom" (Littlebird, "*House*").

The film ends with a low-angle shot of another runner—also played by Littlebird—with long hair and a breechcloth, continuing Abel's dawn run along a ridge (see figure 4.20). Littlebird interprets these final shots as a visual manifestation of what happens in ritual prayer as Abel, searching for a sense of identity and a way to heal, "finds a crack in the door to another realm of feeling": "When we've heard enough stories, our personal lives become mythological . . . and then we embrace a concept of ourselves that is timeless." The long-haired runner is "both ancient and prophetic" because he suggests Abel's transformation or potential for transformation based on access to his ancestors and to the land as a site of renewal.[44]

On the Set

Understanding *House Made of Dawn* in the context of its particular historical moment requires attending to the story of its making. In reinventing the process of film production outside of Hollywood, director Morse, lead actor Littlebird and author Momaday—all new to filmmaking—modeled the way strategic attention to production situations can imaginatively reactivate the cultural values embedded in Indigenous narratives. Building on

Figure 4.20. *House Made of Dawn*, Firebird Productions (1972), the transformation.

their perspectives and stories about the production, in this section I want to delineate the web of opportunities and causalities—the threads leading to the film's production and radiating from that production outward toward other projects—that emerged in the spaces and relationships created between Los Angeles and New Mexico.

Hollywood has always employed Native actors as authenticating elements of Western feature films, and while recent Hollywood productions have more often carefully navigated the politics of authenticity by casting Native actors in Native roles, the structuring story remains one told by non-Natives. When white actors perform in redface, the cinematic territory is emptied of Native presence and heritage, and audiences see a complete expansion of whiteness and white masquerade into the film's symbolic landscape. *House Made of Dawn* is unique for its time because both the story and the circumstances of its production—the script, location shooting, and Native actors—come from Native and non-Native partnerships. Littlebird remembers, "I was scared. I saw what films about Indians do, and how they were manipulated" (Littlebird, "*House*"). But unlike studio productions, on this set all of the participants were "part of the storytelling process." It is this influence of Native actors on the storytelling process that distinguishes *House Made of Dawn* from *Flap*, *Billy Jack*, and other contemporary studio and independent productions. As a production style, the filming of *House Made of Dawn* suggests Jace Weaver's conception of Native literatures as "communitist,"—combining the words *community* and *activist* to describe literatures that participate in "healing of the grief and sense of exile felt by Native communities and the pained individuals in them" (49).

House Made of Dawn, directed in this collaborative way, developed from a form of composite transcultural authorship in both its screenplay and shooting. When discussing his initial involvement with *House Made of Dawn*, Morse stresses his inexperience both with Native communities and as a filmmaker. "The first day I ever spent on a film set was our first day of shooting." Partly because of this inexperience, he was open to new ways of collaborating in the film's production. Although he "felt an immediate empathy with Abel," it was the universality of the story that appealed to him. "It wasn't that I was into Native American culture or anything like that—what I knew about Indians I basically learned from John Ford" (Morse, "*House*"). Morse had purchased the rights to the novel when it was first published in 1968; after the novel won the Pulitzer Prize in 1969, he received several offers from major film studios (including Universal) to buy the film rights, but recalls casting as a major reason why he ended up directing the film himself: "It was clear that they were going to cast Sal

Mineo as Abel, and it wasn't what the book was about. It was dishonest to everything that attracted me to the book in the first place." Instead, Morse broke a cardinal rule in Hollywood and financed the film with his own money: "it was all on the totally high road—I wouldn't let it be turned over to somebody else. . . . It was a time and an era . . . and a belief that we could change the world . . . that our own individual beliefs mattered, and it mattered to hold on to them" (Morse, "*House*").[45] While protecting the role of Abel from the vagaries of studio casting, Morse, wanting to surround himself with professional cast and crew wherever possible, still cast a non-Native actor as Tosamah. How might *House Made of Dawn* have spoken with a different voice if Momaday, who read for the part of Tosamah, had been cast instead of John Saxon? An example is the Los Angeles bar scene in which Tosamah stares down the cop Martinez, which might have taken on an intricately reflexive significance.

The performative work of "speaking from the content of Pueblo people's history" came largely from one extended Laguna–Santo Domingo family's participation in the production. Hopi photographer and filmmaker Victor Masayesva has written of Native experimental filmmaking, "The tribal person's trans-cultural performances . . . are most profound when inherited skills and ancestral knowledge dominate the stage" (239). In his 1986 *The American Indian in Film*, Michael Hilger comments that in *House Made of Dawn* the "real emotional center is the acting" of Littlebird and Varela as Abel and Benally (142).[46] Morse, too, feels that Littlebird's performance anchors the film: "there was a correlation between what [audiences] thought of the film and what they thought of Larry. . . . Basically if the audience was able to understand and empathize with Abel, they liked the film." Distributors did not believe the film could draw a white audience. According to Morse, "the film seemed to be a total failure, artistically and financially. . . . But the one nice thing is that when it was shown, at different Indian celebrations or festivals . . . people always loved it. It always got very strong support from the Native American community" (Morse, "*House*").

Larry Littlebird's participation led to the incorporation of Pueblo dramatic idioms, community aesthetics, and local knowledge, while the production itself became a model of alternative filmmaking for his own later television and documentary production. He describes his work on the set this way: "On this production I was right in there with the people who were making the film, I wasn't off to the side in my little honey wagon all by myself, waiting to be called out onto the set. I was involved in the development of the script, how this was being interpreted" (Littlebird, "*House*"). Some of the most effective scenes in the film resulted from this active collaboration. For example, Morse recalls that the rooftop scene "was basically improvised between Larry and Jay. They knew that there were a few plot points that we wanted to get across in the scene. But basically Larry said 'Listen, I have some ideas for a song' or 'Jay and I have talked,' and I said 'Great, I'll turn on the camera.' That kind of trust was there on the set between Larry and myself" (Morse, "*House*").

In productions such as *The Lone Ranger* (1949–1957) or *Dances with Wolves* (1990), Native actors play roles that are subordinated to the centering consciousness of a white character played by a white star; plots focus on the development of white characters as they journey westward across the landscape, mimicking historical white settlement of Native lands. Yet by becoming involved in Hollywood film production through small roles as extras, actors like Littlebird gained experience in filmmaking precisely because of the interrelated geographies of production in practices such as location shooting. Both Littlebird and filmmaker and scholar Beverly Singer (Tewa and Diné) began their film careers working on the set of *Flap* (then titled *Nobody Loves a Drunken Indian*) (Reed 1970), a Warner Brothers production starring Anthony Quinn in redface. In her history of Native filmmaking, *Wiping the War Paint Off the Lens*, Singer writes:

> During the summer of 1969, the seed of my interest in film-making was planted. I was fourteen years old when a Hollywood film crew came to Santa Clara Pueblo to make a movie starring Anthony Quinn, who portrayed a character named Flapping Eagle, a drunken Indian with a ludicrous plan to protest injustices committed against Indians by stealing a railroad car. . . . That the firsthand opportunity to watch the production of a movie, including the building of a façade, the application of makeup on actors, and hearing the director call out "action," took place about a five-minute walk from my house is still amazing to me. The Pueblo community was allowed to watch the action. I was starstruck, but not by the actors; rather, my soul desired to be a film director. (30)

Littlebird, too, began acting as an extra on the set of *Flap* and later also performed (with Mesa Bird) in *The Man Who Loved Cat Dancing*. He recalls being chosen from the casting lineup because of his hairstyle (in all of Littlebird's screen time in *Flap*, he is filmed from behind so that his hair rather than face is visible to the audience):

They picked me out of the lineup because at the time, my hair was long. I tied it in a traditional manner, and young men in that period of time didn't have hair like that. . . . I was just finding out about the way motion pictures got made. It's pretty dismal being on a big set. So I went to Hollywood and that clinched it for me. I saw the way people were treated, with not much respect behind the scenes, and what an ego center it is. I left that production and just came on home. Seeing how Hollywood makes movies turned my stomach, so when Rick [Morse] came along I really wasn't too interested. I was given the book [*House Made of Dawn*] on the set of *Flap* . . . that book was life-changing for me. It had the ring of truth. I felt that if they made a movie of that I wanted to be around so it didn't get screwed up. I never thought of myself as the lead—I just wanted to be there. (Littlebird, "*House*")

Morse had been trying to cast *House Made of Dawn* in Hollywood and was frustrated by the process: "I sent out the agent, asked him to see Native American actors, and was sent a whole lot of Italians to look over. And I just didn't want to do that" ("*House*"). But in the space of two days, Morse received calls from producer Tony Bill, fresh from the set of *Flap*, and from Momaday in Santa Fe, to suggest Littlebird for the part of Abel (Momaday had seen Littlebird's photo a news article about the Santa Fe Indian Market). Eventually Littlebird's extended family was cast as well—his uncle Mesa Bird played Francisco, and his nephew Teddy Garcia played the young Abel.

The participation of these performers in the production moves *House Made of Dawn* away from Hollywood's reliance upon non-Native audiences' recognition of and relationship to a white star, although John Saxon's performance as Tosamah prevents the film from completing this move. Abel's memories and consciousness structure the film, and his image dominates the screen through repeated close-ups and long-shots. Littlebird's performance necessarily anchors the film's setting and claims its territory—the actor lives in the place and time that he occupies as a character, unlike Westerns in which Native characters only occupy the West of the past, never the modern West.

The combination of professional and non-professional actors, and the casting of Littlebird's extended family in *House Made of Dawn,* integrates the intergenerational relations of production into the work of familial continuity on screen. Mesa Bird did not read English and learned his part aurally rather than from the script. In contrast with the common practice of stagey gestures and narrative framing through voiceover in Indian Westerns such as *Broken Arrow* and *Dances with Wolves*,[47] the relative paucity of explanation and gesticulation, and the lack of full translation of Mesa Bird's Keresan lines, results not in silencing the film's Native characters but rather in a Pueblo relational style. "He's an example of something that's real, just being himself on screen" Littlebird says, "but he's *acting* a character he knows from living where he does. He's not portraying himself. It's second nature" ("*House*"). The phrase "second nature" begins to account for Mesa Bird's acting, which depends on his "being himself" yet not "portraying himself" in dramatizing a character from his cultural community. Littlebird suggests that Bird's performance is analogous to the work of translation between Keresan and English, a process that emphasizes communicating or transmitting knowledge rather than mimesis.

Littlebird describes his own performance in *House Made of Dawn* as a manifestation of his intimacy with his community: "I knew *everybody* in that book first-hand—well . . . these are my people. I had so many close associations with the Abel character, on all levels, everything from his development as a child, to everything that he experienced and I'd witnessed in my own close relations and close friends. I could identify with it" ("*House*"). He describes these "sensibilities" and "presence" as emerging from both everyday experience and cultural training in Pueblo dramatic performance. According to Littlebird:

> [Morse] had an interest in casting right from New Mexico . . . and he took my suggestions of relating it to people of the Pueblo communities, people who had the right sensibilities. . . . From my perspective, for example in the Pueblo culture, there are things that are just correct in the sensibilities. It's ingrained in them, in the people. We have an unspoken understanding of presence. And that presence, if it's going to be brought onto the screen, has to play itself. . . .
>
> Pueblo culture has a great deal of dramatic experience. The dramas that take place in our ceremonies, you have to train for them and you have to prepare for them and you have to understand how to communicate. And that's been going on for thousands of years; it has its own language and its own forms. The people are at ease in it, and I was at ease in it. And I knew that's what I brought with me, and I was just given an opportunity to express them. ("*House*")[48]

Littlebird's songs and improvisations on the set, and his familial relationship and shared language with Mesa Bird, are the most obvious examples of their communication of a local social style. Performances by non-professional actors stage a transaction that privileges and rewards Native audiences' recognition of individuals, and shifts the film's address to its audience away from the model in which white players in redface speak to a mass audience as if it were a white audience.

On the set of *House Made of Dawn*, the collaborators worked to make their mode of production more closely match the film's content. The film encodes its mode of production in one of the first scenes, as Abel is running. He remembers his grandfather's voice describing the time of year of the dawn run, just after the people clean the ditches following the spring rains: "A race, Abelito. It is run at dawn, in the early spring when the ditches are made clean and deep for the water." The voiceover corresponds to Abel's memory, in the novel, of his grandfather's instruction in how to read the position of the dawn sun on the "contour of the black mesa": "just there at the saddle, where the sky was lower and brighter than elsewhere on the high black land, the clearing of the ditches in advance of the spring rains and the long race of the black men at dawn" (173). Littlebird has also referred to this seasonal activity, cleaning the irrigation ditches, to describe the film's production in contrast to his early experiences in the film industry:

> *House Made of Dawn* was a turning point for me, because what I discovered was that it's possible to make motion pictures without the encumbrance of Hollywood production. . . . It was the extreme opposite of Warner Brothers. Here was this little group of people all working together, and what I saw was, "Oh, that's like at the Pueblo when we're going to clean the ditches." The whole community is involved. . . . We know what our common vision is, and the common vision is the flow of water which brings life to our community, and gives us life. That's a common vision, and *everybody* is connected to it. Well, that's when I began to glimpse that . . . you could make movies like that, where everybody that's part of the set is tied into the vision. And if they are, you're going to get better sound . . . better lighting. Productions try to do that, but the reality is that departments are truly departments; they don't overlap in feel or in community. And so I began to see that . . . if you could get enough Native people working together, there was a possibility that a whole new methodology for making film could become available. And

> essentially, that's the project that George [Burdeau] and I later
> went to work on—the *Real People* series. (Littlebird, "*House*")

The work of making films described here is quite different from the work of Native extras on location shoots, and although it is held to a measure of manual labor, it is also unlike the portraits of agricultural day-labor and factory work in *House Made of Dawn*. The material relationships with soil and seasonal rain in a productive system of agriculture, and the imaginative, social, and spiritual ceremonial structures that support dryland farming, are extended to describe Indigenous visual sovereignty. By framing this insight in terms of a specific place and agricultural pattern, Littlebird connects the politics and practices of film production with larger issues of both collective action and land use. Pueblo values and concrete vision of social relations to the land dominate the content and creation of media. Furthermore, the film's off-screen connection to this community is a vision of health in film production (like the water that "brings us life"), whereas Hollywood's disconnection in its departmental production style is seen in the context of illness (in Littlebird's earlier assertion that "seeing how Hollywood makes movies turned my stomach"). This locally, literally "grounded" style also provided Littlebird with experience and training that prepared him for future film and television projects outside of Hollywood.

House Made of Dawn catalyzed Larry Littlebird and George Burdeau's own movement from working as extras in Hollywood's revisionist Westerns into documentary television production. Public television documentaries, facilitated by public interest in bicentennial celebrations, were a primary avenue for Native media production in the 1970s. After further training at the Anthropology Film Center in Santa Fe—a critical source of support for their film work at this juncture—they went on to work together in 1977 on *The Real People*, a series of nine programs about Plateau tribes from eastern Washington, Idaho, and western Montana. With the success of the *Real People* series, George Burdeau and filmmaker Frank Blythe started what would become Native American Public Telecommunications (NAPT), the first national organization devoted to supporting the "creation, promotion and distribution of native media," with an emphasis on educational media for public television and public radio. In addition to the *Real People* series, Burdeau also produced the *Forest Spirits* series in 1975, seven programs on the Oneida and Menominee tribes in Wisconsin. Littlebird made the independent documentary *I'd Rather Be Powwowing* in 1983 (produced by George P. Horse Capture for WNET-TV). Sandra Sunrising Osawa (Makah) had already produced a 10-part series for KNBC-TV in Los Angeles in 1970,

The Native American Series, and Larry Evers produced *Words and Places* in 1978, an 8-part series focused on Native oral traditions and song (one featured the poetry of Harold Littlebird, Larry Littlebird's older brother, who also composed some of the songs for *House Made of Dawn*).[49] Victor Masayesva, whose 1993 film *Imagining Indians* I discussed at length in chapter 3, began making films in the 1980s, with *Hopiit* (1982), *Itam Hakim, Hopiit* (1984), and *Ritual Clowns* (1988). Focusing on educating the public about media stereotypes, Phil Lucas (Choctaw) and Robert Hagopian produced the 5-part series *Images of Indians* for PBS in 1979, with Will Sampson (Muscogee) as the series host and narrator. Part two ("How Hollywood Wins the West") of this series begins with Sampson's intervention in a group of Native children's viewing of "Elbow Room," an animated musical program that depicts U.S. expansion through the Louisiana Purchase by reiterating the doctrine of Manifest Destiny and omitting Indigenous presence on the land.[50] By turning off the on-screen television and calling attention to the problematic construction of U.S. imperialism as an innocent need for "elbow room," *Images of Indians* initiates a reflexive historical consideration of images of Indians in a domestic context. This reflection, signaled by the scene of intergenerational Indigenous spectatorship, reemphasizes generational continuity in the face of Western genre erasure and the reflexive turn in Indigenous media in the coming decades as Indigenous filmmakers became interpreters as well as producers of media.

Departing from the conventions that had structured such representations up to that point, *House Made of Dawn* speaks back to discourses of New Hollywood revisionism—and even amateur, independent productions such as *Billy Jack*—that appropriate cinematic Indians to allegorize generational oppositionality and social revolt in white America. Momaday, Littlebird, Morse, Burdeau, and other filmmakers from this period can be seen as an originary cohort of contemporary Native film storytellers, a generational bridge between the Hollywood's near-total control over screen images of Indians during the studio era and the film-school-educated Native directors such as Chris Eyre (Cheyenne/Arapaho) and Randy Redroad (Cherokee) who emerged in the 1990s. The 1960s–1980s feature films, such as *House Made of Dawn*, *Arrowboy and the Witches*, and *The Exiles*, financed by individual contributions or grants, never saw wide distribution, but their filmmaking efforts dovetailed with other, more visible minority film revivals in the 1970s in African-American and Chicano communities.[51] Decades later, films such as Blackhorse Lowe's (Diné) first feature, *5th World* (2005), and Sterlin Harjo's (Creek/Seminole) second feature *Barking Water* (2009), employ temporal disjuncture and flashbacks to convey characters'

264 / Native Recognition

relationships to one another as they travel over significant landscapes toward their places of origin. Both on-screen and off-screen, the writers, actors, and director of *House Made of Dawn* staged an activist occupation that reclaims and reinvents urban, reservation, and cinematic landscapes, showing us a way to "use this very powerful medium and do it differently."

5

"Indians Watching Indians on TV"

Native Spectatorship and the
Politics of Recognition in *Skins* and *Smoke Signals*

In preparing for his role as Thomas Builds-the-Fire in the 1998 film *Smoke Signals*, actor Evan Adams (Coast Salish) improvised what would become one of the film's signature lines: "You know, the only thing more pathetic than Indians on TV, is Indians watching Indians on TV!" This joke—uttered while the camera tilts and pans away from the small television playing a black-and-white Western film to follow Builds-the-Fire—circulated ubiquitously in reviews as a sign of the film's break from Hollywood's representations of nineteenth-century stoic warriors (see figure 5.1). Promoted as the first film written, directed, and acted by Native filmmakers to gain wide release, *Smoke Signals* was immediately recognized critically as signifying a paradigmatic shift in Native American film history.[1] This marketing locates the film's primary innovation in its relations of production, leaving open a range of questions about an Indigenous audience for the film.[2] Yet the richly suggestive line "Indians watching Indians on TV," referring to the Indian characters in the Western and to the characters in *Smoke Signals*, also privately addresses *Smoke Signals*' Indigenous audiences by reflexively positioning itself in their spectatorial field. And by simultaneously inviting *all* viewers to think about Indigenous spectatorship, director Chris Eyre (Cheyenne/Arapaho), writer Sherman Alexie (Spokane/Coeur d'Alene), and Evan Adams draw our attention to the problematic relationship between the imagined mass audience targeted by television rebroadcasting and Native viewers' apprehension of mediated images of Indians in the context of home

Figure 5.1. *Smoke Signals*, ShadowCatcher Entertainment (1998), a televised Western.

viewing. By characterizing its Indigenous audiences in this way, *Smoke Signals* distances itself from the Western—a genre dedicated to representing the erasure of Native nations—and from the idea of a homogenous mass audience. At the same time, the line embeds *Smoke Signals* in ongoing relation to the larger history of Western genre and documentary images.

Films in which popular media images of Indians recirculate within Native public and private spaces ask viewers to understand media history in terms of Indigenous interpretive frames. Textually embedded, on-screen performances of Native spectatorship involve "retelling the image" or visually reframing aging media through narrative. Visualizing this shift in perception highlights media production and consumption as acts of communication that are socially situated and inevitably engaged politically with relations of power. Staging Native spectatorship and reception on screen, then, distances viewers from Western and documentary fantasies of vanishing and antimodern Indians, aligning audiences instead with Indigenous perspectives through these embodied viewers. This chapter considers instances of this dramatization of spectatorship in Chris Eyre's second feature film, the 2002 drama *Skins*, as well as brief examples from *Smoke Signals* and other contemporary Native feature films in order to explore the pedagogical, genealogical, and possessory aspects of reclaiming and repurposing archival film footage.

In focusing on films from the turn of the twenty-first century, I am interested in filmmakers' processes of retrieval in the historical context of a century of Western genre media saturation. Traversing a media space structured by damaging representations has involved reappropriating, mocking, and taking political leverage from Hollywood representations through specific strategies: recognizing and "recrediting" Native actors in Hollywood productions; embedding references to film production and reception processes in film texts while integrating oral storytelling and testimony as compatible modes of transmission and instruction; reworking genre conventions, including Western genre icons and formulae of familial trauma and masculine vigilantism; and retrieving history by reinterpreting sites of media representation that memorialize the loss or separation of relatives. Since the independent feature films that first departed from Hollywood production of Indian images—Kent Mackenzie's *The Exiles* in 1961, Rick Morse's *House Made of Dawn* in 1972, Leslie Marmon Silko's (Laguna) *Arrowboy and the Witches* in 1980, and Victor Masayesva's (Hopi) *Itam Hakim, Hopiit* in 1984, among others—independent filmmaking practices have continued to present opportunities to speak about the impact of media production and reception on Indigenous families and to dramatize and sometimes actively mediate disrupted relations between family members and generations. Images of Native spectatorship—embedded scenes of critical viewing—model ways of looking that are also forms of Indigenous reclaiming. In reflexive scenes of viewing, Native films and coproductions negotiate and comment on the intrusion of media images of Indians, especially news broadcasts and Westerns, into the homes, families, and childhood experiences of the Indigenous focal characters. They employ a "streaming archive" of television rebroadcasting—a virtual repository of shared and continuously circulating representations—to render the past as a collection of mediated memories.[3]

Chris Eyre's feature films mark a breakthrough for Native American filmmaking both in terms of control over an independent production and in their address of (and access to) a broad Native and non-Native viewership. *Skins* extends *Smoke Signals'* self-conscious claim to Indigenous ownership of cinematic practices and the site of film production as a Native place. Eyre allegorizes Native audiences in both films, demonstrating the potential for Native viewers to claim and resignify Western genre and documentary images of anonymous and stereotyped Native characters through politicized spectatorship. *Skins'* models of viewing unravel the realism and assumed supremacy of older Hollywood representations by revealing them to be constructions. Though far less often studied than *Smoke Signals*, *Skins*, too, engages the Western as a fluid and available sign system while developing a different, more reparative way of viewing the function of images of Indians on television.

Through both formal and thematic aspects of his feature filmmaking—including sound, editing, mise-en-scène, iconic Western genre and nationalist images, and the emotional and realist modes of melodrama and documentary—Eyre's films speak back to the tropes of victimization and narratives of Indian spectrality by envisioning Native consumption of commodity entertainment. The "pathos" in the line "the only thing more pathetic than Indians on TV is Indians watching Indians on TV" refers to the Western's period-based exclusion of Native characters from the apparatus of modernity and to the irony of Indigenous consumption of the very genres that consistently exclude them. That modernity, signaled visually by on-screen technologies of media transmission and consumption, countermands the narratives of primitivism and "vanishing" Indians embedded in the Western's images of savage warriors, and at the same time articulates a coherent integration of assimilation and traditionalism in the narrative.

I am less concerned here with television studies or reception studies per se, or in parsing the differences or similarities between television and film, than in the fluidity of interchange between media as an implicit backstory in representations of reception.[4] Westerns originally shot on film and screened in theaters are later rebroadcast on small television screens situated in Native domestic spaces. This more intimate and relational setting facilitates the image of television reception as an imagined space of encounter and exchange in Eyre's films, which are themselves shown on both theatrical and, later, television screens playing DVDs. These small-screen versions of big-screen Westerns emphasize the context of viewing; Westerns that erase Indian families are screened in Native family homes that exemplify the very intergenerational future that the genre refused to envision for Native nations. Furthermore, in this politicized aesthetic of reception, the location of the "screen" itself becomes malleable, such as at the end of *Skins* when the outsized presidential portraits on Mount Rushmore are made to echo televised images and to exaggerate the cinematic technique of the close-up in a literal "interface" of viewer and screen. The film's play with recognition and disguise and with the scale and location of the face-to-screen encounter emphasizes the role of media screens in the identification and misidentification of Indigenous identity. My understanding of the scene of reception as a relationship with composite media and with the semiotics of commodity culture involves both the specificity of television reception in *domestic* settings and also extends beyond television reception to include other forms of technologically mediated dialectic in public space. This proliferation of screens, as a form of mise-en-abyme, functions as a sign of Indigenous modernity that further disrupts linear narratives of assimilation, situating Native viewers as contemporary consumers of mass culture.

Prefiguring the scenes of television viewing in Eyre's films is the work of Cherokee writer Thomas King, whose 1993 novel *Green Grass, Running Water* includes multiple scenes in which Native characters (including a television salesman) watch the same Western film again and again on televisions in homes, in hotel rooms, and in a television store showroom.[5] Most dramatically, the white owner of the television store, Bill Bursum, creates an enormous sales display consisting of stacked television sets in the shape of a map of North America (Bursum's name plays on the Bursum Bill, a 1922 legislative proposal that would have awarded Pueblo lands and water rights to non-Native squatters). King's complex allusions to figures like Bursum subtly assert a connection between legislation intended to dispossess tribes of their lands and genocidal popular culture images. Yet despite the fact that the novel's characters can never find anything to watch on television except Westerns, they establish ways to expand the meaning and function of this limited menu of popular culture offerings to take account of their lives, such as when one Native character dwells on memories of his father, an actor in Hollywood Westerns who wore a prosthetic nose in his roles in order to look "more Indian." A number of the Native characters actively recredit Westerns on television by recognizing the extras as their relatives and friends. At the novel's climax, spiritual trickster beings magically occupy the televised Western in order to change its outcome, enabling the on-screen Indians to win in battle against settler forces led by John Wayne. King's attention to Indigenous relations across the production and reception of Westerns, to Native viewers' capacity to recredit Hollywood performances, and to the power of imaginative intervention in conventional Western structures to alter the genre's colonial outcomes, all acknowledge the porousness of television's virtual images, their embedded and interdependent relationship to the world off-screen.

Skins' attention to images of Indians in the movies targets Westerns as sites of systematic misrecognition that invasively dislocate and disarticulate both familial and political relationships. The film's Western genre trajectories of masculine action based on the helpless witnessing of trauma followed by vigilantism prove to be self-destructive models of social action for the film's Native communities.[6] Eyre retrieves, amplifies, and ultimately overturns representations of familial separation, dysfunction, and absence embedded in dominant filmmaking practices and in emblematic Western genre constructions: the figure of John Wayne and the weeping face of Iron Eyes Cody. Visual anthropologist Faye Ginsburg describes Indigenous uses of media to access and recover historical events as "screen memories," inverting

Freud's paradigm in which adults "screen out," repress, or make invisible the traumas from the past ("Screen Memories" 40). In their encounter with (and redeployment of) commodity images of Indians originally produced for non-Native consumers, characters in Eyre's films redirect the meaning-making process of spectatorship to do the work of historical pedagogy as well as familial and community remembrance. In *Skins,* contemporary filmic scenes of viewing model and stage an intergenerational recognition across the screen, transforming that historical barrier into a facilitation of familial continuity, even as they interrupt that continuity with images and situations of loss and mourning.

Recognition and Native Spectatorship

Footage and photographs of Native peoples taken by outsiders have often signified cultural appropriation in service of salvage ethnography and Western frontier dramas, indexing the unequal relations of power during production, circulation, and reception. But in documentary films such as *The Return of Navajo Boy*, co-produced by Jeff Spitz and Bennie Klain (Diné), scenes of Native viewing de-exoticize Native characters and extras on-screen through politicized recognition in the context of the history of tourist and ethnographic photography, museum screenings, and the repatriation of footage as a singular event. In film dramas set in contemporary contexts, however, a more subtle and continuous recirculation of footage takes place. Fictional characters register the damage (or *pathos*) of generic images of Indians, or in a more optimistic move, resignify and recredit these images using a variety of popular culture forms.

Examples of the former can be found in scenes from *Smoke Signals* and *The Exiles*, which reveal the way media images exacerbate social oppression and conditions of poverty. An early scene in *Smoke Signals* depicts the impact of pop culture stereotypes on young Native viewers in a wrenching scene that is tonally very different from Thomas Builds-the-Fire's later, flippant comment about "Indians on TV." In one of the film's flashback sequences, the young Victor Joseph (Cody Lightning, Cree) watches a televised Western while his mother and father fight over money and alcohol (see figure 5.2). After striking Victor's mother Arlene (Tantoo Cardinal, Cree), Victor's father Arnold Joseph (Gary Farmer, Cayuga), decides in anger to leave the family and the reservation; Victor will never see him again. Victor's parents, as they fight, share the frame with the television set, so that Victor witnesses both the mass-mediated images of the Western

Figure 5.2. *Smoke Signals*, ShadowCatcher Entertainment (1998), Victor watches television as his parents fight.

and the dissolution of his family at the same time. The film frame links these two scenes of conflict as a single traumatic spectacle, infusing the genocidal violence of the Western with the intimate psychic wounds of domestic violence and vice versa. In a strikingly similar scene from *The Exiles*, a film about members of a Native community in the Bunker Hill neighborhood of Los Angeles, Julia Escalanti (Delos Yellow Eagle) and her children and friends watch a Western on television as her husband Rico (Rico Rodriguez) drops in to get some gambling money to continue a night on the town. The family's bleak circumstances are evident in the cramped apartment, illuminated by the television playing in the bedroom—which doubles as the family's living room—while the couple argue and Rico takes money from Julia's purse.

Television as a form of social disruption takes a different form in James Luna's (Luiseño) performance art piece, as filmed in *The History of the Luiseño People: La Jolla Reservation, Christmas 1990* (Luna and Artenstein, 1993). In the performance, Luna drinks beers, chain smokes, and watches Bing Crosby's 1954 movie *White Christmas* while he calls members of his extended family—his brother, mother, nephew, son, and former girlfriend—on Christmas Eve. The racialized products of contemporary communicative technologies (*White Christmas*) mediate his isolation in the domestic space of his living room while he lies to his mother ("no, I'm not drinking") and exchanges formulaic holiday platitudes with his children ("Santa got your

272 / Native Recognition

Christmas list") on the telephone. His consumption of beer, cigarettes, and television equate and indict these consumables as numbing agents that make social detachment a commonplace banality. Kathleen McHugh notes that Luna's film "uses the light from this composite of industry media (we are seeing a film on television that is recorded on video) as one of its primary illuminations" because it suggests allegorically that "the primary illumination in the history of the Luiseño people, in the history of Native peoples in the Americas in general, has been 'the light' of commercial entertainment media and genres, particularly the 'western,' as a central part of domestic décor" (447).[7] The scene of spectatorship in *History of the Luiseño People* attaches Indigenous domestic life to mass media while signaling its divisive interruption of that same domestic life. Commercial media here is a colonizing, corrosive replacement for human interaction, and the whiteness of its representations has become part of Indigenous collective memory. Jane Blocker writes that Luna's "infinite regress of quotation complicates native memory to show that it does not spring solely from pure origins in venerable ancestors, but that it is constructed in part out of its own representations in popular culture, out of what it inherits and redresses from whiteness" (28).

If Luna's *History* condemns the whiteness of commercial television from outside of its parameters, commercial films such as *Christmas in the Clouds* (Montgomery 2001) encourage genre consumption by using parody. Imagining Native audiences controlling and participating in mainstream images and technologies of communication, *Christmas in the Clouds* organizes viewers' identifications by maneuvering popular culture genres, as *Smoke Signals* and *Skins* do for the Western. In this romantic comedy set on a tribally owned resort (shot on the grounds of the Sundance Film Institute), a paperback Native American romance novel with the fictitious title *Path of Savages* (by the real romance author Cassie Edwards) provides a structuring generic framework. The Native hotel staff avidly consume the book and even quote from it when giving advice to the romantic lead. In one scene, a stylized tableau enacted from a love scene in the book dramatizes the fantasy of the Native hotel manager Mary (Sheila Tousey, Menominee). Mary's mental image of herself (transformed as a blond) in the arms of the warrior Buffalo Thunder (Steve Sandalis)—an image that closely resembles the book's lurid cover art—reveals her identification with the white heroine Vanessa and her appetite for stereotypically hypermasculine and romanticized images of Native men. This theatrical image is followed by a sardonic reading from the novel by handyman Phil (Jonathan Joss, White Mountain Apache), a character who himself later tries to evoke the image of Buffalo Thunder to attract the attention of young women visiting the hotel. In another scene, young children watch cartoon Indians modeled on the Three Stooges, whose distorted dialogue satirizes the integration of business hierarchy and tribal community at the hotel.[8] The film delivers both straightforward romance and comedic parody in the context of a contemporary revision of pop-culture caricatures.

In a more experimental and even campy mode, Mohawk director Shelley Niro's film *Honey Moccasin* (1998) also relies on established genre conventions. A local cable television news program (featuring cultural critic Paul Chaat Smith [Comanche] as an anchorman and talk show host) structures the film's parodic whodunit mystery narrative in which Honey (Tantoo Cardinal) magically transforms from barkeep to sleuth in order to recover stolen powwow costumes.[9] Unlike the look back at the Western that characterizes *Smoke Signals* and *Skins*, in *Honey Moccasin* community television provides an alternative venue for people on the reserve to talk to one another across the screen, expanding the imagined range of television's function from channeling Westerns, romantic comedies, and mysteries into Native homes to amplifying regional communicative networks.

How can we account for the simultaneous oppositionality and accommodation of these images, their ability to draw affective and political power from the same generic conventions they critique? The theorization of reception in cultural studies credits viewers with a complex range of spectatorial strategies including resistant spectatorship, amplifying local rather than universalized models of encounter with mass media. In Althusserian terms, the interpellative or "hailing" function of cinematic texts as ideological state apparatuses would impose a misrecognition on Indigenous viewers, but as Hamid Naficy writes, "in addition to 'hailing,' there is much 'haggling' in cinematic spectatorship" because "oral culture's interaction with the screen is neither passive nor unidirectional" (9). The "various forms of spectator counter-hailing of the screen" can include refusing or disengaging from Western forms as well as consuming or fetishizing them, thereby "resisting the West through its objectification" (21). The latter strategy is politically oppositional but textually articulated to dominant representations.

Confrontations with popular images of Indians have been described by Native critics as formative experiences.[10] Acoma writer Simon Ortiz remembers his own awkward and uncomfortable feelings of "unreality as an Indian" that came from being forced to identify with popular images that were "from a different, unfamiliar, unknown Indian culture and place" (6). Tom Grayson Colonnese (Santee Sioux) asserts:

asking Indians to watch a John Wayne western is like asking
someone if they would like to go back and visit the schoolyard
where they used to get beat up every day. No—that's too unseri-
ous a comparison, though the connection to our childhoods
and bad childhood memories is important . . . for Indians,
watching westerns would be like Jews watching films about
the Holocaust in which the Jews themselves were presented
as the violent, aggressive villains! We were the ones who were
slaughtered and destroyed, but that's not usually how we've been
depicted. (335–36)[11]

And in an article about the importance of *Smoke Signals* as an intervention in media images, N. Bird Runningwater (Cheyenne/Mescalero Apache)
details a childhood encounter with the Western:

I remember the first time I had a connection with an Indian
on television. I was eight years-old, and my cousin Cathy and
I were watching a stereotypical cowboy and Indian western. The
Native characters were dressed like nothing we had ever seen in
our world. At one point, two warrior-type characters entered the
scene, and when asked by the lead Anglo character how many
enemies they had spied, they replied "na'kii."

Cathy and I looked at one another in amazement and
began jumping for joy. We ran to tell our family that we had
just heard an Indian on television speaking our Apache language.
We felt like the world had finally had a glimpse of our lives as
they really were, and from that point on, everything would be
different. We watched more and more Westerns after that, waiting
and hoping that maybe we would see ourselves on television or
hear our language one more time. We never did.

The stories recounted by these artists and intellectuals target what Ortiz
describes as a painful "unreality." Their memories of televised misrepresentation of Indigenous languages, cultures, history, place, dress—the distance
from "our lives as they really were"—comprise a collective story about the
ways that impressionable early viewing experiences helped to catalyze an
active critical voice and oppositional stance.

In his influential essay "Encoding/Decoding," Stuart Hall argues that
television reception involves strategies of audience decoding, including an
"*oppositional* code" in which "it is possible for a viewer perfectly to under-

stand both the literal and the connotative inflection given by a discourse but to decode the message in a *globally* contrary way" (517). While the form of the audiovisual text is fixed, the viewer's consumption of the program represents an equally important "moment of the production process in the larger sense" because the audience's meaning-making interpretive work also "produces" the content of the programming. Hall locates the potential to resignify dominant discourses in these "active transformations" or appropriations of programmatic content into "meaningful discourse" that can then "influence, entertain, instruct or persuade" (509). With Hall's early theories of reception in mind, anthropologist Sam Pack asserts that for Fourth World viewers, television is an important arena where identities are negotiated in the context of power relations: "the question of 'who are they?' directly shapes and informs the question 'who are we?'" (4).

Film scholars working in the area of revisionary identification in cinema have explored oppositional viewing practices in great detail in terms of sexual disidentifications and fantasy. José Esteban Muñoz characterizes "disidentification" as neither assimilationist nor separatist, but rather an interpretive dynamic that works to "transform a cultural logic from within," allowing artists to transform a "B-movie archive" into "antinormative treasure troves."[12] Patricia White, discussing "uninvited" readings of classical Hollywood films by lesbian viewers, describes film reception that is "transformed by unconscious and conscious past viewing experience," a form of "retrospectatorship" (197). I want to explore instantiations of Indigenous viewing in Native cinema by retaining these scholars' attention to oppositionality and the reworking of past cinematic images while moving away from the psychoanalytic models that have dominated film studies paradigms of spectatorship. The lens of a playful and politicized process of spectatorship-as-resistance illuminates the ways in which spectators make meaning and the ways that viewer-driven interpretation constitutes a form of ownership that retrospectively reorganizes the original relations of media production. In the context of Indigenous filmmaking, this process often takes the particular form of attribution, *recrediting* the primary identities of anonymous Native "extras" in cinematic landscapes. Thus, the politicized and familial meanings of recognition converge in acts of "reidentifying" as well as "disidentifying" with the images on screen. The recognition and naming that characterizes many Indigenous cinematic representations of spectatorship and identification has special significance as oppositional work that corrects historical acts of renaming or withholding names from Native students in residential schools, from Native actors in Westerns, and from "anonymous" Native storytellers in books published by non-Native authors.

To describe this way of looking that is also a form of reclamation, I interpret "recognition" and "misrecognition" here as having intersecting familial and political significance. A form of remembering, recognition accesses mediated stories about the past and acknowledges history's persistent value. Recognition is a key aspect of pervasive cinematic modes such as melodrama, which employs the disguise and revelation of identity as standard plot elements. In the legal, political, and activist frameworks in Indigenous studies, recognition refers to and is the basis for diplomatic relations between nations, and it is this recognition of nation-to-nation relationships, formalized in treaty documents, that Native tribes consistently insist that the U.S. government acknowledge (and which is implied in the federal recognition of individual tribes). My interpretation of recognition as a process of recrediting is also influenced by Chadwick Allen's description of Indigenous minority acts of "re-recognition" as strategic, politicized performances that revalue treaties. This description of certain Indigenous performances of identity as "re-recognition" develops the meaning of recognition as a tactical refocusing of colonizing frameworks, in which Indigenous activists and artists reenergize and "*re-recognize* . . . rather than deconstruct, the authority of particular colonial discourses, such as treaties, for their own gain" (18). Considering recognition as an artistic choice based in legal history returns us to Jolene Rickard's definition of sovereignty, "the border that shifts Indigenous experience from a victimized stance to a strategic one" ("Sovereignty" 51), as a fundamental premise of Indigenous art. In cinematic representations, this "shift" is signaled visually in the embodied Native viewer on screen and in cinematic reflections on the visual as a medium of repatriation. Furthermore, political recognition is also intimately *familial* in film dramas and documentaries that chronicle relations between parents and children or between siblings who have been separated or alienated from one another. In Chris Eyre's films, characters watch Westerns and in the process they reclaim its images through simultaneous acts of political and familial recognition. The characters' recrediting models a process of historical recovery and ownership of popular culture and meaning-making through a practice of reception involving recognition, identification, naming. The problem posed for the characters in *Skins*, then, becomes the appropriate response to recognition.

Chris Eyre's "Home Dramas"

Adapted from Paiute author Adrian Louis's novel of the same title, *Skins* dramatizes the difficult love between two Lakota brothers, Mogie (Graham

Greene, Oneida) and Rudy (Eric Schweig, Inuvialuit/Chippewa/Dene)—
other members of the family include Aunt Helen (played by Lakota/Dakota
poet Lois Red Elk) and Mogie's son Herbie (Noah Watts, Crow/Blackfeet).
In frustration over his inability to help his alcoholic older brother and others
in his community, Rudy, a police officer on the Pine Ridge Indian Reservation, turns to vigilantism. In each case, however, he inadvertently victimizes
his own relations, first a distant relation and then, devastatingly, his brother
Mogie, who is already terminally ill. Fulfilling Mogie's dying wish—to deface
the carved figure of George Washington on Mount Rushmore—becomes a
way for Rudy to express his grief over his brother's death and the distress
of the Pine Ridge community that he sees every day as a tribal cop. Like
Smoke Signals, *Skins* dramatizes familial relations in a reservation context,
and like *Smoke Signals* the film ends with a memorial service and images of
a troubled protagonist mourning the death of a family member.[13]

Rudy's turn to vigilantism is, like Abel's extralegal violence in the film
version of *House Made of Dawn*, a manifestation of illness—in fact, Rudy
knows he needs help and seeks it from a young spiritual leader, Ed Little
Bald Eagle (Myrton Running Wolf, Blackfeet).[14] By committing violence
outside of his community's social constraints, Rudy acts out the Western's
assaults on Native families, including his own. The Western representational
formula of masculine "regeneration through violence" on the frontier, as
described by cultural historian Richard Slotkin, is invoked not only through
images of Westerns on-screen but also in casual references to the transposition of Western genre vigilantism to racist urban law enforcement in films
such as *Death Wish* and *Dirty Harry*. In *Smoke Signals*, Thomas suggests
that Arnold Joseph looks like Charles Bronson in *Death Wish V*, and in
Skins Rondella Roubaix (Elaine Miles, Cayuse/Nez Perce) responds to Rudy's
veiled threats with a derisive "fuck you, Clint Eastwood." But as with Abel
in *House Made of Dawn*, Western genre models of masculine regeneration
don't work for Rudy; rather, they lead him to victimize the Lakota people
he wanted to help—his *oyate* (people) and *tiospaye* (clan, family).

Even more strongly than *Smoke Signals* does, *Skins* depicts the fracturing and reconfiguration of families as a product of the way the media tells
stories about history, documents contemporary communities, and influences
the actions of its audiences. *Smoke Signals* and *Skins* both combine a focus on
specific tribes (Coeur d'Alene and Lakota, respectively) with pan-Indian production and casting to focus on issues shared politically across tribes. Both
films were well-received critically, although some critics have argued that
they perpetuate stereotypes.[15] In measuring the distances between intended
and decoded meanings for imagined Native viewers, the films explore the

ways that oppositional viewing might be translated to action. Eyre repeats several of his most successful cinematic techniques from *Smoke Signals* in this film, including flashbacks from the brothers' youth and references to popular media images of Indians through footage of televised Westerns playing in Native homes. Taking up the figure of the "crying Indian" from a televised public service announcement (PSA) in the 1970s, *Skins* both engages and parodies the act of mourning. The film's exploration of grieving is, importantly, different from *Smoke Signals* in its mapping of the characters' feelings of loss onto a monumental icon of American imperialism and a televised performance in redface in the film's closing images of Mount Rushmore. Furthermore, the emotional funeral at the film's end recalibrates both the melodramatic register of the early "Indian dramas" and the media saturation of romanticized representations in the 1970s to serve what director Chris Eyre describes as contemporary "home dramas." Images of "Indians watching Indians on TV" and of televisions themselves are mediating forces that recur throughout the film, seemingly in the background but in fact acting as visual and aural transitions between scenes, sparking conversations between characters, and motivating Rudy's final vigilante act of violence. Several crucial scenes in the film are bracketed by televisions and television screens, which structure and saturate the representation of the characters' lives.

Mogie's identifications have to do with history and with testimony as a document of Indigenous resistance as he invests the male melodrama of the Western[16] with documentary content about Lakota history, just as *Skins* invests its drama about Mogie with documentary footage (which Eyre, in the DVD commentary, characterizes as "sad stuff" but "all true"). Eyre's imagined Indigenous spectatorship involves viewers who engage in a form of retrospection that deemphasizes the fantastic, using oral-storytelling-on-screen to realign Western melodramas with a testimonial realism.

The film's opening images of the Pine Ridge Indian Reservation are almost purely in a documentary mode, comprised of found or stock news footage. This opening sequence powerfully frames the film's dramatic content and invests the family relationships with a larger significance in light of the tribe's historical and ongoing battles for treaty land rights and self-determination. An example is the use of footage donated by Robert Redford from his film about the 1973 occupation of Wounded Knee, *Incident at Oglala* (1992); the borrowed footage is especially significant because of its original place in a documentary about the American Indian Movement's (AIM) confrontation with the Federal Bureau of Investigation (FBI) at Pine Ridge in 1973, a historical activist reoccupation of Lakota land. As images of barbed wire, trash, and weather-beaten trailer homes and government housing flash on the screen, the soundtrack plays a speech by Bill Clinton promising resources "for your children and their future." Then, in voiceover accompanying shots of Mount Rushmore and the Wounded Knee massacre site, Eyre's own voice outlines statistics and facts that again orient viewers to the political and historical contexts for the film, juxtaposing the popular tourist attraction of Mount Rushmore with the Pine Ridge Indian Reservation ("the poorest of all counties in the U.S."), and describing the Wounded Knee massacre of 1890 as viewers see footage of the graveyard and signs. Finally, a news anchorwoman's voice reels off rates of unemployment, death from alcoholism, and other statistics over a montage of news footage depicting Native men being arrested and jailed. Periodically, tracking shots of Pine Ridge houses from the road both recollect this documentary opening and mimic what Rudy sees from his patrol car.

The film's forays into this documentary montage, with its authoritative narrator (the director himself, at one point), borrowed footage, persuasive political agenda, and documentary techniques of location shooting on the reservation in actual homes (not dressed or built for the film), insist that viewers receive this drama differently than the historical fantasies of films such as *Dances with Wolves*, tapping instead into the conventions of social realism. The opening sequence, interspersed with the credits, seems to be directed toward non-Native viewers who might know little about Native American history or politics, or about the particular history of Pine Ridge. But these sequences also represent a dual address: non-Native viewers receive a historical and political briefing and an education in the key issues and motifs of the film, whereas insider viewers are offered recognizable footage and landmarks that outline the parameters of the film as familiar territory.

The realism evoked by these images of the reservation are problematic in the sense that the mobility of the flyover and driving shots of the landscape mimic a totalizing touristic gaze or a form of parachute journalism in which the viewer remains a voyeur. But the trope of driving as a cinematic "overview" also echoes Rudy's point of view as a patrolman, someone whose tasks of surveillance and empathy come into profound conflict, particularly when he tries to correct the systematic failure of institutions to assist the community through law enforcement. Chris Eyre describes these driving shots as disrupting the balance of two characters in the frame of a "50/50" two-shot in an automobile. By panning to create a "split screen" between one character and the open landscape, we see the land as it occupies the character's imagination. Eyre's attention to the landscape reflects both his early training in landscape photography and the practical necessity of driving across distances in the American West, especially on rural reservations: "All reservations are different. They all look different. For me, there's a whole context that you have to place a story in . . . to look at the landscape and try and incorporate that into the volume of the sensibility and feel of the movie."[17]

The film returns midway to this documentary intertext to present a case against the liquor business in the reservation border town of White Clay, Nebraska. Rudy is beginning to pay attention to spiritual obligations by burning sweetgrass and making tobacco ties in his living room. Later, as he watches television there, he is the audience for the news report on White Clay, where a small number of white-owned stores profit enormously from Lakota customers from the reservation. Eyre intercuts shots of the film's characters and a reconstructed newscast production with 15-year-old stock footage from the NBC *Nightly News* with reporter Monica Red Bear (see figure 5.3). Mogie and his friend Verdell Weasel Tail (Gary Farmer) watch as the anchorwoman (here played by Jenny Cheng) delivers the story, filmed by her Native film crew. The self-referentiality of the filming as a metaphor for the Native production of *Skins* inserts the film's characters into actual historical footage, putting Mogie on both sides of the screen (as subject and as viewer) over the course of the film, and putting Rudy in a position to recognize his brother on television (see figure 5.4). From the production of the newscast, Eyre cuts to the outside of Rudy's house and the sound of a Western movie shoot-out; then, inside, to Rudy's face illuminated by the television as he surfs channels, skipping past another Western before

Figure 5.3. *Skins*, First Look Pictures (2002), newscast production.

Figure 5.4. *Skins*, First Look Pictures (2002), Mogie (Graham Greene) on television.

arriving at the newscast, which now includes an inebriated Mogie mocking the interviewer (see figure 5.5). The Western is sonically and metonymically linked to the newscast by Rudy's own editing using his remote. At the same time that the family drama in *Skins* becomes (hypothetically) subject to representation on the news, the segment relates what we see on news broadcasts to the film's "real" or recognizable families.

Figure 5.5. *Skins*, First Look Pictures (2002), Rudy (Eric Schweig) watches Mogie on television.

The final shot of this interior scene, after Rudy has turned off the television, is his silhouetted reflection on the dark screen. This is a classically reflexive image, like the much-remarked shot of Cary (Jane Wyman) entrapped by the "gift" of a television at Christmastime in the Douglas Sirk melodrama *All that Heaven Allows* (1955), and like the shot of Sheriff Ed Tom Bell (Tommy Lee Jones) silhouetted in Llewelyn Moss's (Josh Brolin) trailer-home television screen in Joel and Ethan Coen's *No Country for Old Men* (2007), a shot that revisits the iconography of the Western but signals its emptiness in the face of 1980s cross-border drug trade. These characters' reflections, fixed within deactivated television screens, suggest the alienating narrative confines of melodramas and Westerns and the bankruptcy of their generic promises of emotional fulfillment and cathartic action. A small screen nested within a big screen, television is imagined here as a medium that fluidly extends the reach of mass culture to the domestic spaces of the characters by mirroring their recognizable countenance in a virtual space. The visual image of the face on-screen manifests viewers' ambivalence toward their interpellation within the bounded frame and imposed sign system of television narratives. In *Skins*, the shot forecasts the film's shift in scale from intimate close-up to monumental visage and from faces on-screen to face-as-screen in its closing images.

For Rudy, the problem of television is its content—he is trapped within the boundaries of vigilante narratives—in contrast to Mogie's ability to read such narratives from outside of their parameters in order to make their clichéd images express his own, specifically Lakota feelings of community, history, and kinship.[18] Rudy's identification leads him to act out prewritten scenarios rather than taking control of television's imposed sign system, while the domestic placement of the television and the isolated conditions of his viewing facilitate his decision to act outside of the community's social constraints. The shot of his reflection in the screen functions as a pivot between Rudy's rising anger as he watches his brother on the news and his ill-fated decision to take vigilante action by burning down the liquor store. Thus, the shot traverses the space between the passive anger of even oppositional media reception and viewers' actions in the world. Furthermore, the image "contains" Rudy's silhouette, surrounding his image while implicating television in the film's larger social critique by revealing it to be an organizing force behind Rudy's vigilantism.

This bad-mirror effect is immediately reinforced in the next shot of Rudy reflected in a bathroom mirror, putting on black makeup as part of his disguise. The image suggests the masking essential to the Western vigilante hero's evasion of identification under the law (e.g. *The Lone Ranger*)—a facial barrier to the kind of reparative recognition that *Skins* will later model for viewers.[19] The racialization of Rudy's impending violence as a performance of whiteness-in-disguise further implicates both Western genre scenarios of action and news stories about Native victims in Rudy's illness and his alienation from his brother and community. The theatrical makeup, then, also alludes to the tradition of redface (and even blackface) performance that has characterized Westerns, and that *Skins* and other films counteract in their revaluation of Native actors in the casting process. In this case, Rudy's recognition of his brother at this moment leads to wrong action when his anger spills over into vigilante violence: he burns down the liquor store in White Clay, inadvertently injuring Mogie. In a later scene, however, Mogie himself guides the other characters' strategies of reappropriation in viewing media images toward political and genealogical recovery, using collective memory as well as humor and absurdity to reshape iconic images.[20] By moving between these examples of spectatorship, *Skins* models a range of nonconsenting responses to media images that become decentralized as they are broadcast into individual homes.

Eyre's mainstream film techniques are deployed to cast doubt on conventional film genres and histories. In the scene discussed above, he uses the television as a sound bridge over a cut from the establishing shot of Rudy's house to its interior, framing the private familial space of the home with images from a nationalist film genre. A structurally similar scene takes place later in the film at Aunt Helen's house, where the brothers have gathered for a family dinner with Aunt Helen and Herbie. After an establishing shot of the house, Eyre cuts directly to the television screen playing a Western: men on horseback are engaged in a shoot-out (see figure 5.6). The

Figure 5.6. *Skins*, First Look Pictures (2002), Mogie watches a Western on television.

televised image fills the entire frame, becoming an encompassing "second screen" through which viewers transition into Helen's domestic space.[21] The televised Western is a pivotal reflexive turn both visually and verbally—that is, we enter the scene through Mogie's commentary about what is playing on the television screen, but he speaks only about the actor, not the film itself—as Mogie provides his son Herbie with his own take on the film. "See that retarded knobshiner? That's Joe Thunderboots. Me and him used to be drinkin' buddies, but I haven't seen him for a while. Now, he's supposed to be a direct descendent of American Horse. Least that's what he said after a couple of drinks."[22]

Among the Indians coded as enemies in the Western, Mogie sees friends. Significantly, Mogie recognizes and appreciates the Western on television not for its myth-making fabrications of frontier history—the function the Western is said to have in much criticism of the genre—but rather in terms of his community networks. That is, the uncredited actor who, along with other anonymous extras, signals a generalized Native threat in the Hollywood Western is, for Mogie, an individual with a specific genealogy that links him to the actual events of this period of history (the second half of the nineteenth century) that the Western typically represents. The Lakota lineage embedded in the very same media that denies the presence of Native families becomes for certain audiences both a coded history and corroboration of survival, a reading that, in its historical specificity, repudiates the Western genre's construction of Native characters as ahistorical and atemporal.

In the scene, the Lakota story of Wounded Knee is embedded in a Western story of frontier violence through the genealogy of the Lakota extras and the ability of a contemporary Lakota audience to recognize them on screen as individuals rather than as generic "Hollywood Indians." As the characters move to the kitchen table for dinner, Herbie asks, "So, who's American Horse?" and Mogie's reading of the Western on television then becomes a prompt for a recounting of the events of Wounded Knee and the testimony of Lakota witnesses. Uncharacteristically tense and bitter, Mogie tells Herbie to "listen up" while his Uncle Rudy begins the story of Wounded Knee. But Mogie is unable to restrain his need to tell the story and interrupts Rudy to clarify that the troopers designated to disarm Big Foot's band at Wounded Knee in 1890 were from "Custer's old command." He goes on, "The Seventh Cavalry was called in to escort them to the reservation. Then the soldiers disarmed them. Wounded Knee was nothing but a damned massacre of women and children." "American Horse," he explains, "testified before Congress." The U.S. disavowal of historical

moments of Lakota testimony becomes part of Mogie's story as well when
Herbie asks, "What happened after American Horse testified?" and Mogie
replies, rigid with barely restrained rage, "They [the Cavalry soldiers] were
all given a Congressional Medal of Honor." Aunt Helen tries to break the
tension by talking about Herbie's football game scores, to which Mogie
replies "I don't give a rat's ass!" Mogie's belittling of his son's accomplishments stems directly from his overwhelming feelings of anger when remembering Wounded Knee; the story that brings the family together in this
scene also furthers their estrangement. Significantly, this estrangement is
revealed through close-ups, a cinematic technique designed to elicit audience identification with focal characters' nuanced emotions (usually withheld from "stoic" Native characters in Westerns, who were most often seen
in long-shot). While Mogie has the ability to identify Native "extras" in
long-shot (as opposed to the closer framing given to white stars), Rudy is
forced to recognize his own violence in his brother's disfigured face through
the use of the close-up on Mogie during his retelling of American Horse's
testimony about Wounded Knee. Later in the scene, when Rudy reveals his
vigilante work to Mogie and confesses that he set the fire that burned his
brother, Mogie accuses him of being crazy and Rudy responds, "Don't you
think I know that? All I have to do is look at your face" (see figure 5.7).
Rudy and Mogie's exchange, and Rudy's final act of vandalism (defacing
the George Washington sculpture on Mount Rushmore), intensify the visual
discourse of faces and recognition in *Skins* as form of mediated memory.

Figure 5.7. *Skins*, First Look Pictures (2002), Mogie in close-up.

For Mogie, the cinematic erasure of Native characters, as they're defeated again and again in the Western, retraces a broader historical and geographical violence; specifically, the Congressional disregard of American Horse's testimony in 1891 and the public effort to deface and resignify Lakota sacred land (Paha Sapa/Black Hills) as a white American tourist destination and U.S. national monument (the presidential sculptures on Mount Rushmore). Mogie's recognition of Joe Thunderboots as a descendent of American Horse introduces Mogie's own history lesson in which Natives don't "vanish" from the Western landscape. Instead, the Western on television offers evidence of Native survival through the genealogy of the actors. The "extras" or "remainders" of Hollywood's frontier equations serve as reminders of stories exchanged between generations; Mogie insists that Natives are present even in films that try to erase them.

Eyre's voiceover commentary on the DVD of *Skins* is especially significant in this regard because of his choice to focus on directing viewers' attention to specific people (actors, non-professional actors, and community members) who participated in the production. His narrative recognizes, identifies, and thanks people for contributing their houses, land, and performances to the production, presenting an off-screen parallel to the presentation of Mogie's Indigenizing viewing practices by linking actors' roles to audiences' worlds and narrating the film's political meaning. Connecting the act of viewing with the act of speaking both acknowledges the damage and silencing of older and contemporary media images, and makes those media histories available as resources for recognizing media imperialism and the counterproject of speech.

Mogie's appropriation of the Western movie as a pedagogical prompt or mnemonic device for an oral history lesson also forces a non-Native audience, an audience targeted by some of the film's earlier didactic, documentary-style footage and voiceover, to acknowledge the copresence of an Indigenous audience. The citation of American Horse's testimony further dramatizes the "passionate research" (to quote Frantz Fanon) that can take place in the revisiting or recuperation of the aged products of popular culture, archived not in libraries and special collections but in the process of circulation in television and rebroadcasting. This "streaming archive" facilitates the restaging of encounters between Indigenous viewers and characters on screen through an oral performative reframing of analog or digital transmission. Stuart Hall assesses retrospection in the context of colonialism by drawing on Fanon's concept of the postcolonial "rediscovery" of identity and the concomitant process of "passionate research" into Native pasts that have been distorted or disfigured by colonial oppression. Hall argues that identity resides not in "archaeology" but rather "in the retelling of the past": "Far from being grounded in a mere 'recovery' of the past, which is waiting to be found, and which, when found, will secure our sense of ourselves into eternity, identities are the names we give to the different ways we are positioned by, and position ourselves within, the narratives of the past" ("Cultural Identity" 705–06).[23] While keeping in mind the important distinctions between Fanon's "post-colonial" theory and the circumstances of ongoing colonization for Indigenous minority communities, Hall's description of an identity based on active retellings of the past usefully emphasizes the continuous but changeable nature of "recovered texts," as well as the processes of recovery in and through acts of representation.

Eyre envisions an Indigenous audience's ability (and even obligation) to view film in a distinctive way, finding the Native presence that was already there, detecting political and historical legacies embedded but disguised in the documentation of victimhood on the nightly news and in Hollywood's attempts at erasure through the Western's acculturating chronicles of settlement. The interdependence of oral and electronic discourses in this scene deconstructs binary oppositions between low-tech and high-tech modes of transmission, but those modes are not conflated. Instead, the scene of storytelling moves from the media storytelling in the living room to oral storytelling at the kitchen table, modeling a strategy for the reeducation of youth through the intertextual relations between two narrative forms.

Only as the scene ends and Rudy leaves the house do we see that the small black television, still playing the Western, is stacked on top of an older, larger model that either isn't working or isn't turned on (see figure 5.8). This

Figure 5.8. *Skins*, First Look Pictures (2002), two televisions.

is in fact a long-delayed reverse-shot, since we have been viewing much of the action in this scene from the general position or point of view of the two television sets. The doubled televisions remind us of the nested screens earlier in the film; the plurality and intensification suggested by the reduplication of the television as a media vehicle imply the multiple versions of history that reside in the intertextual relationships between Hollywood and independent media and between media makers and the viewers who make their own meanings from the signals broadcast to their homes. The very composite nature of television rebroadcasting and the tools of its streaming archive seem to facilitate the characters' oppositional readings.

In *Skins*, the scenes of Native viewing work to de-exoticize on-screen Native characters, as both viewers and subjects, through the power of politicized recognition—Rudy *recognizes* his brother Mogie on the news, and Mogie *recognizes* his friend Joe Thunderboots in the Western. Far from stereotyped presentations on screen as threatening or victimized figures, *Skins* presents Native viewers who can generate documentary content from within generic media fantasies of Indians by recognizing the Native actors as part of their families and communities, and by recognizing the historical and contemporary events behind the stories parlayed by Westerns and by the nightly news. Rather than focusing on the recognizable qualities of white stars (playing cowboy heroes or playing villains in redface), the cinematic viewers in *Skins* take the "anonymous" extras as primary figures of community identification.

In imagining Native reception, Eyre stages his own interaction with his viewers, shaping relations to families and lands through film production while simultaneously making such private negotiations visible and accessible to a mixed audience in the broader public. In an interview about making *Skins*, Eyre asserts that the act of filmmaking itself incorporates a particular agenda in its address to viewers and calls the film a "home drama" and "a women's movie for men," referring to the emotional relationship between Rudy and Mogie (*Skins* DVD commentary). "In my movies I'm trying to convince my audiences to . . . go home" (Chaw); "My movie is like me," he says. Adopted by a white family as an infant, Eyre said that seeking his biological family was "something I just knew I was going to do. . . . I had love out there but I didn't know where it was and I think in my movies what's happening is these characters are yearning for each other—they're home dramas, and ultimately I want my audience not to miss each other" (Chaw). Eyre's desire to film a familial "near miss" is manifested in *Skins'* rendering of screens as both sites of rupture and sites of reunion.

Like *Smoke Signals*, *Skins* was made with multiple audiences in mind. Eyre brought *Skins* back "home"—to its site of production—in a physical way by showing it to the communities where it was set on the Pine Ridge Indian Reservation. His Rolling Rez Tour brought the film to reservation communities across the country using a semitrailer equipped with a 100-seat theater, air conditioning, and a 35 mm projector. As a metaphor for the Western's performance of social relations and Hollywood's exclusion of Native voices, the bus as a modern stagecoach and dramatic "stage" that Eyre developed so evocatively in *Smoke Signals* is materialized here quite differently, as a Native space, a physical but mobile location where Indigenous films and Indigenous viewing answer back to the history of cinematic misrecognition.[24] In the content of the film as well as in its exhibition in the Rolling Rez Tour bus, *Skins* explores what it means to resituate media images onto Native lands.

Acting Out (of) Loss: Two Modes of Mourning

Both *Smoke Signals* and *Skins* end with scenes of mourning as Victor (Adam Beach, Salteaux) mourns the death of his alcoholic father Arnold Joseph and Rudy mourns for his brother Mogie. Rudy's signature act of vandalism at the end of *Skins* is defacing the Mount Rushmore national monument. As a private commemoration of his brother, he tosses a bucket of red paint over the carved cliff, inadvertently creating a red tear down George Washington's face that echoes the widely circulated image of Iron Eyes Cody (the Italian-American actor Espera or "Oscar" DeCorti) in his role as the "Crying Indian" from the 1971 PSA. Rudy enacts two mourning rituals for his brother—a formal wake attended by family and community and a private act when he defaces the Mt. Rushmore monument in honor of his brother's request and his own relationship with the Lakota trickster spirit Iktomi. (Iktomi, the spider, is linked with rocks throughout the film and in Lakota mythology is the son of the rock spirit Inyan.)[25]

If Eyre's films ask viewers to mourn lost relatives and damaged families, they also mimic and ridicule other popular culture representations of weeping Indian victims. Scenes of mourning in Native cinema intervene in a popular culture landscape already saturated with taxidermic significations of Indian vanishing in popular culture—the "crying Indian" and other representations of loss. Eyre engages with issues of tragedy and its mediation by insisting that his audience join him in mocking as well as joining in crying as the physical manifestation of loss. Rudy tosses the red paint over the side of the excessive, monumental face of George Washington in an act of mourning that doubles as an activist prank; George Washington is made to weep for humble Mogie. Like the image of "Indians watching Indians on TV" in *Smoke Signals*, images of weeping signal both pathos and parody in *Skins*, registered on intimate and monumental scales.

In carrying out two trajectories for memorializing the familial past, Eyre insists on the interdependence of emotion and its mediation in the presence of popular representations. In particular, Mogie's death brings up the power of reenactment as a meaningful revisiting of traumatic events for actors who share their characters' affiliation and heritage. The actor Graham Greene was initially reluctant to "play dead" for the shot of Mogie in his coffin, and the day after the scene was shot, the crew burned the coffin and prayed together. In the DVD director's commentary, Eyre describes the day that the crew shot the scene of Mogie's wake as "a heavy day on the set": "The mood in this room was real. The mood in this room was too close, I think, for a lot of people. You see this guy crying in the back—he's crying, he's actually really crying. It just brings back memories for so many people, I think. It was a difficult, difficult scene to do." In the same commentary, Eyre declares his wish that *Skins* is "a place hopefully for healing, and to share family experience . . . and family love." In his focus on the memorial scene as a both a traumatic moment in film production and a mode of familial healing for the film's characters, Eyre revisits scenarios of mourning from the media past, a past that is integral to Mogie's character. He reinstates the moral efficacy and urgency of mourning in the act of crying, taking back the work of memorializing as both familial and political recognition and a way to reinterpret mediated images of Indians.

The scenarios and melodramatic tableaux of the silent Indian dramas reemerge here as "disidentifications" that are also reidentifications, projected back on the nationalist, iconic faces of settler culture. The narrative interruption and emotional intensity amplified by the stasis of the monument is similar to that of the close-up. Mary Ann Doane describes the close-up's contradictory functions in film history and criticism as a problem of magnification. The close-up is "inescapably hyperbolic . . . the vehicle of the star, the privileged receptacle of affect" ("The Close-Up" 91) that "underwrites a crisis in the opposition between subject and object" (94) and between the identifiable face and its effacement.[26] For Cherokee scholar Ellen Cushman, the skin color of the face often forms the premise for racial legibility and the surface of closest public scrutiny because "the primary text of authenticity is the face" (390).

In Westerns, the system of facial recognition signaled by close-ups of white stars—such as the famous tracking shot that reintroduces John Wayne to the viewing public in *Stagecoach*—suppresses audience recognition of the Native extras often seen in long-shot while condensing the genre's national history into a few iconic images. In *Smoke Signals*, during Victor and Thomas's bus ride to Arizona, they teach one another the codes of this cinematic regime of authenticity by discussing its facial sign system. Using *Dances with Wolves* as their authoritative text, they practice an "Indian warrior look," the Native version of the vigilante, by monitoring and suppressing facial expressivity ("quit grinning like an idiot—get stoic!") and managing their hair ("you gotta free it! An Indian man ain't nothing without his hair"). When this carefully cultivated "warrior look" fails to prevent racist treatment in the real world, Victor and Thomas begin to dismantle the cinematic "machine of faciality" and the face-as-the-site-of-speech by singing a song, "John Wayne's Teeth," which questions the authenticity of the white face (and mouth) that has most often spoken for the Western: "John Wayne's teeth, John Wayne's teeth, are they false, are they real, are they plastic, are they steel?"[27]

In *Skins*, the close-up of Mogie following Rudy's comment that, "All I have to do is look at your face" in order to recognize his own mistaken action, positions the face in close-up—and the monuments later in the film—not as a disguise or mask but rather as a legible site of rebuke. Damage and illness are literally written on the faces of the characters in the masking, scarring, and painting, the defacement and effacement that seem to disguise but in fact reveal. These close-ups, along with the monumental rock face of the U.S. presidents on Mount Rushmore, infuse intimate family recognition with nationalist discourses. The "white wall" of George Washington's face is the screen on which triumphalist American history is written; by scarring or "tearing" it with red paint, Rudy reveals the white face to be a mask and the history it memorializes to be in fact a cover for deliberate acts of forgetting.

This movement between small and large-scale faces and screens welds affect to its commodification within a sign system structured by the history of popular culture images. In *On Longing*, Susan Stewart writes that the "larger than life" quality of movie stars is a "matter of their medium of presentation . . . and that formation, that generation of sign by means of sign, provides the aesthetic corollary for the generative capacity of commodity relations" (91).[28] Mogie's immersion in and appreciation of popular culture images of all kinds—not just televised Westerns—signals his status as a contemporary consumer; hence his, and later Rudy's, ability to transpose

the specular sign system of commercial culture to Lakota relations of kinship and love is even more radical. Early in the film Mogie expresses his
love for Madonna by wearing his Madonna T-shirt, and Rudy manifests his
affection for his brother in specifically commodity terms at key moments
in the film. While Mogie is dying in the hospital, Rudy is at the gas station buying a T-shirt with an image that replaces the four presidents carved
into the rock of the Paha Sapa/Black Hills with the faces of the leaders
Sitting Bull, Chief Joseph, Geronimo, and Dull Knife. The shirts themselves update a resignaling of the land from the 1970s American Indian
Movement, and Eyre characterizes Rudy's purchase as an "act of self-love."
In identifying with and consuming commodity images of Indians, Rudy
reshapes their meaning-making to do the work of family reunification while
also modeling a Native market for material products carrying Native portraits, much like the modeling of viewership earlier in the film. By purchas-
ing the T-shirt Rudy repositions himself as the driver of cultural products
rather than himself a product. The renegotiation of power at the heart of
Rudy's recirculation of images is in line with the idea (but not always the
practice) of repatriation as a political transfer of ownership. Like the image
of the four portraits on the T-shirt, the PSA of the crying Indian image is
highly context-dependent, functioning in its production, circulation, and
reception rather than in isolation.

The "Crying Indian" PSA that first aired on Earth Day 1971 became
one of the most successful television commercials ever produced (see figure
5.9). A second PSA was developed in which Cody rode into modernity
on horseback, and a "Keep America Beautiful" poster circulated with the
image of Iron Eyes Cody's tear-stained face. The crying Indian weeps in a
mode of sentiment and romanticized nostalgia. Iron Eyes Cody performs in
full costume—including fringed buckskin, braids, and feathers—paddling
a traditional birch-bark canoe through a natural setting shot in soft focus
in a pictorialist style. As he paddles, he enters a modernity signaled by an
industrialized landscape, where through silhouette and superimposition he
becomes a spectral anomaly, a figure out of time moving—visible and yet
unacknowledged—through a contemporary dystopia marked by factories,
cars, highways, and litter. The close-up of Cody's face with its single tear
reactivates the melodramatic mode of the sympathetic Indian drama both
in its silence and in its *melos*. The music that accompanies the ad, dominated by drums and low, rhythmic string music, recalls the "Indian music"
from early Westerns. The image also recalls Edward Curtis's photography,
with its pictorialist use of silhouette, nostalgic narratives of vanishing Indians, and somber portraiture of often anonymous subjects labeled as types

Figure 5.9. Iron Eyes Cody (Espera DeCorti), image courtesy of Keep America Beautiful, Inc., used with permission; from the 1971 public service announcement.

rather than identified as individuals. The close-up of the crying Indian on "Keep America Beautiful" posters draws on the traditional stasis of portraiture and the melodramatic tableaux in which the emotional distress of the character(s) models and triggers an audience's own emotional reactions, reactions intended to "move" the audience to action.

Later, in 1998 (the same year that *Smoke Signals* was released), the PSA was updated with Iron Eyes Cody's image followed by the slogan "back by popular neglect." In keeping with the reflexivity of contemporary advertising, images of people littering as they board a city bus are followed by an image of the crying Indian poster at the bus stop; we see the tear falling on the poster, suggesting a magically conscious portrait, truly an Indian removed from time, suffering in the act of helpless witnessing, a frozen face with a tear that has continued to fall for 25 years. His weeping denotes a powerlessness that suggests political dependency (or wardship). He is a supplicant, and the ad entreats viewers by shaming them through the moral power of melodrama. In codifying Hollywood actors in redface as land stewards, the PSA's producers returned to historical constructions of Native peoples as figures for ethical responsibility (the original slogan was "People start pollution. People can stop it"). While the crying Indian is associated with land in terms of environmental stewardship, he also mystifies land ownership and the transfer of land that is at the heart of his moral efficacy by substituting a generalized emotional appeal to universal good behavior (not littering) for concrete policy analysis and specification of Native land rights.

In returning to the image of the crying Indian and in mapping that image onto the monumental visage of George Washington, Chris Eyre repoliticizes the mystified television Indian, overlaying the PSA rebuke of U.S. land stewardship onto the celebration of manifest destiny and reinserting issues of sovereignty and political autonomy that had been disassociated from images of Indians in the media, especially through Western genre representational displacement. Furthermore, the epic scale of these national symbols is harnessed to do the intimate work of mourning for a single family. At the same time that Eyre repudiates imposed melodramatic sympathy by making a national symbol take back the tears of the televised Indian, he also wields the accumulated power of that figure by claiming this and other televised images as part of a virtual "media past" that is part of a Native experience and thus available for Native use in resisting the very imperialism that it represents. Through the signage of these superimposed portraits, Eyre stages an encounter between symbolic, mediated icons—the crying Indian and the first president—fusing their visages in a fabrication of nation-to-nation interchange. Additionally in this complex exchange, Eyre's image hybridizes the white face of George Washington, which is then made to embody an interracial encounter rather than a purified nationalism (see figure 5.10).

As a closing image, this "close-up" also materializes the disfigurement of colonialism on the face of the nation as it parallels Mogie's scarred face, seen in close-ups earlier in the film. The recognizable tear/scar/paint imposed on the recognizable face of Washington, in turn imposed upon the cliff-face, registers and parodies the history of white actors "playing Indian" in redface. By painting the cliff-face red, Rudy attempts to reIndigenize the rock/screen into which the face is carved, inscribing a complex political history of geographical remapping onto the treaty land of the Black Hills and making the rock of the (resurfaced) cliff into a visual palimpsest onto which disputed boundaries are projected, boundaries that are figured as recognizable faces.

Figure 5.10. *Skins*, First Look Pictures (2002), George Washington's tear.

To return to Doane: "As simultaneously microcosm and macrocosm, the miniature and the gigantic, the close-up acts as a nodal point linking the ideologies of intimacy and interiority to public space and the authority of the monumental" ("The Close-Up" 109). In producing images of crying that move audiences, Eyre seems to assert that cinema itself can be a site of mourning; displaced and replaced icons stand not only for nations and land rights but also for neighbors and relatives. Yet at the same time, he playfully appropriates iconic images of U.S. national collective memory as a malleable semiotic system of mediated commodities. The rock-as-screen in this sequence—a space or "place" of encounter akin to what Mary Louise Pratt describes as a "contact zone"—recognizes a Lakota spiritual order in both contested land and the apparatus or materially "contested ground" of popular culture.[29]

Graham Greene and Eric Schweig are actors who have worked on Hollywood productions that insist on an acting-out of the historically suspended, culturally marked Indian in dramas of settlement. In order to make a living as actors, Greene, Schweig, and others have had to embody film and television roles that represent endless variants on the image of the crying Indian. Greene's long career has included playing a Lakota medicine man in Kevin Costner's *Dances with Wolves*, and Schweig played Uncas in Michael Mann's 1992 adaptation of that classic of U.S. imperialist frontier adventure literature, *The Last of the Mohicans*. If *Smoke Signals* speaks back to *Dances with Wolves* in the media-saturated banter between Victor and Thomas ("This isn't *Dances with Salmon*, you know"), *Skins* answers *The Last of the Mohicans'* powerful nostalgia by projecting back a similarly romanticized, silenced witness, in the figure of the weeping buckskinned Indian. In the *Skins* DVD commentary, Schweig says of his role as Rudy that "I was so happy to get up in the morning and put on a pair of pants and put on a shirt, instead of a loincloth and buckskin and all that nonsense, because all it does is perpetuate all the ignorance that we've had to put up with for 500 years" (*Skins* DVD commentary).[30]

Filmmakers who once watched old Westerns on television are challenging Hollywood's presumptions of an all-white viewing audience's unified beliefs about the history of U.S. settlement. They retrospectively revise the way those films have been interpreted, offering oppositional readings of Westerns from a Native perspective manifested in acts of speaking and listening. These reflexive practices are metaphors for processes of historical, political, and familial retrieval and repatriation, and for self-determination in the arena of media representations. And they are more than metaphors, often linking as parallel processes the production of film texts with social action; in films such as *The Return of Navajo Boy*, as discussed in chapter 3, the work of film production and reception results in the *actual* reunification of disbanded family members. Film footage, as both a material object and a representational symbol, is recirculated and returned to Indigenous provenance. In dramas and documentaries about acculturation in the context of intergenerational or interfamilial relations, issues of heritage and ownership are central to stories of the return of both filmed images and reunited family members. Through these complex exchanges, the films persuasively revise the politics of public memory, both documenting and dramatizing the historical impact of institutional, cultural, and cinematic interventions. Eyre's productions were among the first Native feature films to offer contemporary, complex speaking roles for Native actors, yet these films simultaneously look back on the violence of mapping televised Indians onto real Native peoples, of recognizing ones' self or relatives in the face and genealogy but not the costumed role of the televised Indian, and of the staged encounter between viewers and the Indians on screen as they negotiate the meaning of a media past.

Coda

Persistent Vision

Across the twentieth and into the twenty-first century, Indigenous peoples have been involved in cinema as performers, directors, writers, consultants, crews, and audiences. While both the specificity and range of this Native participation have often been obscured by the on-screen, larger-than-life images of Indians in the Western, recovering historical films reveals the complexity of Native interventions in cinema production and consumption. At the same time, the study of Native American images in cinema need not focus solely on mainstream representations, or on the elements of dominant U.S. culture and values that Hollywood feature films so often reveal. The work of this book has been to complicate discussions of Hollywood Westerns and of Native film production and reception by emphasizing texts in dialogue at moments when dominant cinema tropes and histories are repurposed for Indigenous projects. Not only have Indigenous images mattered to the Western, but Westerns have also mattered to Indigenous filmmakers and viewers, both then and now, in an interrelated and contested field of audiovisual representation. Whether Native filmmakers and their collaborators wield Western genre tropes of their day in feature productions or contemporary filmmakers recover and reframe archival images in the present, Native filmmakers have actively shaped and responded to the Western genre from its beginnings.

Critical revaluation of Indigenous images in cinema responds to Shari Huhndorf's crucial query in American studies: "What happens to American studies if you put Native studies at the center?" (*Mapping* 3). In film studies, such a move facilitates critical recognition of the centrality of Indigenous images and image-making to the birth and expansion of cinema, including not only the generic development of the Western but also the documentary, the melodrama, and the action film—all shaped from the very origins of Hollywood by Native participants—as well as the global circulation of Indigenous features, from the silent-era productions of James Young Deer and Edwin Carewe to the contemporary work of groups such as Isuma Productions. Across this long and ongoing history of Indigenous presence in the cinema has been an emphasis on Native recognition of genealogical continuity as a dynamic and material source for a range of counterimages to cinematic "vanishing Indians." The analyses developed in this book have explored ways that Indigenous filmmakers and performers, while working contrapuntally to public ideologies of vanishing, have also remained engaged with broader systems of popular culture representation and political action.

"Westerns were harmed in the making of this film": Remediation and Experimentalism

The aesthetic reclaiming of early cinematic images by Native communities and individual artists has paralleled a critical recovery of sympathetic silent Westerns as forms of counterdiscourse within the Western genre. A crucial argument for revisiting these films is their renewed relevance for Native youth, the group targeted by the boarding school policies of the past and whose images were so contested in early Westerns. The reframing process in which artists and filmmakers continue to look back to an already-mediated past is exemplified by two twenty-first century experimental productions: the short experimental film *4wheelwarpony* (2008), directed by White Mountain Apache and Diné director Dustinn Craig,[1] which documents the youth skateboarding culture in the Whiteriver community on the White Mountain Apache Indian Reservation in Arizona, and *Tonto Plays Himself* (2010) by Muscogee Creek and Cherokee director Jacob Floyd, which narrates the filmmaker's evolving research into the Western through the personal lens of family history.

    4wheelwarpony has shown at various film festivals and in venues such as *REMIX: New Modernities in a Post-Indian World* (2007–2008), an exhibit produced jointly by the National Museum of the American Indian (NMAI) and the Heard Museum in Phoenix, Arizona, and the NMAI exhibition *Ramp It Up: Skateboard Culture in Native America* (2009). Craig's film aligns contemporary Native experience with historical images, resulting in an aggressive revisualization and manipulation of older visual records in an evocative rather than expository mode. Rapidly edited split screens depict historical photographs juxtaposed with images of tribal members, Craig's family, skateboarders, and still or animated drawings. The young men in the skateboarding group wear costumes replicated from nineteenth-century photographs of Apache scouts for the U.S. military, including guns and rifles, reenacting the scouts' movement over traditional lands. *4wheelwarpony* is characterized by formal experimentation and visual effects, including multiple split screens, iris (masking), animation, slow motion, montage, superimposition, lyric on-screen text, reenactment, and integration of archival and still photographs with contemporary moving footage.[2] The film has no narration, relying instead on a repetitive musical pattern that builds tension and momentum until the final "credit" at the end of the film when skateboarders (dressed in their Apache scout costumes) read the film's title written on their skateboards. This naming, positioned just before the credits and highlighted as the film's only spoken language, frames the entire film in light of this title, which is also the name of the Craig's skateboard company. The film explores both voicelessness and the power of naming through visual experimentalism, the strategic return to silent images, and selective use of sound.

Craig reworks the established cinematic gun/camera trope of the Western and documentary genres through the mediating expressive presence of the skateboard. Toward the end of the film in a sequence of still images, the Apache scouts/skateboarders play with their guns, which are then replaced by skateboards inscribed with the film's title. Contemporary Native youth culture—both in the form of skateboard culture and filmmaking itself—supplants armed violence as a form of resistance when the gun becomes a skateboard. Craig's transformative vision answers the depiction of violent masculinity in Western genre images of Apaches and particularly the pop culture focus on Geronimo as an icon of Indigenous threat to white settlement. At the same time, the film's title indicates the substitution of the skateboard for horses, and the images of the young men reenacting Apache scouts running over their lands function as signs of both mobility and rootedness. The visual spectacle of the skateboarders' own feats also replace stunts of Western genre action sequences—such as Yakima Canutt's stunt work in the climactic "Indian attack" at the end of *Stagecoach*— providing a new center of gravity for spectacular action in the display of skateboarding skills. With its aesthetic abundance stemming from simultaneous actions across the partitioned screen space, *4wheelwarpony*'s formal excess challenges viewers with multiple streams of emotional and intellectual content. The film also expands and explores the space between still images and motion picture film by moving between these modes and by conflating them in stop-motion sequences of still photographs that rapidly reposition figures in the frame into brief narrative sequences, such as when two scouts point their guns back and forth at one another in alternating still shots. Craig's beautifully shot and brilliantly edited 8-minute film reaches backwards to imagine previous generations through reenactment and archival photography, while privileging Indigenous futures in its images of youth and a vibrant, mobile, contemporary Native skateboarding culture.

In the 2010 short film *Tonto Plays Himself*—made under the auspices of New York University's Culture and Media graduate program—Jacob Floyd investigates historical Western genre images of Indians, structuring the film as both personal narrative and pedagogical presentation to the viewer. Catchphrases from the pop culture mediascape mark the progress of Floyd's archive-based research, including the action-film promise of violent revenge ("This time, it's personal") and a warning of impending ghostly revenge gleaned from television signals in *Poltergeist* ("They're here!"). Floyd's appropriation of footage through splicing and editing is accompanied by the assurance, "Westerns were harmed in the making of this film." Floyd's low-budget, personal research film can be seen as a form of didactic experimentalism, involving film clips, voiceover, intertitle screens, and home movie footage, organized by framing footage of Floyd and his family. The family context is important because Floyd's primary discovery is that Creek actor Victor Daniels (stage name Chief Thundercloud) is his cousin, born just a few miles away from his family's home in Oklahoma. Scenes of viewing—Floyd watching movies in his small apartment and a closing scene of his family watching television together—reframe older Western images in the context of Native familial interpretation. The flood of stereotypes in films where Daniels utters lines such as "Me want-um scalp" is tempered by Floyd's discovery of Daniels's activism behind the scenes on behalf of Native actors, and his attempts to change on-screen images. Closing with an overt reference to the gun/camera trope, Floyd "shoots back" at canned Indian images with his small home-movie camera.

Visual Circuits, from "The Indian with a Camera"
to "The Held Image"

Indigenous artists have linked acts of recognition with repatriation to create an alternate hermeneutic space around the concept of Indigenous production and consumption of visual culture. Laguna writer Leslie Marmon Silko connects Indigenous control over the means of visual production with activist reterritorialization by suggesting that these are sequential forms of resistance ultimately oriented toward Indigenous futures. In a widely cited passage from her essay on Victor Masayesva's photography, "The Indian with a Camera," Silko writes, "The Indian with a camera is an omen of a time in the future that all Euro-Americans unconsciously dread: the time when the indigenous people of the Americas will retake their land" (178). While directly countering the discursive assumptions of Indian "vanishing" that undergirded theories of frontier "free land" for colonial settlement—that essential component of Frederick Jackson Turner's thesis on the American frontier—Silko also reasserts the power of Indigenous seeing to set the stage for a future era of renewed land rights. These land rights, signaled by visual mediation, are based on the genealogical continuity of Indigenous peoples into a future that counteracts the "vanishing" of temporal diminishment or before-and-after narratives of assimilation. The Western genre's historical prophecies—the didactic stories Western films tell about the national past in order to explain and legitimate the dominance of contemporary settler landholding—are challenged by the alternative temporalities in texts authored by generations of Indigenous peoples. And yet looking back at the Western, Native films also claim its images as part of their own experience of twentieth-century media by reusing its powers of audiovisual storytelling.

Films that temporally resituate viewers' relationships to images highlight the formal manipulation of time across traditions of photography and film. From the freeze frames in the film *House Made of Dawn* that transition between flashbacks and the present, to the inset photographs held in the hands of on-screen viewers in *The Return of Navajo Boy*, the films discussed in this book reflect on systems and processes of Native seeing and being seen. Visual strategies such as freeze frames and inset photographs, theorist Garrett Stewart argues, summon viewers "into a world beyond and behind the screen world" (13).[3] These strategies rely on the power of film to "awaken" photography, as well as the power of stills excerpted from film to reframe cinematic content, as when documentary images become family portraiture rather than dominant narrative, facilitating Indigenous ownership and recrediting on the basis of intergenerational recognition.

Within the national discourses of the United States, legislative frameworks such as the Native American Graves and Repatriation Act of 1990 (NAGPRA) register a shift in the public recognition of Indigenous ownership of cultural patrimony. Maori director Barry Barclay articulates a discourse of cinematic repatriation beyond the national discourses of the United States in his eloquent chapter "The Held Image," from *Our Own Image*. Barclay describes two moments that illustrated for him "something remarkable about how we collect and save our images, about how we present them and to whom" (83). The first is an exchange with a Native teenager in Maui, who showed him a picture of her daughter: "It was her image. She was holding it" (83). This scene of ordinary possession and sharing quietly counters the circulation of Indigenous images as ethnographic evidence with the inter-personal storytelling prompted by family snapshots. In the second instance, Barclay and his cameraman delivered taped interview material to the elders who had given the interviews: "Handing those tapes across one by one to each elder became some of the most special moments I have ever had in film-making. . . . Like the young woman in the canefields of Maui, they were holding their own image in their own hands" (93). Barclay's emphasis on the image of "holding" another image articulates a concept of Indigenous ownership and archiving that includes sharing and circulation. My analysis of remediation in contemporary Native films extends the concept of Indig-enous provenance, visualized through "the held image," to scenes of view-er-screen encounter or "Indians watching Indians on TV." These on-screen images of Native recognition and critical viewing implicitly acknowledge the right of tribes to be the intended audience of visual representations. Viewing canonical and sympathetic Westerns from Indigenous viewpoints, Native and collaborative films perform interpretive ownership by scrutiniz-ing and reframing—often through processes of crediting or naming—those older visual culture forms of containment and the discursive disintegration of Indian families in the public imagination.

If Hollywood films have tended to nationalize individual experiences, pooling them into one dominant narrative and visual scenario, the inde-pendent, experimental, and documentary films discussed in this book work to bring back the distinct voices of witness and community testimony to the on-screen stories of Native characters. Recent archival retrievals of Hol-lywood films and film fragments as documents of Indigeneity and bicultur-alism have reframed (without erasing) the films' original work. While the originary images may have been deployed in service of imperialist projects, contemporary strategies of retrieval and reengagement demonstrate not only a tactical "raiding of the colonial archive," but also the ways that Indigenous media productions continue to be reflexively embedded in the wider field of national and international mediated images of Indians (Ginsburg and Myers). In their contemporary work of "looking back" and in their deft use of media technologies, generic structures, and historical texts, film-makers such as James Young Deer, Edwin Carewe, Victor Masayesva, Jeff Spitz, Bennie Klain, Rick Morse, Larry Littlebird, and Chris Eyre disrupt the linear temporality underpinning narrative constructions of primitivism, civilizing missions, and assimilation. They do so by invoking audiovisual palimpsests of the West in order to amend its erasures and ruptures through enunciations of intergenerational witness.

The story of Indigenous participation in the cinema is too multifaceted, too long, too large to tell in one book. Rather than attempting to address every relevant text in a comprehensive overview, my aim has been to read individual productions closely and to bring together a wide range of film types and periods—Hollywood and independent productions; feature films, documentaries, and experimental films; silent, studio-era, and contemporary—balancing historical contexts of initial production with the revaluation of texts in the present, weaving these into a conversation about the broader political and cultural work of moving images. At the same time, I have emphasized the importance of archival recovery of silent-era "lost" or largely forgotten films as well as systems and process of media recovery. As very recent revaluations of films such as *Ramona*, *The Exiles*, and *House Made of Dawn* suggest, much archival work remains to be done on Indigenous participation in U.S. and global film production, including biographies and accounts of individual Indigenous film artists and performers as well as attention to Native innovations in new media and youth media, such as IsumaTV and Rezkast. I have argued that one strand of Indigenous audiovisual reclamation has taken place through the discursive reconstruction of familial and community images, inviting us to see national issues of recognition and repatriation in more intimate terms of genealogy and custody. These films complicate the temporal straitjacket of before-and-after images in their geographic and temporal mobility and in the way they highlight the capacity of film to visualize Indigenous continuance. Formal visual and audio strategies and new modes of production reframe commercial footage in a Native media space, activating and disseminating a range of Indigenous systems of classification and laying claim to visual objects originally produced under colonial relations of power. In the face of the Western's vanishing Indians, photography as an emblem of death is reborn into narratives of Indigenous persistence in the cinema.

Notes

Introduction
Before-and-After: Vanishing and Visibility in Native American Images

1. Quoted in the film *Coming to Light: Edward S. Curtis and the North American Indians,* Dir. Anne Makepeace. See Hearne, "Telling and Retelling."

2. A still image from the workshop—filmmaker Darren Kipp (Blackfeet) cleaning the camera lens—has circulated widely as the web portal image for the NMAI, Film and Video Center website and on the cover of Beverly Singer's break-through book, *Wiping the War Paint Off the Lens.*

3. The converging emphasis in Westerns and federal policy discourses on vanishing and, in sympathetic depictions, on metaphors of wardship ignores a wide range of Indigenous relational structures. Tribal nationhood, villages and bands, moieties and clans, and kinship systems may emphasize matriarchy or special relationships with grandparents, siblings, aunts and uncles, and other extended family networks, as well as spiritual relations. These complex formations have also been affected or transformed by colonizing forces and interrupted by the removal of children to military-style institutional settings.

4. In this book I use the term "Indian" when it is part of an established name or phrase, such as "vanishing Indian," "Indian policy," "Indian drama," "pan-Indian," "Indian agent," and so forth, as well as at times to describe Hollywood images (for example, "images of Indians"). I use "Native" or "Native American" to refer to North American Native peoples, and to images of and by Native peoples on screen, and I use the overlapping (but not synonymous) term "Indigenous" to refer more broadly and globally to Indigenous minority peoples and to certain theoretical, historical, or paradigmatic issues that reach beyond the geographic boundaries of Native North America.

5. See Philip French and John Cawelti for descriptions of contemporary revisionist Westerns of the last quarter of the twentieth century as "post-Westerns." Susan Kollin's edited collection *Postwestern Cultures* goes much farther in developing the concept in the context of critical regional studies, and Neil Campbell's work

frames the post-Western as an intertextual but decidedly contemporary phenomenon of "films of the modern West" (such as *The Big Lebowski*).

6. Nanna Verhoeff's extensive study of early cinema Westerns marshals evidence of "considerable inconsistency in the use of genre labels" before 1915, suggestive of an emergent and unstable construction of genre in this period—a time when films were categorized in relational ways, such as when a *New York Times* writer described "the Western film, and its sister, the Indian film" (114–15; 13).

7. See Aleiss, "Native Americans: The Surprising Silents."

8. See, for example, Ward Churchill's *Fantasies of the Master Race*, Angela Aleiss's *Making the White Man's Indian*, Jacqueline Kilpatrick's *Celluloid Indians*, and M. Elise Marubbio's elaboration of the ways that Hollywood films have gendered the trope of vanishing and Indian death as female in *Killing the Indian Maiden*. Many studies of the Western (and of sound-era Westerns in particular) do not include significant discussion of Indian images (Tompkins, McGee, and Stanfield).

9. Slotkin's emphasis on the Western's generic focus on vigilantism is preceded by Leslie Fiedler of course, who makes an eloquent case for the similarity of "the duel and the lynching" as forms of racialized violence:

> It hardly matters, the band of vigilantes against band of outlaws or single champion against single villain—the meaning is the same: a plea for extra-legal violence as the sole bastion of true justice in a world where authority is corrupt and savagery ever ready to explode. And it is, perhaps, quite as much a product of the reaction against Reconstruction as those novels of Thomas Dixon, Jr., *The Leopard's Spots* and *The Clansman*, from which D. W. Griffith made *The Birth of a Nation*. . . .
> [J]ust as Dixon's fictions were an imaginative, almost a mythological, justification for the oppression of the Negro, so those of Wister and his imitators were, though less explicitly, an analogous justification for the extermination of the Indian. (139)

10. See Abel, *The Red Rooster Scare*. Also, in their endeavor to redirect critical apprehension of the Western to address its imperialist origins and legacies, film scholars Ella Shohat and Robert Stam emphasize the genre's educational work: "The Western . . . played a crucial pedagogical role in forming the historical sensibilities of generations of Americans" (115). Contemporary theorists of education continue to see children's films as "teaching machines" in the sense that "children learn from exposure to popular cultural forms" (Giroux 125).

11. Qtd. in Welsh 54.

12. See Huhndorf, *Going Native*, and Deloria, *Playing Indian*, for discussion and specific examples of institutionalized practices of "playing Indian."

13. See Bolter and Grusin, *Remediation*. This concept is discussed briefly in the concluding chapter of this book.

14. For a history of this emergence, see Singer's *Wiping the War Paint Off the Lens*, and Ginsburg's 1996 essay "Mediating Culture: Aboriginal Media and

the Social Transformation of Identity" <http://www.usc.edu/dept/ancntr/pdcomm/ginsburg.html>.

15. "Celebrating," pp. 7, 10. Barclay identifies a list of contemporary feature filmmakers as part of this movement, including Native directors Sherman Alexie (Spokane/Coeur d'Alene) and Chris Eyre (Cheyenne/Arapaho), First Nations director Zacharias Kunuk (Inuit), Sami director Nils Gaup, and Australian Aboriginal directors Tracey Moffatt and Ivan Sen. If it were expanded to television and cinema documentary, the list and timeframe could be radically expanded to include the documentary film work of myriad Indigenous filmmakers from the 1960s onward, as well as many new feature and experimental film directors and amateur productions.

16. Faye Ginsburg uses the term "Parallax Effect," to describe "indigenous media as arising from a historically new positioning of the observer behind the camera so that the object—the cinematic representation of culture—appears to look different than it does from the observational perspective of ethnographic film" (65). A concrete historical moment in this shift came with Sol Worth and John Adair's 1960s fieldwork teaching filmmaking to Diné students and discussing the resulting films' expressive worldview. Published as *Through Navajo Eyes* in 1972, this landmark project, for all its shortcomings, put cameras in Indigenous hands, ceding the old ethnographic order of outsiders filming Native subjects.

17. Ginsburg, "Indigenous Media" 94; Ginsburg, "The Parallax Effect" 168–69.

18. Angela Aleiss writes that although *Motion Picture World* described Young Deer as "a Winnebago from Nebraska (5 August 1911, p. 276) . . . the Winnebago say that there was no tribal member by the name of Young Deer or Youngdeer" according to her correspondence with tribal historian David Smith (*Making* 176n). While I follow Young Deer's claims to Ho-Chunk identity in this manuscript—by referring to him as Ho-Chunk—I want to clarify that he was not an enrolled member of the tribe according to extant tribal records. Young Deer's Native identity remains unconfirmed; it is possible that he was non-Native, although I think it is more likely that he had Ho-Chunk ancestry (as he claimed) without having been recorded or formally enrolled as a tribal member.

19. See Bhabha 117.

20. The origin of the Western film genre in dime novels and Wild West shows has already been well established in film scholarship. For recent work on Buffalo Bill and the Western, see Joy Kasson's "Life-Like, Vivid, and Thrilling Pictures": Buffalo Bill's Wild West and Early Cinema" and Corey K. Creekmur's "Buffalo Bill (Himself): History and Memory in the Western Biopic," both in *Westerns: Films through History*, ed. Janet Walker.

21. See Solnit, *Rivers of Shadows*, and Rony, *The Third Eye*.

22. Rony 36–39. In discussing Regnault's influence on ethnographic film, Rony asserts, "[l]ike ethnography, cinema is also a topos for the meeting of science and fantasy. Cinema, however, eliminated the potentially threatening return look of the performer present in the exposition, thus offering a more perfect scientific voyeurism" (43).

23. Early cinematic documentaries, combining the ethnographic and the exotic, sought to capture a Native "purity" while using Euro-American narrative frameworks. See Edward Curtis's *In the Land of the Headhunters* (1914), the films of Robert Flaherty, and Cooper and Schoedsack's *Grass* (1925).

24. Significant scholarship on boarding schools includes studies of letters from students, publications of the schools, before-and-after photographs, and other primary documents. See Adams, Child, Fear-Segal, Katanski, Lomawaima, and Malmsheimer.

25. Jacqueline Fear-Segal specifies that lighting and white powder were used to lighten students' skin tones in the "after" images taken by Choate (163–64).

26. Although before-and-after photographs focused on children, other photographers (such as Edward Curtis) rarely photographed Native children. Channette Romero notes that ". . . early photographers tried to limit any evidence of the continuation of Native cultures; they often decontextualized their subjects, photographing them alone, removed from their tribal contexts and families, as children are direct evidence of survival and continuation" (51).

27. See Marien, *Photography: A Cultural History* 44. Marien writes that the daguerreotypes were made on commission "for the weekly Paris journal *L'Illustration* . . . with the explicit intention of rushing them to publication as wood engravings" (44).

28. The Getty collection includes images of slave children before and after their removal from slaveowners and education at the Orphan's Shelter in Philadelphia. The images are captioned "As We Found Them" and "As They Are Now," and the children are dressed first in torn rags and then in finer clothes. A brief narrative provides the backstory of the children's mother and of their removal from slavery, and the bottom of each card reads, "Profits from sale, for the benefit of the children." See the Getty collection online <http://www.gettyimages.com/detail/3207142>. I'm grateful to Kristin Schwain for directing me to this image sequence in the Getty collection.

29. In an 1877 court case, Barnardo was accused of manipulating before-and-after images by using child models (rather than the actual children aided by the charity) and by exaggerating their appearance of poverty through costume and pose. Barnardo argued that he should be allowed to create expressive images in service of truths (as painters do), and the case was dismissed with a reprimand. See Marien 157, 160.

30. See, for example, the Duke University Library's digitized collection of images from the Emergence of Advertising in America, 1850–1920 database, in the John W. Hartman Center for Sales, Advertising and Marketing History. An image from the Hawley Scrapbook (n.d.) shows a man's beard before and (revealed by a pop-up) after treatment with Buckingham's Dye: <http://library.duke.edu/digitalcollections/eaa.SB0056/pg.1/>. A photographic image from a 1949 full-page advertisement for the Protam Nutritional Plan shows a "popular New York model" before and after losing 30 pounds on the diet plan (from the Medicine and Madison Avenue database, item number MM0762): <http://library.duke.edu/digitalcollections/mma.MM0762/pg.1/>.

31. See Judith Williamson's study of advertising structures, *Decoding Advertising*.

32. In 1891 Captain Pratt told the Carlisle, Pennsylvania, *Daily Evening Sentinel*, "We have two objects in view in starting the Carlisle School—one is to educate the Indians—the other is to educate the people of the country . . . to understand that the Indians can be educated" (qtd. in Malmsheimer 63). He wrote in his memoir that "the progress of the school and the appreciation of the public went hand in hand" (R. Pratt 276).

33. Qtd. in Malmsheimer 57.

34. Though Butler's theories interrogate gender apart from race, her notion of the constitutive performance of identity suggests that if we are our performances, the performances prescribed for Native people through cinematic representations and through boarding school regulations impose a symbolic violence beyond a simple dissonance between the "Hollywood Indian" and the people represented.

35. See Konkle's discussion of the clichéd commonplace assumption that Native people are "torn between cultures" in *Writing Indian Nations* 288–90.

36. Pratt clothed the Carlisle School students in surplus military uniforms—Union blues left over from the Civil War—and housed them in abandoned military barracks. His reuse of these materials and structures not only repeated the dispersal of low-quality commodity rations on reservations and forecast the penury of Congressional appropriations for later government boarding schools, but also retroactively incorporated Natives into the military, effectively marking the children as awkward remnants of U.S. wars. Pratt describes struggling with Bureau of Indian Affairs (BIA) officials after initially being sent "the shoddiest of shoddy clothing" that "illustrated the ill-considered system of buying the cheapest materials" for Native students. More significantly, Pratt was able to substitute a military rationing system for the per capita allowance granted to most Indian boarding schools: "experience in army service showed that children living on that ration would be hungry all the time." He requested and was granted authority to use the Army ration table instead of the BIA's table, "and for the whole twenty-five years I was superintendent that was the allowance at Carlisle in contradistinction to the varying tables used in other Indian schools" (R. Pratt 233). His subsequent conversations with bureau officials revealed that the reduced BIA rations for Native children at boarding schools were not based on any research into other boarding school systems but rather on the impulse to "economize" (234). Pratt himself was a veteran of frontier conflicts and used his military training in educating the students in marching, flag drills, and other forms of soldierly discipline. His creation of an educational system based on both prison and military models, and his strong advocacy of an "outing" program that resembled the fostering or temporary adoption of Native students in to white homes, coalesced as a mode of institutional intervention in Native families that would persist for almost a century. Resistance to military indoctrination came first from Brulé Sioux Chief Spotted Tail, from the Rosebud reservation, who objected to the use of soldiers' uniforms for his sons at the school. According to Pratt's memory of the incident, "He said he did not

like to have their boys drilled, because they did not want them to become soldiers" (237).

37. See Konkle, "Indigenous Ownership," and Bruyneel on "American Colonial Ambivalence," in *The Third Space of Sovereignty*, 10–19. Konkle offers a detailed discussion of the specific processes of U.S. liberal imperial legal and philosophical thought by which the idea of Indianness was made abstract for the express purposes of territorial dispossession.

38. The Cherokee Nation sued Georgia in 1831 to force the state to adhere to treaty rights and territorial boundaries. The court, under Chief Justice John Marshall, ruled that although the Cherokee were a separate, "domestic dependent nation," it did not constitute a foreign nation and thus could not sue Georgia.

39. Like the ward/guardian relationship, the pact between the U.S. government and Native nations was expected to be temporary, as evidenced in Marshall's phrasing, "[Native Americans] occupy a territory to which we assert a title independent of their will, which must take effect in point of possession *when* their right of possession ceases" (Prucha 59, emphasis added). But unlike ward/guardian relationships, "when" the relationship ceases Native nations were expected to be either extinct or amalgamated into the general population, *losing* rather than *gaining* title, coming out of rather than into an inheritance. The state is thus revealed to be an instrument of what Homi Bhabha describes as a "moment of separation": "what is being dramatized is a separation—*between* races, cultures, histories, *within* histories—a separation between *before* and *after* that repeats obsessively the mythical moment or disjunction" (82). Alcida Ramos outlines a similar trope with regard to South American constructions:

> picturing the Indians as children, an old cliché in the indigenist scene, is nonetheless a potent trope in the discourse of the powerful. In metonymic fashion, it wraps the relationship of the national state with its Indigenous peoples in a cloak of established truths about the nature of the Indian as well as the civilized. It has been the most recurrent message sent forth to the Indians as the way things are and should be. With a single stroke it delivers two of the cardinal commandments of the dominant interethnic truth: (1) whites, i.e. adults, know what is best for the infantile Indians; (2) for Indians to reach adulthood they must relinquish their Indianness. (84)

40. For example, the Indian Removal Act of 1830 mandating relocation west of the Mississippi guarantees the tribes that "the United States will forever secure and guarantee to them, and their heirs or successors, the country so exchanged with them. . . . *Provided always*, That such lands shall revert to the United States, if the Indians become extinct, or abandon the same" (Prucha 53, emphasis in original). According to Marshall's decision in the 1823 *Johnson and Graham's Lessee v. William McIntosh*: "Merely occupants" of the land, Indians are "deemed incapable of transferring the absolute title to others" (Prucha 37).

41. Raheja, *Reservation Reelism.* See my discussion in Chapter 3 of northern Cheyenne elder Charles Sooktis' story about playing Indian (in Cecil B. DeMille's *The Plainsman*) for an example of Indigenous "redfacing" in the trickster tradition.

42. The polyphonic and multicultural amalgamation of signs worn by the cowboy present one example. Jane Gaines and Charlotte Herzog have pointed out the "hybrid nature of the iconography of the Western hero" with component parts made up of Native fringed buckskin, the hat and chaps of Mexican *vaqueros*, and various military elements. Gaines and Herzog read this amalgamation not as "the remnants of lost cultural connection," but rather as the "signs that keep this connection alive, that work against the repression of origins," and that call up "a comparison between cultural miscegenation and interracial mixing" in the continuing hybridization of a figure that paradoxically signifies a suppression of ethnicity in the Anglicization of the frontier (177, 178). If cowboy heroes are culturally and racially signified by their costumes, Native characters are doubly so.

43. See Sobchack, "The Scene of the Screen," 146.

44. Verhoeff's larger point involves the way "othering," as a form of museification in Indian dramas, involves ethnographic elements and displays (such as still images), the "trans-racial transvestitism" of redface, or white actors playing Indian characters, and the structural elements "when assimilation is foregrounded in the theme of the narrative" (56–57).

45. My analysis of scenes of Native viewing in later chapters of this book also builds on Allen's description of the "scene of Indigenous instruction" in post–World War II Native American and Maori activist and literary texts. Allen describes scenes of "idealized grandparent-grandchild relationships" through which characters engage in "rebuilding the ancestor" or "becoming the ancestor" as part of a continuation of Indigeneity into the future (161). I have extended this notion elsewhere in discussions of the "scene of the story" or "scene of storytelling" in Native animated programs for children that visualize storytelling as a framing technique that (re)situates Native creation stories within tribal relationships and epistemological frameworks ("Indigenous Animation").

46. See Arif Dirlik's historicization of Indigenous modernities as "alternative modernities" ("Global Modernity?" 277) and his investigation of Indigenous "claims to a different historicity" (*Postmodernity's Histories* 212).

47. My argument builds on substantial critical attention to Native activism in the 1970s and particularly, as I discuss further in the chapter, is Allen's description of Indigenous activist occupations of dominant discourses in literary texts in *Blood Narrative*.

Chapter 1
Reframing the Western Imaginary: James Young Deer, Lillian St. Cyr, and the "Squaw Man" Indian Dramas

1. The term "Indian dramas" or "Indian films"—an industry description used in trade journals in the first decades of the twentieth century—refers to early

films on "Indian subjects." These films, according to Eileen Bowser, "might be considered a branch of Westerns, but in the early years they constituted a separate genre" (173). I refer to these films in this chapter as "Indian dramas," "silent Westerns," and "frontier melodramas." See Aleiss for a discussion of "sympathetic" images of Native peoples in silent films. See Bataille and Silet for a useful collection of early writings on representations in film (55–70). Marsden and Nachbar, writing about screen stereotypes, employ the useful terms "Noble Anachronism" and "Savage Reactionary" to indicate long-standing stereotypes of Indians in popular culture and the cinema. Stanfield describes Native and Mexican villains in early Westerns, arguing that sexual transgression, cross-racial romance, and cultural assimilation all lead to the destruction of Native characters ("The Western").

2. The first boom in Indian dramas ended around 1914 when public attention turned to World War I. Scott Simmon writes, "Within a year after the release of *The Invaders*, trade journals were informing budding scriptwriters that film companies had begun hanging out 'No Indians Wanted' signs: 'none of the companies will state that they desire Indian dramas. They are played out'" (*Invention* 79).

3. This chapter focuses on selections from the Library of Congress collection, "American Indians in Silent Film," which contains at least 40 films (out of 132) that touch on issues surrounding cross-racial romance and mixed-blood children. In "The Family on the Land," Virginia Wright Wexman explores the way silent Westerns naturalize the Anglo couple as rightful inheritors of the North American continent through images of the body, the landscape, and the law. Wexman asserts that in silent Westerns the romantic couple generates the "family on the land," a trope that sets in motion the Western's primary conflict: its attempt to reconcile democratic parity and Anglo supremacy (162).

4. An iris shot is usually masked (or blacked out) around the edges, sometimes using the circular lens aperture itself, so that only a circular fragment of the frame is visible. In silent film, the circle in an iris shot may expand or contract to open or close a scene (irising-in or irising-out).

5. In his detailed analysis of this film, Scott Simmon notes the emphasis on "the film language of male voyeurism" (*Invention* 75) in the way this scene "relies on the obsessively repeated film grammar of the turn-of-the-century Peeping Tom films, such as *As Seen through a Telescope* (1900)" (68).

6. The image of the gun/camera has been discussed by artists and scholars such as Victor Masayesva (Hopi), Susan Sontag, Donna Haraway, and Cynthia Erb. In *On Photography*, Sontag asserts that photography is "predatory": "Just as the camera is a sublimation of the gun, to photograph someone is a sublimated murder" (14–15). Erb usefully translates this concept to account for images of white visual mastery over territory in imperial adventure films from *Tarzan* to *King Kong*. Masayesva considers this trope in the context of Indigenous media resistance in his essay "Indigenous Experimentalism" (as I discuss in chapter 3). See also Landau and Haraway on the camera as a trope of colonial hunting.

7. See Dippie's discussion of the "heirship problem" implicit in the Dawes Act (178–79). Because Native nations were assumed to be vanishing, no provi-

sion was made under the allotment system for future generations; once the land was parceled out to individuals Native people or families, the remaining land was not held in trust for tribal children and grandchildren but instead distributed to non-Native settlers.

8. Qtd. in Dippie 186. However, Leupp also "endorsed the use of force in bringing children to school when families would not cooperate with voluntary measures" (Child 13). In this sense the government boarding school policy reflected its military origins in the incarceration of Native people who resisted U.S. westward expansion.

9. For a discussion of the impact of coercive education on a specific community (Hopi), see J. Jenkins, esp. 150–51. Gerald Vizenor reflects on the continuing policy of removing children from Native homes in "Stealing Tribal Children" and other essays. For an excellent account of boarding school education in the upper Midwest and its relation to Native families, see Child. For a firsthand narrative of mission school education, see LaFlesche.

10. Jay has discussed Griffith's early Indian films for Biograph as a prelude to *The Birth of a Nation*'s focus on "the white family made whole after its sundering by war"—whether that war is the Indian Wars or the Civil War, and whether the ethnic threat is Native American or African American. Griffith's films, Jay argues, are dominated by lost objects (a white infant, a white woman's body), which must be found to reconstitute the patriarchal family (19–20). Jay's discussion of D. W. Griffith's Indian dramas is an important addition to the extensive scholarship on the performative and narrative innovations of Griffith and Biograph. See, for example, Roberta Pearson's *Eloquent Gestures: The Transformation of Performance Style in the Griffith Biograph Films*, Tom Gunning's *D. W. Griffith and the Origin of American Narrative Film*, Scott Simmon's *The Films of D. W. Griffith*, and Michael Allen's *Family Secrets: The Feature Films of D. W. Griffith*.

11. Andrew Brodie Smith and Philip Deloria have each written excellent accounts of Young Deer and St. Cyr's intervention in the emerging film industry and the "squaw man" film cycle. This chapter contributes closer visual attention to images in the "squaw man" constellation of films, and to Young Deer and St. Cyr's signature interventions, in the context of the broader field of racialized images in Indian dramas and in American popular and political culture at the time.

12. The corporate histories and mergers of the Jesse L. Lasky Feature Play Company—founded by Jesse L. Lasky, his brother-in-law Samuel Goldfish, theater director Cecil B. DeMille, and attorney Arthur Friend—and W. W. Hodkinson's Paramount Pictures (formed in 1914 as a distribution company) is complicated by the fact that the individuals founding the Lasky company later became executives in other major studios. When founding member Samuel Goldfish (later Samuel Goldwyn) was left out of the Lasky Company merger with Adolph Zukor's Famous Players Film Company in 1916, he went on to establish Goldwyn Pictures, which later merged with Loew's-Metro and the "Mayer group" to become Metro-Goldwyn-Mayer (MGM) in the mid-1920s. DeMille, in turn, established and directed the DeMille Studio for five years (having purchased the Thomas H. Ince Studio in Culver City) and

subsequently briefly worked for MGM before returning to Paramount. The story of DeMille's early career and the production of *The Squaw Man* has become an essential part of Hollywood's origin story. See, for example, the various biographies of Cecil B. DeMille, including Higashi's *Cecil B. DeMille and American Culture: The Silent Era*; Birchard's *Cecil B. DeMille's Hollywood*; Koury's *Yes, Mr. DeMille*; and Louvish's *Cecil B. DeMille: A Life in Art*. For an account of Indian stage dramas and their adaptations on film, including *The Squaw Man*, see Friar and Friar.

13. See Bergland for a discussion of the figure of the spectral Indian in nineteenth- and twentieth-century literature.

14. Peter Brooks sketches the historical development and theorization of the "tableau of reaction" (61–65) as a "mute scene" in which the actors come together as a group and each expresses an emotional reaction "at a moment of climax and crisis, where speech is silenced and narrative arrested in order to offer a fixed and visual representation of reactions to peripety" (61).

15. Royle and Faversham's novel takes place primarily in England and accordingly is more concerned with the circumstances leading to Jim's departure than with his life in the American West. However, Jim's work in England's colonies (as a soldier in India and a potential soldier in the Boer War) prepares the reader to view his ranch in the West as a similar endeavor. The West of *The Squaw Man* novel, represented by the Maverick town saloon and the desolate Carston Ranch, is a heterogeneous place populated by "tattered specimens of the various races" (147) in marked contrast to the insular English aristocracy. The novel also contains conflicted views of motherhood, culminating in Nat-u-Ritch's suicide when her son is taken from her. Lady Diana's "maternal instincts" and childless condition contrast with the "childlike" qualities of Nat-u-Ritch, who gives up her son to Diana's care. The first image of motherhood is not Diana or Nat-u- Ritch but Lady Elizabeth, Henry's mother, whom even Henry comes to accuse of marring the English aristocracy: "You've spoiled me, mother" (85). By the end of the novel, on meeting Jim's mixed-race son Hal, Diana holds the child in a way that expresses "all the starved maternity of her barren life" (256). In contrast, Nat-u-Ritch is an "abject slave" (207) to Jim. When Jim tells her that Hal will go away she sobs "like a child who is suddenly asked to face something it cannot understand" (260), underscoring the paternal relationship also implicit in the U.S. government's view of Native peoples as "wards." Unlike Diana, Nat-u-Ritch is never allowed to grow up.

16. Sumiko Higashi attributes DeMille's success to his emphasis on the "intertextuality of feature film" with the more legitimate, genteel theatrical stage, evident in his interest in adapting novels and plays rather than original scenarios. In her words, DeMille "inserted the photoplay into genteel culture by exploiting the parallel discourses deemed highbrow in an era characterized by conspicuous racial, ethnic and class distinctions" (2, 1).

17. The authenticity of the letter is unknown. Both Fear-Segal and Katanski have demonstrated that published letters, stories, and novels, seemingly authored by boarding school students or their parents, were sometimes penned by teachers

and school administrators as part of an organized propaganda effort in support of the schools.

18. Discussing Zane Grey's depiction of Mormonism in *Riders of the Purple Sage*, William Handley writes of Westerns, "the designs of Empire are to a large degree predicated upon the idea that the conquered are both Other (sexually, religiously, racially) and yet culturally 'familiarized,' or made ideologically serviceable and assimilable, for the conquerors" ("Distinctions" 2).

19. Like the story of Pocahontas, *The Squaw Man* was reproduced widely across media at the turn of the century. See Tilton's extensive study of the development and dissemination of the Pocahontas image in early American texts, as well as Rayna Green's analysis of Pocahontas as the locus of a range of popular culture stereotypes. Opposite Pocahontas in this representational schema are "squaw figures," Green argues, which denote a shameful sexuality that extends to the men they associate with (hence the derogatory term "squaw man"). Marsden and Nachbar trace the development of a sentimental Pocahontas figure in *The Squaw Man* and later Westerns. Leslie Fiedler's foundational critical text *The Return of the Vanishing American* traces the echoes of Pocahontas and John Smith, in American literature and revisionist Westerns—as well as the equally mythic male couple, Natty Bumppo and Chingachgook, from James Fenimore Cooper's *The Last of the Mohicans*. The "Indian heroine" persists and, Fiedler argues, is altered, "denigrated or sacramentalized, or both," in the revisionist Westerns of the 1960s.

20. Kolodny has called this feminine figuration of the land the "American pastoral impulse." Drawing on Freudian and linguistic models, Kolodny describes a "yearning" expressed in American literature for the "land-as-woman," which is also "a movement back into the realm of the Mother . . . to begin again . . . in order to experience the self as independent, assertive, and sexually active" (153–54). See Stoler for an account and analysis of institutionalized female concubinage in the nineteenth-century colonized world. Stoler documents a similar association between the colonized landscape and changing gender relations in the Dutch East Indies, from the actual concubinage encouraged by the Dutch East Indies Company to the strict social segregation after the arrival of large numbers of white women to the East Indies. Particularly relevant to my study is her examination of state control over "abandoned" mixed-race children in orphanages, championed by white women whose own fertility was the subject of intense interest at a time when white motherhood was seen as central to the project of empire ("Making Empire Respectable").

21. Higashi writes, "Characteristically, the response of the Anglo-Saxon elite to the centrifugal forces of a market society resulting in fragmentation was to impose cultural and moral order" (9).

22. The article misreads the Allotment policy. Land was allotted to individuals with no additional plots set aside for children or later generations.

23. Millard, SM13. See Susan Courtney's discussion of this article in *Hollywood Fantasies of Miscegenation* (33).

24. See Philip Deloria's introduction to *Indians in Unexpected Places* for a discussion of the ways that tensions between "expectation and anomaly" function in photographic and cinematic images of Native people in contemporary settings.

25. See Gallagher's discussion of the "hyperconsciousness" of the Western genre in its earliest stages, its division into subgenres, and its "cyclicism" rather than "evolution" as a genre (249, 252).

26 Film scholar Nanna Verhoeff reads the film differently, pointing out that the non-Native characters are also stereotypes and that "The Indian woman . . . is the one who is partly 'mobile.' She takes on a subject position in the beginning of the film, and sustains this position to the very end, until her husband punishes her for it. It is not white society that is able to exclude her" (171).

27. It is worth noting that Edison and others also frequently filmed scenes of Native acculturation as a locus of exhibition as well, including *Indian Day School* (1898) at the Isleta Indian School in New Mexico, *Serving Rations to the Indians* (1898), and AM&B Co.'s *Club Swinging, Carlisle Indian School* (1902).

28. The association between gold and the missionary project in the New World is very old. Christopher Columbus wrote in the journal of his fourth voyage, July 1503: "Gold is most excellent. With gold treasure is made, and he who possesses it may do as he wishes in the world. It can even drive souls into paradise" (Sale). Narrative constructions of Indigenous women as translators and cultural mediators for European men also inform *Iola's Promise*. For a discussion of La Malinche, Sacagawea, and other historical figures, see Karttunen.

29. See Verhoeff, *The West in Early Cinema*, especially her section on "Young Wild Women," which includes a discussion of *The Corporal's Daughter* (399). She argues persuasively that in early Westerns "types of characters, type-characters, are conceived as bearers of cultural stereotypes, while simultaneously facilitating the films' undermining of those social categories" (391).

30. "Blood quantum" here refers to the nineteenth-century legal concept that a person's "race" or racial mixture can be measured in percentages of "blood" passed down from various ancestors. Though it has no basis in either scientific study of the body or tribal theories of knowledge, the idea of blood quantum continues to carry great weight in the legal determination of Native identity. For example, U.S. federal Certificate of Degree of Indian Blood (CDIB) cards are often required as documents of Native ancestry in order for individuals to qualify for educational scholarships and other benefits and services. The terms "full-blood" and "mixed-blood" (or the derogatory "half-breed") indicate how deeply this discourse has permeated the way Americans imagine Natives and the assimilation process. See Lomayesva, and Strong and Van Winkle, for discussions of contemporary and historical controversies over racial identity and the idea of blood quantum.

31. See Bhabha, Doane (*Femmes Fatales*), and Fanon.

32. See Schatz, esp. 55.

33. Like the kiss in *Iola's Promise* and the fashionable clothing in *An Up-to-Date Squaw*, the telescope functions as an emblem of European modernity in a Native

encounter, a visual sign articulating what Philip Deloria describes as the tension between expectation and anomaly in representations of Indians.

34. Ann Little, who played Sky Star in *The Invaders*, also played Nat-u-Ritch in DeMille's 1918 version of *The Squaw Man*.

35. Scott Simmon asserts that the actor has been "misidentified" as William Eagleshirt and that the "key roles of the suitor and the chief remain unidentified" (64). Lakota actor William Eagleshirt, after working with the Bison 101 Ranch Wild West Show through the turn of the century, moved to Los Angeles with the troupe to work in motion pictures between 1911 and 1917.

36. In addition to the authenticity of the Native performers, Scott Simmon identifies the landscapes as the source of Ince's films' cinematic authenticity, noting French film historian Jean Mitry's contemporary description of the films as "a kind of dramatization of the real" (67). Yet the "reality" of the landscapes are subject to Western genre imperatives: "bright and wide landscapes are set up as empty spaces that must be filled by racial battles" (66).

37. *White Fawn's Devotion* is now widely available on DVD through the *Treasures from American Film Archives* collection. While James Young Deer is not definitely known to have directed *For the Papoose*, both Scott Simmon and Andrew Brodie Smith attribute the film to him, and it strongly resembles his other work in the casting of Red Wing and in its signature alterations to the "squaw man" plot. See Brownlow (345–50), Deloria (*Indians in Unexpected Places*), Raheja, and Andrew Brodie Smith for discussions of the careers and films of James Young Deer and Lillian St. Cyr/Princess Red Wing.

38. Qtd. in Simmon, *Program Notes* 70.

39. Blaisdell, rev. of *The Squaw Man*, 1243. See also M. Elise Marubbio's discussion of this review (50–51) and of the casting Nat-u-Ritch in the three DeMille versions of *The Squaw Man* (1914, 1918, and 1931).

40. Jackie Huggins in Mellor and Haebich, *Many Voices*. Also qtd. in Kennedy 58.

Chapter 2
"Strictly American Cinemas": Social Protest in *The Vanishing American*, *Redskin*, and *Ramona*

1. Linda Williams argues similarly, "The kind of novelistic, theatrical, or cinematic realism that introduces the look and feel of real city streets, contemporary social problems, or more complex psychological motives is perfectly compatible with what needs to be recognized as an ever modernizing melodrama" (*Playing* 15).

2. See Zitkala-Sa, "School Days"; Eastman; LaFlesche; McNickle, "Train Time"; and Standing Bear.

3. Qtd. in McNickle, 87.

4. See the influential and extensive discussions of the Indian Citizenship Act of 1924 and its relation to the work of Native intellectuals by scholars Robert Warrior (Osage), Lucy Maddox, and Kevin Bruyneel among others. Bruyneel investigates Indigenous responses to the act in *The Third Space of Sovereignty*.

Native American participation has historically been very high in the U.S. military endeavors. Native veterans of World War I were granted citizenship in recognition of their service in 1919, and Congress unilaterally granted all Native Americans born in the U.S. full citizenship in 1924. These acts were intended to further absorb and assimilate Native people into an American "mainstream" and as a step toward resolving their ambiguous legal status. But by the mid-1920s, reformers such as John Collier were advocating for Indigenous cultural preservation rather than assimilation, and many Native people saw the automatic citizenship not as a step toward equality (states such as New Mexico, Arizona, and Maine would deny Natives voting rights until the late 1940s through various legal maneuvers), but rather as a violation of their sovereignty and a threat to their rights as separate nations.

5. The legal principle of *parens patrie* or "parent of the country" dates at least from eighteenth-century England where the king could claim guardianship of the helpless. Although government intervention through the boarding school system was unique to Indigenous communities, it was also part of a wider trend in child welfare policy. Between 1853 and 1929, for example, Methodist minister Charles Loring Brace's Children's Aid Society shipped orphaned, destitute immigrant children from New York City to be adopted by farm families in the Midwest. In 1874 a scandal involving the abuse of a young girl in a New York tenement resulted in the origin of the Society for the Prevention of Cruelty to Children in New York and other locations. After the turn of the twentieth century, government agencies slowly replaced or supplemented these private and missionary organizations.

6. A strong cohort of writers and political activists included literary patron Mabel Dodge Luhan; John Collier, who would later lead the Bureau of Indian Affairs (BIA) from 1933 to 1945; Mary Austin, the regional writer, dramatist, and promoter of Native poetry as a form of American modernism; publisher Charles F. Lummis; and activists such as Dakota teacher and writer Zitkala-Sa, who was herself educated at boarding schools from age eight.

7. A previous Red Cross Survey on Native health from 1924, authored by Florence Patterson, was suppressed by the BIA but became a useful source for the Meriam Report team. Patterson found that at the Rice Boarding School in Arizona, children subsisted on a diet of potatoes, bread, syrup, and black coffee that cost the school 9 cents per day per child, compared to the 35 cents per day per child that reformers argued was a minimum to maintain a healthy diet (Szasz, *Education* 19). The report also noted the overcrowded dormitories and toilet facilities, and the labor required of the students, raising the question of "whether much of the work of Indian children in boarding schools would not be prohibited in many states by the child labor laws, notably the work in the machine laundries" (13). The poor diets, overwork, and overcrowding were blamed in part for the epidemic proportions of tuberculosis and trachoma in the children (201–16). In 1912 a Public Health Service

study of trachoma in reservation communities and schools revealed an infection rate of 29.8% in schoolchildren, with a rate in excess of 50% in many schools; in the 30 boarding schools in Oklahoma, the rate of infection was more than 69%. A jump in congressional appropriations for Native health mitigated the situation somewhat, but after a budgetary contraction during World War I, trachoma rates were up again in the 1920s, including an infection rate of 50% at the Pima and Mescalero Apache schools in Arizona (Adams 132–35).

8. My reading of the politics of race in discussions of Native boarding schools as well as representations of institutional assimilation in popular periodicals and cinema is influenced by Pierre Bourdieu and Jean-Claude Passeron's theorization of educational systems as means through which social divisions are reproduced. Bourdieu and Passeron understand what they call "pedagogic action," a form of symbolic violence, to enable or validate state violence, suggesting that education is "the chief instrument of the transubstantiation of power relations into legitimate authority" (15). Pedagogic work enacts a form of control without physical constraint, Bourdieu and Passeron argue, but it can intersect with the compulsory requirements of institutional environments:

> "total" institutions (barracks, convents, prisons, asylums, boarding schools) unambiguously demonstrate the deculturating and reculturating techniques required by PW [pedagogic work] seeking to produce a habitus as similar as possible to that produced by the earliest phase of life, while having to reckon with a pre-existing habitus. (*Reproduction in Education* 44)

Bourdieu and Passeron's concept of habitus, the internalization of what they call the cultural arbitrary, and their use of the term "reproduction" to refer to the maintenance of social divisions establish a powerful metaphorical link to family and kinship through broad analogy to systems of hereditary privilege. In the process of cultural (and political) conversion in boarding schools, institutional attempts to naturalize a Western cultural arbitrary depended prevalently on deprivation and violence in the educational process, a dependence that exposed the artifice and imposed semiotics of cultural change.

9. The themes of assimilation through boarding school in sympathetic Westerns from the silent era developed in the broader context of Progressivism, school reform, and increasing public debates about the educational value of film as a new medium, as well as its potentially harmful effects on children. The latter debate has been ongoing since the birth of cinema, but late in the 1920s the public focus on children as consumers of cinema reached a climax of sorts with studies intended to provide evidence for censorship efforts. The emphasis on the production of normality in American children and on cinema-going as a site for the education and social engineering of those children closely parallels the concurrent phenomenon of the government run boarding school. The Payne Study and Experiment Fund enabled the Motion Picture Research Council, headed by William H. Short, to conduct five

years of social science research on the effects of cinema on children. The results, published in popular form by Henry James Forman in a *McCall's Magazine* series in 1932 and later as a book, *Our Movie Made Children* (1933), emphasized in broad strokes that "what the screen becomes is a gigantic educational system with an instruction possibly more successful than the present text-book variety" (64–65). Forman singles out *The Covered Wagon* for special praise in the book (31), as well as *The Vanishing American*, *Ben Hur*, and other historical epics. Tellingly, the studies were carried out not in individual family homes but rather in an institutional home run by the Ohio State Bureau of Juvenile Research, because, as Forman put it, "the routine of institutional life offered the regularity and uniformity necessary for scientific investigation" (13). Other publications based on the Payne Study include a series of 12 titles, some combined in one cover, as part of a series titled Motion Pictures and Youth published by the MacMillan Company in 1933. Titles included *The Emotional Responses of Children to the Motion Picture Situation* by Wendell S. Dysinger and Christian A. Ruckmick; *Movies and Conduct* by Herbert Blumer; and *Motion Pictures and the Social Attitudes of Children*, combined with *The Social Conduct and Attitudes of Movie Fans*, by Ruth C. Peterson and L. L. Thurstone. The report by Ruth C. Peterson, summarized briefly in Forman's book, concluded, that "motion pictures have definite, lasting effects on the social attitudes of children and that a number of pictures pertaining to the same issue may have a cumulative effect on attitude" (qtd. in Forman 66). In addition to measuring children's attitudes toward crime, gambling, war, and prohibition, she also addressed issues of social prejudice against ethnic groups. Her most dramatic study involved the screening of a sound version of *The Birth of a Nation* to public school students in Crystal Lake, Illinois: "the conclusion that the motion picture, 'The Birth of a Nation' had the effect of making the children less favorable to the Negro is undoubtedly justified" (38). Film scholar Nicholas Sammond has argued that although the Payne Study had little real impact on the Hays office or censorship practices, their lasting effects included a discursive construction of a "normal" American child as a consumer of Hollywood films (66).

    10. Qtd. in Simmon 79.

    11. In his account of the production, director Myles commented on the financial savvy of the Native actors in their contract negotiations (Kelley 292). Myles had been a leading man for Pathé Studios, and might well have encountered James Young Deer and Lillian St. Cyr during his early work in Hollywood. Richard Banks had grown up in Oklahoma near Kiowa and Comanche communities and drew on this experience for the screenplay. The film failed financially, however, and the print was thought to be lost; its recovery in 2007 led to a collaboration between Michelle Svenson at the National Museum of the American Indian Film and Video Center; Bob Blackburn, director at Oklahoma History Center; Brian Hearn, Oklahoma City Museum of Art; and Leo Kelley, curator at Oklahoma Historical Society. Now with a new score by Comanche composer David Yeagley, the film is scheduled to be shown together with Sleeping Bear's tipi at the Oklahoma Historical Society's "Oklahoma @ the Movies" exhibit during 2013.

12. See Beltrán, "Dolores Del Rio."

13. Greg M. Smith has noted that Talmadge, rather than developing a core persona that carried over from film to film, foregrounded her versatility: "Talmadge did not require culturally coded makeup . . . as if changing ethnicities for her were as easy as changing clothing. . . . Taking advantage of the racial mobility given to her whiteness and the 'natural' masquerade abilities of the feminine, she portrayed an unprecedented variety of ethnicities and promised emotional access into these Other subjectivities" (7).

14. *Just Squaw*, directed by Michelena's husband, George Middleton, failed to make a profit and was one of the last films produced by Michelena's own company, Beatriz Michelena Features. *The Test of Donald Norton* was produced by the short-lived (1924–1928) Chadwick Pictures Corporation, a company started by I. E. Chadwick. Chadwick would have been very familiar with the prewar "squaw man" film cycle and the work of James Young Deer because he had served as the American representative for Pathé Frères in the early 1910s.

15. Strongheart describes a 24-page report correcting a script for Twentieth Century Fox's production of *Pony Soldier* (1952), including the suggested addition of "A Character which is seldom if ever seen in a Movie where Indians are concerned. An old lady whose wisdom would be respected in a Tribal Council. Her wisdom and oratory would solve a great problem" (Strongheart 45).

16. In fact, an intertitle emphasizes the lack of government assistance: "The government will not pay for this training—the tribe must." Later, after several years at college, "Braveheart has written the romance of the Indian—and his royalties have repaid his debt to the tribe." The lead character's fluency in both legal and popular discourses dramatizes the film's formal movement between courtroom drama, social problem film, and Western frontier romance.

17. Strongheart writes, "after much explanation and inducement I fell victim to the job, to persuade the boys and girls to participate in the movie, to inform the Director on customs and mannerisms of the Indian people so the actor could do justice to the part" (11).

18. "A thought came to me of an incident in my young boyhood while attending the Indian School. We had a disciplinarian who always took on to himself the great joy and authority to scold and threaten the boys. One day he approached a small boy and he scolded and yelled at him. The little boy looked at the big husky policeman and said to him, 'You four times my big, all the same, me have no scare of you!'" (Strongheart 45).

19. See the reviews of *The Heart of Wetona*, *Variety*, 10 Jan. 1919, and *New York Times*, 6 Jan. 1919.

20. According to DeMille's secretary's records, *Braveheart* was made for $290,195.39 but only grossed $249,407.70 at the box office (Birchard 365).

21. Films that languished in production and never reached the screen, include an adaptation of *Laughing Boy*, Oliver La Farge's 1930 Pulitzer Prize–winning novel about a Diné couple (the director was to be William Wyler), and Robert Flaherty's failed attempt to make a Hollywood fiction film at Acoma Pueblo.

22. James Cruze was born James Vera Cruz Bosen in Ogden, Utah, and was the descendant of Danish immigrants who followed Brigham Young to Utah to establish the Church of Jesus Christ of Latter-Day Saints (Mormon) community there. His claim to have Ute ancestry was never proven, but Kevin Brownlow writes:

> Remembering that James Cruze had Indian blood, [Jesse] Lasky consigned the project [*The Covered Wagon*] to him. "To this day, I don't know whether he really had some Indian forbears—I never checked on it—but hearsay to that effect was what prompted me to call him in for a conference." Cruze's powerful build and black eyes lead to the belief that he was of Indian extraction. No one could have been more suitable to direct *The Covered Wagon*, for only a generation—if that—separated Cruze from the pioneers, and covered wagons had been a familiar part of his youth. (370)

See also Louise Brooks's description of working with Cruze in Brownlow's *The Parade's Gone By* (360–61).

23. For accounts of Will Rogers's extensive production across media and his formative work in radio in particular, see Justice, Foster, May, Moon, Ware, and Velikova. Rogin also includes a discussion of *Judge Priest* in *Black Face, White Noise*. Ware argues persuasively that Rogers strategically selected assimilationist techniques and codes, integrating his Cherokee nationalism and ranching traditions with American popular forms in his early vaudeville work "playing cowboy" ("Unexpected" 25). Rogers's films are quite different from both his own performances in other media (especially radio) and from the melodramatic forms of the Indian drama and its reformist images of Native familial rupture and reunification.

24. See discussions of Riggs's film work by Marta Weigle and Kyle Fiore, Jace Weaver (*That the People Might Live*; *The Cherokee Night and Other Plays*), and Craig Womack.

25. AMPAS press file, *The Vanishing American* 92. Paramount invested considerable star power in its 1925 adaptation of Zane Grey's *The Vanishing American* by pairing Richard Dix with Lois Wilson, star of *The Covered Wagon*. In the mid-1920s, Dix was one of the nation's top box-office draws with successful roles in Westerns as well as DeMille films such as his 1923 production of *The Ten Commandments* (Lahue 73). He played Navajo protagonists in both *Redskin* and *The Vanishing American*, and later played the part-Cherokee character Yancey in *Cimarron* (Ruggles 1931), a historical drama about the Oklahoma land rush.

26. The excesses and hardships of production were described by producer Jesse Lasky in the *New York Times* article "Producing Indian Film was a Stupendous Task" (25 Sept. 1925). See also Brownlow 344–45, and Aleiss, "Hollywood Addresses" 57. Aleiss also notes that despite Paramount's "massive publicity campaign . . . the film was far from a box-office winner" (peaking at $10,735 in October 1925), easily surpassed by competing films like *Stella Dallas* (which peaked at $15,000 at the end of November 1925) (*Making* 37).

27. Rev. of "The Vanishing American," *Variety* 21 Oct. 1925, AMPAS files.

28. The "lost home" of Indian Westerns can be productively compared to the iconography of the slave cabin in the literary and various performed versions of *Uncle Tom's Cabin*, and to the "home songs" of blackface minstrelsy, which mourned the separation of families under slavery and "spoke to restless migrants moving west, to recently transplanted rural folks in cities, and to rootless urban dwellers beginning to experience the anomie of modern city life" (Williams, "Playing" 58, 71). While the slave cabin linked nostalgic memories to the racially determined experience of slavery and bondage, images of lost Native domesticity in sympathetic Westerns presented familial separation as inevitable and natural, rather than systemic, often through narrative devices such as the death of the child, the death of the mother, the breakup of an interracial marriage, adoption, fosterage, or education as a result of exigencies of the frontier.

29. See Pascal (10–11) for a detailed discussion of the publishing history of *The Vanishing American*.

30. M. C. Lathrop, 8 Apr. 1923, synopsis of serialized novel in *Ladies Home Journal* (Nov. 1922–Apr. 1923), AMPAS script files for *The Vanishing American*.

31. As noted in the introduction to this book, the image was reprinted as a census photo in James C. Faris's book *Navajo and Photography: A Critical History of the Representation of an American People*, which suggests that the "weary census taker" may have been "oblivious to the delight of the man spreading candy among his children" (105). Faris argues that photographs of Navajo represent Western "visualist hegemony" that reduces "all histories . . . to those of the West" (11, 19).

32. For comparative purposes, see Lucy Lippard's extended analysis or "diary" of a Native family photograph in *Partial Recall*. The photo of Sampson, Frances Louise, and Leah Beaver in 1907, taken by Mary Sharples Schaffer Warren, seems to Lippard to establish reciprocity and "intersubjective time" (37) though of course the photograph is clearly posed rather than spontaneous, and Mary Schaffer's "colonial lens" is revealed by her journal descriptions of being at " 'play' in the fields of the conquered" (42–43).

33. The caption for the photograph is "Reverand Smith enumerates Navajo Camp," http://www.archives.gov/press/press-kits/1930-census-photos/reverend-smith-enumerates-navajo-camp.jpg.

34. In Angela Aleiss's account (*Making the White Man's Indian* 34–38), Grey began writing *The Vanishing American* in 1922 at the suggestion of Jesse Lasky, vice president of productions for Paramount, after a trip they took together to Northern Arizona. In the case of *Redskin*, AMPAS files contain a letter from the Office of Indian Affairs to Elizabeth Pickett, who was then the Assistant Manager for Fox Varieties, acknowledging and approving her plans to make a "seven-reel Indian picture," which would "correctly show present-day conditions among the Indians and treat in a sympathetic way the work of the Government for them." Pickett had already directed films for the Red Cross and Fox Varieties, and the letter, dated 11 Dec. 1925, long preceded Paramount's final purchase of the novelized form of "Navajo" from Pickett in 1929, suggesting the project was conceived as a film from the beginning.

35. Rev. of *The Vanishing American*, *Variety*.

36. See "Technology: 'I Want to Ride in Geronimo's Cadillac,' " Philip Deloria's eloquent essay on images of Indigenous peoples and cars in the early twentieth century, in *Indians in Unexpected Places*.

37. Schertzinger's story is also contradicted by early temporary scripts and synopses of the film. As early as August 1928 sequences of the film are listed in "natural colors" and "black and white" (AMPAS files, Redskin First Temporary Script, 18 Aug. 1928).

38 The reference is to Jim Thorpe, the Sac and Fox tribal member, Carlisle graduate, and Olympic athlete and sports hero who went on to act in Hollywood films during the 1930s and 1940s. Films of the 1910s and 1920s depicting Native characters in boarding schools as star athletes capitalized on the public fascination with Thorpe, and many Indian sports mascots date from this period.

39. See Jane Gaines's *Fire and Desire* for an extended discussion of Noble Johnson's career.

40. Elizabeth Pickett, "Redskin First Temporary Script," 18 Aug. 1928, A–7. AMPAS script files, *Redskin*.

41. See Adams.

42. Media studies scholar Cynthia Erb has described the generic trope of gentle contact in imperial adventure films as a "drama of the touch," building on Donna Haraway's analysis of interspecies clasping of hands as an alternative to the aggressive appropriation in the "shooting" trope of the gun/camera.

43. See Pickett, Synopsis treatment of NAVAJO, Master File 1478, n.d., 5, 10. AMPAS files.

44. PCA files, "Redskin," AMPAS.

45. Jackson, *Ramona*, 340.

46. I would like to thank Charles Silver at the Museum of Modern Art for alerting me to the surviving copy of the film in the National Film Archive (NFA) of the Czech Republic, and Veroslav Haba at the NFA for generously facilitating my visit and viewing of the print, and providing a translation of the Czech language intertitles. As of this writing, the film has been repatriated to the U.S. Library of Congress, thanks to the generosity of the Czech Republic and the dedication of Mike Mashon of the Library of Congress Motion Picture, Broadcasting and Recorded Sound Division.

47. Carewe's *Ramona* follows the orientation of the novel in its advocacy of Indian policy reform. The massacre is witnessed by Alessandro in the novel, but it is not described in detail; the reader only learns of the massacre through Alessandro's brief recounting of it to Ramona. In Carewe's film, this elided violence is experienced more directly by both Alessandro and Ramona and fully realized in the film's visual grammar.

48. In fact, in a letter to the Hays office in 1929, Wisconsin viewer and newspaper editor J. E. Halfert objects to pictures in which "a small child has died or where a mother has died and a small child pathetically looks on." "I believe there is enough sorrow, sadness and mourning in this world, without seeing it in

the movies, especially when it comes to mothers and children. I really believe this is wrong. I've made it a point to inquire of mothers and others who had seen such pictures as to what they thought of these scenes. They didn't like them. The picture Ramona was a wonderful picture, but that one scene, the death scene could well have been left out, I believe without destroying the real value of the picture" (*Ramona* 1928, AMPAS file).

49. Scholars Mathes, Senier, DeLyser, and Phillips have situated Jackson's work in the context of the nineteenth-century women's sentimental novel, Indian policy reform, and the General Allotment Act of 1887, including "friends of the Indian" societies such as the Women's National Indian Association (WNIA) with which Jackson was involved. The novel's publication intersected with a Southern California real estate boom and was also aggressively promoted by a burgeoning heritage tourist industry in the region.

50. See DeLyser's cultural geography of Ramona tourism in Southern California, *Ramona Memories*.

51. Griffith himself had opened his screen adaptation of the story with an explicit acknowledgement of the novel and his acquisition of rights to the story from the publisher. Griffith's film is important in adaptation studies as one of the first films for which legal rights were purchased from the publisher to retell a novel on screen; and as numerous scholars have pointed out, Griffith himself played Alessandro in several stage adaptations of *Ramona* before making the film.

52. An example of comedic irony from the 1920s would be Will Rogers's film *Two Wagons, Both Covered*, but more contemporary work in this tradition certainly includes Weise and Vizenor's *Harold of Orange* (1984), and the twenty-first-century comedy sketches produced for internet distribution by the Native group "The 1491s." Carewe engages in a more solemn but equally "tricky" strategy (to invoke Vizenor's trickster paradigm) by deploying the sentimental conventions of melodrama while rearranging the ethnic configuration of aggression and innocence in frontier representation.

53. For references to Carewe's films in studies of silent film, Native American film history, and Dolores del Rio's career, see Brownlow, Singer, Aleiss, Beltrán, and Hershfield.

54. See Sandberg 95 and "Bucharest Goodbye Deeply Stirs Queen."

55. See Ellenberger, "Director Edwin Carewe's Grave Is Marked after More Than 69 Years." Carewe and Inspiration Pictures merged in Tec-Art Studios in 1927. According to the *New York Times*, properties involved in the $10 million deal included "the entire equipment of the old Griffith Studios at Mamaroneck" ("$10,000,000 Merger of Movie Producers"). Carewe made *Ramona* under the auspices of Inspiration Pictures and distributed through United Artists. Inspiration Pictures, run by Charles Duell Jr. and Henry King with Richard Barthelmess, Walter Camp, and John Boyce-Smith as principals, was active before and during the merger with Tec-Art from about 1923 through 1929. See Brownlow, *The Parade's Gone By* 106.

56. See Angela Aleiss's additional confirmation of this in *Making the White Man's Indian* 180.

57. Carewe's profile in the 1927 *Who's Who among Oklahoma Indians*, compiled by J. G. Sanders, appears to be the source for Carewe's listing in Thomas Benton Williams's *Soul of the Red Man* (336), where he and his brother are listed under the names Jay Fox and Finis Fox.

58. Brownlow and Lowrey list different ancestors of Carewe—maternal grandfather versus maternal grandmother—in describing his Chickasaw genealogy. In fact Carewe's father, Frank M. Fox, is listed on the Dawes Rolls as Chickasaw. Ellenberger writes that Carewe "attended the University of Texas and the University of Missouri majoring in dramatics" before joining the Dearborn Stock Company and appearing in Broadway plays and in regional productions in New York, Philadelphia, Washington, Chicago, and Los Angeles. Marion Gridley reports in the 1936 book *Indians of Today* that Carewe attended the Arkadelphia Methodist College in Arkansas, the Polytechnic College in Fort Worth, Texas, and the Missouri State University, but later ran away from home to perform in traveling repertory companies throughout the Midwest.

59. Alexander Walker asserts that the film's profitability stemmed from its hit title song, sung by Del Rio in the film: "The title song of Dolores Del Rio's *Ramona* was credited with helping the film to a large part of its 1,500,000 dollars gross by the end of 1928" (82).

60. A 1940 *New York Times* obituary notes that Carewe's cut from the gross earnings of *Ramona* in one year was $380,000 and from *Resurrection* was $320,000. In 1926 he was in the news for his offer of $25,000 to Queen Marie of Romania to play the part of the Queen in *Resurrection*; her scenes were to be shot in one day and were to be directed by Ilya Tolstoy ("Bucharest Goodbye Deeply Stirs Queen"). Just a year after the release of *Evangeline*, however, Carewe's career had faltered, and he was facing financial ruin and federal charges of income tax fraud. Singer Ernestine Shumann-Heink sued Carewe in 1930 for failure to complete a contract to cast her as the lead in four musicals, and in 1932 Carewe was indicted on charges of tax evasion for the period of his highest earnings, from 1926 to 1929 ("Schumann-Heink Sues" and "Edwin Carewe Surrenders").

61. See Michelle Raheja's extensive research on Native actors in Hollywood in *Reservation Reelism*.

62. "Edwin Carewe, 56, Director of Films," *New York Times*, 23 Jan. 1940. According to the *New York Times* obituary, Carewe took the name "Edwin" from his favorite actor, Edwin Booth, and the name "Carewe" from a character he was playing on stage. This account of Carewe's paternal tribal genealogy differs from Brownlow's assertion of maternal tribal heritage and is supported by documentation in the 1907 Chickasaw tribal rolls.

63. For a more detailed account of this process, see Gibson, *The Chickasaws*.

64. There is no clear evidence that Jackson's *Ramona* had a direct effect on the 1887 legislation, which was passed two years after her death in 1885. Scholars disagree about the extent of Jackson's influence on the Dawes Act through her fiction and nonfiction because she generally advocated for tribal land rights rather than assimilation (Mathes 5–6). In a literary biography of Jackson, Kate Phillips

points out that Jackson's report on conditions among mission Indians did have a direct effect on the passage in 1891 of the Act for the Relief of the Mission Indians (276), but that Jackson would have been unlikely to support legislation that would decimate tribal land bases as the Dawes Act did (although she was friendly with Massachusetts Senator Henry Dawes, who sponsored the legislation) (27–28). Siobhan Senier, in her introduction to the edited edition of *Ramona*, notes that critics such as Michael Dorris and historian Allan Nevins have "traced an almost direct line from *Ramona* to the Dawes Act" based on the novel's broader contribution to public "sentiment" and "agitation" over Native issues (19).

65. Although the version of the film that is available in the National Film Archive in the Czech Republic is silent with intertitles, there is reason to believe that a partial sound version of the film using the early Movietone sound technology may have been in circulation as well, allowing viewers to hear Del Rio's voice for the first time. Hollywood's transition to sound was under way in 1928, and Carewe creates opportunities for music in *Ramona* in a similar way to his partial sound film *Evangeline* (released the following year). For example, the film's first tracking shot moves across the faces of the hacienda staff as they sing religious songs together in morning prayer. The narrative also frequently moves forward through sound cues, such as when Felipe plays his guitar, when Ramona hears Alessandro singing. Later in the film, she hears him sawing wood for their child's coffin.

66. Several biographers suggest that Del Rio and Carewe were romantically involved during their work together in the mid- and late-1920s, through the filming of *Evangeline* in 1929. Del Rio had divorced Jaime by 1928 (the year of his death, in Berlin), and Carewe, who had married Aiken on the trip to Mexico in 1925, separated from her in 1927, and divorced in 1928. Whatever the relationship between Del Rio and Carewe, Del Rio broke her contract with Carewe after *Evangeline*, and she signed a lucrative deal with United Artists (and another contract with RKO). She married MGM art director Cedric Gibbons in early 1930, and Carewe remarried his former wife Mary Aiken in late 1929. See "Edwin Carewes Separate," "Refused to Sue Husband," and "Carewe to Rewed Ex-Wife."

67. Qtd. in Hershfield 15; the review appeared in *Photoplay* in Mar. 1928, 52. "Miss Del Rio Is Sole Star of 'Ramona,'" 19 Feb. 1928. See also Beltrán, *Latina/o Stars* 32.

68. Carewe, "How I Selected Dolores Del Rio's New Starring Role." Ramona press book, Library of Congress (with thanks to Mike Mashon for providing a scan of the press book).

69. Rev. of *Ramona*, *New York Times*, 15 May 1928, 445. Rev. of *Ramona*, *Variety*, 16 May 1928. AMPAS files. *Variety* also assessed Warner Baxter in redface as "a better brave than Dix and some of the other Hollywood male leads who have attempted bronze skinned interpretations."

70. See Hershfield and Beltrán for discussions of Del Rio's career.

71. Because the film is not yet generally available in the United States, my analysis assumes that many readers have not seen it.

72. See Marubbio, *Killing the Indian Maiden*.

73. Alessandro, like Ramona, receives Father Salvierderra's blessing, but displays such conversational ineptitude ("my boys will work like devils") that he must request it again.

74. This lack of concern with regional authenticity adds subtly to the confusion in the later massacre scene: shots mix iconographies that suggest Plains tribes and settled farming tribes, for example, when one posse member lassos a tipi, pulling it down to expose the family hiding inside, while in another image two of the posse surround and shoot down four Native men riding in a small hay wagon pulled by two oxen.

75. Sandwiched between these scenes is Felipe's own failed courtship of Ramona. Yet Roland Drew's on-screen chemistry with Del Rio is far more compelling than Warner Baxter's, and perhaps this explains Carewe's decision to cast him as her Acadian lover Gabriel in *Evangeline* the following year.

76. Carewe's strategy in reversing the ethnic lines of the Indian massacre scene also forecasts the strategies of revisionist Westerns in the late 1960s and early 1970s, particularly in films such as *Soldier Blue* and *Little Big Man*, both of which contains scenes of white soldiers massacring peaceful Native villages with the violence witnessed by white women.

77. "Redskin and National Braid."

78. Melodrama comes from the Greek world *melos* (song) and the French *drame* (drama), and "in its dictionary sense, melodrama is a dramatic narrative in which musical accompaniment marks the emotional effects" (Elsaesser 50).

Chapter 3
"As if I Were Lost and Finally Found": Repatriation and Visual Continuity in *Imagining Indians* and *The Return of Navajo Boy*

1. The project began when an Illinois real estate developer, Bill Kennedy, wanted to learn more about a film that his father, Robert Kennedy, made in the 1950s, called *Navaho Boy*. He hired documentary filmmaker Jeff Spitz to research the film, then to return it to the Diné family—the Cly family of Monument Valley—who were the film's subjects. Robert Kennedy had originally toured with the film *Navaho Boy* in the 1950s and narrated its storyline for audiences. The live accompaniment of the silent footage calls to mind silent cinema exhibitions that involved live music or an on-stage lecturer, and like those silent films, *Navaho Boy's* silence has made it available for contemporary reinterpretation through sound, as in the National Braid soundtrack for the 1929 film *Redskin*, discussed in chapter 2, and Edward Curtis's 1914 silent film, *In the Land of the Headhunters*, which was reclaimed by the Kwakwaka'wakw with their 1972 soundtrack (see Hearne, "Telling and Retelling").

2. According to director Jeff Spitz, Bill Kennedy began the project by "trying to figure out what to do with the old film that his dad had." It was "a very

different type of relationship than the one I would wind up having with Elsie [Elsie Cly Begay], who would look at his dad's old film and not remember his dad, look at it and remember the baby that was taken from their family and remember her grandpa." Kennedy remained involved, however, and continued to make the project possible as it grew. Spitz recalls, "Bill becomes an absolutely essential person in this whole unfolding of a film project, because I didn't have any funds to do this and I went back to him and told him that the people in his dad's film were alive and they would like to see the old film and they'd like to use it as a starting point to tell their own story." Along with the Cly family, a key person to the production was Bennie Klain, then working as a radio journalist, who interviewed Bill Kennedy and Jeff Spitz early in the project's development. Spitz describes the way Klain "got involved in interpreting footage that I'd send to him and then got involved in the editing room and really complex discussions about how to represent both the point of view of the film and the expressions of Navajos that are in their own language and their own context, in terms of subtitles" (Spitz, Interview).

3. Masayesva and Younger 90, 12.

4. In the context of museum studies, "visual repatriation" refers to processes by which Indigenous communities "re-own the knowledge and experiences that the objects embodied" (Fienup-Riordan, "Yup'ik Elders" 56).

5. See Jacobs and Romero.

6. Other contemporary Native films about making or remembering the making of documentaries retrieve Native presence through a similar reflexivity. Prominent among these are Arlene Bowman's *Navajo Talking Picture* (1986), about the filmmaker's attempt to produce a documentary about her grandmother, who is increasingly reluctant to appear on camera; Claude Massot's *Nanook Revisited* (1990) about the return of a film print of *Nanook of the North* to the Inuit community where it was filmed; and George Burdeau's *Backbone of the World* (1997), about Burdeau's return to his own Blackfeet reservation and the community's attempt to protect sacred lands. Victor Masayesva, because he has positioned himself outside of the film industry, has asserted the freedom to function as an independent arbiter of aesthetics, balancing his autonomy as a filmmaker with the restraint that comes with community accountability.

7. The language and assumptions behind the act tacitly acknowledge the unique relationship between Native tribes and the U.S. government. The act recognizes a separate, collective identity for tribal peoples and further registers the importance of objects in sustaining and practicing that identity by connecting tribal members with their genealogical and material past. However, the requirement of a "reasonable trace" to earlier groups touches on the vexed issue of federal recognition of tribes—the presumption of the U.S. government to decide who is and is not Native remains unquestioned. The Native American Graves and Repatriation Act of 1990 (NAGPRA) as a U.S. law is just one iteration in the context of larger international pressures for reparation and restitution. Yet NAGPRA has had enormous and complex consequences for both federally recognized and unrecognized tribes

and for tribal relations with museums. Attempts to repatriate ancestral remains can involve conflict and competing claims, sensitive information, charged emotions, and challenges to the very systems of traditionality that the act was intended to support. For extended discussions of NAGPRA, see Brown, Brown and Bruchac, Weaver, and Fine-Dare, as well as several edited collections: Mihesuah's *Repatriation Reader: Who Owns American Indian Remains?* Bray's *The Future of the Past: Archaeologists, Native Americans, and Repatriation*; and Fforde, Hubert, and Turnbull's *The Dead and Their Possessions: Repatriation in Principle, Policy and Practice*.

8. While voiceover and sound are key to my discussion of cinematic attribution, this chapter is not primarily about sound, but rather the cinematic captioning that links image to voice in a particular colonial context. This work points, however, toward the need for more scholarly attention to the importance of voiceover for Indigenous cinema's extension of oral literature and storytelling (See Knopf, *Decolonizing,* and Evans, *Isuma*). For an extended discussion of cinema voiceover and its relation to technologies such as radio and to oral storytelling, see Kozloff.

9. See Knopf's essay "Imagining Indians—Subverting Global Media Politics in the Local Media" for a discussion of the specific Westerns named in *Imagining Indians*.

10. Barry Brummett's term "shadow texts" is useful in referring to the "familiar texts we bring to our experiences with new texts" (qtd. in Mechling 51).

11. Posterization is a special effect in which the picture is reduced to a small number of colors, removing any fine gradations of color and brightness. Masayesva frequently employs this technique in his images, lending an enigmatic quality to ordinary scenes.

12. From the French, meaning "placing into infinity," "mise-en-abyme" refers to the effect of multiplied images when standing between two mirrors. In film studies the term generally refers to films-within-films, dreams-within-dreams, or other formally embedded reflexive strategies.

13. Fatimah Tobing Rony notes that Masayesva uses computer imagery as "short cuts . . . it's part of the economy of presenting information" ("Victor" 26). She writes that "the combination of text and photographic image is a common element in Masayesva's work: the photograph does not merely illustrate but exists as an independent message, and its meaning often cuts against the text, adding opacity and abstraction" ("Victor" 23).

14. The name "Little Coyote" is unclear in the sound recording and may be inaccurate; Masayesva confirmed that he also heard this name, but could not be sure.

15. Raheja defines "redfacing" as "the cultural and ideological work of playing Indian," a representational strategy in the tradition of "the trickster figure" (*Reservation Reelism* 20). Trickster figures—who engage in hyperbolic and impulsive, destructive, or scandalous behavior—end up creating new systems from the disorder their actions trigger, and trickster stories are often both funny and didactic.

16. Contemporary Indigenous production companies, such as Isuma Productions in Igloolik, Nunavut, offer more permanent community benefits in terms of employment and education as well as locally generated images. Isuma's cinema-

tographer, Norman Cohn, observed that during the filming of *Atanarjuat (The Fast Runner)* (2001), the location camp and the filmed set resembled one another, creating a sense of continuity between film text and production. For a discussion of that film and its funding, production, and marketing, see Evans, *Isuma*; Ginsburg, "Screen Memories" and "*Atanarjuat* Off-Screen"; Kunuk and Cohn, Interview with Eric Peery and "Making *Atanarjuat*"; Bessire; Huhndorf, "*Atanarjuat*"; Raheja, "Reading"; and Hearne, "Telling and Retelling."

17. See John Purdy's discussion of the way this dentist/patient scenario calls up uncomfortable aspects of cross-racial captivity romance and frontier war narratives, both Western genre plots suggested by posters on the dentists' office wall (109).

18. The camera/gun trope is implicit not only in the parallel vocabularies but also the historical development of camera and gun technologies. The global cross-cultural ramifications of the predatory camera have been usefully taken up in discussions of trophy hunting, colonial photography, and imperialist cinema by scholars such as Donna Haraway, Paul Landau, and Cynthia Erb.

19. Photographs are, according to Edwards, "active and dynamic . . . interlocutors in the process of telling histories" (*Raw Histories* 87). "Collaborative visual repatriation thus requires the recognition of differently valid 'visual economies' in which 'the Archive' is decentred, and the visual economy extended and refigured through inclusion, recognition and liberation of the 'Indigenous voice'" (85). Edwards distinguishes the work of film and photography in visual repatriation, however: "Film, whilst sharing some of these characteristics, has a very different narrative effect. The length of quotation from the flow of life being longer, it gives the sense of real time rather than fractured time. It also lacks the intense performative qualities of photographs. The stillness of photographs invites certain ways of weaving stories around them" (84).

20. This is not to deny the harmful effects of Western image-making. Television and movies have directly threatened Indigenous systems of sacred knowledge as Eric Michaels and others have shown. And Philip Deloria emphasizes the reductive effects of sameness that adhere to reproducible copies, pointing to the origin of the word "stereotype" in the printing industry, where it referred to "a printing plate capable of reproducing copies indistinguished by individual difference" (*Unexpected Places* 8).

21. See also Jennifer Deger's insightful expansion of theories of mimesis articulated by Michael Taussig and Walter Benjamin in order to account for Yolngu (Australian Aboriginal) cultural imperatives of intersubjectivity and relatedness. She writes, "Yolngu use mimesis to bind together diverse subjects in webs of relationships laid down by the Ancestral" in order to "efface everyday differences . . . affirming an essential connectedness" (88).

22. Although I shift fluidly from photography to film here, the conjunction of these modes has been theorized extensively in recent publications such as Beckman and Ma's *Still Moving: Between Cinema and Photography*. Christopher Pinney describes still photographs as having "too many meanings" compared to films, which can "constrain meaning through narrative chains of signification" (27).

23. Spitz, interview. Victor Masayesva, in an interview with Fatimah Tobing Rony, describes a similar photographic encounter: "I wouldn't know my grandfather if not for photography, because I never met him and I saw him in a [photograph of] the Snake Dance. So, that's how I met him" (Rony, "Victor Masayesva" 23).

24. See the film website for webisodes: <http://navajoboy.com/webisodes>.

25. For example, John Collier writes in his 1967 text on the use of photography in visual anthropology that "questioning the native [with] the photograph can help us gather data and enhance our understanding" (qtd. in Edwards, *Talking* 87).

26. Ford's Monument Valley Westerns include *Stagecoach* (1939), *My Darling Clementine* (1946), *Fort Apache* (1948), *She Wore a Yellow Ribbon* (1949), *The Searchers* (1956), *Sergeant Rutledge* (1960), and *Cheyenne Autumn* (1964). For further discussion of Ford's use of landscape in these films and for further accounts of his relationships with Diné people and with Goulding, see Leutrat and Liandrat-Guigues, Mitchell ("Why Monument Valley?"), Carmichael, Davis, and Gallagher (*John Ford*). As Andrew Sarris wrote of Ford's films: "*Stagecoach* was not actually the first movie shot in Monument Valley. But Ford made it seem that way" (82). Several scholars note that tourist activity grew in Monument Valley as a result of Ford's seeming "discovery" of it, a trope of discovery embedded in his Westerns (see Colonnese, Carmichael, and Gallagher, *John Ford*).

27. Deborah Carmichael argues that Ford's use of the valley's dry landscape, clearly inappropriate for settler agriculture, "implicitly supports Native Americans' claim on the land" (225). I would argue instead that Ford's use of the valley to tell stories about settler families, not Native families, advocates U.S. territorial appropriation.

28. The point-of-view shot, a formal technique at the center of long-standing disputes over the nature of spectatorship and identification in film studies scholarship, here calls attention to the work of context in making visual meaning. Because of the specific work of gun sights in this formulaic Western genre configuration of shot-reverse-shot, "the possibility of sympathetic identifications with the Indians is simply ruled out by the point-of-view conventions: the spectator is unwittingly sutured into a colonialist perspective" (Shohat and Stam 120). Referring to Tom Engelhardt's analysis of the rifle as a tool of vision, they write, "In essence, the viewer is forced behind the barrel of a repeating rifle and it is from that position, through its gun sights, that he receives a picture history of Western colonialism and imperialism" (120).

29. See Hearne, "The 'Ache for Home,'" and Neale.

30. See Steven Leuthold's discussion in *Indigenous Aesthetics* of Indigenous documentary representations of land through aerial flyover shots, which he argues "act as visual metaphors for religious beliefs and as expressions of Indians' lengthy relationships with the land" (127). He contrasts his own reading with Derek Bousé's analysis of Forest Service wilderness documentaries as an "inventory of natural resources" (127).

31. A thorough reading of Ford's Monument Valley films in light of tourist activity and imagery in the region might offer new interpretations of the films and

of specific scenes that have been the focus of critical debate. For example, in *The Searchers*, a much-discussed scene involves mixed-blood character Martin Pawley (Jeffrey Hunter) believing that he is bartering with Native groups for a red woven blanket, but instead accidentally acquiring a wife, Look/Wild Goose Flying in the Night Sky (Beulah Archuletta) (see, for example, readings of this scene by Peter Lehman and Elise Marubbio). If we think in terms of the daily tourist work that Ford would have witnessed in Monument Valley, these sequences form a surrealistic commentary on the kinds of encounters that Goulding regularly engineered for Ford and others with staged camps where outsiders could take photographs of women weaving rugs and purchase blankets and other objects from Goulding's trading post.

32. Qtd. in Sula n.p.

33. Furthermore, McDougall describes the film as becoming a "compound work" through the multiple cultural forces that structure it; in this case it is an emblem of this recognition or mapping activity: "Here it becomes possible to say that the film is no longer outside the situation it describes, nor has it merely been expanded through self-reflexivity or acknowledgement of fuller meanings. It is inside someone else's story" (163).

34. See Hearne, "Indigenous Animation" 96.

35. Pack, in "Watching Navajos Watch Themselves," calls for greater attention to "how media are creatively interpreted by subaltern audiences to both construct and contest representations of self and other" (111). He offers an informal reception study of a Diné family, the Benallys, watching *The Return of Navajo Boy* (along with a very different, dramatic production—the Hallmark film *The Lost Child* [Arthur 2000]). The Benallys appreciated the familiarity and authenticity of the PBS documentary, particularly the use of the Diné language, familiar locations such as Richardson's Pawnshop and the new Navajo Nation Museum, and even family connections (Pack notes that the Benally family has a clan relationship to the Cly family). While one woman (Grandma Annie) commented that the film was *nizhoni*, "beautiful," others in the family disliked the use of pan-Indian powwow music, the recording of Yeibechei songs and dances meant to be performed only in winter, and the underlying story of the missionary adoption of John Wayne Cly ("It was the white man who took him away and the white man who brought him back") (122–23).

36. Among the many analyses of and references to this scene, see Rony, *The Third Eye*; Ginsburg, "Screen Memories"; Huhndorf, *Going Native*; and Raheja, "Reading Nanook's Smile."

37. Diné clans are matriarchal—a child belongs to his or her mother's clan. Members of a clan are considered to be related, as in a sibling relationship; to marry within one's own clan is tantamount to incest and strictly prohibited. Diné extended family kinship involves many clan brothers and sisters, many grandparents (including the brothers and sisters of biological grandparents), and many aunts and uncles (including the cousins of biological parents).

38. Gaines describes "documentary pathos" as part of a larger theory of "political mimesis" that draws together Linda Williams's focus on film genres

(horror, porn, melodrama) that elicit bodily responses from viewers, Sergei Eisenstein's notion of the "agitational spectacle" or moment of *pathos* in political propaganda films, and Michael Taussig's theorization of the "miraculous reconstitutive powers of mimetic technologies" ("Political Mimesis" 94) as forms of sympathetic magic in which a copy or reproduction has special powers to influence its original source.

39. Worsham writes, "the work of decolonization requires that we change the terms of recognition" and, furthermore, that "the crucial stakes of political struggle are the categories of perception and the systems of classification and conceptualization—in other words, the words, names, and phrases—that construct the social world, the real existing world. In this view, we must fight phrases with phrases" (222).

Chapter 4
Imagining the Reservation in *House Made of Dawn* and *Billy Jack*

1. The film did not circulate beyond film festivals for many years until New Line Cinema purchased it, and eventually released it on VHS for a limited time. It is currently not in wide circulation, although used VHS copies are available from Internet sources including Amazon.com. A 35 mm print of the film has been restored and archived at the National Museum of the American Indian, Film and Video Center.

2. Although I take Momaday's novel and essays into consideration at several points in this chapter and incorporate some of the critical work on the novel, my focus here is primarily on the filmed version of *House Made of Dawn*, which was largely scripted by Momaday. According to director Richardson Morse, "Basically, Scott did the writing of the screenplay . . . certainly 90% of what was put down on paper was originally put down by Scott, with then maybe some editing coming from me." Some alterations to the book's plot and style were deliberate—such as centering the story completely on Abel's point of view rather than the multiple perspectives offered by the novel—while others took place during editing. Parts of the footage were cut from the finished film, such as scenes with the character of Angela St. John, played by former Miss America (1954) Lee Meriwether. The omission of white characters from the novel, such as Angela St. John, suppresses Momaday's exploration of whites' movement to Native lands through mission work and tourism, focusing instead only on Native movement to Los Angeles.

3. See Neale's assessment of the tendency in Western genre criticism to treat Native characters as "ethnic stand-ins" for other minorities.

4. For example, Milestone's restoration and release of *The Exiles* on DVD was co-produced by Spokane/Coeur d'Alene writer-filmmaker Sherman Alexie and filmmaker Charles Burnett.

5. Morse, Littlebird, and Momaday spoke with me about the film in interviews during 2003 and 2004. Edited transcripts of the interviews are available at the

National Museum of the American Indian, Film and Video Center website, "Native Networks": <http://www.nativenetworks.si.edu/eng/rose/hmod.htm>.

6. Momaday, "House Made of Dawn," interview. Other films reached contemporary audiences through representations of cityscapes, and Paula Massood asserts a broad movement of heroes from the Western (such as those played by John Wayne and Clint Eastwood) from rural to urban settings in films of the early 1970s, writing that "it is no accident that Eastwood would move out of the rural West and into the urban frontier in *Dirty Harry* (Siegel 1971) at roughly the same time as the rise of blaxploitation's heroes" (96).

7. In his study of Momaday "in the Movement years," Robert Warrior (Osage) interprets Momaday's interest in Billy the Kid as amendatory: "His embrace of the Billy the Kid story confounds many who read *The Ancient Child*, but when we treat it as one more piece of the complex world of ideas and images that Momaday brings to his work, we can see that he writes Native consciousness and agency into a narrative from which they have been excluded" (*The People* 165).

8. Momaday himself traces this trajectory in an essay written in the early 1960s, "The Morality of Indian Hating," in which he connects contemporary federal Indian policies such as Termination and Relocation—policies which "impose" an "identity of defeat"—to the dynamics and attitudes of the early frontier and events such as the Puritan massacre of the Pequots at Fort Mystic in 1637 (59). He further articulates these ideas in "On Indian-White Relations: A Point of View." Both essays are published in Momaday's collection *The Man Made of Words*.

9. See James, *Allegories of Cinema* 22.

10. My understanding of *House Made of Dawn* as the product of related locations also builds on Ella Shohat's call for critics to broaden their studies of race beyond isolated sites of representation in minority cinema traditions to consider "ethnicities-in-relation." We can see *House Made of Dawn* as articulating "geographies-in-relation"—the speaking of one place in terms of another—in its text and production.

11. Sean Kicummah Teuton, in his analysis of movement in the novel *House Made of Dawn*, argues that the concept of transmotion inaccurately frames Indigenous relationships to homelands as "nonterritorial" or "fabricated" rather than "composed of material facts" (49). Yet Vizenor's description of transmotion depends on both inventive vision and materiality, joining "vision" with "ability," "imagination" with "substantive rights" (*Fugitive Poses*).

12. Littlebird's own childhood experience involved frequent travel between California and New Mexico—his father worked for the Southern Pacific Railroad. He lived with his mother at Laguna Pueblo and still remembers traveling back and forth: "we had a free pass and we could go back and forth just anytime we wanted to" (*"House"*).

13. See the more extensive studies of the novel *House Made of Dawn* by scholars cited elsewhere in this chapter—including Chadwick Allen, Lawrence Evers, Robert Nelson, Louis Owens (Choctaw), Susan Scarberry-Garcia, Sean Teuton (Cherokee), and Robert Warrior (Osage), among others—for discussions of the novel's politics of identity in relation to tribal lands.

14. Sometimes individuals or families participated voluntarily, whereas sometimes their participation was due to economic need or direct government pressure.

15. In the face of the federal narrative of tribal decline signaled by the policy of Termination, demographic figures showed tremendous Native ethnic renewal and sharp increases in Native self-identification: the years between 1960 and 1970 saw a 51% increase in the number of people claiming Native American ethnicity in the U.S. census, and between 1970 and 1980 the increase was 72%. These numbers, of course, represent complex constructions of race on the part of the census bureau and the individuals claiming ancestry. For a discussion of census figures and Native population growth in the twentieth century, see Nagel 83–112.

16. In the case of many Pueblos, reservation boundaries may partly include but are not the same as the boundaries of historical homelands.

17. See Warrior, *The People and the Word*, for a discussion of how Momaday can be seen as "speaking from a specific moment" during these peak years of AIM activism.

18. The early fish-ins were particularly successful due to their strong legal basis in treaty provisions, widespread media coverage, and the support of entertainers such as Marlon Brando. The occupation of Alcatraz Island drew enormous attention and galvanized Native activism as a pan-Indian, largely urban-based movement.

19. For an account of Native American experiences in Vietnam, see Holm, esp. 171–83, on Native Vietnam veterans in activist movements and at the 1973 Wounded Knee occupation. Holm argues that the participation of more than 40,000 Native soldiers (1.4% of the Native population of the United States) in Vietnam led to a renewal of Native warrior traditions in the context of a national crisis and that many veterans brought their experiences in Vietnam to bear on the conflicts between tribes and the U.S. government. Chadwick Allen situates Holm's work in the context of the Native American literary and activist renaissance in *Blood Narratives* (117–18).

20. Qtd. in Churchill and Vander Wall 121–22. See Vine Deloria's account of the problems in the occupation of Alcatraz Island in the essay "Alcatraz, Activism and Accommodation" (in *Spirit and Reason*) where he outlines the organizers' focus on "awakening the American public to the plight of Indians" (247). See Paul Chaat Smith and Robert Warrior's detailed account of three major AIM protests in *Like a Hurricane*.

21. Examples include *Tell Them Willie Boy Is Here*, *Billy Jack*, and *Flap*. The ethnic vigilante figure wasn't limited to revisionist Westerns but rather pervaded the emergent action film, including productions such as *Shaft*, *Sweet Sweetback's Baadasssss Song*, *Enter the Dragon*, and of course the Rambo movie *First Blood* in the early 1980s.

22. See, for example, Lenihan, Corkin, and Slotkin. Steve Neale offers a cogent critique of this critical trend in which Native characters on screen "are made to function as signifiers of a preoccupation with racism, race and ethnicity in such a way as to exclude them from this same preoccupation" (9).

23. Film scholar Armando José Prats writes that revisionist Westerns engage the master narrative of westward expansion—what he calls the Myth of Conquest—

to the extent that the representation of "the Indian depends utterly not on *tribal memory* but on the white man's remembrance" (129).

24. Richard Slotkin's analysis of these Westerns emphasizes their allusions to the Vietnam War and especially the My Lai massacre (and its exposure in *Life* magazine), suggesting that the "Mylai counter-myth" lead to the "re-emergence of a new 'Cult of the Indian'" that took the forms of counterculture, neorealist depictions of American Western history (581–91). Prats theorizes further that Indian Westerns of the Vietnam era—such as *Ulzana's Raid* and *Chato's Land*—represent instances of "racio-cultural ambivalence" in which dominant categories of Other and Same become confused (231).

25. Merritt writes that *Billy Jack* was made for only $650,000 and moved through various companies during production, including AIP, Avco-Embassy, Twentieth Century-Fox, and Warner Brothers. The film was released in 1971, then rereleased in 1973 with equal success, especially in rural, "smaller-market communities" (it grossed in excess of $30 million with each release) (224–25).

26. By "ethnic vigilante," I have in mind characters such as Sweet Sweetback from *Sweet Sweetback's Baadasssss Song*, and Lee from *Enter the Dragon*. In these films, after leaving isolated, hermetic refuges from which they bring their special abilities (Sweet Sweetback's brothel, Lee's Shaolin Temple, or Billy Jack's cliff-dwelling hideaway), Sweetback, Lee, and Billy Jack become so enraged by a scene of ruthless racial injustice that they are driven to demonstrate almost superhuman powers. Sweet Sweetback witnesses two police officers beating a young black activist to whom he is handcuffed. Once unlocked from his "partner" he proceeds to beat the police officers with the handcuffs, symbols of his own uneasy connection to the larger black community. Sweetback denies and then finally accepts a fraternity with those oppressed, understanding that what he sees happening to his cuff-mate is in some way also happening to him. Lee (Bruce Lee) in *Enter the Dragon* is motivated to fight by his enemy Han's crimes against the Shaolin Temple and his own sister. Lee's ally Roper (John Saxon) witnesses his black friend Williams hung from chains in a scene that alludes to southern lynchings. Both Lee's spiritual and familial communities have been violated, and Lee's "trigger"—tasting his own blood during his fight with Han—connects his one-on-one confrontation with the evil Han to his role as a member of these communities, signaled by the replication of his image in the mirrored chamber of the film's climactic fight.

27. For example, *Devil's Doorway* (Mann 1950). For an example of 1950s political rhetoric about reservations, see Carlos B. Embry's book *America's Concentration Camps: The Facts about Our Indian Reservations Today*, published in 1956 (the year *The Searchers* was released). See Hearne, "The 'Ache for Home.'"

28. See Merritt 224–25.

29. See Vizenor, "Stealing Tribal Children."

30. The Paiute visionary Wovoka, or Jack Wilson (1856–1932), drew from both Christian and Native religious traditions (including the Northern Paiute prophet Tavibo, who in the 1870s prophesied that the earth would swallow whites and resurrect the Native dead) in his pan-Indian, millenarian Ghost Dance religion. Wovoka claimed that, in a series of visions in the late 1880s, God taught

him a ceremonial dance that would allow the dancers to see dead relatives and hasten the coming of the afterlife, gave him power over the weather, and instructed him to preach moral behavior. According to ethnographer James Mooney, who interviewed Wovoka, the prophet preached that people "must be good and love one another, have no quarreling, and live in peace with the whites; that they must work, and not lie or steal; that they must put away all the old practices that savored of war; that if they faithfully obeyed his instructions they would at last be reunited with their friends in this other world, where there would be no more death or sickness or old age" (qtd. in Hittman 17). Although much of the public associated the Ghost Dance movement with Native militancy and resistance, Wovoka preached that Natives "not refuse to work for the whites and do not make any trouble with them until you leave them" (Mooney BAE 14, part 2, 1896). The panicked, aggressive government and military reaction to the Ghost Dance as practiced among the Lakota led to the massacre of Big Foot's band at Wounded Knee in 1890.

31. Marsha Kinder, drawing together theoretical work by Linda Williams, Tom Gunning, and Mary Ann Doane, describes a pattern of "narrative orchestration of violence in which action sequences function like performative 'numbers,' interrupting the linear drive of the plot with their sensational audio and visual spectacle yet simultaneously serving as dramatic climaxes that advance the story toward closure" (68).

32. Arif Dirlik reminds us that the idea of the primitive or "premodern" is "itself a product of modernity" ("Globalization" 4).

33. Critic Jason Stevens rearticulates that privileged center in terms of pulp Westerns and the figure of Billy the Kid, arguing that Momaday appropriates the American outlaw-hero's capacity for self-creation by "envisioning the Kiowa as both his elders and quintessential American heroes" (624).

34. James's emphasis on location is relevant to my analysis as well, since Native urban experiences informed the production of *House Made of Dawn* as well as its content. James recognizes cinema as social practice in terms of cultural landscapes or what he calls the "geography of production": "the relation between a given film's representation of the city and the actual urban resources that supply and govern its manufacture" ("Toward" 3).

35. See Allen on Momaday's discussion of ancestry or "memory in the blood" (161).

36. 49s are social gatherings with informal songs and dances that take place during or after a powwow, often on its margins.

37. In its low production values, amateur cast and crew, and geographic marginality to Los Angeles, *House Made of Dawn* shares some of the social practices of neorealist production and that informed the 1960s manifestos of Latin American "Third Cinema" and "imperfect cinema."

38. Morse minimized the roles of white characters who live temporarily on the reservation, Father Olguin and Angela St. John.

39. Morse describes many of his production choices—such as avoiding the expense of a 1950s period set by adapting the film as a contemporary story—as

"simply practical." Most of the Los Angeles scenes were "shot on the run," although he had the alleys shut down for the long alley scenes (Morse, *"House"*).

. 40. As David James has observed of ethnic self-representations and "geographies of production," "the double voicings of minority cinemas . . . reflect the combination of their invisibility or misrepresentation by Hollywood and their exclusion from its apparatuses" (Hollywood, 11).

41. Teuton, in accord with Larry Evers's early work on *House Made of Dawn*, describes the way Abel's actions depart from Walatowa community norms in the novel. For example, returning from World War II, Abel "does not undergo the ritual cleansing of warriors used in Pueblo tradition to deactivate the power to kill" (52); and he kills the albino in a "crime of individuality" by acting "without the consent of the community"; Abel "comes to learn that he should not attempt to destroy individualistically that which denies meaning, but should instead confront negative forces within the interpretive context of the tribal community" (67).

42. As Deborah Madsen has shown, contemporary trauma theory assumes an integrationist or "assimilationist" process of healing based on a model that "fails to account for the inherited nature of certain forms of historical trauma and equally for the traumatic nature of everyday life for vulnerable people" (63).

43. Scenes of Abel singing constitute an important difference from the novel. In Momaday's text Abel is unable to sing aloud even as he imagines a song at the end of the novel. The songs in the film were composed by Larry Littlebird's brother, the poet, potter, and storyteller Harold Littlebird, whose poetry and songs were later featured in a 1978 *Words and Places* series documentary, *Songs of My Hunter Heart: Laguna Stories and Poems* (Carr).

44. Littlebird (*"House"*). Littlebird also understands the Diné chants in the novel as the white dawn house or "house of emergence for human beings" from his own Pueblo tradition. The people who went to see *Billy Jack*, he argues, were really looking the spiritual dimension articulated in *House Made of Dawn*: "It's both ancient and prophetic; the dawn run is prophetic of people's recognition of their identity, what they've been . . . he's able to go inward and re-discover all these things that are present."

45. The total cost of the film, according to Morse, was approximately $700,000.

46. Jacqueline Kilpatrick, in *Celluloid Indians,* acknowledges *House Made of Dawn* as a "serious attempt" but compares it unfavorably to the novel: ". . . much of the novel's greatness is lost" in the film, she writes, which is "disappointing to those who know the book" (181). The film's primary failing, according to Kilpatrick, is its inaccurate representation of Pueblo and Diné philosophies regarding evil and "the power of words" to create reality. The film suffers, she suggests, from a failure in "translating this novel into film," which leads to misunderstandings on the part of non-Native audiences (181).

47. See Prats, "His Master's Voice(over)."

48. Littlebird describes his childhood education in his autobiographical work *Hunting Sacred*.

49. See Beverly Singer's landmark history of these developments in Native film and television production in *Wiping the War Paint Off the Lens*.

50. The segment, part of the popular "School House Rock" program, was sponsored by Xerox and first aired in 1976 on ABC-TV.

51. Chon Noriega outlines the emergence of Chicano documentary cinema and television in *Shot in America*; David James provides a detailed analysis of "No Movies" performances in "Hollywood Extras." These productions questioned the ability of individuals, wavering between unified and fragmented subjectivities, and of collective action, to affect social change and enforce social justice, and reflected on the power of performance to critique, escape, and intervene in systems of social power. The films take sociological accuracy as a source of authority by incorporating a visual language (from film, photographs, and news media) to indicate specific moments in the history of American race relations.

Chapter 5
"Indians Watching Indians on TV": Native Spectatorship and the Politics of Recognition in *Skins* and *Smoke Signals*

1. For more extensive discussions of *Smoke Signals*, see Alexie, *Smoke Signals*; Hearne, *Smoke Signals: Native Cinema Rising*; Cummings; and Gilroy, "Another Fine Example" and "Conversation." See Cox, *Muting White Noise*, for further discussion of popular media images in Native American literature and in Sherman Alexie's writing in particular.

2. Native American viewers comprise 1.5% of the "potential audience inside the USA," according to Edward Buscombe (*Injuns!* 143).

3. By "streaming media archives" I mean not physical libraries or collections but rather a common heritage of popular images, accumulated memories of images circulated and transmitted through photographs as well as television, advertising, movies, and other modes of broadcasting. The wide availability of images for Indigenous repurposing results from this commodified cultural saturation.

4. Theories of new media may best describe this intersection—Henry Jenkins's replacement of models of passive spectatorship with one of active "participatory culture," and Jay David Bolter and Richard Grusin's theorization of new media as "remediation." Bolter and Grusin use this term to argue that the defining characteristic of new media is the enfolding of one medium within another—a "formal logic by which new media refashion prior media forms" (273). While Bolter and Grusin reject another connotation of remediation—that new media "remedy" inadequacies of older media—in my analysis, images of mediated intimate domestic space provides Indigenous audiences with opportunities to remedy, append, or amend the *content* of Hollywood's misrepresentations even when deploying its conventional forms.

5. In addition to the pervasive references to visual culture in his novels, King has himself worked as a photojournalist and still actively pursues professional photography projects, including an ongoing series of portraits. His 1989 novel *Medicine River*, which he adapted with a cowritten screenplay for the 1993 television movie of the same title, features a protagonist who is a photographer, played in the film by Graham Greene.

6. *Stagecoach* offers an example of this classic Western narrative in the back-story of Ringo Kid (John Wayne). Having witnessed his brother's murder by the Plummer gang, Ringo seeks revenge outside of the law. Among many, many other exemplars: Linn McAdams (Jimmy Stewart) in *Winchester 73* (1950), Jeb (Robert Mitchum) in *Pursued* (1947), and even the Stranger (Clint Eastwood) in *High Plains Drifter* (1973).

7. As Blocker argues, Luna's performances illustrate the way that "the con-sumption of whiteness is toxic . . . it devitalizes the native population." In targeting white fantasies about Natives, she writes, Luna "disillusions their fantasy by showing just what native memory now includes: the remembrance of whiteness remembering nativeness" (*Seeing Witness* 22).

8. A caricatured cartoon Indian says, "If we botch this job the chief is gonna transfer us from the raiding party to the skinning and tanning tent!"

9. Casually embedded scenes of television in other contemporary films include Cufe Smallhill (Cody Lightning) watching television to pass the time and avoid socializing in *Four Sheets to the Wind* (Harjo 2007). And in Blackhorse Lowe's film *5th World* (2005), the young couple Andrei (Sheldon Silentwalker) and Aria (Liva'ndrea Knoki) are first seen bathed in blue light from the television set as they watch a French New Wave film. During their subsequent road trip across the Navajo Nation, Andrei and Aria's relationship develops around their shared love of film and popular culture, from John Ford films to the Simpsons. *Medicine River* (Margolin 1993) engages in a similarly reflexive relationship with photography. In that film, Will (Graham Greene) uses his career in photojournalism to avoid returning to his Native community, but his professional assertion that "I don't do portraits" gives way to his eventual reintegration into his home community through a series of calendar portraits depicting individuals from the reserve.

10. In exploring the figure of the Indigenous spectator, I am referring neither to psychic spectatorship—the spectator as a subject of cinematic apparatus—nor to empirical studies of the spectator-as-viewer, but rather to an imagined specta-tor, an embodied viewer modeled in the audiovisual text itself. Studies of actual Native reception and of general audience perceptions of screen Indians have gener-ally involved focus groups. JoEllen Shively, for example, compared Native and Anglo perceptions of *The Searchers*, finding that although Native audiences appreciated "the fantasy of being free and independent like the cowboy" and "the familiarity of the setting," Anglos responded to the film as an affirmative history, as "a story about their past and their ancestors" (357). S. Elizabeth Bird's useful study, *The Audience in Everyday Life*, moves away from text-based studies to consider the ways that audiences take up media scenarios, whereas anthropologist Sam Pack's "Watching Navajos Watch Themselves" describes one Diné family's appreciation for representa-tions that accurately reflect cultural details and language use.

11. Colonnese goes on to describe his and his colleagues' reactions to view-ing *The Searchers*, in which he notes the historical and economic conditions of the Diné "extras" working in movies "about their own subjugation by whites," as well as the unacknowledged Native prior ownership of the land that makes the Comanche attack on the white ranch in *The Searchers*, in fact, a counterattack (336–37). He

describes the temporal manipulation at the core of the story of settlement in *The Searchers* this way:

> Where did that ranch *come from?* Indian viewers are aware that these supposedly peaceful ranchers, interested only in making a living through raising cattle, are living on land that has been seized. The "first attack," here, does not come from the Comanches; the first attack has already taken place, though we are not permitted to see it: it was a white attack, a successful white attack, that captured this land from the Indians by violence. Scar's attack, in which the Edwards ranch is destroyed, much of the Edwards family killed, and Lucy and Debbie captured, is in fact a *counterattack*. But for white audiences, it appears to lack clear motivation, and is merely an act of senseless cruelty. (337)

12. Muñoz, *Disidentifications* 26, 11. Muñoz's theorization of disidentification, like Judith Butler's politicization of "the experience of misrecognition, this uneasy sense of standing under a sign to which one does and does not belong," is also engaged (though more distantly) with revisions of Lacanian models (12). Lacan's model of *meconaissance*—an infant's misrecognition of itself in the mirror— has been powerfully taken up in film studies to theorize a spectator's gendered identification with the gaze of the cinematic apparatus and with the star on screen. Emerging from ideas about the formation of individual identity and the (western) child's psychosexual development, Freudian and Lacanian paradigms generally exclude non-European kinship, economic and social relations, and the ways that Indigenous relational systems have been disrupted or reorganized in the wake of colonization.

13. See Wood 27–40 for a discussion of *Skins* in the context of Chris Eyre's career and his other film and television work.

14. In the novel, Rudy's problems are even more closely connected with his masculinity—his initial impotence and his wife's abandonment of him is transformed by his interaction with the Lakota trickster Iktomi; his temporary derangement after hitting his head on a rock is manifested not only by vigilantism but also by lustiness.

15. Edison Cassadore (Western Apache) describes a screening of *Skins* on a college campus in which, "in a racially mixed audience, young Indian college students found this film unsettling. They deplored the stereotype of the drunken Indian and the impoverished economic conditions." These spectators also felt that the film "should only be viewed by other Indian people" (155). Cassadore also asserts that "the conditions represented in *Skins* . . . on reservations are 'real' though the film's limitations are that it lapses and fixates too long on the theme of angry revenge and regret" (155).

16. See David Lusted's *The Western*, esp. 181–84 for a discussion of the Western as male melodrama.

17. Eyre describes the shot this way: "I have a 50–50 shot that's a landscape and a character . . . you put the camera on the hood, you frame up the character,

and you say 'Now I want to pan more to the right' and the DP says 'Well, there's nothing out there.' That's the point" (Eyre, Interview).

18. Frank B. Wilderson III offers a different reading of this scene, in which Rudy is aligned with hegemonic forces, and Mogie, not Rudy, is contained by the mise-en-scène, within the "small box" of the television that works to "ameliorate the otherwise murderous gesture of the genocided 'Savage'" (205).

19. The image also powerfully recalls the cinematic tradition of blackface performance, particularly the shot of Jakie Rabinowitz/Jack Robin (Al Jolson) "blacking up" in a dressing room mirror before a minstrel show in the 1927 film *The Jazz Singer* (Crosland). The specific use of blackface to signal both disguise and masquerade also expands the film's racial discourses to stereotypical African-American representations, a visual reference amplified by the film's young criminals, Teddy Yellow Lodge/Mr. Green Laces (Michael Spears) and Black Lodge Boy (Gerald Tokala Clifford), who identify the vigilante (Rudy in disguise) as a "ghost" or "*wanase*" with "mud on his face, like part nigger, *hasapa* guy." The derogatory racial epithet alongside the Lakota words *hasapa* (black skin) and *wanase* (ghost) suggest the young men's confusion about the identity of their attacker (they don't recognize Rudy) while also framing Rudy's vigilantism as a racialized performance. See Wilderson's discussion of this moment as evidence of "Eyre's inability to (a) meditate on Blackness's grammar of suffering and (b) meditate on how the ethical dilemmas of that grammar of suffering are incompatible with the world's grammar" (241).

20. As George Lipsitz describes the work of collective memory in American popular culture, "the very forms most responsible for the erosion of historical and local knowledge can sometimes be the sources of reconnection in the hands of ingenious artists and audiences" (261).

21. Director Chris Eyre commented, "I like to show the difference in houses" on the reservation, to counter non-Native viewers' assumptions and stereotypes about how Native people live (*Skins* DVD commentary). Locations for the film were all actual residences with the exception of the liquor store, which was built and then burned down for the scenes shot in White Clay, Nebraska.

22. Joe American Horse is cast in a bit part in the film as a panhandler standing outside of a liquor store in White Clay; Rudy hands him a cigarette in a scene near the end of the film. Other important appearances in the film are activists Winona LaDuke as Rose Two Buffalo and Milo Yellow Hair as "Drunk # 1." Chris Eyre makes an appearance early in the film as an unnamed tribal cop in the scene after Rudy is knocked unconscious by a rock (in its incarnation as Iktomi). For some audiences, recognizing these activists in their parts as "extras" in the film mimics Mogie's on-screen model of film viewing as recognition.

23. Hall calls identity a production "which is never complete, always in process, and always constituted within, not outside, representation" ("Cultural Identity" 704).

24. See Hearne, *Smoke Signals: Native Cinema Rising* for an extended discussion of the bus as a symbol, and of scenes on the bus, in *Smoke Signals*.

25. Zitkala-Sa, *American Indian Stories,* 13. Iktomi is a Lakota trickster spirit, a shapeshifter associated with spiders and with language and innovation. His elaborate attempts to trick others often fail or backfire, making him appear foolish even as he sets powerful forces in motion.

26. In *A Thousand Plateaus*, Deleuze and Guattari imagine this face-as-screen to be the very construction of whiteness: "concrete faces cannot be assumed to come ready-made. They are engendered by an abstract machine of faciality (*visage-ite*), which produces them at the same time as it gives the signifier its white wall and subjectivity its black hole" (168). Doane writes of Deleuze's theory of faciality that "the face becomes the screen upon which the signifier is inscribed, reaffirming the role of the face as text, accessible to a reading that fixes meaning" ("The Close-Up" 105).

27. See Hearne, *Smoke Signals: Native Cinema Rising*, for an extended discussion of this scene.

28. Qtd. in Doane, "Close-Up" 109.

29. M. Pratt 4; Hall, "Notes" 239.

30. An example of film representation that conveys Indigenous modernity while retaining the Western genre period costuming of the late nineteenth century—what Schweig calls "buckskin and all that nonsense"—would of course be Jim Jarmusch's 1995 independent feature *Dead Man*, which serves as a crucial transitional film between the industry return to the Western epic mode in 1990 with *Dances with Wolves*, and the Indigenous responses that came towards the end of the decade with *Smoke Signals, Naturally Native, Tushka* (all 1998), and other films. *Dead Man* achieves this sense of shared modernity particularly through the figure of Nobody (Gary Farmer), whose extended backstory of capture and European education makes him a far more worldly, widely educated "sidekick" than the focal character, William Blake (Johnny Depp).

Coda
Persistent Vision

1. Son of the late Vincent Craig (the Diné singer-songwriter and creator of the comic strip "Muttonman"), Craig began making amateur skateboarding videos in his teens, moving on to short personal documentaries, commission, and installation films for institutions such as the National Museum of the American Indian (NMAI) and the Heard Museum in Phoenix. He codirected (with Sarah Colt) a 2009 feature-length documentary, *Geronimo*, produced as part of the WGBH-TV miniseries *We Shall Remain*, focused on events and leaders in Native American history.

2. According to Edward Small, experimental film exists as a separate genre from both narrative feature films and nonfiction documentary. His list of eight technical and structural qualities of experimental films include "economic independence, brevity, a collaborative construction, an affinity for ongoing technological developments, an affinity for the phenomenology of mental images, an avoidance of

verbal language, an exploration of nonnarrative structures, and a pronounced (often quintessential) reflexivity" (xv). Indigenous experimental films—such as Masayesva's *Imagining Indians* or Craig's *4wheelwarpony*, revise some of these characterizations of experimentalism by using voiceover and collaboration with Native and non-Native crew and subjects. Interestingly, Victor Masayesva's emphasis (in his essay on Indigenous experimentalism) is not on technical qualities but rather on the political and spiritual qualities of Indigenous experimental art.

3. Film studies theorist Garrett Stewart, in his investigation of the photogram (the individual photographic imprint) as an emblem of the relation of photography to film, theorizes the arrested or "seized" freeze frame and the lateral pan across "inset photos" (13) as tropic "exceedings of narration" that take viewers "from stylistic inflection back to mechanical processes" (16).

Works Cited

Research Archives

Cinema Television Library and Archives of the Performing Arts, University of Southern California, Los Angeles.

Cultural Resource Center, National Museum of the American Indian Archives, Suitland, MD.

Film and Television Archive, University of California, Los Angeles.

Film and Video Center, George Gustav Heye Center, Smithsonian/National Museum of the American Indian, New York.

Margaret Herrick Library, Academy of Motion Picture Arts and Sciences, Beverly Hills, CA (AMPAS)

Motion Picture, Broadcasting, and Recorded Sound Division, Library of Congress, Washington, DC.

National Film Archive, Prague, Czech Republic.

Published Sources

$10,000,000 Merger of Movie Producers; Carewe and Inspiration Pictures Are Combined with the Tec-Art Studios." *New York Times* 9 Nov. 1927, Amusements 23.

"$25,000 Offer for Day in Movies; Bucharest Goodbye Deeply Stirs Queen." *New York Times* 4 Oct. 1926, 1, 6.

Abel, Richard. *The Red Rooster Scare: Making Cinema American, 1900–1910*. Berkeley: University of California Press, 1999

Adams, David Wallace. *Education for Extinction: American Indians and the Boarding School Experience, 1875–1928*. Lawrence: University Press of Kansas, 1995.

Aleiss, Angela. "Hollywood Addresses Indian Reform: *The Vanishing American*." *Studies in Visual Communication* 10.4 (Fall 1984): 53–60.

———. *Making the White Man's Indian: Native Americans and Hollywood Movies.* Westport, CT: Praeger, 2005.

———. "Native Americans: The Surprising Silents." *Cineaste* 21 (1995): 34–35.

———. "'The Vanishing American': Hollywood's Compromise to Indian Reform. *Journal of American Studies* 25.3 (1991): 467–72.

Alexie, Sherman. *The Lone Ranger and Tonto Fistfight in Heaven.* New York: Harper Perennial, 1993.

———. *Smoke Signals: A Screenplay.* New York: Hyperion, 1998.

Alison, Jane, ed. and introduction. *Native Nations: Journeys in American Photography.* London: Barbican Art Gallery, 1998.

Allen, Chadwick. *Blood Narrative: Indigenous Identity in American Indian and Maori Literary and Activist Texts.* Durham, NC: Duke University Press, 2002.

Allen, Michael. *Family Secrets: The Feature Films of D. W. Griffith.* London: BFI, 1999.

Allred, Christine Edwards. *Harper's Indians: Representing Native America in Popular Magazine Culture, 1893–1922.* Diss. University of California, Los Angeles, 2001.

Babcock, Barbara. "First Families: Gender, Reproduction and the Mythic Southwest." *The Great Southwest of the Fred Harvey Company and the Santa Fe Railway.* Ed. Barbara Babcock and Marta Weigle. Phoenix, AZ: Heard Museum, 1996. 207–17.

Barclay, Barry. "Celebrating Fourth Cinema." *Illusions* 35 (2003): 7–11.

———. *Mana Tuturu: Maori Treasures and Intellectual Property Rights.* Honolulu: University of Hawai'i Press, 2005.

———. *Our Own Image.* Auckland, NZ: Longman Paul, 1990.

Barkan, Elazar, and Ronald Bush. *Prehistories of the Future: The Primitivist Project and the Culture of Modernism.* Stanford, CA: Stanford University Press, 1995.

Barthes, Roland. *Camera Lucida: Reflections on Photography.* Trans. Richard Howard. New York: Farrar, Straus and Giroux, 1981.

Bataille, Gretchen M., ed. *Native American Representations: First Encounters, Distorted Images, and Literary Appropriations.* Lincoln: University of Nebraska Press, 2001.

Bataille, Gretchen M., and Charles P. Silet, eds. *The Pretend Indians: Images of Native Americans in the Movies.* Ames: Iowa State University Press, 1980.

Beckman, Karen, and Jean Ma. *Still Moving: Between Cinema and Photography.* Durham, NC: Duke University Press, 2008.

Beltrán, Mary. *Latina/o Stars in U.S. Eyes: The Makings and Meanings of Film and TV Stardom.* Urbana: University of Illinois Press, 2009.

———. "Dolores Del Rio, the First 'Latin Invasion,' and Hollywood's Transition to Sound." *Aztlán* 30.1 (Spring 2005): 55–85.

Bendix, Regina. *In Search of Authenticity: The Formation of Folklore Studies.* Madison: University of Wisconsin Press, 1997.

Benjamin, Walter. *Illuminations: Essays and Reflections.* 1955. New York: Harcourt, Brace, Jovanovich, 1968.

Bergland, Renée L. *The National Uncanny: Indian Ghosts and American Subjects.* Hanover, NH: University Press of New England, 2000.

Berkhofer, Robert F. *The White Man's Indian: Images of the American Indian from Columbus to the Present*. New York: Random House, 1979.

Bernardi, Daniel, ed. *The Birth of Whiteness: Race and the Emergence of U.S. Cinema*. New Brunswick, NJ: Rutgers University Press, 1996.

Bernardin, Susan, Melody Graulich, Lisa MacFarlane, and Nicole Tonkovich, eds. *Trading Gazes: Euro-American Women Photographers and Native North Americans, 1880–1940*. New Brunswick, NJ: Rutgers University Press, 2003.

Bessire, Lucas. "Talking Back to Primitivism: Divided Audiences, Collective Desires." *American Anthropologist* 105.4 (2003): 832–37.

Bhabha, Homi. *The Location of Culture*. London: Routledge, 1994.

Birchard, Robert S. *Cecil B. DeMille's Hollywood*. Lexington: University Press of Kentucky, 2004.

Bird, S. Elizabeth. *The Audience in Everyday Life: Living in a Media World*. New York: Routledge, 2003.

Blaisdell, George. "A Man with the Bark On." Rev. of *The Squaw Man*. *Moving Picture World* 28 Feb. 1914. AMPAS files.

Bliss, Michael. " 'Back Off to What?' Enclosure, Violence, and Capitalism in Sam Peckinpah's *The Wild Bunch*." *Sam Peckinpah's* The Wild Bunch. Ed. Stephen Prince. Cambridge, Eng.: Cambridge University Press, 1999. 105–29.

Blocker, Jane. "Failures of Self-Seeing: James Luna Remembers Dino." *PAJ: A Journal of Performance Art* 23.1 (2001): 18–32.

———. *Seeing Witness: Visuality and the Ethics of Testimony*. Minneapolis: University of Minnesota Press, 2009.

Bogle, Donald. *Toms, Coons, Mulattoes, Mammies, and Bucks: An Interpretive History of Blacks in American Films*. 1973. New York: Continuum, 2000.

Bolt, Christine. *American Indian Policy and American Reform: Case Studies of the Campaign to Assimilate the American Indians*. London: Allen and Unwin, 1987.

Bolter, Jay David, and Richard Grusin. *Remediation: Understanding New Media*. Boston: MIT Press, 2000.

Bourdieu, Pierre. *The Logic of Practice*. Trans. Richard Nice. Cambridge, Eng.: Polity Press, 1990.

Bourdieu, Pierre, and Jean-Claude Passeron. *Reproduction in Education, Society and Culture*. Trans. Richard Nice. London: Sage, 1977.

Bowser, Eileen. *The Transformation of Cinema, 1907–1915*. Berkeley: University of California Press, 1990.

Bray, Tamara, ed. *The Future of the Past: Archaeologists, Native Americans, and Repatriation*. New York: Garland, 2001.

Briggs, Charles. "Metadiscursive Practices and Scholarly Authority in Folkloristics." *Journal of American Folklore* 106 (1993): 387–434.

Brooks, Peter. *The Melodramatic Imagination: Balzac, Henry James, Melodrama, and the Mode of Excess*. New Haven, CT: Yale University Press, 1995.

Brown, Alison K., and Laura Peers. "Pictures Bring Us Messages," *Sinaakssiiksi aohtsimaahpihkookiyaawa: Photographs and Histories from the Kainai Nation*. Toronto, ON: University of Toronto Press, 2006.

Brown, Michael F. *Who Owns Native Culture?* Cambridge, Eng.: Cambridge University Press, 2003.

Brown, Michael, and Margaret M. Bruchac. "NAGPRA from the Middle Distance: Legal Puzzles and Unintended Consequences." *Imperialism, Art and Restitution.* Ed. John Henry Merryman. Cambridge, Eng.: Cambridge University Press, 2006. 193–217.

Brownlow, Kevin. *The Parade's Gone By . . .* Berkeley: University of California Press, 1968.

———. *The War, the West, and the Wilderness.* New York: Knopf, 1979.

Bruyneel, Kevin. *The Third Space of Sovereignty: The Postcolonial Politics of U.S.-Indigenous Relations.* Minneapolis: University of Minnesota Press, 2007.

Buscombe, Edward. *Injuns! Native Americans in the Movies.* London: Reaktion Books, 2006.

Butler, Judith. *Gender Trouble: Feminism and the Subversion of Identity.* New York: Routledge, 1990.

Campbell, Neil. "Minor Cinema, Critical Regionalism, and the Post-Western." 18 May 2012 <http://critical-regionalism.com/2011/03/30/minor-cinema-critical-regionalism-and-the-post-western-neil-campbell/>.

Carewe, Edwin. "Directorial Training." *Hollywood Directors, 1914–1940.* Ed. Richard Koszarski. New York: Oxford University Press, 1976. 187–90.

———. "How I Selected Dolores Del Rio's New Starring Role." *Ramona* press book. Washington, DC: Library of Congress, 1928.

"Carewe to Rewed Ex-Wife. Film Director Obtains Chicago License for Ceremony." *New York Times* 16 June 1929. <http://query.nytimes.com/mem/archive/pdf?res=F50D1EF73C55127A93C4A8178DD85F4D8285F9>.

"Carewes Will Remarry. Film Actress and Producer Were Divorced in Mexico a Year Ago." *New York Times* 14 June 1929. 18 Apr. 2012 <http://query.nytimes.com/mem/archive/pdf?res=FA0716FC3B5C177A93C6A8178DD85F4D8285F9>.

Carmichael, Deborah A. "The Living Presence of Monument Valley in John Ford's *Stagecoach* (1939)." *The Landscape of Hollywood Westerns: Ecocriticism in an American Film Genre.* Ed. Deborah Carmichael. Salt Lake City: University of Utah Press, 2006. 212–28.

Cassadore, Edison Duane. *Re-Imagining Indians: The Counter-Hegemonic Representations of Victor Masayesva and Chris Eyre.* Diss. University of Arizona, 2007.

Cawelti, John. *The Six-Gun Mystique Sequel.* Bowling Green, OH: Bowling Green State University Popular Press, 1999.

Census Bureau, "Reverend Smith Enumerates Navajo Camp." 18 Apr. 2012 <http://www.archives.gov/press/press-kits/1930-census-photos/reverend-smith-enumerates-navajo-camp.jpg>.

Chaw, Walter. Interview with Chris Eyre, 2 Oct. 2002. *Film Freak Central.* 24 Apr. 2012 <http://filmfreakcentral.net/notes/ceyreinterview.htm>.

Child, Brenda J. *Boarding School Seasons: American Indian Families, 1900–1940.* Lincoln: University of Nebraska Press, 1998.

Churchill, Ward. *Fantasies of the Master Race: Literature, Cinema, and the Colonization of American Indians*. New York: City Lights Press, 2001.

Churchill, Ward, and Jim Vander Wall. *Agents of Repression: The FBI's Secret Wars against the Black Panther Party and the American Indian Movement*. Boston: South End Press, 1988.

Clifford, James. "Indigenous Articulations." *The Contemporary Pacific* 13.2 (2001): 468–90.

———. *The Predicament of Culture: Twentieth-Century Ethnography, Literature, and Art*. Cambridge, MA: Harvard University Press, 1988.

———. "Traditional Futures." *Questions of Tradition*. Ed. Mark Salber Phillips and Gordon Schochet. Toronto, ON: University of Toronto Press, 2004. 152–68.

Colonnese, Tom Grayson. "Native American Reactions to *The Searchers*." *The Searchers: Essays and Reflections on John Ford's Classic Western*. Ed. Arthur M. Eckstein and Peter Lehman. Detroit: Wayne State University Press, 2004. 335–42.

Columpar, Corinn. *Unsettling Sights: The Fourth World on Film*. Carbondale: Southern Illinois University Press, 2010.

Connolly, Vera. "The Cry of a Broken People." *Good Housekeeping* 1 Feb. 1929, 30–31, 226–37.

———. "The End of the Road." *Good Housekeeping* 3 May 1929, 44–45, 153–70.

———. "We Still Get Robbed." *Good Housekeeping* 2 Mar. 1925, 34, 35, 250–59.

Cook, David A. "Ballistic Balletics: Styles of Violent Representation in *The Wild Bunch* and After." *Sam Peckinpah's* The Wild Bunch. Ed. Stephen Prince. Cambridge, Eng.: Cambridge University Press, 1999. 130–54.

Corkin, Stanley. *Cowboys as Cold Warriors: The Western and U.S. History*. Philadelphia: Temple University Press, 2004.

Courtney, Susan. *Hollywood Fantasies of Miscegenation: Spectacular Narratives of Gender and Race, 1903–1967*. Princeton, NJ: Princeton University Press, 2005.

Cox, James H. *Muting White Noise: Native American and European American Novel Traditions*. Norman: University of Oklahoma Press, 2006.

Crary, Jonathan. *Suspensions of Perception: Attention, Spectacle, and Modern Culture*. Boston: MIT Press, 2000.

Creekmur, Corey K. "Buffalo Bill (Himself): History and Memory in the Western Biopic." *Westerns: Films through History*. Ed. Janet Walker. London: Routledge, 2001. 131–50.

Cushman, Ellen. "Faces, Skins and the Identity Politics of Rereading Race." *Rhetoric Review* 24 (2005): 378–82.

Danius, Sara, and Stefan Jonsson. "Interview with Gayatri Spivak." *Boundary 2* 20.2 (1993): 24–50.

Davis, Ronald L. *John Ford: Hollywood's Old Master*. Norman: University of Oklahoma Press, 1995.

Debo, Annette. "Interracial Modernism in Avant-Garde Film: Paul Robeson and H. D. in the 1930 Borderline." *Quarterly Review of Film and Video* 18.4 (2000): 371–83.

Deger, Jennifer. *Shimmering Screens: Making Media in an Aboriginal Community.* Minneapolis: University of Minnesota Press, 2006.

Deleuze, Gilles, and Felix Guattari. *A Thousand Plateaus: Capitalism and Schizophrenia.* Trans. and Forward by Brian Massumi. Minneapolis: University of Minnesota Press, 1987.

Deloria, Philip J. *Indians in Unexpected Places.* Lawrence: University of Kansas Press, 2004.

———. *Playing Indian.* New Haven, CT: Yale University Press, 1999.

Deloria, Vine, Jr. "Alcatraz, Activism and Accommodation." *Spirit and Reason: The Vine Deloria, Jr., Reader.* Ed. Barbara Deloria, Kristen Foehner, and Sam Scinta. Golden, CO: Fulcrum Publishing, 1999. 241–48.

———. *Custer Died for Your Sins, an Indian Manifesto.* 1969. Norman: University of Oklahoma Press, 1988.

DeLyser, Dydia. *Ramona Memories: Tourism and the Shaping of Southern California.* Minneapolis: University of Minnesota Press, 2005.

Denise Cummings. "'Accessible Poetry'? Cultural Intersection and Exchange in Contemporary American Indian and American Independent Film." *Studies in American Indian Literatures* 13.1 (2001): 57–80.

Dippie, Brian W. *The Vanishing American: White Attitudes and U.S. Indian Policy.* Lawrence: University Press of Kansas, 1982.

Dirlik, Arif. "Globalization, Indigenism, and the Politics of Place." *ARIEL* 34.1 (2003): 15–30.

———. "Global Modernity? Modernity in an Age of Global Capitalism. *European Journal of Social Theory* 6.3 (2003): 275–92.

———. *Postmodernity's Histories: The Past as Legacy and Project.* Lanham, MD: Rowman and Littlefield, 2000.

Doane, Mary Ann. "The Close-Up: Scale and Detail in the Cinema." *Differences: A Journal of Feminist Cultural Studies* 14.3 (2005): 89–111.

———. *Femmes Fatales: Feminism, Film Theory, Psychoanalysis.* New York: Routledge, 1991.

Downes, Randolph C. "A Crusade for Indian Reform, 1922–1934." *Mississippi Valley Historical Review* 32.3 (1945): 331–54.

Duke University Library, John W. Hartman Center for Sales, Advertising and Marketing History. "Emergence of Advertising in America, 1850–1920" database. Hawley Scrapbook, pop-up image. 16 Apr. 2012 <http://library.duke.edu/digitalcollections/eaa.SB0056/pg.1>.

———. "Medicine and Madison Avenue" database. Protam Nutritional Plan advertisement, "Popular New York Model." 16 Apr. 2012 <http://library.duke.edu/digitalcollections/mma.MM0762/pg.1>.

Eastman, Charles. *From the Deep Woods to Civilization: Chapters in the Autobiography of an Indian.* 1916. Lincoln: University of Nebraska Press, 1977.

Edwards, Elizabeth. *Raw Histories: Photographs, Anthropology and Museums.* Oxford, Eng.: Berg Press, 2001.

———. "Talking Visual Histories: Introduction." *Museums and Source Communities: A Routledge Reader.* Ed. Laura Peers and Alison K. Brown. London: Routledge, 2003. 83–99.

"Edwin Carewe, 56, Director of Films; Leader in Silent Era, Noted for Productions of 'Ramona' and 'Resurrection,' Dies." *New York Times* 23 Jan. 1940, Obituaries, 27.

"Edwin Carewe Surrenders; Film Director in Los Angeles Answers Tax Fraud Indictment." *New York Times* 1 Apr. 1932. 18 Apr. 2012 <http://query.nytimes.com/mem/archive/pdf?res=F10715F83D5A13738DDDA80894DC405B828FF1D3>.

"Edwin Carewes Separate. Director Says He and Former Mary Akin are Incompatible." *The New York Times* 13 Oct. 1927. 18 Apr. 2012 <http://query.nytimes.com/mem/archive/pdf?res=F00E17FF3F591B7A93C1A8178BD95F438285F9>.

Ellenberger, Allan R. "Director Edwin Carewe's Grave Is Marked after More Than 69 Years." 12 Sept. 2009. 18 Apr. 2012 <http://allanellenberger.com/book-flm-news/edwin-carewe-marked-at-hollywood-forever/>.

Elsaesser, Thomas. "Tales of Sound and the Fury: Observations on the Family Melodrama." *Home Is Where the Heart Is: Studies in Melodrama and the Women's Film.* Ed. Christine Gledhill. London: BFI, 1987. 43–69.

Embry, Carlos B. *America's Concentration Camps: The Facts about Our Indian Reservations Today.* New York: McKay, 1956.

Erb, Cynthia. *Tracking King Kong: A Hollywood Icon in World Culture.* Detroit, MI: Wayne State University Press, 1998.

Evans, Michael Robert. *Isuma: Inuit Video Art.* Montreal, ON: McGill-Queen's University Press, 2008.

———. "Sometimes in Anger: The Struggles of Inuit Video." *Fuse* 22.4 (2000): n.p.

Evers, Lawrence J. "The Killing of a New Mexican State Trooper: Ways of Telling an Historical Event." *Critical Essays on Native American Literature.* Ed. Andrew Wiget. Boston: G. K. Hall, 1985. 246–61.

———. "Words and Place: A Reading of *House Made of Dawn*." *Western American Literature* 11.4 (1977): 297–320.

Eyre, Chris. Telephone interview. 4 July 2008.

Fabian, Johannes. *Time and the Other: How Anthropology Makes Its Object.* New York: Columbia University Press, 1983.

Fahys, Judy. "A Legacy of Uranium, a Prayer for Healing." *Salt Lake Tribune* 1 Jan. 2011. 13 Jan. 2011 <http://www.sltrib.com/sltrib/politics/50949776-90/uranium-begay-died-epa.html.csp?page=1>.

Fanon, Frantz. *Black Skin, White Masks.* New York: Grove Press, 1967.

Faris, James C. *Navajo and Photography: A Critical History of the Representation of an American People.* Salt Lake City: University of Utah Press, 2003.

Fear-Segal, Jacqueline. *White Man's Club: Schools, Race, and the Struggle of Indian Acculturation.* Lincoln: University of Nebraska Press, 2007.

Fforde, Cressida, Jane Hubert, and Paul Turnbull, eds. *The Dead and Their Posses-sions: Repatriation in Principle, Policy and Practice*. London: Routledge, 2002.

Fiedler, Leslie. *The Return of the Vanishing American*. New York: Stein and Day, 1968.

Fienup-Riordan, Ann. *Freeze Frame: Alaska Eskimos in the Movies*. Seattle: University of Washington Press, 1993.

———. "Yup'ik Elders in Museums: Fieldwork Turned on Its Head." *Arctic Anthro-pology* 35.2 (1998): 49–58.

Fine-Dare, Kathleen S. *Grave Injustice: The American Indian Repatriation Movement and NAGPRA*. Lincoln: University of Nebraska Press, 2002.

Forman, Henry James. *Our Movie Made Children*. 1933. New York: Bowen Press, 2007.

Foster, Tol. "Of One Blood: An Argument for Relations and Regionality in Native American Literary Studies." *Reasoning Together: The Native Critics Collective*. Ed. Craig S. Womack, Daniel Heath Justice, and Christopher B. Teuton. Norman: University of Oklahoma Press, 2008. 265–302.

Foucault, Michel. *Discipline and Punish: The Birth of the Prison*. 1975. New York: Random House, 1995.

French, Philip. *Westerns*. New York: Viking, 1973.

Friar, Ralph E., and Natasha Friar. *The Only Good Indian . . . The Hollywood Gospel*. New York: Drama Book Specialists/Publishers, 1972.

Gaberscek, Carlo. "On Location at Canyon de Chelly and Acoma Pueblo." *Griffi-thiana* 73/74 (2005): 5–17.

———. "Westerns Filmed in Arizona 1912–1929." *Griffithiana* 73/74 (2005): 19–57.

Gaines, Jane M. "Costume and Narrative: How Dress Tells the Woman's Story." *Fabrications: Costume and the Female Body*. Ed. Jane Gaines and Charlotte Herzog. New York: Routledge, 1990. 180–211.

———. *Fire and Desire: Mixed-Race Movies in the Silent Era*. Chicago: University of Chicago Press, 2001.

———. "Political Mimesis." *Collecting Visible Evidence*. Ed. Jane M. Gaines and Michael Renov. Minneapolis: University of Minnesota Press, 1999. 84–102.

———. "White Privilege and Looking Relations: Race and Gender in Feminist Film Theory." *Screen* 29.4 (1988): 12–27.

———, and Charlotte Herzog. "The Fantasy of Authenticity in Western Costume." *Back in the Saddle Again: New Essays on the Western*. Ed. Edward Buscombe and Roberta E. Pearson. London: BFI Publishing, 1998. 172–81.

Gallagher, Tag. *John Ford: The Man and His Films*. Berkeley: University of California Press, 1986.

———. "Shoot-Out at the Genre Corral: Problems in the 'Evolution' of the West-ern." *Film Genre Reader II*. Ed. Barry Keith Grant. Austin: University of Texas Press, 1995. 246–60.

Getty Images. "Slave Children." 16 Apr. 2012 <http://www.gettyimages.com/detail/3207142>.

———. "As They Are Now." 16 Apr. 2012 <http://www.gettyimages.com/detail/news-photo/portrait-of-an-african-american-brother-and-sister-both-of-news-photo/74441181>.

Gibson, Arrell Morgan. *The Chickasaws.* Norman: University of Oklahoma Press, 1971.

Gilroy, Jhon Warren. "Another Fine Example of the Oral Tradition? Identification and Subversion in Sherman Alexie's *Smoke Signals.*" *Studies in American Indian Literatures* 13.1 (2001): 23–42.

———. "A Conversation with Evan Adams." *Studies in American Indian Literatures* 13.1 (2001): 43–56.

Ginsburg, Faye. "Atanarjuat Off-Screen: From 'Media Reservations' to the World Stage." *American Anthropologist* 105.4 (2003): 827–31.

———. "Indigenous Media: Faustian Contract or Global Village?" *Cultural Anthropology* 6.1 (1991): 92–112.

———. "Mediating Culture: Aboriginal Media and the Social Transformation of Identity." University of Southern California, Conference on Communication and Empowerment, 1996. 16 Apr. 2012 <http://www.usc.edu/dept/ancntr/pdcomm/ginsburg.html>.

———. "The Parallax Effect: The Impact of Indigenous Media on Ethnographic Film." *Collecting Visible Evidence.* Ed. Jane M. Gaines and Michael Renov. Minneapolis: University of Minnesota Press, 1999. 156–75.

———. "Screen Memories: Resignifying the Traditional in Indigenous Media." *Media Worlds: Anthropology on New Terrain.* Ed. Faye Ginsburg, Lila Abu-Lughod, and Brian Larkin. Berkeley: University of California Press, 2002. 40–56.

———, and Fred Myers. "A History of Aboriginal Futures." *Critique of Anthropology* 26.2 (2006): 27–45.

Giroux, Henry A. *Breaking into the Movies: Film and the Culture of Politics.* New York: Wiley-Blackwell, 2002.

Gledhill, Christine. "The Melodramatic Field: An Investigation." *Home Is Where the Heart Is: Studies in Melodrama and the Women's Film.* Ed. Christine Gledhill. London: BFI, 1987. 5–39.

Gopnik, Adam. "The Unreal Thing." *New Yorker* 19 May 2003, 66–73.

Gorbman, Claudia. "Drums along the L.A. River: Scoring the Indian." *Westerns: Films through History.* Ed. Janet Walker. New York: Routledge, 2001. 177–95.

Gould, Stephen Jay. *The Mismeasure of Man.* 1981. New York: Norton, 1996.

Grant, Madison. *The Passing of the Great Race.* New York: Scribner's, 1916.

Green, Rayna. "The Pocahontas Perplex: The Image of Indian Women in American Culture." *Massachusetts Review* 16 (Fall 1975): 698–714.

Grey, Zane. *The Vanishing American.* New York: Grosset and Dunlap, 1925.

Gridley, Marion E., ed. *Indians of Today.* Crawfordsville, IN: Lakeside Press, R. R. Donnelly, 1936.

Griffiths, Alison. "Science and Spectacle: Native American Representations in Early Cinema." *Dressing in Feathers: The Construction of the Indian in American*

Popular Culture. Ed. S. Elizabeth Bird. Oxford, Eng.: Westview Press, 1996. 79–95.

———. *Wondrous Difference: Cinema, Anthropology, and Turn-of-the-Century Visual Culture.* New York: Columbia University Press, 2002.

Gunning, Tom. "The Cinema of Attraction: Early Film, Its Spectator, and the Avant-Garde." *Wide Angle* 8 (1986): 63–74.

———. *D. W. Griffith and the Origins of American Narrative Film: The Early Years at Biograph.* Urbana: University of Illinois Press, 1991.

Halfert, J. E. Letter to the Hays office, 1929. AMPAS file, *Ramona,* 1928.

Hall, Stuart. "Cultural Identity and Cinematic Representation." *Film and Theory: An Anthology.* Ed. Robert Stam and Toby Miller. Oxford, Eng.: Blackwell Publishers, 2000. 704–14.

———. "Encoding/Decoding." *Culture, Media, Language: Working Papers in Cultural Studies, 1972–1979.* Ed. Centre for Contemporary Cultural Studies. London: Hutchinson, 1980. 128–38.

———. "Notes on Deconstructing 'The Popular.'" *People's History and Socialist Theory.* Ed. Samuel Raphael. London: Routledge and Kegan Paul, 1981. 227–40.

Handler, Richard, and Jocelyn Linnekin. "Tradition, Genuine or Spurious?" *Journal of American Folklore* 97 (1984): 273–90.

Handley, William R. "Distinctions without Differences: Zane Grey and the Mormon Question." *Arizona Quarterly* 57.1 (2001): 1–33.

———. "*The Vanishing American* (1925)." *America First: Naming the Nation in U.S. Film.* Ed. Mandy Merck. London: Routledge, 2007. 44–64.

Haraway, Donna. "Teddy Bear Patriarchy: Taxidermy in the Garden of Eden, New York City, 1908–1936." *The Haraway Reader.* London: Routledge, 2003. 151–98.

Hearne, Joanna. "The 'Ache for Home': Assimilation and Separatism in Anthony Mann's *Devil's Doorway.*" *Hollywood's West: The American Frontier in Film, Television, and History.* Ed. Peter C. Rollins and John E. O'Connor. Lexington: University Press of Kentucky, 2005. 126–59.

———. "'The Cross-Heart People': Race and Inheritance in the Silent Western." *Journal of Popular Film and Television* 30.4 (2003): 181–96.

———. "*House Made of Dawn*: Restoring Native Voices in Cinema." Four interviews. 8 Dec. 2005 Smithsonian Institution, National Museum of the American Indian, Film and Video Center. Native Networks / Redes Indígenas. 24 Apr. 2012 <www.nativenetworks.si.edu>.

———. "Indigenous Animation: Educational Programming, Narrative Interventions, and Children's Cultures." *Global Indigenous Media: Cultures, Poetics, and Politics.* Ed. Pamela Wilson and Michelle Stewart. Durham, NC: Duke University Press, 2008. 89–108.

———. "*Smoke Signals*": *Native Cinema Rising.* Lincoln: University of Nebraska Press, 2012.

———. "'John Wayne's Teeth': Speech, Sound and Representation in *Smoke Signals* and *Imagining Indians*." *Western Folklore* 64:3-4 (2005): 189–208.

———. "Telling and Retelling in the 'Ink of Light': Documentary Cinema, Oral Narratives, and Indigenous Identities." *Screen* 47:3 (Autumn 2006): 307–26.

Hershfield, Joanne. *The Invention of Dolores Del Rio*. Minneapolis: University of Minnesota Press, 2000.

Herzbert, Bob. *Savages and Saints: The Changing Image of American Indians in Westerns*. Jefferson, NC: McFarland, 2008.

Higashi, Sumiko. *Cecil B. DeMille and American Culture: The Silent Era*. Berkeley: University of California Press, 1994.

Hilger, Michael. *The American Indian in Film*. Metuchen, NJ: Scarecrow Press, 1986.

———. *From Savage to Nobleman: Images of Native Americans in Film*. Lanham, MD: Scarecrow Press, 1995.

Hittman, Michael. Ed. Don Lynch. *Wovoka and the Ghost Dance*. Yerington Paiute Tribe, 1990. Expanded ed. Lincoln: University of Nebraska Press, 1997.

Hobsbawm, Eric, and Terence Ranger, eds. *The Invention of Tradition*. Cambridge, Eng.: Cambridge University Press, 1983.

Holm, Tom. *Strong Hearts, Wounded Souls: Native American Veterans of the Vietnam War*. Austin: University of Texas Press, 1996.

hooks, bell. *Black Looks: Race and Representation*. Boston: South End Press, 1992.

Hopkins, Candice. "Making Things Our Own: The Indigenous Aesthetic in Digital Storytelling." *Leonardo* 39.4 (2006): 341–44.

Horsman, Reginald. *Race and Manifest Destiny: The Origins of American Racial Anglo-Saxonism*. Cambridge, MA: Harvard University Press, 1981.

Huggins, Jackie. "Preface." *Many Voices: Reflections on Experiences of Indigenous Child Separation*. Ed. Doreen Mellor and Anna Haebich. Canberra: National Library of Australia, 2002. ix–xi.

Huhndorf, Shari. "*Atanarjuat, The Fast Runner*: Culture, History, and Politics in Inuit Media." *American Anthropologist* 105.4 (2003): 822–26.

———. *Going Native: Indians in the Cultural Imagination*. Ithaca, NY: Cornell University Press, 2001.

———. *Mapping the Americas: The Transnational Politics of Contemporary Native Culture*. Ithaca, NY: Cornell University Press, 2009.

Jackson, Helen Hunt. *A Century of Dishonor: A Sketch of the United States Government's Dealings with Some of the Indian Tribes*. 1881. Minneapolis: Ross and Haines, 1964.

———. *Ramona*. 1884. Introduction by Michael Dorris. New York: Penguin, 1988.

Jacobs, Karen. "Optic/Haptic/Abject: Revisioning Indigenous Media in Victor Masayesva, Jr., and Leslie Marmon Silko." *Journal of Visual Culture* 3.3 (2004): 291–316.

James, David. *Allegories of Cinema: American Film in the Sixties*. Princeton, NJ: Princeton University Press, 1989.

———. "Hollywood Extras: One Tradition of 'Avant-Garde' Film in Los Angeles." *October* 90 (Fall 1999): 3–24.

———. *The Most Typical Avant-Garde: History and Geography of Minor Cinemas in Los Angeles.* Berkeley: University of California Press, 2005.

———. "Toward a Geo-Cinematic Hermeneutics: Representations of Los Angeles in Non-Industrial Cinema—*Killer of Sheep* and *Water and Power*." *Wide Angle* 20.3 (1998): 23–53.

Jay, Gregory S. " 'White Man's Book No Good': D. W. Griffith and the American Indian." *Cinema Journal* 39:4 (2000): 3–26.

Jenkins, Henry. *Convergence Culture: Where Old and New Media Collide.* New York: New York University Press, 2006.

Jenkins, Jennifer Lei. "Hearths and Minds: Violence and Domesticity in Hopi Life." *Paradoxa* 15 (2001): 146–57.

Jhally, Sut. *The Codes of Advertising: Fetishism and the Political Economy of Meaning in the Consumer Society.* London: Routledge, 1990.

Johnson, E. Pauline. *The Moccasin Maker.* 1913. Tucson: University of Arizona Press, 1987.

Jojola, Ted. "Absurd Reality II: Hollywood Goes to the Indians." *Hollywood's Indian: The Portrayal of the Native American in Film.* Ed. Peter C. Rollins and John E. O'Connor. Lexington: University Press of Kentucky, 1998. 12–26.

Justice, Daniel Heath. *Our Fire Survives the Storm: A Cherokee Literary History.* Minneapolis: University of Minnesota Press, 2006.

Kalinak, Kathryn. "How the West Was Sung." *Westerns: Films through History.* Ed. Janet Walker. New York: Routledge, 2001. 151–76.

———. " 'Typically American': Music for *The Searchers*." *The Searchers: Essays and Reflections on John Ford's Classic Western.* Ed. Arthur M. Eckstein and Peter Lehman. Detroit, MI: Wayne State University Press, 2004. 109–43.

Kaplan, Amy. "Manifest Domesticity." *American Literature* 70.3 (1998): 581–606.

Karttunen, Frances. *Between Worlds: Interpreters, Guides and Survivors.* New Brunswick, NJ: Rutgers University Press, 1994.

Kasson, Joy S. "Life-like, Vivid, and Thrilling Pictures: Buffalo Bill's Wild West and Early Cinema." *Westerns: Films through History.* Ed. Janet Walker. London: Routledge, 2001. 109–30.

Katanski, Amelia V. *Learning to Write "Indian": The Boarding-School Experience and American Indian Literature.* Norman: University of Oklahoma Press, 2005.

Kelley, Leo. "The Daughter of Dawn: An Original Silent Film with an Oklahoma Cast." *The Chronicles of Oklahoma* 77 (Fall 1999): 290–99.

Kennedy, Rosanne. "The Affective Work of Stolen Generations Testimony: From the Archives to the Classroom." *Biography* 27.1 (Winter 2004): 48–77.

Kilpatrick, Jacqueline. *Celluloid Indians: Native Americans and Film.* Lincoln: University of Nebraska Press, 1999.

Kinder, Marsha. "Violence American Style: The Narrative Orchestration of Violent Attractions." *Violence and American Cinema.* Ed. J. David Slocum. New York: Routledge, 2001. 63–100.

King, Thomas. *Green Grass, Running Water.* New York: Bantam Books, 1993.
———. *Medicine River.* 1989. Toronto, ON: Penguin, 1991.
———. *The Truth about Stories: A Native Narrative.* Minneapolis: University of Minnesota Press, 2003.
Kollin, Susan, ed. *Postwestern Cultures: Literature, Theory, Space.* Lincoln: University of Nebraska Press, 2007.
Kozloff, Sarah. *Invisible Storytellers: Voice-Over Narration in American Fiction Film.* Berkeley, CA: University of California Press, 1988.
Knopf, Kerstin. *Decolonizing the Lens of Power: Indigenous Films in North America.* Amsterdam, Neth.: Rodopi, 2008.
———. "Imagining Indians—Subverting Global Media Politics in the Local Media." *Global Fragments: (Dis)Orientation in the New World Order.* Ed. Anke Bartels and Dirk Wiemann. Amsterdam, Neth.: Rodopi, 2007. 117–38.
Kolodny, Annette. *The Lay of the Land: Metaphor as Experience and History in American Life and Letters.* Chapel Hill: University of North Carolina Press, 1975.
Konkle, Maureen A. "Indigenous Ownership and the Rise of U.S. Liberal Imperialism." *American Indian Quarterly* 32.3 (2008): 297–323.
———. *Writing Indian Nations: Native Intellectuals and the Politics of Historiography, 1827–1863.* Chapel Hill: University of North Carolina Press, 2004.
Koszarski, Richard. "Edwin Carewe (1883–1940)." *Hollywood Directors, 1914–1940.* New York: Oxford University Press, 1976. 186.
Koury, Phil A. *Yes, Mr. DeMille.* New York: Putnam, 1959.
Koven, Mikel. "Folklore Studies and Popular Film and Television: A Necessary Critical Survey." *Journal of American Folklore* 116 (2003): 176–95.
Kunuk, Zacharias, and Norman Cohn. "Interview with Eric Peery." *Celluloid Fever.* Videocassette. Access Tucson Cable Television, 2002.
Kunuk, Zacharias, and Norman Cohn. "Making *Atanarjuat*." *Brick* 70 (2002): 17–23.
LaFlesche, Francis. *The Middle Five: Indian Schoolboys of the Omaha Tribe.* 1900. Lincoln: University of Nebraska Press, 1978.
Lahue, Kalton C. *Gentlemen to the Rescue: The Heroes of the Silent Screen.* New York: Barnes, 1972.
Landau, Paul. "Empires of the Visual: Photography and Colonial Administration in Africa." *Images and Empires: Visuality in Colonial and Postcolonial Africa.* Ed. Paul S. Landau and Deborah D. Kaspin. Berkeley: University of California Press, 2002. 141–71.
Langer, Mark. "Flaherty's Hollywood Period: The Crosby Version." *Wide Angle* 20.2 (1998): 38–57.
Lathrop, M. C. Synopsis of *The Vanishing American*, as serialized in the *Ladies Home Journal* (Nov. 1922-Apr. 1923) 8 April 1923. AMPAS script files for The Vanishing American.
Lehman, Peter. "Texas 1868/American 1956: *The Searchers*." *Close Viewings: An Anthology of New Film Criticism.* Ed. Peter Lehman. Tallahassee: Florida State University Press, 1990. 387–415.

Lenihan, John H. *Showdown: Confronting Modern America in the Western.* Urbana: University of Illinois Press, 1985.

Leuthold, Steven. *Indigenous Aesthetics: Native Art Media and Identity.* Austin: University of Texas Press, 1998.

Leutrat, Jean-Louis, and Suzanne Liandrat-Guigues. "John Ford and Monument Valley." *Back in the Saddle Again: New Essays on the Western.* Ed. Edward Buscombe and Roberta E. Pearson. London: BFI Publishing, 1998. 160–69.

Limerick, Patricia. *The Legacy of Conquest: The Unbroken Past of the American West.* New York: Norton, 1987.

Lewis, Randolph. *Alanis Obomsawin: The Vision of a Native Filmmaker.* Lincoln: University of Nebraska Press, 2006.

Lincoln, Kenneth. *Native American Renaissance.* Berkeley: University of California Press, 1983.

Lippard, Lucy R., ed. *Partial Recall.* New York: New Press, 1992.

Lipsitz, George. *Time Passages: Collective Memory and American Popular Culture.* Minneapolis: University of Minnesota Press, 1990.

Littlebird, Larry. *"House Made of Dawn."* Interview by Joanna Hearne. Native Networks. 4 Sept. 2003 and 25 Sept. 2003. <http://www.nativenetworks.si.edu/eng/rose/littlebird_l_interview.htm>.

———. *Hunting Sacred: Everything Listens: A Pueblo Indian Man's Oral Tradition Legacy.* Santa Fe, NM: Western Edge Press, 2001.

Lomawaima, Tsianina K. *They Called It Prairie Light: The Story of Chilocco Indian School.* Lincoln: University of Nebraska Press, 1994.

Lomayesva, Frederick K. "Indian Identity and Degree of Indian Blood." *Red Ink* 3 (Spring 1995): 33–36.

Louis, Adrian. *Skins.* New York: Ellis Press, 2002.

Louvish, Simon. *Cecil B. DeMille: A Life in Art.* New York: St. Martin's, 2007.

Lowrey, Carolyn. *The First One Hundred Noted Men and Women of the Screen.* New York: Moffat, Yard, 1920.

Ludlow, Helen. "Indian Education at Hampton and Carlisle." *Harper's New Monthly Magazine* 42 (1881): 659–75.

Lusted, David. *The Western.* London: Pearson Education, 2003.

MacCannell, Dean. *The Tourist: A New Theory of the Leisure Class.* 1976. Berkeley: University of California Press, 1999.

MacDougall, David. *Transcultural Cinema.* Ed. and Introduction Lucien Taylor. Princeton, NJ: Princeton University Press, 1998.

Maddox, Lucy. *Citizen Indians: Native American Intellectuals, Race, and Reform.* Ithaca, NY: Cornell University Press, 2006.

Madsen, Deborah L. "On Subjectivity and Survivance: Rereading Trauma through *The Heirs of Columbus* and *The Crown of Columbus.*" *Survivance: Narratives of Native Presence.* Ed. Gerald Vizenor. Lincoln: University of Nebraska Press, 2008. 61–88.

Malmsheimer, Lonna M. "'Imitation White Man': Images of Transformation at the Carlisle Indian School." *Studies in Visual Communication* (September 1985): 54–75.

Marez, Curtis. "Aliens and Indians: Science Fiction, Prophetic Photography and Near-Future Visions." *Journal of Visual Culture* 3 (2004): 336–52.

Marien, Mary Warner. *Photography: A Cultural History.* New York: Prentice Hall, 2010.

Marks, Laura U. *The Skin of the Film: Intercultural Cinema, Embodiment, and the Senses.* Durham, NC: Duke University Press, 2000.

Marsden, Michael, and Jack Nachbar. "The Indians in the Movies." *Handbook of North American Indians.* Washington, DC: Smithsonian Institution, 1988. 607–16.

Marubbio, M. Elise. *Killing the Indian Maiden: Images of Native American Women in Film.* Lexington: University of Kentucky Press, 2006.

Masayesva, Victor, Jr. *Husk of Time: The Photographs of Victor Masayesva.* Tucson: University of Arizona Press, 2006.

———. "Indigenous Experimentalism." *Magnetic North.* Ed. Jenny Lion. Minneapolis: University of Minnesota Press, 2001. 228–39.

Masayesva, Victor, Jr., and Erin Younger, eds. *Hopi Photographers, Hopi Images.* Tucson: Sun Tracks and University of Arizona Press, 1983.

Massood, Paula J. *Black City Cinema: African American Urban Experiences in Film.* Philadelphia: Temple University Press, 2003.

Mathes, Valerie Sherer. *Helen Hunt Jackson and Her Indian Reform Legacy.* Austin: University of Texas Press, 1990.

Mathews, John Joseph. *Sundown.* 1934. Norman: University of Oklahoma Press, 1988.

Matthew, Henry. "He Is a 'Bad Mother*$'!#': Shaft and Contemporary Black Masculinity." *Journal of Popular Film and Television* 30:2 (Summer 2002): 114–19.

May, Lary. *The Big Tomorrow: Hollywood and the Politics of the American Way.* Chicago: University of Chicago Press, 2000.

McClintock, Anne. *Imperial Leather: Race, Gender and Sexuality in the Colonial Contest.* New York: Routledge, 1995.

McGee, Patrick. *From Shane to Kill Bill: Rethinking the Western.* Malden, MA: Blackwell, 2007.

McHugh, Kathleen. "Profane Illuminations: History and Collaboration in James Luna and Isaac Artenstein's *The History of the Luiseño People.*" *Biography* 31.3 (Summer 2008): 429–60.

McNickle, D'Arcy. *The Surrounded.* 1936. Albuquerque: University of New Mexico Press, 1986.

———. *Native American Tribalism: Indian Survivals and Renewals.* Oxford, Eng.: Oxford University Press, 1973.

———. "Train Time." *Indians at Work* 3 (15 Mar. 1936): 45–47.

McQueeney, Kerry. "Extraordinary 1920 Silent Film with an All-Indian Cast Re-Released after a Painstaking Restoration Project." *Daily Mail* 16 July 2012. 17 July 2012 <http://www.dailymail.co.uk/news/article-2174260/The-Daughter-Of-Dawn-Footage-restored-1920-silent-film-Indian-cast.html>.

Mechling, Jay. "Picturing Hunting." *Western Folklore* 63 (2004): 51–78.

Mellor, Doreen, and Anna Haebich, eds. *Many Voices: Reflections on Experiences of Indigenous Child Separation*. Canberra: National Library of Australia, 2002.

Memmi, Albert. *The Colonizer and the Colonized*. Boston: Beacon Press, 1965.

Meriam, Lewis, et al. *The Problem of Indian Administration*. Institute for Government Research. Baltimore, MD: Johns Hopkins Press, 1928.

Merritt, Greg. *Celluloid Mavericks: A History of American Independent Film*. New York: Thunder's Mouth Press, 2000.

Michaels, Eric. *Bad Aboriginal Art: Tradition, Media and Technological Horizons*. Minneapolis: University of Minnesota Press, 1994.

Mihesuah, Devon, ed. *Repatriation Reader: Who Owns American Indian Remains?* Lincoln: University of Nebraska Press, 2000.

Millard, Bailey. "Indian Brides Who Have Made Their Husbands Rich." *New York Times* 8 May 1910, magazine section SM13. <http://query.nytimes.com/mem/archive-free/pdf?res=9901E6D61539E433A2575BC0A9639C946196D6CF>.

"Miss Del Rio Is Sole Star of 'Ramona.' Helen Hunt Jackson's Novel of Early California Indians Is Brought to Screen." *The New York Times* 19 Feb. 1928. 18 Apr. 2012 <http://query.nytimes.com/mem/archive/pdf?res=F50B15FA3858167A93CBA81789D85F4C8285F9>.

Mitchell, Lee Clark. *Westerns: Making the Man in Fiction and Film*. Chicago: University of Chicago Press, 1998.

———. "Why Monument Valley? (And Why Again and Again?): John Ford's *Stagecoach* and the Landscape of Time." *Paradoxa* 19 (2004): 116–46.

Mix, Tom. Letter to Kane and Michaelson, 1 Nov. 1910. AMPAS files, "Selig."

Momaday, N. Scott. *House Made of Dawn*. 1968. New York: Perennial Classics, 1999.

———. "*House Made of Dawn*." Interview by Joanna Hearne. 11 Mar. 2003. Native Networks. 24 Apr. 2012 <http://www.nativenetworks.si.edu/eng/rose/momaday_n_interview.htm>.

———. *The Man Made of Words, Essays, Stories, Passages*. New York: St. Martin's, 1997.

———. *Poetics and Politics*, Seminar transcript, 30 Mar. 1992, University of Arizona. 24 Apr. 2012 <http://poeticsandpolitics.arizona.edu/momaday/momaday.pdf>.

Moon, Michael. "A Long Foreground: Re-Materializing the History of Native American Relations to Mass Culture." *Materializing Democracy: Toward a Revitalized Cultural Politics*. Ed. Russ Castronovo and Dana D. Nelson. Durham, NC: Duke University Press, 2002. 267–93.

Mooney, James. *The Ghost Dance Religion*. 14th Report, Part 2. Washington, DC: Smithsonian Bureau of Ethnology, 1896.

Morse, Richardson. "*House Made of Dawn*." Interview by Joanna Hearne. 28 Jan. 2004. Native Networks. 24 Apr. 2012 <http://www.nativenetworks.si.edu/eng/rose/morse_r_interview.htm>.

Mourning Dove. *Cogewea, The Half-Blood*. 1927. Lincoln: University of Nebraska Press, 1981.

Muñoz, José Esteban. *Disidentifications: Queers of Color and the Performance of Politics.* Minneapolis: University of Minnesota Press, 1999.

Muntz, Lori Lynn. "Representing Indians: The Melodrama of Native Citizenship in U.S. Popular Culture of the 1920s." Diss. University of Iowa, 2006.

Naficy, Hamid. "Theorizing 'Third-World' Film Spectatorship." *Wide Angle* 18.3 (1996): 3–26.

Nagel, Joane. *American Indian Ethnic Renewal: Red Power and the Resurgence of Identity and Culture.* Oxford, Eng.: Oxford University Press, 1996.

Naremore, James. *Acting in the Cinema.* Berkeley: University of California Press, 1988.

Native American Graves and Repatriation Act, 25 U.S.C. 3001 et seq (16 Nov. 1990). 31 July 2009 <http://www.nps.gov/history/nagpra/MANDATES/INDEX.HTM>.

Neale, Steve. "Vanishing Americans: Racial and Ethnic Issues in the Interpretation and Context of Post-War 'Pro-Indian' Westerns." *Back in the Saddle Again: New Essays on the Western.* Ed. Edward Buscombe and Roberta Pearson. London: British Film Institute, 1998. 8–28.

Nelson, Robert. *Place and Vision: The Function of Landscape in Native American Fiction.* New York: Lang, 1993.

Nesbit, John. "Bennie Klain, Navajo Producer (2002 Interview)." Old School Reviews. 10 Jan. 2011 <http://oldschoolreviews.com/articles/klain.htm>.

Nicholson, Heather Norris, ed. *Screening Culture: Constructing Image and Identity.* Lanham, MD: Lexington Books, 2003.

Noriega, Chon. "Birth of the Southwest: Social Protest, Tourism, and D. W. Griffith's *Ramona.*" *The Birth of Whiteness: Race and the Emergence of U.S. Cinema.* Ed. Daniel Bernardi. New Brunswick, NJ: Rutgers University Press, 1996. 204–26.

———. *Shot in America: Television, the State, and the Rise of Chicano Cinema.* Minneapolis: University of Minnesota Press, 2000.

North, Michael. *The Dialect of Modernism: Race, Language, and Twentieth-Century Literature.* Oxford, Eng.: University of Oxford Press, 1994.

Office of Indian Affairs. Letter to Elizabeth Pickett. 11 Dec. 1925. AMPAS files, *Redskin.*

Ortiz, Simon. "History Is Right Now." *Beyond the Reach of Time and Change: Native American Reflections on the Frank A. Rinehart Photograph Collection.* Ed. Simon J. Ortiz. Tucson: University of Arizona Press, 2004. 3–8.

Owens, Louis. "Acts of Imagination: The Novels of N. Scott Momaday." *Other Destinies: Understanding the Native American Novel.* Norman: University of Oklahoma Press, 1992. 90–127.

———. "As If an Indian Were Really an Indian: Native American Voices and Postcolonial Theory." *Native American Representations: First Encounters, Distorted Images and Literary Appropriations.* Ed. Gretchen M. Bataille. Lincoln: University of Nebraska Press, 2001. 11–24.

Pack, Sam. "Reception, Identity, and the Global Village: Television in the Fourth World." *M/C: A Journal of Media and Culture* 3.1 (2000). 14 May 2009 <http://www.uq.edu.au/mc/0003/fourth.php>.

———. "Watching Navajos Watch Themselves." *Wicazo Sa Review* Fall (2007): 111–27.

Parish, James Robert, and George H. Hill. *Black Action Films: Plots, Critiques, Casts and Credits for 235 Theatrical and Made-for-Television Releases*. Jefferson, NC: McFarland, 1989.

Pascal, Richard. "'Proof against White Blood': The White Indian in *The Vanishing American* and *Laughing Boy*." *Australian Journal of American Studies* 19.2 (1999): 3–22.

Pearson, Roberta. *Eloquent Gestures: The Transformation of Performance Style in the Griffith Biograph Films*. Berkeley: University of California Press, 1992.

Peers, Laura, and Alison K. Brown. *Museums and Source Communities: A Routledge Reader*. London: Routledge, 2003.

Peyer, Bernd, ed. *The Singing Spirit: Early Short Stories by North American Indians*. Tucson: University of Arizona Press, 1989.

Phillips, Kate. *Helen Hunt Jackson: A Literary Life*. Berkeley: University of California Press, 2003.

Pickett, Elizabeth. *Redskin*. New York: Grosset and Dunlap, 1929.

———. "Redskin First Temporary Script." 18 Aug. 1928. A-7. AMPAS script files, *Redskin*.

———. "Synopsis Treatment of Navajo." Master File 1478, n.d., 5.10, AMPAS files.

Pinney, Christopher. "The Lexical Spaces of Eye-Spy." *Film as Ethnography*. Ed. Peter Ian Crawford and David Turton. Manchester, Eng.: Manchester University Press, 1992. 26–49.

Prats, Armando José. "His Master's Voice(Over): Revisionist Ethos and Narrative Dependence from *Broken Arrow* (1950) to *Geronimo: An American Legend* (1993)." *ANQ: A Quarterly Journal of Short Articles, Notes and Reviews* 9.3 (1996): 15–29.

———. *Invisible Natives: Myth and Identity in the American Western*. Ithaca, NY: Cornell University Press, 2002.

Pratt, Mary Louise. *Imperial Eyes: Travel Writing and Transculturation*. London: Routledge, 1992.

Pratt, Richard Henry. *Battlefield and Classroom: Four Decades with the American Indian, 1867–1904*. Ed. and Introduction by Robert M. Utley. New Haven, CT: Yale University Press, 1964.

Prins, Harald. "Visual Media and the Primitivist Perplex: Colonial Fantasies, Indigenous Imagination and Advocacy in North America." *Media Worlds: Anthropology on New Terrain*. Ed. Faye Ginsburg, Lila Abu-Lughod, and Brian Larkin. Berkeley: University of California Press, 2002. 58–74.

"Producing Indian Film Was a Stupendous Task." *New York Times* 20 Sept. 1925, X5.

Prucha, Francis Paul, ed. *Documents of United States Indian Policy*. Lincoln: University of Nebraska Press, 2000.

Purdy, John. "Tricksters of the Trade: Reimagining the Filmic Image of Native Americans." *Native American Representations: First Encounters, Distorted Images, and Literary Appropriations*. Ed. Gretchen Bataille. Lincoln: University of Nebraska Press, 2001. 100–18.

Raevouri, Saskia, ed. *The Making of Are We Civilized?* E-book. Voorheesville, NY: Square Circles Publishing, 2011.

Raheja, Michelle. "Reading Nanook's Smile: Visual Sovereignty, Indigenous Revisions of Ethnography, and *Atanarjuat (The Fast Runner)."* *American Quarterly* 59.4 (2007): 1159–185.

———. *Reservation Reelism: Redfacing, Visual Sovereignty, and Representations of Native Americans in Film.* Lincoln: University of Nebraska Press, 2010.

Ramos, Alcida. "From Eden to Limbo: The Construction of Indigenism in Brazil." In *Social Construction of the Past: Representation as Power.* Ed. George Clement Bond and Angela Gilliam. New York: Routledge, 1994.

"Redskin." Program, *Le Giornate Del Cinema Muto,* XXII edizione, Sacile, 11–18 Oct. 2003. 17 Apr. 2006 <http://www.cinetecadelfriuli.org/gcm/previous_editions/edizione2002_frameset.html>.

"Redskin and National Braid." *La Cineteca del Fruili.* 30 July 2009 <http://www.cinetecadelfriuli.org/gcm/ed_precedenti/edizione2003/Redskin.html#cliff>.

"Redskin." AMPAS PCA files.

"Refused to Sue Husband. Mary Aiken Says Film Director Carewe Asked Her to Divorce Him." *New York Times* 1 April 1928. 18 Apr. 2012 <http://query.nytimes.com/mem/archive/pdf?res=FA0610FC3E5C177A93C3A9178FD85F4C8285F9>.

The Return of Navajo Boy Webisodes. 18 Apr. 2012 <http://navajoboy.com/webisodes/>.

Rev. of *The Heart of Wetona. New York Times* 6 Jan. 1919. 30 Jul 2009. <http://www.stanford.edu/~gdegroat/NT/oldreviews/wetona.htm#variety>.

Rev. of *The Heart of Wetona. Variety* 10 Jan. 1919. 30 July 2009 <http://www.stanford.edu/~gdegroat/NT/oldreviews/wetona.htm#variety>.

Rev. of *Ramona. New York Times* 15 May 1928, 445. AMPAS files.

Rev. of *Ramona. Variety* 16 May 1928. AMPAS files.

Rev. of *The Vanishing American. Variety* 21 Oct. 1925. AMPAS files.

Rickard, Jolene. "The Occupation of Indigenous Space as 'Photograph.'" *Native Nations: Journeys in American Photography.* Ed. Jane Alison. London: Barbican Art Gallery, 1998. 57–71.

———. "Sovereignty: A Line in the Sand." *Aperture* 139 (Nov. 1996): 51–54.

Riley, Michael. "Trapped in the History of Film: Racial Conflict and Allure in *The Vanishing American." Hollywood's Indian: The Portrayal of the Native American in Film.* Ed. Peter C. Rollins and John E. O'Connor. Lexington: University Press of Kentucky, 1998. 58–72.

Riggs, Lynn. *The Cherokee Night and Other Plays.* Forward by Jace Weaver. Norman: University of Oklahoma Press, 2003.

Rogin, Michael. *Blackface, White Noise: Jewish Immigrants in the Hollywood Melting Pot.* Berkeley: University of California Press, 1996.

Romero, Channette. "The Politics of the Camera: Visual Storytelling and Sovereignty in Victor Masayesva's *Itam Hakim, Hopiit." Studies in American Indian Literatures* 22.1 (Spring 2010): 49–75.

Rony, Fatimah Tobing. *The Third Eye: Race, Cinema and Ethnographic Spectacle.* Durham, NC: Duke University Press, 1996.

———. "Victor Masayesva, Jr., and the Politics of Imagining Indians." *Film Quarterly* 48.2 (1994–1995): 20–33.

Rosaldo, Renato. *Culture and Truth: The Remaking of Social Analysis.* Boston: Beacon Press, 1989.

Rosenthal, Nicolas G. "Representing Indians: Native American Actors on Hollywood's Frontier." *The Western Historical Quarterly* 36.3 (2005): 31 pars. 30 July 2009 <http://www.historycooperative.org/journals/whq/36.3/rosenthal.html>.

Royle, Edwin Milton, and Julie Opp Faversham. *The Squaw Man.* New York: Harper and Brothers, 1906.

Runningwater, N. Bird. "Smoke Signals." *Yes!* (Winter 1999). 24 Apr. 2012 <http://www.yesmagazine.org/issues/education-for-life/801>.

Rushing, W. Jackson. *Native American Art and the New York Avant-Garde: A History of Cultural Primitivism.* Austin: University of Texas Press, 1995.

Russell, Catharine. *Experimental Ethnography: The Work of Film in the Age of Video.* Durham, NC: Duke University Press, 1999.

Sale, Kirpatrick. *The Conquest of Paradise: Christopher Columbus and the Columbian Legacy.* New York: Knopf, 1990.

Sammond, Nicholas. *Babes in Tomorrowland: Walt Disney and the Making of the American Child, 1930–1960.* Durham, NC: Duke University Press, 2005.

Sandburg, Carl, Dale Fetherling, and Doug Fetherling. *Carl Sandburg at the Movies: A Poet in the Silent Era, 1920–1927.* Metuchen, NJ: Scarecrow Press, 1985.

Sanders, J. G. *Who's Who among Oklahoma Indians.* Oklahoma City: Trane, 1927.

Sandos, James, and Larry E. Burgess. "The Hollywood Indian versus Native Americans: *Tell Them Willie Boy Is Here* (1969)." *Hollywood's Indian: The Portrayal of the Native American in Film.* Ed. Peter C. Rollins and John E. O'Connor. Lexington: University Press of Kentucky, 1998. 107–20.

Sandweiss, Martha. "Undecisive Moments: The Narrative Tradition in Western Photography." *Photography in Nineteenth-Century America.* Fort Worth, TX: Amon Carter Museum and Harry N. Abrams, 1991.

Sarris, Andrew. *You Ain't Heard Nothin' Yet: The American Talking Film History and Memory, 1927–1949.* Oxford, Eng.: Oxford University Press, 1998.

Scarberry-Garcia, Susan. *Landmarks of Healing: A Study of House Made of Dawn.* Albuquerque: University of New Mexico Press, 1990.

Schatz, Thomas. *Hollywood Genres: Formulas, Filmmaking and the Studio System.* New York: McGraw-Hill, 1981.

Scherer, Joanna Cohan. "You Can't Believe Your Eyes: Inaccuracies in Photographs of North American Indians." *Studies in the Anthropology of Visual Communication* 2.2 (1975): 67–79.

"Schumann-Heink Sues." *New York Times* 6 Apr. 1930. 18 Apr. 2012 <http://query.nytimes.com/mem/archive/pdf?res=FB0B10F9355D157A93C4A9178FD85F448385F9>.

Senier, Siobhan. "Introduction." *Ramona*. Helen Hunt Jackson. Ed. Siobhan Senier. Peterborough, ON: Broadview Editions, 2008. 15–31.

Sherman, Sharon. *Documenting Ourselves: Film, Video, and Culture*. Lexington: University Press of Kentucky, 1998.

Shively, JoEllen. "Cowboys and Indians: Perceptions of Western Films among American Indians and Anglos." 1992. *Film and Theory: An Anthology*. Ed. Robert Stam and Toby Miller. London: Blackwell, 2000. 345–60.

Shohat, Ella. "Ethnicities-in-Relation: Towards a Multicultural Reading of American Cinema." *Unspeakable Images: Ethnicity and the American Cinema*. Ed. Lester D. Friedman. Urbana: University of Illinois Press, 1991. 215–50.

Shohat, Ella, and Robert Stam. *Unthinking Eurocentrism: Multiculturalism and the Media*. London: Routledge, 1994.

Siegel, Jeff. "Shaft." *Mystery Scene* 59 (Spring 1999): 23–25.

Silko, Leslie Marmon. "The Indian with a Camera." *Yellow Woman and a Beauty of the Spirit: Essays on Native American Life Today*. New York: Simon and Schuster, 1996. 175-179.

———. *Yellow Woman and a Beauty of the Spirit*. New York: Simon and Schuster, 1997.

Simmon, Scott. *The Films of D. W. Griffith*. Cambridge, Eng.: Cambridge University Press, 1993.

———. *The Invention of the Western Film: A Cultural History of the Genre's First Half-Century*. Cambridge, Eng.: Cambridge University Press, 2003.

———. Program Notes. *Treasures from American Film Archives: 50 Preserved Films*. National Film Preservation Foundation, 2000.

Simon, Roger I. "The Touch of the Past: The Pedagogical Significance of a Transactional Sphere of Public Memory." *Revolutionary Pedagogies: Cultural Politics, Instituting Education, and the Discourse of Theory*. Ed. Peter Pericles Trifonas. London: Routledge, 2000. 61–80.

Singer, Beverly. *Wiping the War Paint Off the Lens: Native American Film and Video*. Minneapolis: University of Minnesota Press, 2001.

Sklar, Robert. *Movie-Made America: A Cultural History of American Movies*. 1975. Rev. ed. New York: Vintage, 1994.

Slotkin, Richard. *Gunfighter Nation: The Myth of the Frontier in Twentieth-Century America*. Norman: University of Oklahoma Press, 1991.

Small, Edward S. *Direct Theory: Experimental Film/Video as Major Genre*. Carbondale: Southern Illinois University, 1994.

Smith, Andrew Brodie. *Shooting Cowboys and Indians: Silent Western Films, American Culture, and the Birth of Hollywood*. Boulder: University Press of Colorado, 2003.

Smith, Greg M. "Silencing the New Woman: Ethnic and Social Mobility in the Melodramas of Norma Talmadge." *Journal of Film and Video* 48.3 (1996): 1–19.

Smith, Linda Tuhiwai. *Decolonizing Methodologies: Research and Indigenous Peoples*. Dunedin, NZ: University of Otago Press, 1999.

Smith, Paul Chaat. "Luna Remembers." *James Luna, Emendatio*. Ed. Truman T. Lowe and Paul Chaat Smith. Washington, DC: National Museum of the American Indian, Smithsonian Institution, 2005. 25–48.

Smith, Paul Chaat, and Robert Warrior. *Like a Hurricane: The Indian Movement from Alcatraz to Wounded Knee*. New York: New Press, 1997.

Sobchack, Vivian. "The Scene of the Screen: Envisioning Photographic, Cinematic, and Electronic 'Presence.'" *Materialities of Communication*. Ed. Hans Ulrich Gumbrecht and K. Ludwig Pfeiffer. Stanford, CA: Stanford University Press, 1994: 83–106.

———. "'Surge and Splendor': A Phenomenology of the Hollywood Historical Epic." *Film Genre Reader II*. Ed. Barry Keith Grant. Austin: University of Texas Press, 1995. 280–307.

Solnit, Rebecca. *Rivers of Shadows: Eadweard Muybridge and the Technological Wild West*. New York: Penguin, 2003.

Sontag, Susan. *On Photography*. New York: Picador, 1973.

Spitz, Jeff. Interview. 30 May 2007.

Stam, Robert. "Bakhtin, Polyphony, and Ethnic/Racial Representation." *Unspeakable Images: Ethnicity and the American Cinema*. Ed. Lester D. Friedman. Urbana: University of Illinois Press, 1991. 251–76.

Standing Bear, Luther. *My People, the Sioux*. New York: Houghton Mifflin, 1928.

Stanfield, Peter. *Hollywood, Westerns and the 1930s: The Lost Trail*. Exeter, Eng.: University of Exeter Press, 2001.

———. "The Western 1909–1914: A Cast of Villains." *Film History* 1 (1987): 97–112.

Stevens, Jason. "Bear, Outlaw, and Storyteller: American Frontier Mythology and the Ethnic Subjectivity of N. Scott Momaday." *American Literature* 73.3 (Sept. 2001): 599–631.

Stewart, Garrett. *Between Film and Screen: Modernism's Photo Synthesis*. Chicago: University of Chicago Press, 2000.

Stewart, Susan. *On Longing: Narratives of the Miniature, the Gigantic, the Souvenir, the Collection*. Durham, NC: Duke University Press, 1993.

Stocking, George W., Jr. "The Turn-of-the-Century Concept of Race." *Modernism/ Modernity* 1.1 (1994): 4–16.

Stoler, Ann Laura. "Tense and Tender Ties: The Politics of Comparison in North American History and (Post) Colonial Studies." *Haunted by Empire: Geographies of Intimacy in North American History*. Ed. Ann Laura Stoler. Durham, NC: Duke University Press, 2006. 23–67.

———. "Making Empire Respectable: The Politics of Race and Sexual Morality in 20th-Century Colonial Cultures." *Imperial Monkey Business: Racial Supremacy in Social Darwinist Theory and Colonial Practice*. Ed. Jan Breman. Amsterdam: VU University Press, 1990.

Strickland, Rennard. *Tonto's Revenge: Reflections on American Indian Culture and Policy*. Albuquerque: University of New Mexico Press, 1997.

Strong, Pauline Turner, and Barrik Van Winkle. " 'Indian Blood': Reflections on the Reckoning and Refiguring of Native North American Identity." *Cultural Anthropology* 11.4 (1996): 547–76.

Strongheart, Nipo T. "History in Hollywood." *The Wisconsin Magazine of History* 38:1 (Autumn 1954): 10–16, 41–46.

Sula, Mike. "Mystery in the Desert." *Chicago Reader* 21 (20 Jan. 2000). 24 Apr. 2012 <http://www.chicagoreader.com/chicago/mystery-in-the-desert/Content?oid=901252>.

Sweeney, Russell C. *Coming Next Week: A Pictorial History of Film Advertising*. New York: Barnes, 1973.

Szasz, Margaret Connell. *Education and the American Indian: The Road to Self-Determination since 1928*. 1974. Rev. 3rd ed. Albuquerque: University of New Mexico Press, 1999.

Szasz, Margaret. "Federal Boarding Schools and the Indian Child 1920–1960." *South Dakota History* 7.4 (1977): 371–84.

Tall Chief, Russ. "Rescue 'Dawn.' " *Slice* (June 2002). July13, 2012 <http://www.sliceok.com/June-2012/Rescue-Dawn/>.

Taylor, Diana. *The Archive and the Repertoire: Performing Cultural Memory in the Americas*. Durham, NC: Duke University Press, 2003.

Teuton, Sean Kicummah. *Red Land, Red Power: Grounding Knowledge in the American Indian Novel*. Durham, NC: Duke University Press, 2008.

Tilton, Robert S. *Pocahontas: The Evolution of an American Narrative*. Cambridge, Eng.: Cambridge University Press, 1994.

Tompkins, Jane. *West of Everything: The Inner Life of Westerns*. Oxford, Eng.: Oxford University Press, 1992.

Tuska, Jon. *The American West in Film: Critical Approaches to the Western*. New York: Greenwood Press, 1985.

Velikova, Roumiana. "Will Rogers's Indian Humor." *Studies in American Indian Literatures* 19.2 (Summer 2007): 83–103.

Verhoeff, Nanna. *The West in Early Cinema: After the Beginning*. Amsterdam: Amsterdam University Press, 2006.

Vizenor, Gerald. *Fugitive Poses: Native American Indian Scenes of Absence and Presence*. Lincoln: University of Nebraska Press, 1998.

———. *Manifest Manners: Postindian Warriors of Survivance*. Hanover, NH: Wesleyan University Press, 1994.

———. "Stealing Tribal Children." *Crossbloods, Bone Courts, Bingo, and Other Reports*. Minneapolis: University of Minnesota Press, 1990. 271-74.

Walker, Alexander. *The Shattered Silents: How the Talkies Came to Stay*. 1978, Elm Tree Books. New York: Morrow, 1979.

Walker, Janet. "Captive Images in the Traumatic Western: *The Searchers, Pursued, Once Upon a Time in the West*, and *Lone Star*." *Westerns: Films through History*. Ed. Janet Walker. Routledge: New York, 2001. 219-52.

Ware, Amy. "Unexpected Cowboy, Unexpected Indian: The Case of Will Rogers." *Ethnohistory* 56.1 (Winter 2009): 1–26.

———. "Will Rogers's Radio: Race and Technology in the Cherokee Nation." *American Indian Quarterly* 33.1 (Winter 2009): 62–97.

Warrior, Robert Allen. *The People and the Word: Reading Native Nonfiction.* Minneapolis: University of Minnesota Press, 2005.

———. *Tribal Secrets: Recovering American Indian Intellectual Traditions.* Minneapolis: University of Minnesota Press, 1994.

Weatherford, Elizabeth. "To End and Begin Again: The Work of Victor Masayesva, Jr." *Art Journal* 54.4 (1995): 48–52.

Weaver, Jace. *That the People Might Live: Native American Literatures and Native American Community.* Oxford, Eng.: Oxford University Press, 1997.

———. *Other Words: American Indian Literature, Law, and Culture.* Norman: University of Oklahoma Press, 2001.

Weigle, Marta, and Kyle Fiore. *Santa Fe and Taos: The Writer's Era, 1916–1941.* Santa Fe, NM: Sunstone Press, 2008.

Welsh, Robert E. "David W. Griffith Speaks." *New York Dramatic Mirror* 14 Jan. 1914, 49, 54.

West, Dennis, and Joan M. West. "Sending Cinematic Smoke Signals: An Interview with Sherman Alexie." *Cineaste* 23.4 (1998): 28–31, 37.

Wexman, Virginia Wright. "The Family on the Land: Race and Nationhood in Silent Westerns." *The Birth of Whiteness: Race and the Emergence of U.S. Cinema.* Ed. Daniel Bernardi. New Brunswick, NJ: Rutgers University Press, 1996. 129–69.

White, Patricia. *UnInvited: Classical Hollywood Cinema and Lesbian Representability.* Bloomington: Indiana University Press, 1999.

Wilderson, Frank B., III. *Red, White and Black: Cinema and the Structure of U.S. Antagonisms.* Durham, NC: Duke University Press, 2010.

Willemen, Paul, and Jim Pines, eds. *Questions of Third Cinema.* London: BFI, 1989.

Williams, Linda. *Hard Core: Power, Pleasure and the "Frenzy of the Visible."* Berkeley: University of California Press, 1989.

———. *Playing the Race Card: Melodramas of Black and White from Uncle Tom to O. J. Simpson.* Berkeley: University of California Press, 1995.

Williams, Thomas Benton. *The Soul of the Red Man.* Oklahoma City: Private printing, 1937.

Williamson, Judith. *Decoding Advertisements: Ideology and Meaning in Advertising.* London: Marion Boyars, 1978.

Wilson, Pamela, and Michelle Stewart. "Introduction: Indigeneity and Indigenous Media on the Global Stage." *Global Indigenous Media: Cultures, Poetics, and Politics.* Ed. Pamela Wilson and Michelle Stewart. Durham, NC: Duke University Press, 2008. 1–35.

Wollen, Peter. "Popular Culture and the Avant-Garde." *Wide Angle* 7:1–2 (1985): 102–04.

Womack, Craig S. *Red on Red: Native American Literary Separatism.* Minneapolis: University of Minnesota Press, 1999.

Wood, Houston. *Native Features: Indigenous Films from Around the World.* New York: Continuum, 2008.

Worsham, Lynn. "Going Postal: Pedagogic Violence and the Schooling of Emotion." *JAC: A Journal of Composition Theory* 18.2 (1998): 213–45.

Worth, Sol, and John Adair. *Through Navajo Eyes: An Exploration in Film Communication and Anthropology.* 1972. Albuquerque: University of New Mexico Press, 1997.

Zitkala-Sa. *American Indian Stories, Legends, and Other Writings.* New York: Penguin Classics, 2003.

———. "School Days of an Indian Girl." *Atlantic Monthly* 85 (1900): 185–94.

Filmography

4wheelwarpony. Dir. Dustinn Craig. BetterOnes Productions, 2008. http://vimeo.com/1776390

5ᵗʰ World. Dir. Blackhorse Lowe. Blackhorse Films, 2005.

The Aborigine's Devotion. World Film Mfg. Co., 1909.

All that Heaven Allows. Dir. Douglas Sirk. Universal International, 1955.

The American Indian: Government Education. Harmon Foundation, 1933.

Are We Civilized? Dir. Edwin Carewe. Raspin Productions, 1934.

Arrowboy and the Witches. Dir. Tony Schmitz. Screenplay Leslie Marmon Silko and Denny Carr. Laguna Film Project, 1980.

Atanarjuat (The Fast Runner). Dir. Zacharias Kunuk. Igloolik Isuma Productions/Lot 47 Films, 2001.

Backbone of the World: The Blackfeet. Dir. George Burdeau. Rattlesnake Productions, 1997.

Barking Water. Dir. Sterlin Harjo. Dirt Road Productions/Dolphin Bay Films/Indion Entertainment Group, 2009.

The Battle of Elderbush Gulch. Dir. D. W. Griffith. Biograph, 1913.

Battleship Potemkin. Dir. Sergei Eisenstein. Goskino, 1925.

Billy Jack. Dir. Tom Laughlin. National Student Film Corp./Warner Bros., 1971.

The Birth of a Nation. Dir. D.W. Griffith. D. W. Griffith Corp./Epoch Producing Corp., 1915.

Bonnie and Clyde. Dir. Arthur Penn. Warner Brothers, 1967.

Box of Treasures. Dir. Chuck Olin. Olin Films/Documentary Educational Resources, 1983.

Braveheart. Dir. Alan Hale. Cinema Corp. of America, 1925.

Broken Arrow. Dir. Delmer Daves. Twentieth Century-Fox, 1950.

Buck's Romance. Dir. William Duncan. Selig Polyscope, 1912.

The Call of the Wild. Dir. D. W. Griffith. Biograph, 1908.

Chang: A Drama of the Wilderness. Dir. Meriam Cooper and Ernest Schoedsack. Paramount Pictures, 1927.

Chato's Land. Dir. Michael Winner. Scimitar Films/United Artists, 1971.

Cheyenne Autumn. Dir. John Ford. Warner Brothers, 1964

The Chief's Daughter. Dir. D. W. Griffith. Biograph, 1911.

Christmas in the Clouds. Dir. Kate Montgomery. Random Ventures/Stockbridge Munsee Band of Mohican Indians, 2001.

Cimarron. Dir. Wesley Ruggles. RKO, 1931.

Club Swinging at Carlisle Indian School. Dir. Arthur Marvin. AM&B, 1902.

Comata, The Sioux. Dir. D. W. Griffith. Biograph, 1909.

Coming to Light: Edward S. Curtis and the North American Indians. Dir. Anne Makepeace. Anne Makepeace Productions/WNET Channel 13 New York/PBS/ Seventh Art Releasing, 2000.

The Corporal's Daughter. Dir. Langdon West. Edison, 1915.

The Covered Wagon. Dir. James Cruze. Famous Players-Lasky Corp./Paramount, 1923.

Dances with Wolves. Dir. Kevin Costner. Majestic Film/Tig Prods., Orion Pictures, 1990.

The Dark Wind. Dir. Errol Morris. Carolco Pictures/New Line Cinema/Silver Pictures, 1991.

The Daughter of Dawn. Dir. Norbert Miles. Texas Film Company, 1920 and the Oklahoma Historical Society, 2012.

A Day in Santa Fe. Dir. James Hughes and Lynn Riggs. 1931. Anthology Film Archives/Image Entertainment, 2005.

Dead Man. Dir. Jim Jarmusch. Pandora Filmproduktion/JVC Entertainment Networks/Newmarket Capital Group/12 Gauge Productions/Miramax, 1995.

Death Wish. Dir. Michael Winner. Dino De Laurentiis Co./Paramount Pictures, 1974.

Death Wish V: The Face of Death. Dir. Allan A. Goldstein. 21st Century Film Corp./ Death Wish V Prods., 1994

Devil's Doorway. Dir. Anthony Mann. MGM, 1950.

Dirty Harry. Dir. Don Siegel. The Malpaso Co./Warner Brothers, 1971.

Duel at Diablo. Dir. Ralph Nelson. Cherokee Productions/United Artists, 1966.

Enter the Dragon. Dir. Robert Clouse. Concord Productions/Golden Harvest Co./ Sequoia Productions/Warner Brothers, 1973

Evangeline. Dir. Edwin Carewe. Edwin Carewe Productions/Feature Productions/ United Artists, 1929.

The Exiles. Dir. Kent MacKenzie. 1961. Milestone Film & Video, 2008.

Familiar Places. Dir. David MacDougall. 1977/1980. Australian Institute of Aboriginal Studies/RAI (Royal Anthropological Institute).

Finding Christa. Dir. James Hatch and Camille Billops. Hatch-Billops Productions/ Third World Newsreel, 1991.

First Person Plural. Dir. Deanne Borshay Liem. National Asian American Telecommunications Association/Independent Television Service, 2000.

Flaming Star. Dir. Don Siegel. Twentieth Century-Fox, 1960.

Flap. Dir. Carol Reed. Cine Vesta Associates/Warner Brothers, 1970.

For the Papoose. Dir. James Young Deer [?]. Pathé, 1912.

Fort Apache. Dir. John Ford. RKO/Argosy, 1948.

Foster Child. Dir. Gil Cardinal. National Film Board of Canada, 1987

Four Sheets to the Wind. Dir. Sterlin Harjo. Dirt Road Productions/Indion Film/ First Look International, 2007.

The Gambler of the West. Klaw and Erlanger, 1914.

The Girl and the Outlaw. Dir. D. W. Griffith. AM&B, 1908.

Grass: A Nation's Battle for Life. Dir. Merian C. Cooper and Ernest B. Schoedsack. Paramount/Famous Players-Lasky, 1925.

The Half-Breed. Dir. Allan Dwan. Fine Arts Film, 1916.

Harold of Orange. Dir. Richard Weise. Film in the Cities/VisionMaker Video, 1984.

The Heart of Wetona. Dir. Sidney Franklin. Norma Talmadge Film Corp./Select Pictures Corp., 1919.

Her Indian Mother [*The White Man Takes a Red Wife*]. Dir. Sidney Olcott. Kalem, 1910.

High Noon. Dir. Fred Zinnemann. Universal/Malpaso, 1952.

The History of the Luiseño People: La Jolla Reservation, Christmas 1990. Dir. Isaac Artenstein. Perf. James Luna. 1993.

Hombre. Dir. Martin Ritt. Hombre Productions/Twentieth Century-Fox, 1967.

Hondo. Dir. John Farrow. Warner Brothers/Wayne-Fellows Productions, 1953.

Honey Moccasin. Dir. Shelley Niro. Women Make Movies, 1998.

Hopiit. Dir. Victor Masayesva. IS Productions/Electronic Arts 6, 1982.

House Made of Dawn. Dir. Richardson Morse. Firebird Productions, 1972.

I'd Rather Be Powwowing. Dir. Larry Littlebird. Public Broadcasting Service/Buffalo Bill Historical Center, 1983.

Imagining Indians. Dir. Victor Masayesva. IS Productions/Electronic Arts Intermix, 1992/1993.

Incident at Oglala. Dir. Robert Redford. Spanish Fork Motion Pictures/Miramax Films, 1992.

The Indian. Klaw and Erlanger, 1914.

The Indian Massacre [*The Heart of an Indian*]. Dir. Francis Ford [?]. Prod. Thomas Ince. New York Motion Picture Co./101-Bison, 1912.

The Indian Runner's Romance. Dir. D. W. Griffith. Biograph, 1909.

In the Days of the Thundering Heard. Dir. Colin Campbell. Selig Polyscope Co., 1914.

In the Land of the War Canoes [*In the Land of the Headhunters*]. Dir. Edward S. Curtis. Continental Film Company, 1914.

Iola's Promise. Dir. D. W. Griffith. Biograph, 1912.

The Invaders. Dir. Francis Ford [?]. Prod. Thomas Ince. New York Motion Picture Co./Kay-Bee, 1912.

The Iron Horse. Dir. John Ford. Fox, 1924.

Itam Hakim, Hopiit. Dir. Victor Masayesva. Perf. Ross Macaya. IS Productions/ Electronic Arts Intermix, 1984.

The Jazz Singer. Dir. Alan Crosland. Warner Brothers, 1927.

Judge Priest. Dir. John Ford. Fox Film Corporation, 1934.

Just Squaw. Dir. George E. Middleton. Beatriz Michelena Features/Exhibitors Mutual Distributing Company, 1919.

Kentuckian. Dir. Wallace McCutcheon. AM&B, 1908.

The Last of the Line. Dir. Jay Hunt. Domino Film Company/Mutual Film, 1914.

The Last Hunt. Dir. Richard Brooks. MGM, 1956.

The Last of the Mohicans. Dir. Maurice Tourneur and Clarence Brown. Associated Producers/Maurice Tourneur Productions, 1920.

The Last of the Mohicans. Dir. Michael Mann. Twentieth Century-Fox/Morgan Creek Productions, 1992.

Laughing Boy. Dir. W. S. Van Dyke. MGM, 1934.

Leather Stocking. Dir. D. W. Griffith. Biograph, 1909.

Little Big Man. Dir. Arthur Penn. Cinema Center 100/National General Pictures, 1970.

Little Dove's Romance. Dir. Fred Balshofer. New York Motion Picture Co./Bison, 1911.

The Lone Ranger. ABC-TV, 1949–1957.

The Lost Child. Dir. Karen Arthur. Hallmark Hall of Fame Productions, 2000.

The Lure of Woman. Dir. Travers Vale. World Film Corp., 1915.

A Man Called Horse. Dir. Elliot Silverstein. Cinema Center 100/National General Pictures, 1969.

The Man Who Loved Cat Dancing. Dir. Richard C. Sarafian. MGM, 1973.

The Man Who Shot Liberty Valance. Dir. John Ford. Ford Productions/Paramount, 1962.

Massacre. Dir. Alan Crosland. First National/Warner Brothers, 1934.

The Massacre. Dir. D. W. Griffith. Biograph, 1912.

Maya, Just an Indian. Frontier, 1913.

Medicine River. Dir. Stuart Margolin. Academy Entertainment, 1993.

The Mended Lute. Dir. D. W. Griffith. Biograph, 1909.

Moana: A Romance of the South Seas. Dir. Robert J. Flaherty. Paramount/Famous Players-Lasky, 1926.

A Mohawk's Way. Dir. D. W. Griffith. Biograph, 1910.

Mr. Skitch. Dir. James Cruze. Perf. Will Rogers. Fox Film Corp., 1933.

My Darling Clementine. Dir. John Ford. Twentieth Century-Fox, 1946.

Nanook of the North. Dir. Robert Flaherty. Les Frères Revillon/Pathé Exchange, 1922.

Nanook Revisited. Dir. Claude Massot. IMA Productions/Films for the Humanities and Sciences. 1990.

Navajo Talking Picture. Dir. Arlene Bowman. Arlene Bowman Productions/Women Make Movies. 1986.

No Country for Old Men. Dir. Joel and Ethan Coen. Paramount Vantage/Miramax Films/Scott Rudin Productions/Mike Zoss Productions, 2007.

Oklahoma! Dir. Fred Zinneman. Rodgers and Hammerstein Productions/Magna Theatre Corporation/RKO Radio Pictures, 1955.

The Plainsman. Dir. Cecil B. DeMille. Paramount, 1936.

Pony Soldier. Dir. Joseph M. Newman. Twentieth Century-Fox Film Corporation, 1952.

A Pueblo Legend. Dir. D. W. Griffith. Biograph, 1913.

First Blood. Dir. Ted Kotcheff. Anabasis N.V./Elcajo Productions/Orion Pictures Corporation, 1982.

Ramona: A Story of the White Man's Injustice to the Indian. Dir. D. W. Griffith. Biograph, 1910.

Ramona. Dir. Donald Crisp. Clune Film Producing Co., 1916.

Ramona. Dir. Edwin Carewe. Inspiration Pictures, 1928.

The Red Girl. Dir. D. W. Griffith. Biograph, 1908.

Red Love. Dir. Edgar Lewis. Lowell Film Productions, 1925.

The Redman and the Child. Dir. D. W. Griffith. Biograph, 1908.

The Redman's View. Dir. D. W. Griffith. Biograph, 1909.

Redskin. Dir. Victor Schertzinger. Paramount, 1929.

The Return of Navajo Boy. Dir. Jeff Spitz. Groundswell Educational Films, 2001.

Ritual Clowns. Dir. Victor Masayesva. IS Productions/Electronic Arts Intermix, 1988.

A Romance of the Western Hills. Dir. D. W. Griffith. Biograph, 1910.

The Searchers. Dir. John Ford. Warner Brothers/C.V. Whitney Pictures, 1956.

Sergeant Rutledge. Dir. John Ford. Warner Brothers/John Ford Productions, 1960.

Shane. Dir. George Stevens. Paramount, 1953.

She Wore a Yellow Ribbon. Dir. John Ford. RKO/Argosy, 1949.

The Silent Enemy. Dir. H. P. Carver. Paramount-Publix/Burden-Chanler Prods., 1930.

Shaft. Dir. Gordon Parks. MGM/Shaft Productions, 1971.

The Squaw Man. Dir. Cecil B. DeMille and Oscar Apfel. Jesse L. Lasky Feature Play Co., 1914.

The Squaw Man. Dir. Cecil B. DeMille. Paramount, 1918.

The Squaw Man. Dir. Cecil B. DeMille. MGM, 1931.

Skins. Dir. Chris Eyre. First Look International/Grandview Pictures/Starz! Encore Entertainment, 2002.

Smoke Signals. Dir. Chris Eyre. Shadow Catcher Entertainment/Miramax, 1998.

Soldier Blue. Dir. Ralph Nelson. AVCO Embassy/Katzka-Berne Productions, 1970.

A Son of the Sahara. Dir. Edwin Carewe. Edwin Carewe Productions/Associated First National Pictures, 1924.

Songs of My Hunter Heart: Laguna Poems and Stories. Dir. Denny Carr. Prod. Larry Evers. Perf. Harold Littlebird. Arizona Board of Regents, 1978.

The Spoilers. Dir. Edwin Carewe. Paramount, 1930.

The Stalking Moon. Dir. Robert Mulligan. The Stalking Moon Co./National General Pictures, 1969.

Stagecoach. Dir. John Ford. United Artists/Walter Wanger Productions, 1939.

Strongheart. Dir. James Kirkwood and D. W. Griffith [?]. Biograph/Klaw and Erlanger, 1914.

Sweet Sweetback's Baadasssss Song. Dir. Melvin Van Peebles. Yeah/Cinemation Industries, 1971.

Tangled Lives: A Strange Culmination of the Seminole War. Dir. Sidney Olcott. Kalem, 1911.

Taza, Son of Cochise. Dir. Douglas Sirk. Universal Pictures, 1954.

Tell Them Willie Boy Is Here. Dir. Abraham Polonsky. Universal Pictures, 1969.

Te Rua. Dir. Barry Barclay. Pacific Films/Trans Tas Entertainment, 1991.

The Test of Donald Norton. Dir. B. Reeves Eason. Chadwick Pictures Corporation, 1926.

Two Wagons, Both Covered. Dir. Rob Wagner. Perf. and script, Will Rogers. Hal Roach Studios, 1924.

Thunderheart. Dir. Michael Apted. Tribeca Prods./TriStar Pictures, 1992.

Tonto Plays Himself. Dir. Jacob Floyd. 2010. Distribution by Jacob Floyd

Totem: The Return of the G'psgolox Pole. Dir. Gil Cardinal. National Film Board of Canada, 2003.

The Tourists. Dir. Mack Sennett. Biograph/General Film Company, 1912.

The Trail of the Shadow. Dir. Edwin Carewe. Rolfe Photoplays/Metro Pictures Corporation, 1917.

Ulzana's Raid. Dir. Robert Aldrich. Universal/Carter de Haven/Robert Aldrich, 1972.

Unidentified Pac/House No. 5: *The Friendly Indian.* Dir. James Young Deer [?]. Melies/Lubin, 1909.

An Up-to-Date Squaw. Pathé Frères, 1911.

The Vanishing American. Dir. George B. Seitz. Famous Players-Lasky Corp./Paramount, 1925.

Viewing Sherman Institute for Indians at Riverside, California. Dir. Mack Sennett. Keystone, 1915.

War on the Plains. Dir. Thomas Ince. New York Motion Picture Co.,/101-Bison, 1912.

Way Down East. Dir. D. W. Griffith. D.W. Griffith Productions/United Artists, 1920.

White Dove's Sacrifice. Dir. Sawyer [?]. Gem Motion Picture Company/Universal Film Manufacturing Company, 1914.

White Fawn's Devotion. Dir. James Young Deer. Pathé Frères, 1910.

The Wild Bunch. Dir. Sam Peckinpah. Warner Bros./Seven Arts Prods., 1969.

Within Our Gates. Dir. Oscar Micheaux. Micheaux Book and Film Company/Quality Amusement Corporation, 1920.

Television series

Forest Spirits series. Dir. George Burdeau. Native American Public Telecommunications/Vision Maker Video, 1975.

The Native American series. Dir. Sandra Sunrising Osawa. KNBC-TV Los Angeles, 1970.

Words and Place series. Dir. Denny Carr. Prod. Larry Evers. Arizona Board of Regents, 1978. 21 April 2012 <http://parentseyes.arizona.edu/wordsandplace/index.html>.

Images of Indians series. Dir. Phil Lucas and Robert Hagopian. KCTS-9 Seattle/United Indians of All Tribes Foundation, 1979.

The Real People series. Dir. George Burdeau and Larry Littlebird. KSPS-TV Spokane, 1976.

Index